Always with Honor

Pyotr Wrangel

ISBN: 9798695956818

v. I

NOTE FROM THE PUBLISHER

The Russian Revolution and subsequent Civil War were perhaps the most significant events in the 20th century. The political turmoil in the 1920s and '30s, cataclysm of the Second World War, and nuclear standoff between the Soviet Union and United States all flow directly from the collapse of the Russian Empire and rise of international communism.

Although the ascent of the Bolsheviks and subsequent Red Terror has been given a great deal of attention in Western media, the struggle of the "White" anti-communist movement is relatively unexplored. Many titles that offer invaluable insights into these world-shaping events are prohibitively expensive or unavailable altogether.

Always with Honor was, until the release of this edition, one of those lost books. First published in 1928 in the German magazine *White Cause*, Wrangel's account of the early days of the Russian Revolution through the final evacuation of White forces from Crimea was quickly translated into English under the title "The Memoirs of General Wrangel." This edition included a note from the translator, Sophie Goulston, as well as General Wrangel's preface to the Russian edition. It fell out of print in just a year.

In 1957 a reprint containing a forward from former President Herbert Hoover, whose institute still produces an admirable amount of scholarship on Russian history, was released under the title "Always with Honor." This edition lacked the translator's note (or any reference to Goulston) and Wrangel's preface. It also quickly fell out of print. Before this edition, copies of Always with Honor were extremely rare and had been known to sell for over $800. This new edition of this classic work unites the translator's note, preface from the author, and former President Hoover's forward for the first time.

Wrangel closes his book by urging readers to remember the lessons of men who fought and sacrificed for civilization. We hope this edition will allow a new generation of readers to do just that.

Thank you for reading!

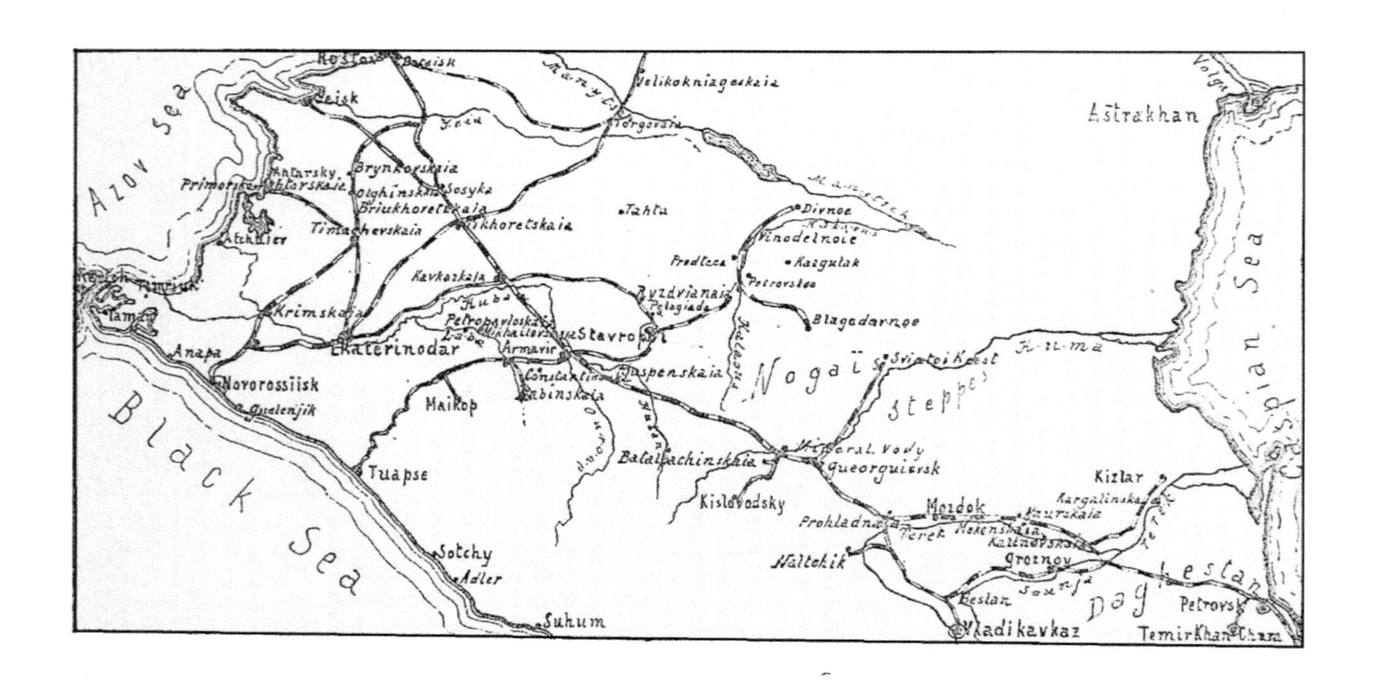

THE THEATRE OF WAR IN NORTHERN CAUCASIA; 1918.

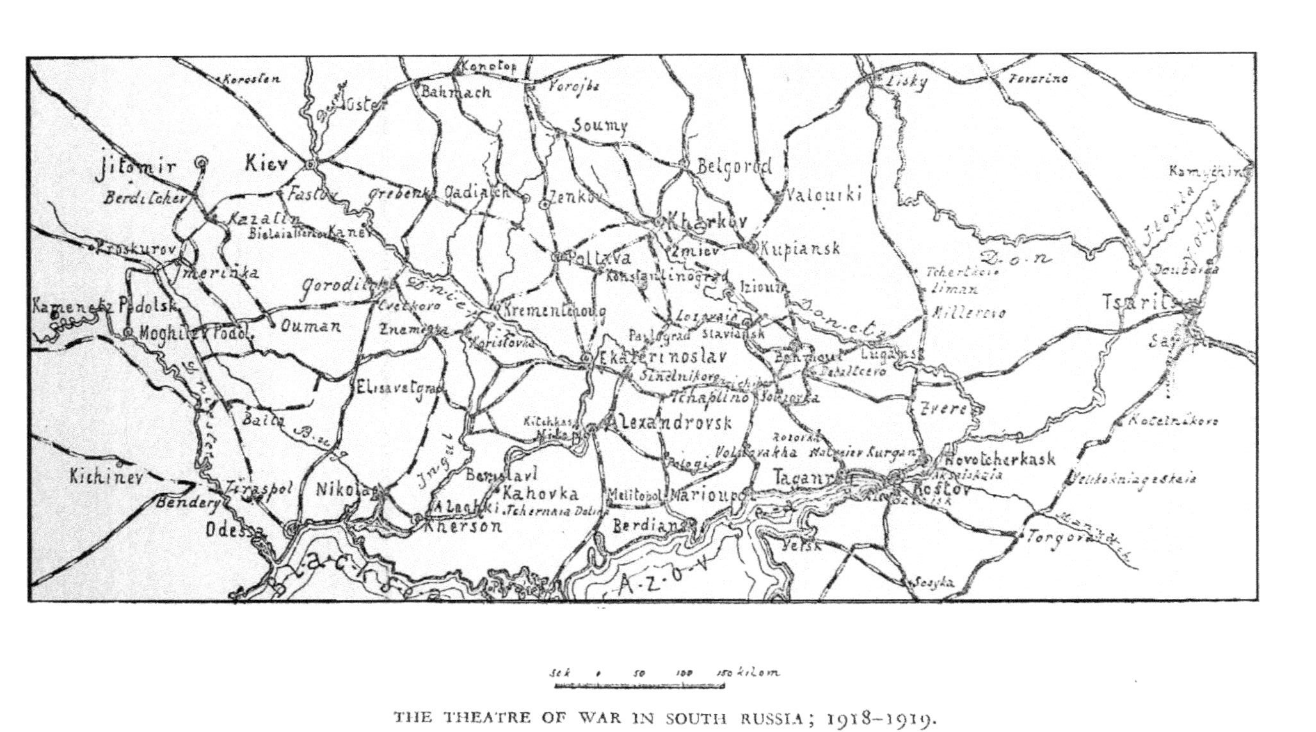

THE THEATRE OF WAR IN SOUTH RUSSIA; 1918–1919.

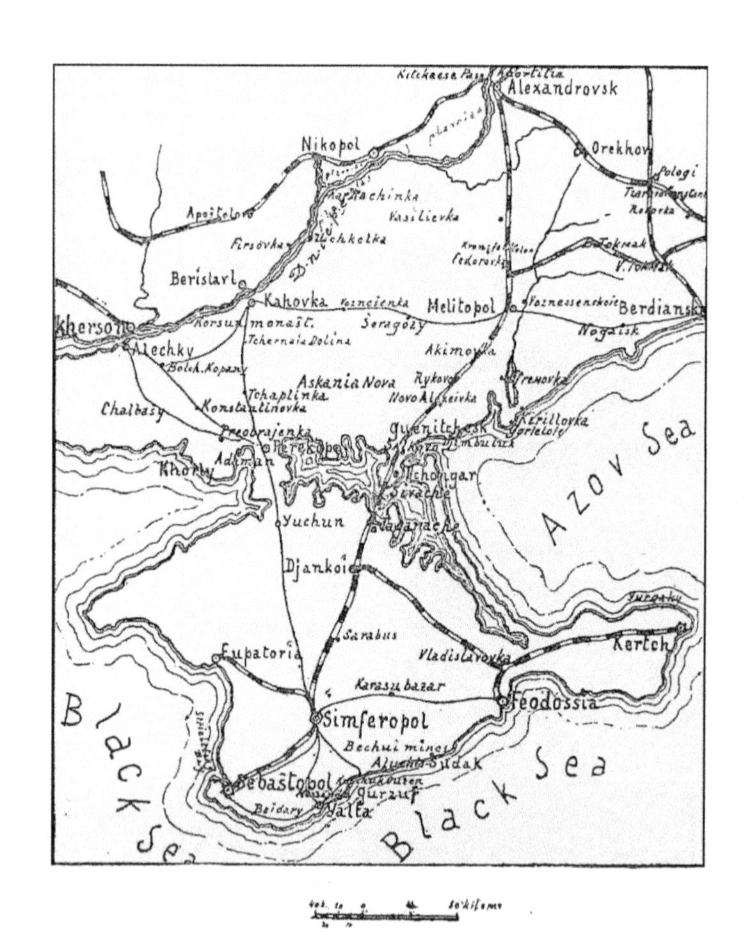

THE THEATRE OF WAR IN THE CRIMEA; 1919–1920.

FORWARD

I am glad that General Wrangel's memoirs are being made available to the American people. The title "Always with Honor" envisages the man.

General Wrangel was educated as an engineer. He departed from that profession to serve his country in war. His first military service was in the Russo-Japanese War in 1904 as an officer in a Cossack regiment. In the First World War he rose rapidly in the Russian Army to the rank of Major General.

I did not know General Wrangel personally. But having charge of European relief and reconstruction measures on behalf of the Allies after the First World War, my duties extended to the Black Sea region. I was therefore familiar with the anti-Communist military operations in South Russia and particularly the army commanded by General Wrangel.

General Wrangel was one of the first of the Russian leaders to realize the dangers of the Communist revolution to the Russian people and the world. Immediately after the seizure of the Government by the Communists he joined the "White" armies under General Denikin in South Russia as one of his principal commanders. I was informed at that time by the Allied military authorities that General Denikin was wholly inadequate to his task and that General Wrangel, who was his subordinate, had the military and personal qualities which might bring victory over the Red armies.

After Denikin's defeat General Wrangel took command of the small disorganized remnants. Starting with an army no better equipped than Washington's at Valley Forge, he recovered the Crimea against ten to one odds. But in the end he was compelled to withdraw through Sevastopol to foreign countries in order to save the remnants of his army and a host of Russian refugees. American Admiral McCauley, who was in Sevastopol at this moment, said:

> "Without any disorder Sevastopol was quickly evacuated at 3 PM. General Wrangel was the last to leave."

Until his death in 1928 General Wrangel devoted all his resources to the service of Russian refugees dispersed over Europe. His wife Olga took a devoted part.

In an address six months before his passing, he said:

> History, which knows no favoritism, will tell the importance of our struggle, the capacity of our sacrifices. It will know that the fight we carried on for the love of our country, for the resurrection of Russia as a nation, was indeed at the same time to safeguard the culture of Europe, the struggle for an age-long civilization, for the defence of Europe against the Red terror.

General Wrangel's memoirs are the story of that great devotion.

HERBERT HOOVER

TRANSLATOR'S NOTE

In writing his Memoirs, General Wrangel does not appear to have aimed at producing a polished literary narrative, but at telling a story from a particular point of view, and telling it as plainly and simply as he could. The greater part of the book is written in the form of a diary, interspersed with despatches, telegrams, and edicts.

Unconsciously, General Wrangel has achieved a vividness and burning sincerity which more than compensates for any lack of nicety in style and form.

The English version is translated from the French, in which detailed accounts of events of purely Russian interest were omitted, in accordance with instructions given by General Wrangel himself.

PREFACE TO THE RUSSIAN EDITION

These Memoirs do not pretend to be a historical work based on scientific research. I have narrated events in which I took part, or of which I was a witness. As I approached the crisis of my story, I have relegated the personal element in these Memoirs more and more to the background, giving general political questions first consideration.

Throughout I have been careful to cite authentic documents to substantiate my own account of the various events. For the most part I have quoted such documents in full. This detracts from the liveliness of the narrative, but ensures its impartiality.

These Memoirs cover the period from the beginning of the Russian Revolution to the end of the armed struggle in Southern Russia. After the Russian Army had evacuated its native land, the contest took other forms. This struggle is still going on, and will go on until the collapse of the Power which is so hateful to the Russian people.

P. WRANGEL

TABLE OF CONTENTS

PART I

THE BIRTH OF THE COUNTER-REVOLUTION

CHAPTER I

THE REVOLUTION AND THE COLLAPSE OF THE ARMY

I - On the Verge

Towards the winter of 1916 the bloody struggles which had been waged throughout the summer and autumn drew to a close. We consolidated our position, filled in the gaps in our effective forces, and reorganized generally.

The experience gained from two years of warfare had not been acquired in vain. We had learnt a great deal, and the shortcomings for which we had paid so dearly were now discounted. A number of generals who had not kept pace with modern needs had had to give up their commands, and life had brought other more capable men to the fore. But nepotism, which permeated all spheres of Russian life, still brought unworthy men into important positions too often. Convention, routine, and fear of disregarding the custom of promotion by seniority still held sway, especially amongst the higher military staff.

After two years of warfare, the Army was not what it had been. The majority of the original officers and men, especially in the infantry, had been killed or put out of action.

The new officers, hastily trained, and lacking military education and *esprit de corps*, could not make satisfactory instructors for the men. They knew how to die bravely for the honor of their country and their flag, like all the staff-officers, but they felt that they had been uprooted from their normal, and anything but military, work and had neither the mentality nor the spirit of the true soldier. They found difficulty in enduring the dangers, fatigue, and privations of life at the front, and war to them meant nothing but suffering. It was impossible for them to inspire the troops and put fresh heart into their men.

Neither were the troops what they had been. The original soldiers, inured to fatigue and privation, and brave in battle, were better than ever; but there were few of them left. The new contingents were by no means satisfactory. The reserve forces were primarily fathers of families who had been dragged away from their villages, and were warriors only in spite of themselves. For they had forgotten that once upon a time they had been soldiers, they hated war, and thought only of returning to their homes as soon as possible.

Before they were sent to the front these men were passed through the *cadres* and given some preliminary training, but it was very inadequate. There were not enough *cadres*, and the barracks allotted to them were too small to house all the men. Furthermore, the instructors, both commissioned and noncommissioned officers, were not up to their work. They were either disabled and worn out from active service, or else very young officers who themselves had much to learn.

The infantry, whose losses were heaviest of any, suffered most from this arrangement. But nevertheless, in spite of everything, the Army was still strong and impressive. The morale of the troops was excellent, and the discipline perfect. I never once saw or even heard of the slightest expression of disaffection or disorder; indeed, before this could happen, the very idea of authority had to disappear, and the generals themselves had to set the example of breaking the bonds of loyalty which existed between officers and men.

It is obvious that after two years of warfare the moral standards of the army could not but have slackened, and respect for the law diminished. Requisitioning, an inevitable consequence of any war, had lessened the soldiers' regard for other people's property. Base instincts were aroused, but I repeat that they would not have been set in motion but for an external shock.

A great deal of work was being done, especially in the wake of the Army, behind-the-lines, by a numerous class of people which was on the increase during these last months. The individuals of this class had been mobilized and were in perfect health, but they had an unconquerable aversion from the endless whining of bullets and the bursting of shells; and so, secure in the protection and support of a quieter atmosphere, they sat on all kinds of committees and occupied themselves with the organization of reading-rooms and canteens for the trenches.

These men, dressed in absurd uniforms, all spurted and laced, took great pains with the main body of the Army, especially the ensigns, for the staff and soldiers of the technical units were recruited from amongst the intelligentzia.

Most of the Army, rank and file as well as officers, took no part at all in politics: they had other things to do, and, besides, they lacked newspapers and information. One party amongst the officers echoed the gossip of the neighboring General Staff. They believed that General Headquarters were *au courant* with events in the country, and prophesied that the disorder in the interior would finally react on the Army and so lead to its defeat.

We continually told one another that things would not come to this pass in Petersburg.

Those of us who loved our country and the Army were terribly anxious at the continual changes in the Ministry, the conflicts between the Government and the Duma, the ever-increasing number of petitions and appeals addressed to the Czar by many influential organizations, each one demanding popular control, and, above all, by the alarming rumors concerning certain persons in the Czar's entourage.

The patriots amongst the High Command suffered deeply as they watched the Czar making fatal mistakes whilst the danger grew and came ever nearer; they held mistaken views, but they believed in them sincerely; they contemplated the possibility of a revolution from within the Palace to be effected by means of a bloodless *coup d'état.* General Krymov, my immediate superior, was one of those who was strongly in favor of this plan. He was commander of a division of Oussourian Cossacks in which I commanded a regiment of Nerchinsk Cossacks.

During the long discussions we had on many an evening he tried again and again to prove to me that things could not go on as they were, that we must prevent a catastrophe, and that we ought to find men who, without a day's delay, would remove the Czar by means of a revolution from within the Palace.

There were other commanders who also agreed that things could not go on as they were, but they realized how inopportune a change in time of war would be, and saw that it would inevitably entail the collapse of the Army and the ruin of the country.

Others, again, desired a revolution for purely personal reasons, hoping to find in it scope for their ambitions, or to profit from it and settle their accounts with such of the commanders as they hated.

I am firmly convinced that if, from the beginning of the revolutionary movement, Headquarters and the generals at the front had forgotten their personal interests and acted unanimously and resolutely, the Army would not have collapsed nor the interior fallen prey to anarchy, or at least that things would have been checked in time.

The Czarevitch's regiment of Nerchinsk Cossacks, which I commanded during the winter of 1916, was part of a division of Oussourian Cossacks. This division, recruited from Eastern Siberia, enjoyed a high reputation in the Army. It had covered itself with glory many times, and recently my regiment had been signally rewarded for distinguished conduct in Galicia. His Majesty had appointed his son honorary commander of the regiment, which was henceforth known as the Czarevitch's Own.

During the Civil War the majority of the officers of the Oussourian division, and of the Nerchinsk regiment in particular, were in Admiral Koltchak's army, and met again under the command of Ataman Semenov and General Ungern. At the time of which I am speaking, these two generals, who have since played such a prominent part in the Civil War, were captains of the fifth and sixth squadrons of the Nerchinsk regiment.

Semenov was a Transbaikalian Cossack—dark and thickset, and of the rather alert Mongolian type. His intelligence was of a specifically Cossack caliber, and he was an exemplary soldier, especially courageous when under the eye of his superior. He knew how to make himself popular with Cossacks and officers alike, but he had his weaknesses—a love of intrigue and indifference to the means by which he achieved his ends. Though capable and ingenious, he had received no education, and his outlook was narrow. I have never been able to understand how he came to play a leading role.

Captain Baron Ungern Stenberg, or simply "the Baron," as his troops called him, was more complex and interesting. He was of the type that is invaluable in wartime and impossible in times of peace.

At the beginning of the Russo-Japanese War, though still almost a child, he had left school and joined up as a volunteer in an infantry regiment. He was wounded many times and was decorated. After the war he went back to Russia, where his relatives made him enter a military school. He passed his officers' examinations only with great difficulty.

Longing for adventure and feeling out of his element in the regular Army, he set out for Siberia and joined a Cossack regiment. He did not remain with it long. One night, in a fit of drunken anger, he picked a petty quarrel with one of his comrades and struck him. The man dealt him a sword-blow on his head, and he felt the effects of this wound for the rest of his life—it undoubtedly upset his mental balance.

He returned to Russia and decided to travel from Vladivostok to Kharbin on horseback. He left his regiment, swung himself into the saddle, whistled to his dog, and set off with a fowling-piece slung over his shoulder. Hunting for his food and sleeping in the open air, he took a whole year to reach Kharbin. There he learnt that war had just broken out between the Chinese and the Mongols. He remounted his horse, pushed on to Mongolia, and offered his services; and there he was, commander of the whole cavalry force of Mongolia!

At the outbreak of the World War he came back to Russia and joined up as sub-lieutenant in the Nerchinsk regiment; from the first he won distinction by his courageous exploits. He was wounded many times, and decorated with the St. George's Cross (the highest honor a soldier can win), and by the end of the year he was a captain and in command of the squadron. He was of medium height, fair and puny-looking, with a long reddish moustache, but he possessed an iron constitution and ruthless energy. War was his natural element.

He was not an officer in the ordinary sense: he knew nothing of system, turned up his nose at discipline, and was ignorant of the rudiments of decency and decorum. He was not an officer, but a hero out of one of Mayne Reid's novels. He was dirty and dressed untidily, slept on the floor with his Cossacks, and messed with them. When he was promoted to a civilized environment his lack of all outward refinement made him conspicuous. I tried in vain to awaken his conscience to the need for adopting at least the external appearance of an officer. He was a man of queer contrasts. He had an original, penetrating mind, but at the same time an astonishing lack of culture, an extremely narrow outlook, the shyness of the savage, a foolish swagger, and an unbridled temper. He was very extravagant, though his means were exceptionally small.

In accordance with an old custom, we had to offer the new honorary commander a horse and the uniform of the regiment which was to bear his name. Consequently I left for the capital at the head of a deputation from the regiment, taking with me a small Maudjourian horse just big enough for the young Czarevitch.

Scarcely two months before this I had been in Petersburg recovering from a wound I had gotten in the famous charge which had earned us the signal honor which was the cause of my returning to Petersburg today.

Confusion was rife in all circles, there seemed to be a presentiment abroad of the nearness of the terrible events which destiny was preparing for Russia. In the Duma and the Imperial Council and in different political groups, a pretense of stern authority was reduced to a matter of public-speaking-matches and political debates; while in artisan circles and urban associations there was subterranean propaganda at work, fed no doubt by Germans. Yet, at the same time, the majority of the population remained absorbed in its little daily cares, the queues lined up outside the shops, the theatres and cinemas were full, and the same old trivial conversations were to be overheard in the crowd.

Court circles appeared to be paying no heed to the approaching storm. High society and the upper bureaucracy remained absorbed in their usual "weighty" questions, such as the appointment of someone to some post, or the opinions held by the Grand Duke's or the Empress's party.

Social life followed its usual course, and it seemed as if these people were merely to be the spectators and not the victims of the drama to come.

Some days after my arrival, I entered the service of the Czar as his aide-de-camp. I have had many opportunities of meeting the Czar and chatting with him. He produced an impression of extraordinary simplicity and unusual kindliness on everyone who met him—the result of the outstanding traits of his character, his perfect education, and his complete self-mastery. He had an alert mind, was skilled in the art of innuendo, and possessed an amazing memory. He remembered not only events but names and dates. One day he spoke to me of the battles in which my regiment had taken part, although it was a long time ago and we had done nothing noteworthy, he even mentioned the villages in which the regiments of our division had been quartered.

I began my service as aide-de-camp to the Czar one Saturday, relieving Duke Nicholas of Leuchtenberg. That day dinner was served in the Empress's apartments. There were only the Imperial Family and myself at table, their Majesties kept me part of the evening for a chat. The Czar was merry and vivacious, the Grand Duchesses and the Czarevitch laughed together and exchanged badinage; but I was struck by the expression of suffering on the Empress's face. She had grown much thinner in the two months since I had last seen her, and I particularly noticed the expression in her eyes, it was sad, I might say absent-minded. She was especially interested in the organization of medical relief in the Army, and also asked me detailed questions about the new type of gas-mask.

The next day being Sunday, I accompanied their Majesties to church. The little temple, built in the old Russian Style, was packed. Watching the Imperial couple at prayer, I involuntarily compared the Czar's expression of pious contemplation with the Empress's look of sorrowful ecstasy.

Some days later I presented the deputation from my regiment to His Majesty. I little dreamt that this was the last time I was to see the Czar.

II - On the Rumanian Front

That same evening I received a telegram from General Krymov. Our division was to leave for Rumania, so I was to rejoin my regiment immediately, taking back with me all the officers and men on leave in Petersburg. We left the next day.

As far as the Rumanian frontier, the trains were running much as usual, but across the frontier things were very different. The Rumanian troops were retreating, and the line was blocked by trains full of refugees, wounded, and munitions. I saw for the first time what I saw daily after this, passengers sitting on the roofs of the carriages, on the buffers, and even on the engines.

At a branch line not far from the terminus our two carriages were hooked on to an express. So that we might have more chance of keeping warm, I had with great difficulty extracted a promise that we should be put on at the front of the train. I do not know how it happened, but they hooked us on at the back after all. This saved our lives. Dashing along at full speed, our train crashed into a train in front of us, and the first fourteen carriages were wrecked, there were several hundred killed and injured.

We found our division on the march, making for the line of the Sereth, from where we were to make for Galatz, where great masses of cavalry were to be concentrated. Then came a counter-order, and we retraced our steps through driving rain, soaked to the skin.

During the march an orderly came to inform me that General Krymov, who was marching at the head of our column, wanted me. I found him with our General Staff near a wood-house, busily reading a letter which had just come. Whilst I was still some way off he called out to me: "Great news! At last they've killed that scoundrel Rasputin!"

The newspapers announced the bare fact, letters from the capital gave the details. Of the three assassins, I knew two intimately: the Grand Duke Dimitri

Pavlovitch and Prince Youssoupoff. What had been their motive? Why, having killed a man whom they regarded as a menace to the country, had they not admitted their action before everyone? Why had they not relied on justice and public opinion instead of trying to hide all trace of the murder by burying the body under the ice? We thought over the news with great anxiety.

In the first days of 1917 I was made commander of the brigade of which my old Nerchinsk regiment was a part. I was genuinely sorry to part from my gallant comrades-in-arms with whom I had shared victory, fatigue, and danger for fourteen months.

As my brigade was stationed behind-the-lines for the time being, I took the opportunity to spend a few days in Jassy. I stayed with Mossolov, our Minister-Resident there, an old fellow-officer of mine. The town was full of refugees and behind-the-line organizations, and it was almost impossible to find lodgings. They were expecting the Grand Duchess Cyril, the Queen of Rumania's sister. Never having belonged to the Grand Duchess's intimate circle, I refrained from calling on her to pay my respects. But on the very day of my arrival the Court-Marshal, M. Hartung, called to inform me that the Grand Duchess expected me the next day at ten o'clock at the Queen's Palace. They had not been able to find a building in Jassy roomy enough to house the entire Royal Family of Rumania, so the Queen and her children were living in one house, the King in another.

At the Grand Duchess's I met the commander of the town, General Kasakevitch, formerly aide-de-camp to the Czar. The Grand Duchess kept us for more than an hour. She gave me details of all the latest events in Petersburg, of the arrest and banishment to Persia of the Grand Duke Dimitri Pavlovitch, of the joint letter which all the members of the Imperial Family had sent to the Czar, begging for mercy for the Grand Duke; of the Czar's refusal, and of the disgrace of the Grand Duke Nicholas Mikhailovitch because he had sent a violent letter to the Czar in which he had given expression to certain bitter truths.

According to the Grand Duchess, all the members of the Imperial Family, even the Czar's closest relations, realized very clearly the danger that was threatening the dynasty and the whole of Russia. The Czarina alone could not or would not see it. Her sister, the Grand Duchess Elizabeth, the Grand Duchess Cyril herself, and Princess Youssoupoff, the mother of Rasputin's murderer, had all tried in vain to open her eyes.

"I know Russia better than you do, and I have known it much longer; besides, there is a Russia whose existence you do not even realize. You only hear what is said in Petersburg in corrupt, aristocratic circles; they are not speaking for the people. If you had been with the Czar and myself at the front, you would have seen how the people and the Army adore him."

The Czarina had opened a drawer, taken out a bundle of letters and shown them to the Grand Duchess. "All these letters are from officers and soldiers, simple Russian men. I receive a similar pile every day; they all adore the Emperor and beg him not to yield an inch to the intrigues of the Duma."...

The Grand Duchess gave us to understand that the majority of the members of the Imperial Family, especially the family of the Grand Duchess Maria Pavlovna (mother of the Grand Duke Cyril) considered it necessary to modify the existing order of things, and that many influential members of the Duma shared this view.

This long interview with the Grand Duchess Cyril left a painful impression on my mind. I had met her many times in Petersburg, but I had never been one of her circle. Her desire to see me, and the confidences with which she had honored me, seemed to me a trifle unusual.

Subsequent events, and the part that the Grand Duke Cyril played at the head of the "revolutionary" Marines-of-the-Guard in the first days of the Revolution perhaps explain many things.[1]

The following day I was invited to dine with the Queen of Rumania, who placed me beside her at the table, and was as charming as she is beautiful. Fortunately no one reopened the subject of events in Petersburg.

On my return to the Embassy I found a telegram informing me that I had been promoted to the rank of general. As our divisional general was ill, I was to deputize for him. The same evening I left to rejoin the Army.

At the end of January we received orders to present ourselves at Kichinev. Bessarabia is a very fertile country, provisions and provender were plentiful, and at last our troops could obtain all they needed. We marched by long stages. The winter was very severe and we had heavy snow-falls; this made the march doubly laborious, but our Transbaikalian horses were used to such conditions, and we arrived speedily and without excessive discomfort.

The pretty little town of Kichinev, usually so quiet and sleepy, was unrecognizable. It was humming with life.

Our division, Count Keller's cavalry corps, and Prince Bagration's division were quartered in the town itself, or in the nearest suburbs. The theatres and restaurants too were full of officers of Cossack and cavalry regiments.

The nobility, the municipality, and the merchants vied with one another in making us welcome. Dinners, balls, and tea-dances followed one another in rapid succession, and the officers, who had been deprived of all these things for the last two years, gave themselves up to gaiety whole-heartedly. The hardships of the winter were forgotten, and we were far from foreseeing the horrors of the morrow.

---

[1] During the February Revolution, rather than put down the revolt Grand Duke Cyril led his men, who had been assigned to protect the Czarina, to Tauride Palace and swore allegiance to the Provisional Government. —PUBLISHER

III - At the Front and in the Interior During the Revolution

Our divisional headquarters were eighteen versts[1] from Kichinev, but we had a modest *pied-à-terre* in the town itself. When General Krymov returned and had settled down there, I went back to Headquarters.

At the beginning of March rumors of trouble in Petersburg were going round the town, there was talk of strikes, disturbances, and risings. But as all the rumors were extremely vague, we paid very little attention to them.

On March 4th or 5th, about eight o'clock in the evening, I was having supper quietly at home when General Krymov telephoned me. I gathered from his tone of voice that something serious had happened. He said "The Revolution has broken out in Petersburg, and the Czar has abdicated. I am going to read you his Manifesto, and that of his successor, the Grand Duke Michael.[2] Tomorrow the troops must be told."

I begged the General to wait a moment, and fetched the chief of our General Staff. As Krymov spoke, he wrote down the text.

The General finished reading the Czar's Manifesto and began on the Grand Duke Michael's. At the first words I said to the Chief of the General Staff: "This is the end of everything, this is anarchy."

Certainly the very fact of the Czar's abdication, even though it was provoked by social discontent, would absolutely stagger the people and the Army. But this was not all. The danger lay in the destruction of the monarchical idea and the disappearance of the monarch. During the last few years many loyal hearts had become alienated from the Czar. The Army as well as the country realized that he had endangered his throne by his own actions.

If he had abdicated in favor of his son or his brother, such an act would not have roused much painful feeling in the country. The Russian people would have sworn allegiance to the new Czar and continued to serve him and their country to the death, as they had always done—"For the Faith, the Czar, and the Homeland."

But in the present circumstances,[3] with the disappearance of the Czar the very idea of authority and all the age-old obligations vanished, and nothing could take the place of either in the minds of the Russian people.

What the officers and the Russian soldiers must have felt! Brought up on the monarchic principle, and loyal in their allegiance to the Czar, they had

---

[1] A "verst" is a Russian measure of distance, roughly equivalent to 2/3rds of a mile or slightly more than one kilometer—PUBLISHER

[2] The Czar abdicated on his own behalf and on that of his son, thus making his brother, the Grand Duke Michael, his successor—TRANSLATOR

[3] The Grand Duke Michael, in favor of whom the Czar had abdicated, had given up his power to the Provisional Government—TRANSLATOR

acted on their principles all their lives, and saw the chief meaning of the war in them. . . .

I must admit that the High Command remained absolutely passive, doing nothing to help the Army though this crisis, to keep up the spirits of the troops, or to make them realize their duty. They issued no orders, and each general had to do what he thought was for the best. One or two stupid things were done. One colonel of an infantry regiment could find nothing more intelligent to say to his men than that the Czar had gone mad.

I decided to communicate the two Manifestos to the soldiers and to explain things as I saw them myself. I informed them of the disturbances in the interior and of the general discontent, a natural result of the abuses committed by the officials who had duped the Czar, or who had been too incompetent to do their duty and to cope with the difficulties of the war. I told them I did not know why the Czar had considered it necessary to abdicate, but here were the Manifestos of the Czar and the Grand Duke, the will of the Czar, to whom we had sworn allegiance, and that of his successor ought to be sacred to us, and since he commanded us to obey and be loyal to the Provisional Government, our duty was to do so.

In the morning the two Manifestos were read to the regiments. The first impression can be described in one word—stupefaction. It was a staggering blow. Officers and men were dumbfounded and could scarcely pull themselves together. For some days the camp was gloomy, everyone trying to understand what had happened. Only in the units where the intellectuals were leaders, and especially behind-the-lines (ambulances, depots, etc.), cheerfulness reigned supreme, and the new regime was celebrated joyfully.

The crisis safely over, I went along to see General Krymov. He took an optimistic view of things, believing that we were on the eve of a renaissance and not of a disaster.

The town was already given over to popular political meetings: groups of people were marching about under the red flag; at the cross-roads, orators sprung from goodness knows where, were haranguing the people. But the General continued to be optimistic. He was convinced that the Army would keep out of politics altogether, and said that since a change of government was inevitable, it was better that it should happen now, and not after the demobilization. Then the Army could return, weapons in hand, to dictate the law of the land in its own way.

He told me the names of the members of the Provisional Government. Goutchkov, the Minister of War, was the only one who had any idea of the needs of the Army. He had been at the head of the Red Cross during the Russo-Japanese War, and President of the Committee for National Defence in the Duma. Now he was Chairman of the Technical Revictualling Committee. Krymov, who knew him intimately, had full confidence in him.

Nevertheless, the appointment of a civilian to the post of Minister of War in the middle of a campaign was a risky proceeding.

"Yes," Krymov said to me, "he is a real statesman, and, furthermore, he knows as much about the Army as you and I do. You will see how things go. He is not to be compared with those damned old routine-mongers who have spent their whole lives in ministries. He is worth the whole lot of them put together."

The head of the Government, Prince Lvov, had been President of the United Zemstvos.[1] He was reputed to be a staunch patriot and an honest man. Miliukov and Chingarev had been eloquent leaders of the Opposition, but of the rest, Terechtchenko, Nekrassov, and the others, we knew little or nothing. . . . We were justified in doubting whether the necessary men, capable of taking the power into their hands, were to be found amongst them.

The General gave me the newspapers which had just arrived from Petersburg. They were scarcely reassuring. It was clear that the Government was already drifting from its original course, taken in tow by the Soviet of the Deputies of the Workmen and Soldiers. I was especially angry to hear for the first time that "soldiers and officers would end by understanding one another, and officers would be forced to respect the soldiers who were men like themselves."

This humbug was not only repeated by nobodies, but by such men as M. Miliukov in his speech at the Tauride Palace on March 2nd.

My fears were only too well founded. The Provisional Government's first measures showed that the disorder in the interior had gone too far to be suppressed, and that these incompetent men, strangers to the Army, could do nothing to prevent things from going to ruin. One morning Krymov telephoned me, saying—

> Get together whatever you need for a few days' absence, you must leave today for Petersburg. Come over here and I will tell you what it is all about.

An hour later I was in Kichinev. I found the General in his shirt-sleeves and red breeches, surrounded by crumpled newspapers which were torn to pieces and trampled underfoot. He was beside himself.

"Read that!" he said, thrusting a newspaper into my hands. "They have lost their heads, God knows what is happening there! I cannot believe that this is really Goutchkov. How can he allow those scoundrels to touch the Army? I have written to him. I cannot leave my division without the permission of my immediate superior. You can go, because I am your superior and I give you permission. Go to Petersburg and see Goutchkov."

---

[1] Zemstvos = local representative assembles—TRANSLATOR.

He began to read his letter to me. In words expressive of sorrow and the deepest indignation, he drew attention to the danger that threatened the Army, and the whole of Russia with it. The Army ought to remain outside politics altogether, and all those who meddled with it were committing a crime against their country. . . . In the middle of reading the letter he clasped his head in his hands and burst into sobs. The letter ended by begging the Minister to regard everything that I said as coming from himself.

The same evening I left for Petersburg. On the way, at one of the stations, we met an express coming from the north. General Baron Mannerheim (who later commanded the White Army in Finland) was on it. He was the first eye-witness to give me details of the popular risings in the capital, the treason of the troops and the murder of officers which had been going on since the beginning of the Revolution. Baron Mannerheim himself had been forced to hide for three days, slipping from one lodging to another. Amongst the victims of the frenzied mob and the soldiery were a number of my friends—old Count Stackelberg, Count Mengden, formerly a colonel in the Horse-Guards, Count Klenmichel, a Hussar of the Guard, and others too . . . the two last mentioned had been murdered at Louga by their own soldiers, reservists of the Guard.

Whilst waiting for our connection at Kiev, we visited the town. The Statue of Stolypin had been knocked down and several houses sacked. It was here that I first heard people praising Kerensky; his admirers believed that he was the only member of the Government with any control over the populace, they said it was he who had put an end to the massacres which had begun in the first days of the Revolution.

At Bakhmatch, Colonel Count Mengden got into the train. He was the brother of the Mengden who had just been assassinated, and aide-de-camp to the Grand Duke Nicholas whom the Czar had appointed Generalissimo when he himself had abdicated. He told us he had just left the Grand Duke, who had already been advised that the Provisional Government desired him to give up his command to General Alexeiev. The Grand Duke had decided to comply with this request to avoid complications. Personally I considered this to be a fatal decision. The Grand Duke was very popular with the Army, with the men as well as the officers. The Supreme Command and the generals at the front would have bowed to his authority. He alone would have been able to save the Army from imminent ruin. The Provisional Government dared not even enter into direct conflict with him.

Tsarskoie Selo Station was swarming with drunken, disorderly soldiers decorated with red ribbons. They were shouting, fooling around, splitting their sides with laughter, and behaving as though they were conquerors. They jostled the train-drivers and climbed into the carriage and the restaurant-car in which I was having lunch. A shock-headed little horror with a cigarette in his mouth and a red ribbon on his breast installed himself unceremoniously at the table of a lady dressed as a hospital nurse and began ogling her. The lady repulsed his attempts, and he gave vent to obscene insults. I took him by the scruff of his neck, carried him to the door, and kicked him out, sending him rolling down the corridor. I heard the men muttering, but no one made even a show of defending him against me.

The first thing I noticed in Petersburg was the profusion of red ribbon. Everyone was decorated with it, not only soldiers, but students, chauffeurs, cab-drivers, middle-class folk, women, children, and many officers. Men of some account, such as old generals and former aides-de-camp to the Czar, wore it too.

I expressed my astonishment to an old comrade of mine at seeing him thus adorned. He tried to laugh it off, and said jokingly: "Why, my dear fellow, don't you know that it's the latest fashion?"

I considered this ridiculous adornment absolutely useless. Throughout my stay in the capital I wore the Czarevitch's badge, the distinguishing mark of my old regiment, on my epaulettes, and, of course, I wore no red rag, and not a soul ever sought to molest me because of it.

The Duma also trembled before the Soviet of the Deputies of the Soldiers and Workmen, and soon let itself be dismissed docilely enough.

This faint-heartedness and servile kowtowing to the new power had been apparent from the first, not only among the soldiers, officers, and minor officials, but also in the Czar's entourage, and even within the ranks of the Imperial Family itself.

From the very first hour of danger the Czar had been abandoned by everyone. During the terrible time which the Czarina and her children had spent at Tsarskoie Selo not a member of the Imperial Family had gone to their aid.

The Grand Duke Cyril Vladimirovich had led the Marines-of-the-Guard to the Duma in person, hastening to present himself to M. Rodzianko.[1] Interviews with him and with Nicholas Mikhailovitch appeared in many newspapers, in which they spoke about the Czar in a vile way. I read these interviews with the utmost indignation.

The struggle for power between the Duma and the Soviet of the Deputies of the Workmen and Soldiers still went on; the Provisional Government, finding that it had no forces with which to fight openly, took more and more to the fatal course of compromise.

Goutchkov, the Minister of War, was away. I told his chancellor's office to advise me when he returned. The next day they let me know that the Minister for Foreign Affairs, Miliukov, had requested me to call and see him.

He received me very politely. "I am in constant communication with Goutchkov. I can forward him the letter which you bring and send him a

---

[1] Rodzianko = President of the Duma—TRANSLATOR.

verbatim account of all that you say. He and I belong to different parties, but today we should all be unanimous, should we not?"

I told him that today iron discipline was more indispensable than ever, that we ought to strengthen and not discredit the authority of the leaders, and that the Government's orders were intended to undermine the foundations of the Army. In short, I said all that I should have said in my military capacity.

He listened to me very attentively and made some notes.

"You interest me very much, but I will not conceal from you that the information we have received from the representatives of the Army does not coincide with what you have just told me," he said.

"That I can well believe," I replied. "But would you be good enough to tell me, sir, to what representatives of the Army you are referring? To those who have been elected by nobody but themselves, and today lord it with the Soviet, or to those who stroll about the Streets, adorned with red ribbons? In Petersburg now the only real soldiers are those lying in the hospitals. It is not they, obviously, who have given you your information. I have no doubt that the others I have mentioned hastened to throw in their lot with the Revolution as soon as it broke out."

"Well, since it is not my province," he concluded, "I will refrain from expressing an opinion. M. Goutchkov is more competent than I to deal with these questions. In any case, I will inform him of our interview, and when he returns he will probably see you himself."

I found a telegram from General Krymov awaiting me at home. The Minister of War had summoned him to Petersburg, so I was to go back to take his place. When I arrived at Kichinev, Krymov had already left for the capital, taking Samarin, his chief-of-staff, with him, for he had been appointed chief of the Minister of War's Cabinet. He was replaced by Colonel Polkovnikov, who later on, after General Kornilov's rebellion, played such a disastrous part during the days when the Provisional Government was falling from power. As chief of the Divisional Staff he was a good worker and a conscientious officer.

We went through bad times. The Provisional Government continued to lose ground to the Soviet, which soon began to lay down the law to it.

The Army realized that this was happening, and instinctively tried to supply a remedy. A number of regiments informed the Government, through their commanders, that they would support it in order to ward off anarchy. All the regiments of our division were of the number.

Unfortunately the Government did not know how to take advantage of the proffered help, or did not wish to. Goutchkov, who paid a visit to the Army at this time, adopted a very haughty tone, saying that the Provisional Government was quite strong enough to dispense with all external support, that there had been no division of power, and that the Soviets and the Government were acting in complete agreement.

Each commanding officer did as he pleased, without consulting his colleagues of the other forces and divisions. Whilst Count Keller refused to swear allegiance to the Provisional Government, and made his troops march past to the strains of the old Imperial Hymn when he took leave of them, General Broussiloff had himself carried at the head of his troops in an arm-chair decorated with red ribbons. . . .

On March 17th I went along to a fete which one of my Cossack regiments was holding. This regiment was brave enough in battle, but rotten at heart. As I approached on horseback I saw that most of the squadrons had replaced their battalion colors with red flags. Passing down the ranks, I noticed that one of these flags was spotted with black, and was made out of a skirt such as the peasant women wear.

I asked the Colonel the meaning of this unseemly farce, "General, the Cossacks ordered it." I replied that in the Army the Cossacks had to obey orders, and not make them. I saluted the regiment in the usual way, then added: "I came here to drink to the glory of your regiment under your glorious old flag for which, so many brave men have died. But now I have changed my mind. It would disgust me to drink to the health of gallant soldiers beneath the shadow of a red petticoat,' and I turned back.

I censured the Colonel in the general orders. With the connivance of one of the captains with whom I was also dissatisfied, he tried to stir up the officers and Cossacks against me, pretending that because I myself was not a Cossack by birth I wanted to disparage all those who were. When I heard of this, I dismissed him from his command, and ordered him and his partner to leave the division that very day and present themselves behind-the-lines, where both of them were brought up for trial.

Except for this incident, order was maintained throughout the division.

General Krymov came back on March 30th. He had been appointed commander of the 3rd Cavalry Corps in place of Count Keller.

Since M. Goutchkov had been at the War Office, one hundred and forty-three of the higher commanders had been dismissed from the military staff, and had been replaced regardless of the custom of promotion by seniority. This proceeding was a very grave mistake. It is true that a number of the higher commanders lacked ability, but the mass-changes, the replacing of old generals by men who were unknown to the troops, especially at such a critical moment, had a disastrous effect on the internal order and the fighting-power of the Army.

General Krymov told me of the massacres at Kronstadt, which had put a period to the life of the best officers of the Baltic Fleet. The sailors had assassinated them.

Krymov had just seen the new members of the Provisional Government, several of them were his friends, and he had regained his courage. According to him, the Provisional Government was strong enough to make itself master of events, in spite of its appearance of weakness. The members of the Government fully realized the necessity for this. They expected to be supported by large sections of society and of the Army, but its principal support, according to Krymov, would be the Cossacks.

Also, the General had managed to get my Oussourian division transferred to this Army Corps, in place of the gallant 12th division of regular cavalry.

I was far from sharing the hopes he entertained concerning the Cossacks. I had spent part of my youth in the district where the Don Cossacks live, I had gone through the Russo-Japanese War in a Cossack regiment, and had since commanded a regiment, a brigade, and a division of Cossacks. I knew them through and through, and I knew that they could easily become the tool of Cossack political cliques.

The separatist tendencies among the Cossacks were a serious danger at this time, because Cossack units formed part of many of the regular divisions.

I believed that there were other ways of combating disorder; that there was no need to rely on only one section of the Army for support, but that we could achieve agreement amongst the command and weld the Army into one unit. But I failed to convince General Krymov, he had passionate faith in his new idea. The troops understood it, and began to distinguish between Cossack and non-Cossack officers straight away. Several officers who were not Cossack asked to be transferred to other regiments.

I told the General that even admitting that I was mistaken and he right (and I would to God it had been so!), we must be consistent and avoid anything which might hinder the success of his plans in the smallest degree, that I, not being a Cossack by birth, and having always served in the regular Army in peace-time, could not possibly be a suitable colleague for him.

General Krymov understood me, and did not argue the point. As our appointments had not yet been published, I could obtain another division without any difficulty. The General wrote to the Minister of War to this effect, and on April 5th I left for Petersburg.

CHAPTER II

THE PROVISIONAL GOVERNMENT

In Petersburg I found that excitement had reached a higher pitch than ever. From morning till night and from night till morning the streets were crowded, especially with soldiers, who were strolling about aimlessly. Red ribbons had gone out of fashion, but untidiness and carelessness were increasing noticeably. The soldiers passed their time in eating sunflower seeds, staring at the officers without saluting them, and jostling passers-by.

Endless meetings were held all over the place—at the Tauride Palace, in the riding-schools, the barracks, the Town Hall, the schools, and elsewhere, especially in public places and at the cross-roads.

Those who had been forced to be silent for centuries now burned to make up for lost time. In the theatres and the cinemas there was invariably some babbler who would stand on a chair and harangue the audience during the intervals. The Press was overflowing with articles, and it was always the same old story, "the peaceful Revolution," "the struggle for liberty," "the safeguarding of the privileges already won." There was no longer any mention of the welfare of Russia, only of the welfare of the "conquests of the Revolution."

The struggle between the Government and the Soviet went on. To give the demagogues their due, they made for their goal straightforwardly, while the right wing of the Government shuffled and vied in cunning with the Bolsheviks, supported and subsidized as they were by Germany. They had seized the Hotel of the Dancer Kchesinska in broad daylight, and were preaching peace from its balcony. The Government trembled and took no action. The old ministers and the former higher officials were in prison, not because they had been accused of sedition against the new Government, but simply because such was the good pleasure of the revolutionary democracy.

The Government, or rather the Soviet, suppressed the Conservative newspapers, whilst the Press of the Left continued its campaign against the Army.

Investigations were the order of the day. A search was made even in the house of the Dowager-Empress, who lived in the Crimea, and this, mark you, by order of the authorities.

And these gentlemen of the Government, who till recently had been reproaching the Czar for his weakness and despotism, now showed themselves to be far weaker, far more irresolute than he had been, and much more foolish than the high officials of the regime they had overthrown.

On April 20th the Red Guard marched against the Government for the first time, and the Government did not yield an inch. At the corner of the Nevsky and the Mikhailovskaia some passers-by were killed. I saw it all from the restaurant where I was having lunch. The crowd scattered at top speed, the cab-drivers lashed their old hacks to a gallop. The scoundrels, with faces like gallows-birds, marched off to the strains of the International. The public, furious with the Red Guard, were loudly accusing the Government of weakness.

I walked along to the Ministry of War, where I found the leader of the Cabinet, Colonel Samarin, our former chief-of-staff.

"Well, Colonel," I said, "so you are not offering any resistance!"

"The Government cannot shed Russian blood," he answered. "If blood is spilt, the Government will lose its moral prestige in the eyes of the people for good and all."

The next day the Soviet published a signed order forbidding the troops to leave their barracks without permission. On May 5th a demonstration was made by the troops which were still loyal to the Government, but that apathetic and impotent power did not know how to use them.

To be absolutely truthful, I must admit that almost the entire population of the capital remained quite passive in the face of everything that happened. They did not seem to notice anything. Some posed as conspirators and spoke of the necessity for organizing themselves, but no one ever dreamt of doing it.

In the Army, thanks to the initiative of Generals Alexeiev and Denikin, there were already officers societies: there was one in Petersburg too, but it did more harm than good. It was scarcely established before it was divided into two hostile camps. Those who hoped to fish in troubled waters declared their adherence to the Revolution.

In some way or another the confusion had to be checked, and, above all, a man had to be found whom the majority would accept as leader—a man popular with the Army, who could lead the troops if necessary, and rely on the support of their bayonets. I considered only two men suitable tor this role—General Letchitsky, the Commander-in-Chief of the 9th Army, and General Kornilov, both of them brave, enterprising, distinguished men, and both adored by the Army. Letchitsky, disgusted with the course things had taken, had sent in his resignation, and was living as a private person. Kornilov at this time was commanding the troops in the capital, a particularly favorable circumstance.

I got into touch with other officers on whom I could rely, and soon we were numerous enough to be able to begin work.

Suddenly, at the beginning of May, General Kornilov definitely broke with the Soviet and left his post. He accepted the command of the 8th Army, which was in Galicia. Amongst others, General Letchitsky was nominated as successor to General Kornilov. I decided to speak to him.

I explained the position, and said that we were at his disposal, and that we had money enough to meet the initial expenses. I added that, once Kornilov had left, he would be nominated as before to replace him, and I begged him not to refuse the post.

"I agree with your point of view," Letchitsky said to me. "I support your programme, as every soldier will. But I will not succeed Kornilov. I have left the Army for good. I am only an old soldier, and nothing more than a soldier. To make a success of the task you have outlined to me, it is not enough to be firm and honest, you must be able to adapt yourself to circumstances. No, it needs a younger man than I."

I knew the General too well to insist.

A few days later General Kornilov left the capital, and was replaced by General Polovtsev, of the Caucasian division.

Although he had gone away, Kornilov still kept in touch with the capital. A certain Zawoiko, his orderly officer, was his go-between. I did not know this gentleman personally, but Colonel Count Pahlen and Lieutenant Count Schuvalov, who shared my opinions, knew him well. They introduced us. Zawoiko seemed to me to be intelligent and energetic, but insincere. Did the sequel prove me wrong? Nevertheless, as I knew him to be Kornilov's confidant, I spoke freely to him, and told him what we had already succeeded in doing. And from that time on Kornilov was kept informed of our actions and movements.

The Army of the day after tomorrow would have to take the offensive again, and the whole town as well as the enemy knew it. Goutchkov had resigned, and the new Minister of War, Kerensky, had struggled into possession. He harangued the troops, urging them in ringing tones to "save the Revolution." New contingents and many reinforcements were on the march, preceded by placards with such inscriptions as "War to the finish," "Death is better than slavery," and similar tags. But it was only rarely that these reinforcements reached their destination. Usually the contingents which were "ready to die to save the Revolution" took themselves off on the way.

On June 18th the Armies on the south-west front attacked the enemy. Kornilov's 8th Army invaded Galicia. A breach was made in the enemy's ranks, and the Russian Army was master of Galitch and Stanislavov. It seemed that after long months of anguish we were at last to be victorious.

On June 30,1917, a telegram from Headquarters informed me that at last I had been appointed commander of the 7th cavalry division in Kornilov's Army. That same day I went to join my division, leaving Count Pahlen at the head of the group of which I have spoken earlier, and taking Schuvalov with me in order to leave him with Kornilov, who needed him.

II - The Revolutionary Army on the Offensive

I reached Kamenetz-Podolsk on July 6th, and found bad news awaiting me. There was a telegram from Kerensky, couched in the following words—

> The Revolutionary Army's admirable beginning has ended in the treason of the Grenadiers-of-the-Guard and the general rout of the 11th Army, which is marching towards the interior. The enemy have taken Tarnopol and are threatening the flank and rear of the 8th Army which Kornilov is commanding. The battalions in the encounter, mostly composed of officers, died like heroes, but the "Democratic Army" saw no point in imitating them or in dying to save the Revolution, and have scattered like a flock of sheep. The generals, deprived of all their forces, are powerless.

In face of the danger which threatened them, the inefficient Provisional Government seemed to realize that "*revolutionary élan*" was not enough, and that discipline also was necessary. The appointment of General Kornilov as Commander-in-Chief of the south-eastern front seemed to confirm this. I had hoped to find General Kornilov still with the Army, and Count Schuvalov and I went immediately to Kolomea, where I thought we should find him. Colonel Count Heyden, who was on his Staff, told me that the General was still at the front, would not be back till the evening, and was leaving the next day for his new Headquarters.

I learnt from Count Heyden that my division (Olviopol Lancers, White Russian Hussars, Kinbourn Dragoons, and the 2nd Don Cossacks) had not yet been completely disorganized by democratization. My predecessor, as well as one of the colonels, had already been forced to leave, but as the officers' corps was excellent, and the regiments were sound on the whole, it would not be difficult to take them in hand again.

Whilst we were talking, a young civilian in a brand new tunic, with a rakish cap and a soldierly manner, came into the room. The Count introduced us. It was M. Philonenko, commissioner and delegate from the 8th Army.

There and then, with extraordinary self-assurance, he began to speak of our military operations and strategy. According to him, he had helped considerably in the maintenance of discipline, and he implied that he was largely responsible for the appointment of the Commander-in-Chief. He promised me his help and protection too, if, by any chance, I wanted to get rid of any officers and soldiers or of any committees of the troops, he was at my service.

I knew Kornilov personally through having dined with him once at the Czar's table in Moghilev, and I had spent an hour or two in the same railway-carriage with him.

Small, spare, swarthy, of the Mongolian type, with a little goatee beard and a black moustache, he spoke in short, abrupt sentences. One had only to see him to realize that he was a man of indomitable energy and great breadth of mind.

I told him that I was proceeding with the organization of the capital, and offered to leave Schuvalov with him, if he cared to have him. He kept him as his orderly officer.

The General, who was due to leave for his new Headquarters in a few hours' time, invited me to dinner and introduced me to his successor, General Tcheremissov, who struck me as being intelligent, but who never looked one straight in the face. My impressions were limited to these, for during the meal we spoke only of unimportant matters.

After dinner, General Kornilov set out for his Headquarters and I for my division.

When I arrived, I had barely had time to review the Hussar regiment, when there came an order from General Tcheremissov ordering me to go immediately to Stanislavov, which he had just reached. My division was to proceed towards this town and cover the flank of the 8th Army which was retreating all along the line. I gave the necessary orders to the brigade-commander who was to take my place whilst I was away, and set off in my car.

I arrived at nightfall. The General Staff was just leaving, they were looking for wagons, removing telephones, and striking camp. The tram which was to take the General away was in the station. About a hundred wagons and lorries followed one after the other. General Tcheremissov explained the situation to me. The whole Army was in full retreat, harassed by the enemy, who was at its heels. The only position it was possible to take up was at Zbioutch. I was put at the head of two divisions, my own and the 3rd division of Caucasian Cossacks; together they formed a cavalry troop which was to manoeuvre on the flanks of the 7th and 8th Armies and to cover their retreat.

I wanted to await the arrival of my own division, which was marching on Stanislavov, so that I could give them the necessary orders, and then to rejoin the Caucasian division, which was operating in the Monastergisk zone, where I intended to concentrate the whole corps.

That night I was awakened by a fiendish din; there were screams and shots. I ran to the window—the town was on fire. I was dressing hastily when an orderly came in, "Your Excellency—it's a pogrom; the retreating soldiers are ransacking the town!"

In the hall, leaning against the wall, was an old man with a long white beard all covered with blood. A dishevelled and almost naked young woman was weeping and wringing her hands. She seized my hands and tried to kiss them, screaming, sobbing, and speaking a dialect I could not understand. I appealed to the porter to act as interpreter.

He told me that the old man was a Jew, the owner of a shop which had been looted, he had been roughly handled and had escaped death only by a miracle.

There were only my orderly and two Hussars near at hand. We went into the street.

Pillaging was going on everywhere: windows were being broken, doors smashed in, furniture destroyed, boxes forced open, materials and household articles covered the roadways and obstructed the ammunition-wagons, lorries, and ambulances. Fires were smouldering all over the place; a spark was enough to cause severe trouble.

An artillery officer I met gave me some men, and I attempted to restore order. Coming upon a group of fugitives engaged in rifling a shop, I struck one of them violently with my fist and felled him to the ground. My two Hussars also hit out. I called out. "Cossacks, see that this scoundrel is flogged." And the whole lot took themselves off.

With the assistance of the gunners, the streets were cleared in two hours, and the artillery and transport were able to get on the march. In the side-streets looting still went on. I had done so much shouting that I had lost my voice.

With the dawn a squadron of lancers arrived I commanded the colonel who was with them to put an end to the pogrom, no matter what the cost. He had a few of the pillagers shot down, and order was restored.

I got into a car and set off to rejoin my Cossack division. Amongst the officers attached to the Divisional Staff, I came across the former Minister of War, Goutchkov, who had just joined up.

The Army was in retreat all along the line. As for Monastergisk, which was occupied by one of my regiments, there was a big munition depot there, and Headquarters had sent along an engineering officer with orders to destroy it.

I was just having dinner when I learnt that my Ossetines[1] were at grips with the enemy in Monastergisk, I motored over there with my chief-of-staff. As we approached the town we saw a huge column of smoke mounting skywards. Then there was an explosion which shook the ground, it was followed by a second and a third. The town was on fire. We met about a hundred men with herds of cattle in full flight. On inquiry, we discovered that the engineering officer, seeing the enemy approaching, had set fire to the depots without first warning the troops, who were skirmishing on the

[1] The Ossetine regiment belonged to the Caucasian division, and was named after one of the numerous Caucasian tribes.—TRANSLATOR

outskirts of the town. More than a dozen of the cavalry and the colonel of the regiment had been killed, victims of a piece of criminal negligence.

That evening the enemy entered the town, and I took up a position some versts to the east.

At dawn the enemy attacked all along the line. For hours all their efforts were in vain. Towards evening the Germans managed to make themselves masters of a village occupied by a detachment of my Kinbourn Dragoons, and threatened us with a breach. I ordered the other squadrons of the regiment to attack. The Germans were beaten.

We took some prisoners and captured some machine-guns. By nightfall the danger was over, and I retired, covering the infantry.

The infantry was still retreating all along the line. Discipline was gone, and numerous stragglers were looting every place they passed through. My corps was maneuvering on the flanks of the 7th and 8th Armies, and was gradually passing over to the offensive.

This went on for some days. I had not yet got to know my regiments, nor they me, so I marched sometimes with one, sometimes with another, so that I could watch them at work.

The Army crossed the Zbroutch and took up its position on the right bank, in close touch with the enemy. My men remained half a day's march to the west of the Zbioutch.

I was under orders to stay there till nightfall if possible, so as to give the infantry time to dig trenches, after which I was to cross the river and concentrate my two divisions behind the line occupied by the infantry. At dawn I learnt that my Cossack division was retreating, hard-pressed by the enemy. An Austrian cavalry brigade, profiting by this retreat, deflected the right flank of the 7th division, with which I was marching at the time, I ordered three regiments into the saddle, leaving the fourth to cover the artillery.

From the top of a hill I watched the enemy approaching at full trot. Shortly afterwards a shell passed over our heads. The enemy had probably sighted our group of officers and was firing on us.

I ordered the artillery to open an *enfilade*, and then set the three regiments on to the Austrians. The enemy turned tail without waiting for an encounter. At this moment another brigade was turning our left flank. Leaving one regiment to pursue the enemy, I commanded the three regiments which remained to charge for the second time, and again the enemy withdrew before the onslaught.

In the meanwhile the Cossack division also went over to the offensive, overthrew the enemy, and again took up the position it had occupied the evening before.

Until night-time the enemy would not attempt to attack us again, but would merely send over some large calibre shells. I went down to one of my brigades which was resting in the forest. The officers were sitting at table near a forester's hut. I had scarcely dismounted when a shell fell not far away. A wounded man groaned, a horse covered with blood galloped off at top speed. Several troopers came out of the wood in great haste, others ran to their horses. There was nearly a panic. I gave the command "eyes front," sat down at the table, and, picking up a fragment of a newly burst shell which had fallen quite near. I turned to the soldiers, saying: "Who wants some hot rolls? Catch!" and I threw it to one of them. Then faces brightened, and a laugh ran along the ranks. They were no longer panicky.

The firing soon ceased. We had only had two men killed and several horses wounded. The regiments set out for their camps.

Then afterwards I passed them at the gallop. I shouted a few words to them, and they cheered me enthusiastically. It was one of those psychological moments when officer and soldiers seem to be of one flesh.

I have lived through other such unforgettable moments before and since—in Manchuria, in Eastern Prussia, in Galicia, in the Kuban, and in the Crimea. I do not know how these bonds are forged on the spur of the moment, always spontaneously and often without any apparent reason. One feels these things instinctively, though one cannot explain them. Without these bonds there would be no army. It is not enough to have your men well in hand, they must be yours, so that they will follow you, not only from a sense of duty, but because something stronger than themselves stirs in their hearts, and makes it impossible for them to do otherwise.

The next day we crossed the Zbroutch. The operations with which we had been entrusted were over: my cavalry was mentioned in dispatches.

One fine day the chief of the Army Staff telephoned me. One of our Caucasian infantry regiments had left its post, and the enemy could profit by this to make a breach and threaten Kamenetz.

Headquarters had been there, but had broken camp. I was ordered to save the situation. The 79th infantry division was to relieve me.

I saw that the cavalry got on the march, and found some ambulances and thirty cars in the car-park, also ten lorries for the General Staff, then I ordered a skirmishing regiment of the 7th division to mount, and we set off. One of my Cossack regiments was already at grips with the enemy and master of a village which the Caucasians had abandoned.

The Caucasians, who had retreated, were camping four kilometres from the battlefield. I ordered them to attack simultaneously with a brigade of the 7th division which was deployed on to the skirmishers.

The enemy's artillery opened an *enfilade*, and suddenly I saw our Caucasians waver and take to flight all along the front. Our artillery sent over some shells, but this only hastened their retreat. I despatched my Lancers, who, with their lances and the flat of their swords, rounded up the men as if they had been a flock of sheep.

I let them get their breath back and have some food, then I made an encouraging speech to them, put myself at their head, and led them to the charge. At first they marched half-heartedly, then with spirit, and finally they charged with fixed bayonets. We took three hundred prisoners and four machine-guns.

Unfortunately, my aide-de-camp and two of my orderly officers were seriously wounded.

After the attack, I said to the chief of my General Staff; "Now we can feel easy about the Caucasians. After such a success, the regiment will fight well."

I was mistaken. That same night they abandoned their position and took themselves off to the interior. . . .

Nevertheless, our cavalry succeeded in holding the head of the Khotin bridge until the expected reinforcements came up. After this affair (whilst we are still on the subject) I received a telegram from the Commander of the Army—

Honor and glory to your cavalry corps— TCHEREMISSOV.

Shortly afterwards General Tcheremissov was superseded by General Sokovnin. On July 16th General Kornilov was appointed Commander-in-Chief of the Russian Army.

III - KORNILOV

When Kornilov was made Generalissimo, the Army realized that at last it had a real leader, the High Command felt that its authority would be restored, and the soldier that he was going to be forced to obey. The powers of the Soldiers' Committees were curtailed.

The men who made up these Committees were not at all bad on the whole. After talking to them on many occasions, I came to the conclusion that if they were properly influenced and left politics alone, dealing only with practical questions, they might even be useful.

Thus the democratized Commissariat frequently refused to hand over material when the commanders of formations asked for it, even when the troops were in pressing need; but they supplied the company delegates at the first demand.

Zawoiko wrote to me frequently. I learnt from him that in view of the desertions in the Army, which were steadily on the increase in certain companies, Kornilov had demanded, amongst other things, that the death-penalty (abolished by the Provisional Government) should be reestablished for deserters and traitors at the front as well as in the interior.

The letter finished with these words —

> The General charges me to tell you to be patient, and not to accuse us falsely of letting things slide. It is impossible to embark on anything before the winter.

To my great astonishment, on August 10th or 12th, I received a telegram from Supreme Headquarters—

> As you are to be appointed to a new post, you have now been put at the disposal of the Commander of the Armies on the Rumanian front, at the same time you are to keep the command of your cavalry corps.

I could not make head or tail of the extremely strange wording of this telegram, so I telephoned Count Schuvalov, and asked him to explain to me what it was intended to convey. He answered that nobody knew at Supreme Headquarters. The Generalissimo was at Moscow and was not returning for a few days. Then I received a telegram from Zawoiko—

> The Generalissimo is very pleased with you. An important post has been entrusted to you.

The same day the order came to send off a brigade of the 3rd Caucasian division to rejoin the Caucasian division stationed at Dno.[1]

On August 27th I joined the General Staff as directed. I found them in an uproar. They had just received a proclamation from Kornilov addressed to the troops. In it he spoke of "infamous treason," and forbade the reception of any communications whatsoever from the President of the Ministerial Council (Kerensky's telegram accusing Kornilov of rebellion arrived some hours later). At the same time Headquarters ordered all the wireless apparatus to be taken away.

The Army Committee protested against this order, and were supported by Levitzky, the Quartermaster-General. The Commander of the Army, General Sokovnin, and his chief-of-staff, had lost their heads. With great difficulty I obtained a copy of the Generalissimo's order. The Commander of the Army proposed that we should not let it become public until the situation was more settled. But he could not stand out against the Committee, and ordered the Quartermaster not to "allow the removal of the wireless."

As I left the General Staff, I saw General Levitzky triumphantly announcing his decision to members of the Committees. I could not refrain

---

[1] An important group of railways on the road to St. Petersburg.—TRANSLATOR.

from telling General Levitzky very sharply that I considered the non-execution of an order from the Generalissimo to be a crime, and that I would immediately order the removal of the apparatus from my General Staff.

The next morning my aide-de-camp came and told me that the Soldiers' Committee of my 3rd Cossack division was sitting, presided over by a demagogue priest whom I had tried to get removed many times.

I went down, and found General Odintzov, the commander of the division, there too. As I entered I saluted the men, as I always do: "Good morning, Cossacks."

The Cossacks answered me as usual. Then the priest-president said: "Will you please note, General, that the members here assembled are not Cossacks, as you call them, but citizens."

"You are quite right, Father; we are all citizens. But that does not prevent my being a General, your being a priest, and their being brave Cossacks. That they are brave I know very well, because I have seen them in battle more than once. That they are Cossacks. I also know, for I myself have worn their uniform for years, and am proud of it."

And turning to the assembly, "Once more, good morning, Cossacks "

"Greetings, Your Excellency," they shouted as one man.

I took my place at the president's table, and requested Brigadier-General Odintzov to acquaint me with the order of the day. He told me that they had just read Kerensky's telegram, and were about to deliberate on the terms in which they were to let him know that the Committee would support him.

"Splendid. And does the Committee know about the Commander-in-Chief telegram?"

A fellow in a tunic, who was not a soldier at all, interrupted "The Army Committee, of which I am the delegate, does not consider it necessary to communicate the telegram to the Company Committees."

"This telegram," I said, "has been sent to me by the Commander of the Army, and I must communicate it to my brothers-in-arms. I will take the responsibility."

The members of the Army Committee protested, but the majority shouted, "We want to hear it!"

I read the proclamation from Major-General Kornilov.

"And now, my men, you know all there is to know. I feel certain that you will do your duty as soldiers, and that you will reach a decision compatible with your conscience and your duty. As for myself, I am a soldier, and have nothing to do with politics. My Generalissimo's orders are law to me. I am sure that your divisional commander will tell you the same thing."

I looked at Odintzov. At last he stammered out, dropping his eyes: "I . . . like all the Cossacks . . . my children." With great difficulty I restrained myself from supplementing this faint-hearted remark, and taking leave of the Cossacks, I went out to my car.

As I was getting into my car Odintzov dashed up: "Er. . . Er . . . I was so startled . . . that really."

Without answering him, I told the chauffeur to drive off.

After long consultations, the 3rd Cossack division declared for Kerensky. The 7th division did not come to any decision until the evening.

The next day Headquarters, which was losing more and more ground to the Committees, decreed that the telephones and telegraphs were to be put under the direct control of the Soldiers' Committees. Furthermore, no orders coming from the commanding officers were to be valid unless countersigned by a member of the Committee.

It was the last straw. I galloped over to Headquarters and procured an interview with the Commander of the Army. "Your Excellency, your decree is a crime for an officer. I cannot possibly obey it, so I beg you to let me resign my commission."

"General! You are not thinking of doing that.'"

"I am thinking of doing one of three things: either of giving a counter-order, or of resigning my duties, or of saddling the 7th division and having a little chat with the Committees face to face."

General Sokovnin said that he would try and arrange something. That same day he sent me what was in effect a counter-order.

On September 5th a telegram from General Sherbatchov, Commander-in-Chief on the Rumanian front, ordered me to go at once to Jassy.

Sherbatchov had been the head of the Military College where I had studied, he told me that, knowing my relations with Kornilov, he had sent for me so that should any unforeseen contingency arise, I should be with him, and therefore, according to him, safe.

Two days later a telegram from the chief-of-staff at Supreme Headquarters informed me that, by an order of September 9th, the Generalissimo had appointed me Commander of the 3rd Cavalry.

The following days were a nightmare to me.

Kornilov was convicted of rebellion and imprisoned. General Krymov, who had been put at the head of the troops which were marching on the capital, committed suicide.

Kerensky the barrister, the "revolutionary Generalissimo," "democracy's hostage" in the Provisional Government, was at the head of the Army.

All these events had shaken the morale of the troops very badly.

The projected appointment of General Alexeiev as chief of the Supreme General Staff was the only glimmer of hope left. If Alexeiev had consented to this appointment, all would not have been lost.

Anxious for the fate of Count Pahlen and the officers of our organization, I made a hasty journey to the capital.

III - The Last Days of the Provisional Government

The first thing I did when I arrived was to call on the General Staff of the military district of Petersburg. There I met General Krasnov, whom I had known during the Russo-Japanese War.

When I told him of my recent appointment, he was lost in astonishment. "But, my dear fellow, I have just been appointed to that very post!"

It was somewhat disconcerting, but it did not surprise me. At this period, when everything was going to the devil, incidents like this often occurred.

To get the matter cleared up I asked the chief of the military district, Colonel Polkovnikov (who had been chief-of-staff in my Oussourian division) what the cause of the mistake was.

He told me that, in his opinion, the order appointing me was of a more recent date than that appointing Krasnov, and that therefore, probably, it was I who should take the command; but he knew nothing definite.

He gave me the details of Krymov's suicide. It was said that the breach between the Minister-President and the Generalissimo had been absolutely unexpected by Krymov himself and by his troops. It was only whilst he had been stationed at Dno that he had received Kerensky's telegram, proclaiming General Kornilov a traitor. According to Polkovnikov, if Krymov had continued his advance on the capital resolutely, Petersburg could have been taken. Unfortunately, General Krymov, taken unawares, worn out by recent events, and distracted by private affairs, had begun to lose his head. He had delayed, and sent to Headquarters for instructions, thus losing precious time. Just a day too late he had realized that success was not a foregone conclusion. General Krymov agreed to go to Petersburg to negotiate with Kerensky, who had sent him an invitation via General Samarin, the leader of the Minister of War's Cabinet. He had gone to Kerensky's house, and a stormy interview had ensued. He had then gone straight on to see an officer he knew. There he had asked for writing material and begged leave to be left alone. A few minutes later an explosion had been heard. They found the General with a bullet in his chest. He had left a letter for his wife. When asked why he had taken his own life, he answered "I want to die because I love my country too much." He died the same evening.

I left the General Staff and went on to the New Club to get news of Count Pahlen. He had come back the day before. According to him, Krymov's movement on Petersburg had come at a moment when his organization was quite unprepared. At the time no one had expected a conflict between the Government and the Generalissimo, and consequently no one had been prepared for it. Immediately after the rupture, an absolutely unknown colonel, who was unfurnished with documents and refused to give his name, had appeared in Petersburg, saying that Krymov had sent him. Pahlen, fearing that he was nothing more nor less than an *agent provocateur*, had promptly refused to negotiate with him.

Polkovnikov begged me to spend the evening with him. Verkhovsky, the new Minister of War, found it impossible to give me a command near the capital in view of my "personal character" and for political reasons. Therefore I was to be given another somewhere else. I demanded my discharge. It was refused. "There is no discharge in the war."

I took the matter to the Minister of War. He told me the same thing. Finally I went to the chief of the General Staff. I was ordered to report at Supreme Headquarters immediately. There they offered me various appointments. I refused, realizing that I could be of no service to my country in the existing circumstances.

At the end of October the Bolshevists broke up the Provisional Government. Kerensky fled, disguised as a sailor, deserting his colleagues, the Army, and Russia.

At last I received my discharge papers, and left Moghilev for the Crimea to join my wife and children as a private individual.

CHAPTER III

UNDER THE YOKE OF BOLSHEVISM

Coming straight from the turmoil of Supreme Headquarters in Moghilev, I was struck by the peaceful atmosphere in the Crimea.

Since the outbreak of the Revolution, many people had fled from the capital cities and taken refuge in the Crimea. Most of them were wealthy people with independent means, who kept right out of politics.

The Empress-Mother and her daughters, the Grand Duchesses Xenia and Olga, and also the former Generalissimo, Grand Duke Nicholas, his brother, Grand Duke Peter, and Grand Duke Alexander, the Empress's son-in-law, were all living at Yalta. Many of our friends too were in the town or near it, and we often saw them. There was nothing for it but to lead a normal life.

Only the news which reached us from time to time made us remember grim realities. Thus we heard of the horrible murder of Dukhonin, the last Generalissimo, and of Kornilov's escape from Bykhov prison.

We also received news of the Ukrainian Rada, which was leaning towards the Left, and of the counter-revolution which was said to be brewing in the neighborhood of the Don.

I very much doubted if it could have spread this far so soon. On the contrary, it seemed more probable that the Cossacks would want to adopt Communism, susceptible as they were to its charms.

Our peaceful life did not last long. In Taurida, which had been quiet up till now, country mansions were being pillaged. One day I happened to be in the town of Melitopol, near our own estate, and there I saw Bolshevist soldiers and sailors for the first time. They were retreating after having been defeated at the mouth of the Don. They were like wild beasts rather than men. Armed to the teeth, they ill-treated and struck the railway officials, boarded the trains, and turned out the passengers, women, children, and all.

The Crimea, like the Ukraine and the Don, wanted to organize itself as an independent State. A provisional Tartar Government had been set up. As a garrison for the little towns of the peninsula it had at its command an old regiment of Tartar dragoons, some companies of officers, and two field-batteries. The garrison in Sebastopol had already gone Red.

The new Crimean Government had ordered a general mobilization. They requested me to become Commander-in-Chief of this army. Before giving my answer I went to Simferopol to find out if this new Government had any justification for its existence, and if it was likely to be stable.

On investigation, I found it to be a bad imitation of Kerensky's new Government, so I refused the honor and went back to Yalta.

On the morning of January 8, 1918, we learnt that during the night a skirmish had taken place between two of the Tartar squadrons and some Reds. The dragoons had retired to the mountains, the Reds had taken possession of the town, and the Soviet Republic was proclaimed the same day. The residents were commanded to give up their arms, a torpedo-boat manned by Red sailors arrived at Sebastopol, and domiciliary searches began.

A gang of these ruffians came to search our house without any kind of a warrant. I let them get on with it, and went on playing with my six-year-old son, taking not the slightest notice of their movements.

They did their utmost to make me lose my temper: seeing that they could not do so, they went away. Since then I have often used this method and found it effective.

On January 10th I was awakened by the sound of firing. The dragoons had come back from the mountains and were occupying a part of the town. I went out on to the balcony, where my brother-in-law, a former Captain of Hussars, joined me. The firing was in full swing, and soon the guns boomed out. Two shells fell in our garden.

At midday I was informed that half a platoon of Reds was stationed near our terrace. I went out to them.

"Which of you is in charge?"

"I am," said a sailor.

"Good. Let me tell you that I am a General and this gentleman is a Captain. Understand that we are not hiding."

"We are only fighting against Tartars," said another. "The poor beggars belong to the age of Catherine the Great; they have sworn allegiance to Russia, and now they want to be independent."

Many times since then I have thought of those words, spoken by an anti-nationalist and a conscious disciple of the International.

Towards evening the dragoons drew off.

At dawn I heard sounds of smashing doors, trampling feet, and shouting. My door opened, several men dashed towards my bed, and a little spotty-faced sailor pointed his revolver at my heart.

"Don't move, I arrest you."

"Send your men away," I said to him. "You can see that I am alone and unarmed. I will get dressed, and then I'll follow you."

I dressed quickly and we went out of the room. Our servants were weeping. My brother-in-law was also arrested. In the courtyard, amongst about fifteen sailors, I saw one of our gardeners whom I had recently taken by the scruff of his neck and thrown out of the house because he had insulted my wife.

I learnt later that he had been responsible for bringing the party along. The wretch shouted, "I swear that this man is a General and has been backing up the Tartars, he is the people's enemy and a counter-revolutionary."

We were hooted by the crowd of idlers which had collected in the street.

Then a Greek said, "I swear that they are innocent and took no part at all in the battle. I live only a stone's throw from here."

"That's all right. We will see about it," a sailor said to him.

Two cars were waiting. We got into one of them, and at the same moment my wife rushed out and hung on to the door. I implored her to go back to the house, and the sailors pushed her off, but she stood there weeping, and begged to be allowed to get into the car.

"If she goes, so much the worse for her," said a sailor. "Let her go."

She leapt into the car and we were off.

We reached the pier, which was crowded with people. A torpedo-boat was moored there. As soon as the crowd saw us, they began to yell: "Look out! Here come the bloodsuckers! To the water with them! To the water!"

I saw several corpses, all covered with blood, but we were safely on the bridge of the torpedo-boat. We were made to go below into a cabin. One sailor remained on guard outside, the others went back to the bridge.

A naval officer appeared. He looked pale and worn out, a pitiable object:

My wife darted over to him, "What are you going to do?"

"Do not be alarmed, Madame. If you are innocent, you will get out of this. I am the captain, but unfortunately I can do nothing."

More sailors appeared bawling: "Let's have these scoundrels! To the water! To the water!"

The captain, supported by a few men, succeeded in persuading them, after a great deal of trouble, that the Revolutionary Tribunal ought to deal with us. At last they went away.

Another prisoner was brought in, a colonel of Engineers. The worthy fellow was very anxious, not for his own fate, but because he had some money belonging to his men at his own home, and "you realize what a fuss they will make if this money is lost."

I have seen death at close quarters many a time, and I am not afraid of it. But the idea of dying at the hands of Russian soldiers, of being shot like a spy or a common thief before the eyes of my wife, was horrible to me. Therefore I did all I could to induce her to go back to our children.

"Besides, you can be of more use to me in the town than here. Tell our servants to come and bear witness to my innocence."

This decided her. She was given permission to go. But I spoilt everything. I felt that I should never see her again, so I gave her back the watch-bracelet she had given me, which I always wore. She went away in tears, and then I saw her coming back. "I realize from this bracelet that you believe you are going to die." As the poor woman had started off, she had seen the crowd tear an officer to pieces. The colonel of Engineers was set free, but he also was soon back. He returned to retrieve a pocket-book which had been taken from him. Naturally he was unsuccessful. As he was starting off again, he whispered to us that the workmen from his woodyard had come to rescue him, and that there was quite a large crowd there demanding that we too should be set free.

At nightfall we were made to leave the ship, and were cooped up in the Customs-house, which was already full of prisoners. It was dirty and windowless and almost unfurnished. The floor was filthy and much spat upon. Our companions in misfortune were of all social grades: there were generals, young officers, students, schoolboy Tartars, and common loafers. The hall was full of sailors and Red Guards: we could hear their obscene swearing.

Although everybody lay down on the floor in the end, in spite of their disgust at its filthy condition, nobody slept. We spoke in whispers and listened to our neighbors sighing.

The examination lasted the whole night. A long-haired untidy little student played the part of police-magistrate.

My turn came at last.

After the formal questions as to my name, age, civil position, etc., he asked me:

"Do you plead guilty?"

"To what?"

"Why have you been arrested?"

"I was just going to ask you that, but I can see that you do not know either. I can guess the cause of my arrest."—and I told him the incident of the gardener, adding. "I do not know if you are a married man, but I suppose, if you are, you would have done the same as I did."

He passed on to another prisoner.

It went on all through the night and into the next day, when fresh prisoners appeared. Some people we knew very well were of the number. There was young Prince Mechtchersky, and old retired General Yartzeff, an octogenarian who could scarcely walk.

About eight o'clock in the evening a tall, fair, good-looking sailor with an intelligent face came into our prison. Several men were with him, including the student who had examined us the night before, and the commissioner who I had seen on the torpedo-boat.

"That's Comrade Vakula, President of the Tribunal," said one of our warders. "He is going to examine you immediately."

The "Revolutionary Tribunal" passed from one prisoner to another, We watched old General Yartzeff, Prince Mechtchersky, a student, and some others being led away.

Comrade Vakula came up to us. I heard the student who had examined me whisper to the President: "This is the one I told you about."

"Why were you arrested?" he asked me

"Probably because I am a Russian General. It is the only crime of which I am guilty."

"Why are you not wearing the decorated uniform which you were probably flaunting yesterday?" And without waiting for an answer he turned to my wife.

"And why were you arrested?"

"I was not arrested, I am here of my own free will."

He feigned surprise.

"Then why are you here?"

"I have always lived happily with my husband, and I want to stay with him until the end."

Vakula, enjoying the theatrical effect in advance, glanced rapidly at the prisoners who were all about us.

"Such women are not to be found every day. You owe your life to your wife. Go!" and with an emphatic gesture he pointed to the door.

But we were kept there for another terrible night. The convicted prisoners were shot at the very door of the prison, and then bodies were thrown into the water. I learnt later that more than a hundred people were executed, including young Mechtchersky and old General Yartzeff.

Once the Reds were masters of the Crimea, the Terror began in Simpferopol, Eupatona, and Yalta. More than a thousand men, officers for the most part, were shot or massacred and thrown into the sea. Domiciliary visits were the order of the day, and money, jewels, and clothing were taken away.

Fortunately all this was done without any system. The residents were obliged to declare their wealth and to pay a contribution proportional to it. My mother-in-law, who was on the list as one of the chief contributors, declared that she possessed absolutely nothing, and could not pay. She was threatened with imprisonment. She stuck to her point, and never paid a halfpenny.

Countess Tolstoy conscientiously gave the amount of her fortune, and sold her jewels, keeping nothing but a few trifles. Her maid denounced her, and she and her daughter were imprisoned.

They searched my house many times, but they found nothing at all. The jewels and money were hidden in the stomachs and heads of my little daughter's dolls, the furs and laces under a heap of charcoal.

Far from denouncing us, my old servants even helped us to deceive the Red bloodhounds. We probably owed our safety to them, because on the day of our arrest they, together with some poor people my wife had helped, had come to demand our release.

A decree was passed forbidding anyone to draw out more than a hundred roubles from his current account—it was impossible to keep a large family on this amount. Our servants complained many times to the Commissar that they had not been paid for months and claimed their due. The bank was ordered to pay the "proletariat" their wages, deducting the sum from our current account. And our loyal "proletariat" brought to their "oppressors eager for their blood" the money which after great trouble they had succeeded in wringing from the "grasping bourgeois."

On more than one night we were forced to go and seek a lodging in a distant part of the town. Everybody stayed indoors and avoided showing themselves in the streets. Provisions became increasingly scarce, life more and more impossible.

We left the town, taking with us those of our servants whom we could trust, and went to live in a flat on the outskirts of Miskhor, where the Reds seldom came. My wife had succeeded in getting me a permit to reside there, on which I was described, not as a General, but as a "certified engineer".

Our neighbors were Tartars, sworn enemies of the Reds, and most of them were Mahometans, they used to warn us of the slightest danger which threatened us.

We lived like this for about three months. Then we heard a rumor that the Germans were in the Ukraine. We saw less and less of the Reds, and one fine morning, we saw a column of Prussian soldiers on the highway, marching in good order.

Deeply grieved as I was to see the enemy master of Russia, and my country disgraced, I was nevertheless happy at being free from the humiliating yoke of those blockheaded idiots.

II - In the Ukraine and White Russia

I must give the Germans their due: they behaved with decency and did their best to avoid annoying the inhabitants of the country they were about to occupy. All the decrees and orders of their predecessors were annulled, except the one concerning permission to leave or enter the Crimea.

The *Kommandatur* helped those who had been robbed to get their possessions back again, and had those Red thieves and murderers who had not been able to get clear in time, arrested and delivered up to justice. The only Bolshevists to whom they gave a helping hand were the leaders, and these they enabled to return to Moscow safe and sound.

The day after the troops arrived, delegates from the German Command presented themselves at Dulber Castle, where all the members of the Imperial Family were in residence, and requested Grand Duke Nicholas to receive them. The Grand Duke sent his answer by his aide-de-camp . If he was to consider himself as a prisoner of war, he believed that he was forced to obey, but if their visit was one of courtesy only, he found it impossible to receive them.

The Prussian officers replied that they quite appreciated his Imperial Highnesses answer, and that they were at his service and ready to put a bodyguard at his disposal.

The Grand Duke refused on the score that the handful of Russian soldiers who were with him were quite sufficient.

Life at Yalta resumed its normal course. The Empress-Mother came over nearly every day to see her old friend, Princess Dolgorouky, and they would sit on a seat on the beach for hours at a time. Grand Duke Nicholas was the only one who shut himself up in the house.

I made up my mind to go and inspect an estate we had in Lithuania, and as Kiev was on the way, I decided to stop and see Skoropadsky, who had just been proclaimed Hetman (Chief of State) of the Ukraine. We were old friends, had served in the same brigade when we were young officers, and had later gone through the Russo-Japanese War together.

At the beginning of the World War he had been a colonel in the Horse Guards and I had been a major. After a few months he had risen to the rank of major-general, and I had been his chief-of-staff. Now I was curious to see him at work.

Kiev, the cradle of Russian Orthodoxy, was now transformed into the "ancient capital of the Ukraine" and the town of residence of the new Hetman, but it had changed very little. The people continued to speak Russian, although the signboards and street names were written up in a dialect which neither the Russians nor the Little Russians understood. The Hetman had given instructions that the official language was to be the Ukrainian tongue. The best of the thing was that the Hetman, although of Little Russian descent, could understand neither the Little Russian language nor his own native tongue, the so-called "Ukrainian."

Skoropadsky's first words were. "I am relying on you: would you like to be my chief-of-staff? We will soon have a powerful Ukrainian army."

I answered that since I had no stake in the Ukraine and knew nothing about local conditions, it would not be right for me to occupy the position.

The two of us talked at great length. I was sure that the World War, which was still going on, would end in the defeat of Germany, and that the Germans, who were supporting the Hetman, would be forced to evacuate Russia. Once this happened, the Hetman's Government would fall, and furthermore, since Germany was lending her support for purely selfish reasons, she would never tolerate the formation of a strong Ukrainian army.

Skoropadsky, however, held very firmly to the contrary opinion. According to him, the Ukraine, supported by Austria and the Slav countries, would become very powerful and play a leading part in the future.

We returned to this question many times. I discussed it with people who were familiar with the situation, and in the end I was convinced that Skoropadsky was not sincere in his venture. Therefore I turned down all his proposals.

Kiev was packed full of officers, who had escaped death by some miracle. Almost the whole of my 7th division was there too. As I have already said, I had not been in at the final breakdown of the Army, and had only seen the beginning. I learnt from them how things had gone since I had left them. They told me of the outrages they had had to endure, and of the life of martyrdom they had led. Most of the officers had been loyal to their duty and their colors until the last, and had been present at the dissolution of their regiments and the collapse of the Army. They had watched the final exhaustion of the worthy fellows with whom they had lived like brothers for years, sharing their joys and sorrows, men who, at their command, had faced death unflinchingly.

And now these last fragments of the Great Russian Army had met at Kiev at the risk of their lives.

Some had come on foot, others by railway, and all had been hounded about like wild animals. Some hoped to go on fighting for Russia under the Ukrainian flag, others to get to the region of the Don, where the Cossacks had renounced Bolshevism and elected the Czarist General Krasnov as Ataman. The rest intended to join the Volunteer Army, which, it was said, was in course of formation. The names of Generals Alexeiev, Kornilov, and Denikin, were enough to create the belief that the undertaking was a serious one.

The flag was certainly in good hands, but there was neither ammunition, arms, nor money. The section of the population from which this new army should have been formed had not yet made up its mind. Were we justified in putting our faith in an undertaking which had such a slight chance of success?

General Svetchin had recently arrived from the Don, he was very well informed as to the situation, and caused me much distress. I heard from him that Krasnov, who had been appointed Ataman, was doing everything in his power to hasten the resurrection of the Army, but that the Cossacks, who were more chauvinistic than ever, refused to have officers in their regiments if they were not Cossacks by birth.

After Kornilov's death and his defeat at the Kuban, it was hardly possible that the reorganization of the Army should go on, especially as it was rumored that the Generals were far from being in agreement with one another.

Several days later I heard that a delegation from the Soviet Government had just come to Kiev to propose some sort of alliance between the ruler of the Ukraine and the "Republic of Workmen and Peasants." It was led by the former Brigadier-General of the 7th division, Odintzov, of whom I have spoken before, and who had been one of the first to join the Red ranks.

One fine day my door opened to admit this gentleman, who came in smiling and with outstretched hand. "What a pleasure to see you again; I heard that you had been killed. I hope you are well?"

I got up without shaking hands with him.

"Yes, thank you. I won't ask how you are, because I know that you are doing very well in the service of your new masters."

Odintzov interrupted me. "Every man has a right to a hearing before he is judged I don't care a damn for public opinion, but I do value that of men I like and respect. You must hear what I have to say."

"I am listening."

"I have sacrificed myself for my country, I have given more than my life, for I have sacrificed my honor."

"Excuse my interrupting you, but I don't quite follow. You are saying that you sacrificed your honor and went over to the Bolsheviks for the good of your country?"

"Yes, I am a monarchist, but to achieve monarchy we must go through anarchy, and serve the Bolshevists that we may overthrow them."

"And you think you can work with Trotsky, who is the paid representative of our enemies? I suppose you realize that he is a German spy?"

"He is not the only one, but there is a topsy-turvy scale of values in politics, and ends justify means."

I opened the door. "If that is all you have got to say to me, please get out."

I will not say much more about my short stay in White Russia. The Germans were in occupation there too, and their discipline was much severer here than in the Crimea. The day after my arrival, Lieutenant Ohnemuller, the commanding officer of the platoon, which was quartered on us, presented himself to me. He was a young man of good family, intelligent, cultured, and very well bred. He noticed my setters, and asked me if I went in for shooting and if I expected to get any here. I told him I had hoped for some, but that it was impossible, as cartridges had been forbidden. The next day he brought me some cartridges. We went out shooting together more than once. I have never been able to understand those chauvinists who regard as an enemy every man belonging to the nation with which his country is at war. You fight your enemy's Army, but you can respect the individuals who compose it.

I heard that a White Army was being formed in the Don and in Caucasia, so I set out for Kiev again.

At Kiev I received confirmation of the news. One of my friends had just had a letter from Alexeiev himself. The Allies had promised arms and money.

I hurried back to Yalta, where I gave my children into the care of their grandmother, after which I set out for Rostov on the Don, accompanied by my wife, who wanted to go on nursing the wounded as she had done during the Great War. The very same day, four years earlier, I had left the capital at the head of my squadron of Horse Guards to go and fight the Germans. The town had been decked with flags, bands had played the National Anthem, and the people had cheered the Czar and his troops wildly.

Today this same people had vilely assassinated the man whom they had then cheered, and had deluged in fire and blood the country for which they had then been so ready to fight. The Army had murdered its officers and destroyed itself.

Nearly all my comrades who had marched off with me then had died on the battlefield. Those who had survived had had to hide themselves like criminals, so that they might be faithful to their duty and rejoin the old flag; they had sought to obtain permits from the German authorities on false pretenses so that they could continue the struggle for their honor, their freedom, and their country.

And to think that Russian men, their own comrades of former days, were trampling this freedom and honor underfoot! It is true that the enemy had brought things to this pass with agents and gold.

Germany had failed to conquer by force of arms, but had succeeded in corrupting her enemy. It is maintained that everything is fair in war. Bernhardi says it. I admit it. But there are ways and ways—some honorable, some base. Quite often the end justifies the means, but the nation which uses unworthy means always gets a bad reputation.

The grim shadow of Civil War fell over Russia.

CHAPTER IV

THE LIBERATION OF NORTHERN CAUCASIA

We sailed on the *King Albert.* It was crowded. Since the Volunteers had been occupying the port of Novorossiisk and the town of Ekaterinodar, the people who had fled from the Red Terror had gone back home. There were a large number of Germans amongst the passengers. I made friends with a German professor, an inspector of the military hospitals used by the Army of Occupation.

The German Command did not officially prohibit officers from joining the Volunteer Army, but in actual practice they put all kinds of difficulties in the way. At Kertch our passports were examined. As I was with the German professor, they did not even glance at our papers.

Rostov was full of people and humming with life. The town had become a temporary capital for Southern Russia as Kiev had for the Ukraine. The streets were full of life, and nothing had changed. Even the policemen at the railway station still wore their old uniforms. Some German uniforms in the streets were the only things that reminded one of the real situation.

At Ekaterinodar we could feel that we were in the rear of an army. There were nothing but uniforms on all sides. I found several acquaintances easily enough, but only with the greatest difficulty did I find a lodging.

I knew neither the chief-of-staff at Supreme Headquarters nor the quartermaster-general, but I recognized one or two old comrades amongst the officers. They told me that Kornilov had tried to find me, and had written to me twice from Petersburg. Neither of his letters had reached me.

When I arrived, the Volunteer Army did not exceed thirty-five thousand men and eighty guns. The infantry, artillery, and engineers were almost entirely composed of officers, the cavalry, with the exception of two regiments which were attached to infantry units, of Kuban Cossacks and Circassians. Most of the officers were unknown to me.

The only arms and ammunition the army had were those it had captured from the enemy. The re-equipping was done at the expense of the people. Our enemy numbered eighty thousand and had a hundred guns, they had the reserve stores of the old Army at their disposal, and arms and munitions to spare, but on the other hand they were badly organized, badly led, and ill-disciplined.

The next day I went to present myself to Generals Alexeiev and Denikin. The former was seriously ill and could not see me. I only knew General Denikin through having met him several times in Manchuria, during the

Japanese War, and at Supreme Headquarters. He received me in the presence of General Romanovsky, his chief-of-staff.

General Denikin was a man of average height and powerful build, with a grizzled beard and moustache. He gave me the impression of being thoughtful, resolute, well balanced, and a thorough-going Russian. He was known to be courageous and honest, and very well versed in military science. During the ill-fated existence of the Provisional Government he had been chief-of-staff to Supreme Headquarters, and had since then commanded the armies in the south-west.

He had never been afraid to speak his mind freely, and to defend the honor of the Army and of the officers' companies in public.

He reminded me of our meeting in Manchuria, and told me that Kornilov had spoken of me many times.

"Well, General," he said, "what are we going to do? I really do not know what you propose. Our effective force is not very large."

"As Your Excellency knows," I replied, "in 1917 I was commanding a cavalry troop, but back in 1914 I commanded a squadron. I am not yet too old to do so again."

'That nonsense," he said, "a squadron! If you would be content with a brigade?"

"Certainly, Your Excellency."

"That's splendid. The General"—indicating Romanovsky—"will tell you all you want to know about the situation."

The next day I called on Romanovsky. He seemed to be intelligent and well-informed, but the favorable impression which he had made on me at first was somewhat modified, for he had a way of never looking straight at anyone, and would always avoid your eyes. He gave me my appointment, not as brigadier-general, as I was expecting, but as lieutenant-general. The next day I went to find my division, which was operating in the Maikop district.

The by-roads along which we drove were good, the going excellent. As far as the eye could see stretched fields stacked with great wheat-sheaves, orchards, and kitchen gardens overflowing with golden melons. The large villages, the white houses with their red-tiled roofs, the churches with their gilded domes, and the steam-mills all bore witness to the wealth and fertility of the countryside. The old fellow who was guiding us told us of the horrors perpetrated by the Reds, he said that the people blessed the day when the Volunteer Army had come to help them get rid of their oppressors.

In a village I ran into a platoon of Cossacks. They turned out to be the escort of the Lieutenant-General I was to succeed. He told me that the division was in the thick of an attack. We hastily swallowed a mouthful of food, and then got into the saddle again and went to join the troops. I discovered several old comrades-in-arms amongst the officers and soldiers.

In the evening we went along to my Headquarters, and I spent the night working with my chief-of-staff.

Technical equipment was almost entirely lacking. We had nothing but a wireless apparatus, no telegraph and no telephone. We re-equipped ourselves with munitions at the enemy's expense, though occasionally the General Staff sent us cartridges and shells from the Don.

For our Medical Service, we had a surgeon and two Sisters of Charity, but there was no linen for dressing wounds and no drugs. The casualties were enormous, and the gaps were filled by volunteers who had to go straight into battle without any preliminary training. Each individual soldier fought well, but as a corporate entity the Army left much to be desired.

My whole division numbered only two thousand five hundred men and three field batteries.

As the land was won back, the village assemblies met and elected communal councils which took over the commissariat and means of transport. They also dispensed justice, and handed over Bolshevists to the authorities. This gave rise to many abuses, too often the people used their authority to square private accounts and take vengeance on their enemies. But we had to restore a certain amount of order somehow. To make matters worse, we were short of staff and time, yet, although this semblance of order was very imperfect, it was better than anarchy.

The Bolshevists had twelve to fifteen thousand infantry, twenty-five or thirty guns, and several hundred horsemen, and were well provided with ammunition and technical equipment. The Red soldiers themselves fought well, but their commanders were hopelessly inadequate.

To our right, in the Maikop district, General Pokrovsky's cavalry division was operating, but our communications were imperfect. To our left, along the line of the Kavkazskaia-Armavir railway, Colonel Drosdovsky's infantry division was in constant communication with us. Our division was to drive back the enemy, who were occupying Ourop on the other side of the river.

The enemy's position which we had to take was near the village of Mikhailovskaia, protected by the deep river Laba, on the left bank of which the enemy held a bridge-head, a range of hills, and swamps. As, in addition, they had far more artillery than we, and were abundantly supplied with ammunition, which we lacked altogether, all our efforts to advance were in vain. I made up my mind to alter things. A brigade defeated the enemy and succeeded in advancing through Mikhailovskaia and occupying the line of the Armavir-Tuapse railway. But this did not lead to anything. The Reds wheeled round, and by using a large number of trains and armored motor-lorries forced the brigade to retreat.

For three weeks we tried in vain to drive off the enemy. During this time Supreme Headquarters bombarded me with dispatches demanding "energetic action and an attack at all costs." But in spite of my urgent entreaties they did not send me supplies of ammunition.

During September there were some unimportant engagements, sometimes the enemy harassed us, sometimes we fell upon them. Our total losses were large. In August and September my division lost two hundred and sixty officers and two thousand four hundred and sixty men, that is to say, one hundred per cent of its effective force. The gaps were filled immediately with recruits from the recently freed territory.

In the middle of the night of October 1st I was told that the enemy had blown up the railway bridge and were concentrating their forces on the right bank of the Laba. I gave the order for an offensive.

From that day on operations took place in the open country and were of the kind in which maneuvering is more important than numerical strength. We won victory after victory.

We advanced in double column. On October 2nd I entered Mikhailovskaia, where an enormous crowd had assembled to receive me. The "ancients" (as the Caucasians call the most respected men of their country) offered me bread and salt, according to custom. Many of them wept as they told me of all they had had to suffer from the Reds. The Bolshevists had taken away with them as hostages the richest men in the district, also the family of the inspector of the local school and a priest. Several "ancients" had been shot on the eve of the departure of the Reds.

October 1st was the date of the village church festival. I went to Mass, and it was more than ordinarily moving. Everyone prayed with unusual fervour and affecting sincerity. When I came out of church I found a brigade of Cossacks and Circassians in the market square. On their left flank, under the green Mahometan flag, was a detachment of Circassian "ancients" who had come down from the mountains to join us. The *aouls*[1] had suffered cruelly at the hands of the Bolshevists: several had been burnt out, and many Circassians had been tortured and shot. In one of the *aouls*, half a score of men had been buried alive. The "ancients" told me that they were putting their sons under my command, though they themselves wished to return to their villages, they promised, however, that they would come at the first appeal and fight side by side with their sons. I thanked them, and at their earnest request handed over to them a couple of dozen prisoners, that they might bring them to justice on the spot where their crimes had been committed. But I had scarcely set off with my troops before the Circassians threw themselves upon the prisoners and cut them to pieces before the eyes of the villagers.

In a neighboring village I came upon the Cossacks of Pokrovsky's division robbing the villagers. To my indignation I perceived several Cossack officers

---

[1] Mahometan mountain villages.—TRANSLATOR

amongst the marauders. I sent for them and told them that if I found them still within the boundaries of my division in half an hour's time they would be shot. In half an hour there was not a single Cossack in the village. I reported their conduct to General Pokrovsky.

Unfortunately, I suspected (and my suspicions were soon justified) that the General not only took no measures against the marauders, but even tacitly encouraged them. The Cossacks had themselves been robbed of everything they possessed, so that it was difficult, indeed impossible, to rid them of their desire to get back an equivalent wherever they could find it.

Considerable sums of money were to be found on almost every enemy, the baggage was packed full of all manner of things, from sugar and tobacco to furs, rugs, cut-glass, furniture, and pianos. At the beginning of the Civil War, before the Bolshevists had begun raising recruits, their army had been composed solely of escaped convicts, out-and-out riff-raff and the scum of the old Army. They had robbed and massacred the populace, killed off the wounded, and raped the women. When our units saw this, they could not be made to behave decently. Since they had no base and were completely surrounded by the enemy, they could not take any prisoners either.

Destitute of everything, they re-equipped themselves at the expense of the countryside, showing not the slightest respect for other people's property. And it was impossible, at any rate at the beginning of the Civil War, to prevent such outrages. I contented myself with demanding that the booty seized from the enemy should be divided equally between all the soldiers, and I appointed supervisory committees. Afterwards, when, thanks to the help of the Allies, the Army could obtain its supplies in a normal manner, I arranged that all the spoils of war should be handed over to the Commissariat. But from the first I had been ruthlessly opposed to all marauding, and had caused offenders to be arrested.

General Pokrovsky (and, unfortunately, he was not the only one) either could not or would not follow my example, and consequently I had to give up the idea of prohibiting this lawlessness. Everything was considered permissible. The result of this state of affairs was disastrous.

The enemy put their infantry into wagons and retreated all along the line, covering forty to fifty-five kilometres a day. One of our columns attacked them fiercely, and captured their baggage, a number of machine-guns, and some ammunition.

I slept in the village of Costantinovka. The master of the house, a fine old man with a long white beard, threw himself at my feet and wept. He was a very rich man, and was held in great respect throughout the district. Three of his sons had fled from the Reds, two had been shot, and his eldest son had been hiding in a cave with several friends for four months. He took me to see them. The sight of the poor devils made me shudder. The old man himself had had to be hidden in the straw for days to save his life. He discovered that one of his fugitive sons had been in my escort, another in one of my regiments. It is impossible to describe the father's joy.

In the morning the troops continued the pursuit. I remained behind for an hour or two, as I had orders to give, then I got into a car and went to rejoin one of my columns. I found the men having a meal I learnt that the other column was fighting with the Red rearguard six kilometres farther on. I got into my car again and went to join it.

The officer in charge of the column, Colonel Toporkov, and his General Staff were on a hillock behind which a battery was posted. A couple of hundred paces away, two Cossack squadrons were covering it. The enemy were in a hollow about one thousand five hundred paces away, their shells almost reached us. I got out of the car and went over to the battery with two of my orderlies. I had scarcely reached it when I heard a cry of "the cavalry!" and saw my Cossacks gallop up furiously, hotly pursued by a great mob of enemy cavalry. The battery commander ordered an *enfilade*, but it did not stop the Reds. The Cossacks who were covering the artillery had come up already, the enemy at their heels. We attempted to stop them in vain. The whirlwind of horsemen swooped down upon us.

The enemy fell upon the battery, one of the guns was done for. I saw an artillery officer fire point-blank at a Red, but another of them struck him down with one blow of his sword. Colonel Toporkov, surrounded by foes, was slashing to right and left. I ran to my car, but it had been wrecked. The chauffeur and his assistants were a long way off. I hurried into a maize field. On both sides of me Cossacks were dashing by; the gunners, too, were in flight. Shooting and slashing was still going on near the battery. An officer offered me his horse, but I refused it. As he insisted, I directed him to go to the village and bring back my escort and my horses which he would find there. He set off at the gallop. I kept on running. Looking behind me, I saw three Reds galloping up. One of them caught up with one of our foot-soldiers and attempted to cut him down, but the soldier fell upon his horse at close quarters, and the two other Reds fell upon him. I wanted to rush to his aid, but I was unarmed. I had no sword, and had given my revolver to an officer who was without one. At this moment an ambulance-car passed me at full speed. I ran after it as fast as I could, and, managing to catch up with it, leapt on board. I was beside myself. The loss of the battery, the flight of the Cossacks, the failure of my efforts to stop them, all contributed to overwhelm me. My men no longer existed.

We passed a soldier riding one horse and leading another. I took it, mounted, and hurried on to meet the Cossacks I had sent for. A brigade appeared at the trot. I ordered it to deploy, and we went in search of the enemy; but the Reds had already fallen back, taking with them two guns, my car, and some clothes which they had stripped from the bodies of our dead.

They followed the line of their general retreat, crossed the River Ouroup, and entrenched themselves on the right bank.

Pokrovsky's division was maneuvering on our right, and on its right flank was Colonel Chkouro and his Cossacks. To our left, between the Ouroup and the Kuban, General Kasanovitch's division was to try and force the River Ouroup and throw the enemy back on to the farther bank of the Kuban.

For two weeks all our efforts were in vain.

On October 19th the enemy crossed the Ouroup and launched an offensive against the junction of my division and General Kasanovitch's.

The engagement was a brisk one, and lasted for twelve hours. There were heavy losses on both sides. At last, towards night, we perceived that the enemy were beginning to retreat, and had crossed the river again. I decided to wheel and attack them from the rear. Four regiments crossed the Ouroup and the movement succeeded. We took three thousand prisoners and a large number of machine-guns. As a final result, the enemy evacuated the whole of the left bank of the River Kuban.

On October 22nd I reached the village of Ouspenskaia, where fighting was still in progress. At the sight of my pennon loud hurrahs rang out from the Cossack ranks. Consciousness of victory and the intoxication of success gives spontaneous birth to confidence in the commander, and creates that bond which is the strength of armies. From that moment on I "held" my units, and our division knew no more defeats.

One section of the enemy was in flight along the railway track towards Stavropol, the other towards Armavir. One of my brigades had started off in pursuit, the other went to reinforce the neighboring division. I remained in the village of Ouspenskaia with two regiments. In that night's work we had taken considerable amount of booty from the enemy, besides many prisoners, and it all had to be cleared up.

My division, on its formation, had been reinforced by the *cadres* of a Cossack infantry division. There was nothing left of it but a score or two of men. All the rest had been killed. For a long time I had been wanting to reinforce it, but how? I decided to make my first attempt with our prisoners.

I ordered three hundred and seventy of the Bolshevists to line up. They were all officers and non-commissioned officers, and I had them shot on the spot. Then I told the rest that they too deserved death, but that I had let those who had misled them take the responsibility for their treason, because I wanted to give them a chance to atone for their crime and prove their loyalty to their country.

Weapons were distributed to them immediately, and two weeks later they went into the fighting-line and behaved with great courage. Later this battalion became one of the best in the whole Army, and covered itself with glory.

We continued to advance on Stavropol, fighting almost every day. Things grew warm not far from the little railway station of Pelagiada, some kilometres from the town. The enemy was firmly entrenched, having beaten back our infantry division. I wheeled my forces during the night, and at dawn fell upon the Reds from the cover of a wood. They broke and took to their heels in a panic, pursued by my regiments. Followed by several squadrons, I reached the suburbs of the town, where the fighting had already begun. The Reds had entrenched themselves in a convent, which we outflanked. Some Cossacks and horses were killed. I deployed my squadrons, drew my sword, and putting myself at their head, led the charge. The streets and the cloister were cleared of Reds and we entered the suburbs, cutting down anyone who tried to stop us.

Our horses were tied up in the precincts of the convent. The wounded came pouring in. The cloister door opened and a priest came out followed by nuns. Bullets were still raining down, crashing against the walls, but the priest and nuns did not seem to notice them. They tended the wounded, and gave them food and drink, whilst the priest sprinkled the Cossacks with holy water. It was a beautiful and touching sight.

In the cloisters we discovered two officers who had succeeded in escaping from the town. The Father Superior had disguised them as nuns, and when the Reds had come to the convent they had not even suspected their identity.

On November 2nd I entered Stavropol to the sound of bugles, followed by my escort. There was still skirmishing going on in some directions. The streets were littered with corpses, dead horses, and overturned wagons. As they heard the sound of the bugles, the citizens came out of doors weeping, clapping their hands, cheering, and bringing the Cossacks wine, cigarettes, and money. One old lady caught hold of my stirrup and tried to kiss my hand.

The town had been through a terrible time. The Bolshevist authorities had fallen out amongst themselves and had shot the commander of their troops. Anarchy was at its height. One and all were free to rob, pillage, and shoot. In the courtyard of the house where I was to lodge lay dozens of corpses, their fingers cut off and their eyes gouged out. We took an immense amount of booty, but I forbade anyone to touch it until the civil authorities arrived. The citizens were forced to give up their weapons.

But it was difficult to re-establish even a semblance of order, for passion and hatred was still running wild. On the following day the Circassians broke into a hospital where several hundred of the enemy's wounded were lying, and massacred seventy. I sent my orderly officer to arrest the culprits. According to the doctors, one of them was an officer, but, unfortunately, we did not succeed in arresting him.

A short time after we had taken the town, an officer who had been commander of the Governor's guard before the arrival of the Reds, had put himself under my orders. I had appointed him Governor of the prison to which the Bolshevists had been sent. A few hours later I was informed that he had shot them. I ordered his arrest, but a score or so of men had already been executed. When the Governor arrived I handed him over, but I do not know what happened to him.

II - In the "Nogais" Steppes

The Reds were retreating northwards. We followed hard on their heels.

One night, after a fairly lively engagement in which we had taken thousands of prisoners and all the rolling-stock held by an enemy division, I received a dispatch ordering me to go and meet General Denikin, who had just arrived at Rvzdvianaia Station. I rode over there on horseback. The moonlight was trickling through a thick mist. Villages, trees, and fields had all taken on the livid hue of corpses, which gave them a weird, dismal appearance. The road was not only strewn with the dead bodies of men and horses, but was also churned up by the rain. As I was splashing through a large pool my horse reared. A grinning corpse was staring at me, its head alone visible, for the water hid its body. A few paces farther on an arm was stretched out towards me. My horse trembled, snorted with fear, and shied from side to side.

The General thanked me for my division's success, and told me that I had been appointed to the command of a cavalry corps consisting of my division and Colonel Ulagay's 2nd division.

The Reds were retreating, but nevertheless they contested every inch with stubborn tenacity. My men were a good way ahead of the other troops. One night the Reds succeeded in wheeling round on us, and one of their platoons entered the village where we were sleeping. I had only thirty Cossacks with me, the rest having been left behind to cover the train, and thirty more men in my escort. There was not the smallest chance of putting up a resistance. If the Reds had acted more boldly they could have taken us all. But they hesitated, confining themselves to shooting down on us, and could not make up their minds to attack. Our transport was ready for instant departure. We dressed hastily, the horses were saddled, and we left the village at full speed. Unfortunately, the equipment belonging to two regiments, and also my wife's ambulance cars, fell into the hands of the enemy. The doctor managed to escape, but one of the sisters was taken prisoner. Providence was watching over my wife; the evening before, she had left the captured ambulance in order to convey the wounded from the town.

Meanwhile the enemy was attacking Colonel Ulagay's units. We held our position throughout the day, but by evening we had run out of ammunition and had to retreat.

I took the necessary measures, and then rode off with my orderly officer, Captain Prince Obolensky, my old comrade in the Horse Guards, to rejoin

Colonel Ulagay. During the night we reached a village which seemed to be empty, but passing through it at a brisk trot we heard sounds of firing in one of the streets. The Reds hidden in the village were opening fire near the bridge. When we reached the spot, we had the devil of a time. I was riding a grey horse—an excellent target, and the bullets simply rained down. The Prince edged his horse close up to mine, seeking to cover me with his own body. "Get back at once!" I shouted, "I command you to go back!" But I shouted in vain. He continued to gallop by my side, boot to boot, and we got through safe and sound.

At dawn the enemy attacked us. We held out until the evening, but we used all our ammunition. I was brought some enemy dispatches which had been found on one of the bodies. At six o' clock in the morning the Reds were going to attack us all along the line. I decided to attack them first before they had time to concentrate. I collected from the men all the cartridges they had left and distributed them among two regiments, who then deployed in skirmishing order. The rest of the troops remained on our left flank, and at dawn, before the enemy had finished concentrating, we charged. We penetrated the enemy's front line and the Reds broke, making off at top speed most of them were slain, and many were drowned in the river.

I decided to profit from the advance my troops had made and lend a hand to General Kasanovitch, who was operating on my right. We marched all through the night, and at dawn on November 22nd I turned on the Reds and attacked them from the rear. The enemy scattered, we took two thousand prisoners, seven guns, forty machine-guns, and all their transport. That evening we took up our position alongside the Kalaous.

On the morning of the 24th the enemy resumed the offensive, for they had obtained reinforcements. They succeeded in driving back our right wing, and came right up to the railroad.

But at midday our first division made a counter-attack. The enemy were worsted and fled. We took one thousand five hundred more prisoners, a battery complete with horses and ammunition wagons, and thirty machine-guns.

As a result, my corps was mentioned in dispatches, and I was promoted to the rank of Lieutenant-General.

I requested that Colonels Toporkev and Ulagay be promoted to the rank of General. Both were excellent officers. Toporkev, a simple Cossack, had begun his career as a private. Endowed with an innate flair for military matters, uncommon courage, elasticity and trustworthy steadiness, he lived the same life as his men, slept in the same room, and ate at their mess. His every order had to be obeyed, and always was, cost what it might. But sometimes he expected too much, and sacrificed too many men to achieve his ends.

Colonel Ulagay had a much more complex nature, vigorous and ambitious to a fault, but honest and noble-hearted, a man of exemplary courage and great military talents. He had a high reputation amongst his officers and Cossacks. He understood the art of getting out of difficult situations, and knew how to take advantage of them, he could also take the initiative when necessary. Though he was a cavalry officer of great merit, he nevertheless had his faults, his was an unbalanced nature, and he was extremely touchy. His mood would change easily from enthusiasm to apathy. When he was beginning a task, he seemed to look for obstacles which would hinder its completion, but once he had made up his mind, he would carry out his decision brilliantly.

In the course of the last few months my command had received considerable reinforcements. In spite of heavy losses, its strength was almost normal. We were well supplied with artillery, technical equipment, telephones, telegraphs, and so on, which we had taken from the enemy. When the Reds had succeeded in making themselves masters of the Kuban district, they had had recourse to conscription there. Now these forced recruits were deserting *en masse*, and coming over to us to defend their homes. They were good fighters, but once their own village was cleared of Reds, many of them left the ranks to cultivate their land once more.

It was unlikely that the enemy would be able to continue the offensive for some time, for they had been completely demoralized by these last defeats. Nor were we in a position to continue our advance until we had reorganized. I took advantage of this respite to ask the Commander-in-Chief for leave to go to Supreme Headquarters and confer with the General Staff on questions of re-equipment, future action, etc., which had been left undecided.

Having got General Denikin's authorization, I delegated the command to Ulagay, who had already been made a General, and set off with my wife, who had to attend to the needs of her ambulance at Ekaterinodar, where Supreme Headquarters were situated.

General Denikin could not have received me more warmly. He said the most flattering things, and acquiesced in all my demands, telling me to settle the details with General Romanovsky, his chief-of-staff. He also was very polite, but persistently refused to say yes or no, neither refusing nor promising anything, his colleagues followed his example.

Headquarters was snowed under with work; there was a deluge of waste-paper. Forgetting or holding over the execution of less urgent measures, Supreme Headquarters was busy with questions which, though perhaps essential, were out of date so far as the present situation was concerned; they were revising and elaborating regulations and organizing committees of study for the great military formations.

I was invited to sit on one of these committees which dealt with questions concerning the cavalry. In my opinion, a strong cavalry force is even more necessary in a Civil War than at any other time. The cavalry of the Volunteer Army consisted solely of Cossacks, who, once their native village was won back, would fight far less whole-heartedly.

It was absolutely necessary to recreate the old regular cavalry, which was, if I may say so, the finest in the world. We had the necessary *cadres* at hand, and also hundreds of old cavalry officers who were actually serving as privates in the infantry. But since the Commander-in-Chief and all his advisers were infantry officers, they were indifferent, not to say hostile, to the idea of organizing regular cavalry units. I drew up a memorandum in which I dealt with the question thoroughly, and submitted it to the committee, which accepted it unanimously. But still General Romanovsky would say neither yes nor no.

I reached Ekaterinodar on the eve of the election of the Ataman by the district Rada.[1] The Right's candidate was Filimonov, the Ataman already in office, the Left's, one Bytch, President of the Rada. Party conflict was at its height, but the Cossack units and most of the population were indifferent to it.

Political strife directly in the rear of an army in war time, especially when it was war to the death, could not be anything but injurious. In my opinion it was most urgent that the Commander-in-Chief should do something to check it. A very little firmness would be enough; too much abstinence from action would seem to indicate weakness.

I broached the subject to General Denikin, but he turned a deaf ear. General Pokrovsky and Colonel Chkouro, who thoroughly understood the Cossacks, also spoke to him, but General Denikin had his own opinion.

Colonel Filimonov was re-elected, he was ingenious and cautious, but lacking in resolution and incapable of coping with the circumstances, as later events showed.

The campaign which Generals Alexeiev and Kornilov had undertaken grew in extent and gained stability; the Allies seemed to understand it. Their representatives appeared in Ekaterinodar—the English General Poole and the French Captain Fouquet. They had come to inspect the troops and see what they lacked.

On November 11th the Armistice was signed between the Allies and Germany. The German Army which was occupying Russia collapsed and fled hurriedly, selling its arms and ammunition, for it also was infected with the Bolshevist poison.

In the Ukraine things fell out as we had foreseen. The Hetman Skoropadsky had been put in power by the Germans, and had maintained himself solely by their support; now he decamped and took refuge in

---

[1] The local Diet for the Kuban district.—TRANSLATOR

Germany. One of our best Generals, Count Keller, was assassinated at Kiev.[1] The officers who had managed to escape went to Caucasia and the Don to continue the struggle. General Krasnov was there; having fooled the Germans and wormed all he could out of them, he was now treating directly with the Allies. He and Denikin had not yet managed to come to an agreement, and each was negotiating separately.

Denikin's Headquarters were furious. They were saying that Krasnov would have to submit to Denikin. At Krasnov's Headquarters they were probably saying the same things about General Denikin.

The fight against Bolshevism flared up in other parts of Russia. Admiral Koltchak's Army was fighting in Siberia, General Miller's in the north, General Youdenitch was trying to form one on the Baltic. It seemed as though the dawn of the resurrection was at hand.

I realized that I was not doing any good at Headquarters, and returned to my command.

By mid-December the enemy had concentrated fresh troops. They took the initiative, attacked General Kasanovitch's army corps, and forced it to retreat to Kalaous. I obtained permission from Headquarters to go to his relief. General Toporkov with his six regiments was to deflect the enemy and attack them.

On the 20th I heard that the Commander-in-Chief had left Headquarters with the Allied Missions to go to the front. The same day Denikin telephoned me. He told me that Kasanovitch had informed him that in view of the critical situation in which his column—which was on the march—found itself, he could not possibly concentrate his troops for Allied inspection.

The General said to me "Can I bring them along to you?" "With pleasure, Your Excellency," I replied. "What can you show them?" he asked. "I can only show them," I said, "how we pound the Reds. Do try and arrive tonight, so as to be able to march with the troops."

I spent the night making the necessary arrangements, and drawing up a detailed report of the situation and of the orders which had been given to the troops, with explanatory diagrams. I had the whole thing translated into English and French, then sent a picket of honor to meet the Commander-in-Chief. When I was told that the train was coming into the station, I too went along.

The day was still young, it was raining, there was a watery sun, and puddles covered the ground. We moved at a walking pace, chilly in the mist. As far as the eye could see stretched the bare, black, unfriendly steppe. All along the road, wagons stuck fast in the mud showed that we had had to abandon our transport. Many were dumped there, all without horses, for General Toporkov had taken them to supplement those drawing the artillery carts

---

[1] Kiev had once more fallen into the hands of the Bolshevists. —TRANSLATOR

which could not go on because of the mud. The mud was certainly terrible. The plastounes[1] had difficulty in following the horses.

As early as four o'clock that same afternoon the column with which we were marching managed to turn the enemy's flank and open fire. We had eaten nothing for twelve hours, and had been in the saddle most of the time. The Commander-in-Chief, his staff, and the foreign agents were unused to the fatigue of war and were feeling quite weak. I found a good observation-post, and suggested to the Commander-in-Chief that they should remain there, though I asked permission to go to my troops. I left my escort and my chief-of-staff with the General. My chief-of-staff was under orders to wait for half a battery and the plastounes to take command of them and to turn the enemy out of a certain village.

Our column, en route for the valley, filed past the Commander-in-Chief, who shouted a few words of encouragement to them as they passed.

Our regiments deployed in battle order under enemy fire, and climbed the right bank of the river. Rather a long way to their right, firing could be heard. On our left, our 2nd division could be seen approaching.

A regiment commanded by a young man who had only the evening before been made a colonel, was climbing the hill. I shouted to him. "Remember that you *earned* the rank of colonel." He immediately gave the word for the charge, and off they dashed at full speed. The firing was terrible, the horses constantly slipped and fell on the churned-up ground, but nothing could stop the gallant fellows. They continued to pursue the enemy and took a village by storm, hunting cavalry, infantry, vehicles, and ambulance cars into it. The 2nd brigade, coming up at a brisk trot, cut them off from the road. Night drew on, reports came in from all sides the Reds were routed all along the front, we had taken more than a thousand prisoners, twelve guns and sixty-five machine-guns, and an immense amount of booty. The position which General Kasanovitch had abandoned had been won back.

I returned to the railway station to which General Denikin and the Allies had already gone. The journey seemed interminable, our horses were at the end of their tether. I found General Denikin and the Allied Mission having supper. They gave me a great welcome as I came in, for they already knew the result of the day's work.

As soon as my guests' train had gone, I went to bed. I had had no sleep for forty hours, and had ridden more than a hundred kilometres in the last twenty-four hours.

By the end of December the enemy's army was utterly destroyed and its remnants scattered over the steppe.

On December 26th a convention was signed between General Denikin and the head of the Don Cossacks' Government. The Don kept its

[1] Cossack infantry.

autonomy, but gave up the supreme command of its army to General Denikin, who became not only Commander-in-Chief of the Volunteer Army, but also Commander-in-Chief of the Armed Forces of South Russia.

The next day a telegram from General Denikin informed me that I had been appointed Commander-in-Chief of the Volunteer Army, whilst General Pokrovsky was to take over the command of my cavalry division.

The Volunteer Army was to continue the pursuit of the routed army, seize the town of Sviator Krest, the Reds' principal base, and then attack the 11th Red Army in the rear whilst it was still covering the group of spas in Caucasia; after this it was to join our cavalry, which was advancing by way of the railway, and finish off the enemy.

After a few days of desperate fighting, the enemy army was routed and we occupied the spas.

III - The Liberation of Terek

As I had no one in mind for my chief-of-staff, the Commander-in-Chief suggested my having General Yusefovitch. I did not know him personally, but only by reputation—and a very good reputation it was. I accepted the suggestion, and have never regretted so doing. I could not have had a better man.

On January 8th I heard that the Commander-in-Chief was arriving the next day at the spas, where I wanted to establish my Headquarters. For the last few days I had been feeling ill, and had not left my railway-carriage. As I was attempting to do so, in order to go and call on the General, one of his messengers came to tell me that he was coming to see me.

He told me that the troops operating in the coal-mining district of Donetz and in the Crimea were to be amalgamated and called the Volunteer Army, those that I commanded were to take the name of the Caucasian Army. I refused to give up the title hallowed by the names of Generals Kornilov and Alexeiev, and as a concession my army was called the Volunteer Caucasian Army.

I entered upon my duties on January 10th, and issued a general order to my troops.

In the early days of the Revolution a large number of people—most of them society folk—had left the capital cities and taken refuge at the spas. As soon as the Reds got to Caucasia, the refugees were persecuted in every conceivable way, but when it was known that the Whites were coming, the real terror began, and got worse daily. The Bolshevists shot hundreds of men, including General Ruzsky, the former Commander-in-Chief of the Armies on the northern front, and Radko-Dmitriev, the hero of Galicia. Everyone who had escaped death had lost a brother, son, or father, and most of them all their worldly possessions too. Great numbers of these poor devils were terrified that the Reds would return, and fled to the rear of our Army, crowding out the railway stations and the trains.

The spas were still overrun by Bolshevists who had not been able to escape in time, and were now trying to break through our lines, thinking that they would be safer there than on the scene of their crimes.

Typhus was raging, there was practically no medical service, and a complete lack of drugs. The epidemic spread terribly. For lack of hospitals, the sufferers were packed together in private houses, stations, and railway-carriages. Having no one to nurse them, the poor wretches dragged themselves out into the streets to look for food, and died there. We did everything in our power to bring a little order into this confusion, ordered the disinfecting of the stations and vehicles, and turned shops and cinemas into new hospitals.

General Pokrovsky, who was to take over the command of my corps, came and presented himself to me. He knew I was prejudiced against him, but showed great tact and dignity in his awkward position, and did not attempt to be pleasant to me at all costs. In short, he behaved like a sensible man.

The Commander-in-Chief called a council of war consisting of his adjutant for civil affairs, General Dragomnov, Romanovsky, his chief-of-staff, General Liakhov, General Yusefovitch, my chief-of-staff, and myself. He outlined his plan of campaign. All the troops which could be spared, after Northern Caucasia had been freed, were to be concentrated in the Donetz coalfield which was being occupied by General May-Mayevsky. Only those which were really needed to cover the Manytsch line were to be left behind. The rest were to operate near Kharkov. However, I proposed that the available troops should not be moved towards the Donetz coalfield area, but into the Manytsch lake district, there to undertake a joint operation with Admiral Koltchak's Army, which was coming up from the Volga. General Romanovsky objected that the coalfield area was indispensable to us, and that since Moscow was our ultimate goal, the shortest way to get there was by way of Kharkov.

General Yusefovitch seconded my scheme, but it was of no avail. General Denikin stuck to his point of view.

I saw the General several times daily. Together we went for a day's trip to the Kislovodsky baths, and as we talked of this and that, I got to know him. I have already said Denikin was one of the best generals in the old Russian Army, a man of high military rank, who had won his excellent reputation during the World War. He distinguished himself many times at the head of his "iron division." Later, as chief of the Supreme General Staff at the very beginning of the Revolution, he had made a courageous attempt to check the dissolution by grouping all the officers round the Supreme Command. Everyone knows his brilliant closing speech at the Officers' Congress at

Moghilev. He was an exceptionally fine speaker, but could only be appreciated by an intelligent audience. He did not know how to grip the troops, and his personal appearance was no help to him. He had not a commanding presence, in fact there was nothing of the great chief about him. He lacked that indefinable something which fires the imagination and stirs the heart. He came from a lower middle-class family, had spent his childhood in the country, and most of his time since in little garrison towns, he owed his success in his career to stubborn hard work. He had developed what he believed to be infallible powers of judgment, and would credit no one's opinion but his own. Yet he was often less clear-sighted than men who were otherwise his inferiors.

He was the son of a minor officer of the line, and he had made up his mind to back the humbler classes against "the aristocrats," "the courtiers," and "officers of the guard." He was morbidly sensitive, and took meticulous care to safeguard his dignity against slights which were sometimes purely imaginary.

Destiny had laid upon his shoulders the burden of a gigantic task in a sphere quite foreign to him, and had plunged him into a whirlpool of passions and political intrigue. He felt lost, he said, at this unsuitable work, was afraid of making mistakes, trusted nobody, and yet failed to find sufficient strength in himself to enable him to navigate the ship of state with a firm hand over the stormy waters.

The struggle went on. The enemy made vain efforts to stop our advances, and managed to avoid a decisive defeat. General Pokrovsky was still pursuing them. At Mozdok, Mekenskaia and Kalmovskaia, the remnants of the enemy's army which had formerly numbered one hundred and fifty thousand men, were absolutely destroyed. A few cavalry troops were all that managed to escape to the Steppes of Astrakhan. But all that was left of the infantry and artillery fell into our hands. The road along which the Reds had retreated was choked with cars, guns, wagons, dead, and wounded. Our cavalry took thirty-one thousand prisoners, eight armoured cars, two hundred cannon, and three hundred machine-guns. Our advance-guard was at Kizlar, our outposts on the shores of the Caspian. In twelve days our cavalry had covered a distance of three hundred and fifty kilometres.

Once Pokrovsky was in occupation of Kizlar, I went off to thank the troops. Halfway there, finding that the railway lines had been destroyed, I made the rest of the journey by car. Traces of the disorderly retreat of the Red Army were to be seen everywhere. The highway was covered with corpses, derelict carts, and dead horses. All the houses and sheds were full of wounded.

At Mozdok, sixty-five kilometres farther on, there were not only guns, carts, ambulances, and vast numbers of corpses, but also convoys of prisoners, marching by one after the other in an uninterrupted stream.

Ragged, starving, with bare, bleeding feet, thousands of these poor creatures dragged themselves along with an escort of only a few Cossacks. Two Cossacks were enough to guard several thousand prisoners, ill or wounded as most of them were. There were many stragglers. They marched along, stumbling and falling, getting on to their feet again with the greatest difficulty and attempting to go on, then sinking down, never to get up again. I went into a signalman's hut at an abandoned railway station. Eight men were lying there, pressed close against one another. I asked one of them where the station-master was. He did not answer. I questioned one of the others—no reply. I stooped down to them. They were all dead except one who was in the last throes, he was clasping a dying dog to his chest, trying to get some warmth from it.

The stations and sidings were crammed with abandoned trains, the engines burnt out, the carriage doors stoved in. The people of the neighborhood were looting them. All mixed up with guns, carpets, and a hundred and one lovely things, were the dead and wounded. In one of the trains I saw a dying man with his head pillowed on his comrade's dead body.

In one station I was shown an ambulance train. There were forty-four carriages full of dead bodies, and not one live man amongst them. One carriage was devoted to Sisters of Charity and doctors—dead, too, of course. General Pokrovsky had sent a score or two of men to clear the stations of the dead and wounded. They were shovelling them on to the handcarts as though they were coals and throwing them into sandpits. From Kargalmskaia Station to Kizlar, a distance of twenty-five kilometers, the line was obstructed by the debris of rolling-stock and piles of merchandise. It must have been worth millions. There was no one to guard all this wealth, and everyone was taking what he wanted. Some trucks full of ammunition had just been overturned, the wreck was still smouldering, and masses of corpses, including those of women and children, were lying on the ground.

The Terek had been freed and was coming to life again. In the streets through which we passed many houses had been destroyed, but the streets were crowded. The people laughed and sang and cheered us. The Cossacks were galloping about, the women in their beautiful peasant dresses were taking their children for walks. My chauffeur pulled up to ask the way. A crowd of children collected to take a look at us at close quarters. About a dozen little urchins, the eldest of whom could not have been more than fourteen or fifteen, were shouldering rifles twice as big as themselves.

"Hello, children, what are you doing with those things?" I called.

"Hunting the Reds," was the reply, "they're hiding down in the reeds by the river "

"I've killed seven of them today," said a twelve-year-old in a big fur cap.

Never before during our Civil War had the full horror of this fratricidal struggle struck me so clearly.

The town of Groznoy, centre of the petrol wells, had been won back, so had the bigger town of Vladikavkaz. After some bloody encounters, the last remnants of the Reds who had taken refuge in the mountains had been killed off or taken prisoners. One of our divisions by itself had taken more than ten thousand.

Northern Caucasia was free.

General Denikin's armies now had a base, an extraordinarily rich piece of territory, a big reserve force, and everything that was necessary for the troops.

I had only just gone back to the spas when I was taken ill. I forced myself to get about as usual and do my work, but in the end I had to take to my bed. Typhus set in, and complications developed, owing to an old wound. I received first-class attention from two famous doctors, both professors from Petersburg, who were also refugees in Caucasia, but to no avail. The doctors declared that I could not pull through. My wife arrived, but I did not recognize her; the doctors told her that she must be prepared for the worst, they told General Yusefovitch that I could not live through the night. The Last Sacrament was administered to me. Then at seven o'clock in the morning came the crisis, and I turned the corner.

My convalescence was a slow business. I was not allowed to get up until the middle of March. The Commander-in-Chief wrote me a very kind letter. I was so weak that it took me hours to write him a reply.

I cannot sufficiently praise the kindness of my friends and of perfect strangers. General Denikin knew that I was in financial difficulties, and charged up the expenses of my illness to the Government. The doctors refused to take their fees, and strangers sent me wine, fruit, and other things.

Whilst I was ill, my army was transferred to the coalfield area in Donetz. General Ulagay and his cavalry corps were the only ones left behind to cover the Sviator-Krest district, a few regiments under General Chatilov were still at Daghestan, clearing the villages of Reds. My Headquarters had been transferred to Rostov on the Don, where General Yusefovitch was taking my place during my absence, I still had my special escort and some of my staff-officers with me.

The doctors forbade me to do any work, so my wife and I went to Sotchy, a spa and seaside town on the Black Sea. We took my escort with us, and also one or two orderly officers. A delightful villa had been put at our disposal, and the country round about was beautiful. I kept in touch with my Headquarters by telegraph. Yusefovitch sent me the report which he had presented to the Commander-in-Chief in which he had again stressed the absolute necessity of joining up with Admiral Koltchak's Army.

I did not stay in the country very long. The news was bad. The Reds had driven back General Borovsky's troops and advanced into the Crimea. Relations between our Commander-in-Chief and the Government of Georgia had grown very bitter, and a complete rupture seemed likely.

Hostilities were expected to begin on the frontier near Sotchy in a day or two. In the neighboring mountains bands of deserters from the Red and White armies, known as "Greens," were organizing themselves at the instigation of the Georgians.

As the Greens became aggressive, the commander of the little garrison in Sotchy asked me to let my escort reconnoitre on the outskirts of the town. I told one of the officers to take some men and do as requested. Twelve kilometres from the town the Greens fell upon them, killing a Cossack and two horses.

The commander of the garrison sent out a detachment to drive the Greens back. The officer and a number of men were killed. Headquarters got to hear of this, sent reinforcements for the garrison, and ordered me to leave the town immediately. As the railway was already threatened, a torpedo-boat was sent to fetch me.

Many of my officers had their wives and children with them, and my escort was mounted. It was impossible to get everybody, horses and all, on board a small torpedo-boat and I hated the thought of leaving anyone behind, so I decided to travel by train, come what might. I had machine-guns put on the engine, and when night had fallen, we started off. The Greens sent some bullets after us, but they had not destroyed the permanent way, and we arrived safely.

On the way I had the train stopped on the Kuban frontier and went to thank some towns and villages who had elected me an "honorary Cossack".

Life had resumed its normal course everywhere. There had been a good harvest, and the country was getting rich again. The Cossacks gave me a cordial welcome and talked to me as if I had been one of themselves. The Cossack proletariat is much more civilized than the Russian peasantry, always having had self-government of a kind. They one and all complained of "our government," meaning the Kuban Government. They thought that the Rada talked too much and quarrelled too often, formulating policies, but not really considering the true needs of the country.

A little while before Easter I arrived at Ekaterinodar, where the doctors sent me to bed again. But before I obeyed them I forced myself to go and see the Commander-in-Chief, who also prescribed a complete rest for me until I was quite well again.

Headquarters took a rosier view of things than ever, in spite of the Red invasion of the Crimea, the complications with Georgia, and the bitter and fruitless struggles in the coalfields. The question of military operations seemed to have been relegated to a secondary place. Important political matters had come to the fore.

The help which France and England had promised had begun to materialize. Boats laden with war materials and drugs, things of which the Army was in great need, had arrived at Novorossiisk. They promised us tanks and aeroplanes. Northern Caucasia was unanimous in recognizing General Denikin as Commander-in-Chief. In his secret conflict with the Ataman of the Don, it was Denikin who came off best. Krasnov fell, and a new Ataman, Bogarevsky, came into power, he was a pusillanimous man, and Headquarters could do as they liked with him. In the Terek and the Kuban Denikin's power was almost absolute, though it is true that his relations with the Government of Ekaterinodar, with Ataman as well as Rada, were rather strained, since they disagreed on most questions.

Headquarters showed the rankest intolerance towards the Cossacks and all others who did not blindly endorse their point of view. Denikin's motto, "Russia, one and indivisible", a vague and obscure phrase on the whole, was to be everyone's watchword. Those who held any other opinion, or were reputed to do so, were stigmatized as separatists. Anyone was called a separatist who had fought the Reds under the Ukrainian flag, or who had taken service with the Hetman, this included a very large number of officers who were now serving in the Volunteer Army. These officers did not give a thought for Headquarters' high politics, but were ready to fight the Bolshevists whatever their leaders' motto might be. But Headquarters regarded them almost as traitors. Before they were admitted to the service they had to pass through a purgatory called the "Committee of Rehabilitation," an unjust, severe, and unintelligent proceeding.

Admiral Koltchak's Army was coming up the Volga. The enemy had concentrated their forces on the eastern front, and tried in vain to stop it. Operations had been impossible on this front for some time owing to the snow. In the south we had not been very successful during the last four months, though we were still occupying the south bank of the Manytsch. In the Donetz coalfield area we had been obliged to withdraw our left wing to Marioupol. Our Crimean troops had been driven back towards the Isthmus of Kertch. The Commander-in-Chief and his General Staff were not satisfied with General Yusefovitch, and hoped that once I took up the reins again our luck would turn.

I still disapproved of their plan of campaign. The crying need to join forces with Koltchak's Army simply stared us in the face. As all my attempts to reopen the subject were fruitless, I sent the Commander-in-Chief a report in which I detailed the situation from my point of view.

In my opinion, since the enemy's forces were infinitely superior to our own, we ought not to operate simultaneously in several directions, but should take decisive action against their weakest spot. Actually, this spot could only be Tsaritsin on the Volga. From there we could effect a junction with Koltchak's Army. I decided that we would have to give up our operations in the coalfields. If we shortened our front on the right bank of the Don by about one hundred and fifty kilometres and took the initiative in the direction

I had indicated, it would be all that we could manage. Otherwise, the initiative would fall to the enemy, and they would be threatening our base.

My prophecies soon came true. On April 12th I learnt from Headquarters that the enemy had stormed Manytsch and moved up to the line of the Vladikavkase-Rostov railway. Our units retreated, scarcely putting up any resistance.

On the 13th I was awakened during the night. The chief of Headquarters' General Staff and the quartermaster-general were there and wanted to see me. Romanovsky told me that there was disastrous news from the front. We had got to do something desperate. He asked me to take command of all the troops we could possibly muster and send to Manytsch. As Yusefovitch was still at Rostov, deputizing for me, I would have to leave him my General Staff, but I could form another. It was impossible to do anything with the forces they proposed to give me, and I could not form an efficient General Staff from men selected anyhow from all over the place.

I told him that under such conditions I must refuse the command, and I pointed out to him where the troops necessary to stop the Red advance were to be found. But he did not agree with me. He thought that if the troops were moved from one place to another we should be risking a panic at Rostov. I told him that there was no fear of this, because, in the circumstances, I would leave for the town immediately, ill as I was, my Headquarters was there already, and I would resume my command straight away.

"Your refusal," said Romanovsky, "will force the Commander-in-Chief himself to take the Manytsch command which he offered to you."

I replied that this would be all to the good. The Commander-in-Chief could transfer troops from wherever he thought proper, whereas I would have had to make do with whatever troops had been given to me. Moreover, circumstances would compel him to use some of those I had.

Romanovsky, Pluchtchevsky-Pluchtchik (the quartermaster-general), and I were not on very good terms when we parted. The next day, the Commander-in-Chief asked me if I had not changed my mind. I answered that, with the troops that his chief-of-staff was willing to allow me, it was impossible to carry out his plan, and I asked his permission to return to my Headquarters and resume my command. That evening I left for Rostov.

CHAPTER V

THE MARCH ON MOSCOW

I. - HARD AT THE DON

In the spring of 1919 the position of General Denikin's Armies was as follows—

The French, who had been occupying Odessa after the fall of the Hetman, had evacuated the town without any warning at the end of March, and the pretence of a Russian Army which was just being formed there had dwindled away to nothing.

The Crimea was abandoned, all but the isthmus of Kertch, where General Schilling had concentrated some troops, which the Allied fleet were supporting with their artillery.

In the Donetz area the Volunteer Corps, under General May-Mayevsky, was still holding out against the enemy, who were doing their utmost to make themselves masters of the coalfields. There was some very heavy fighting, and our forces were diminishing daily. On the left flank, near Marioupol, a small group or our troops were face to face with the Reds. We intended to concentrate a cavalry corps, commanded by General Chkouro, on May-Mayevsky's right flank. This corps was in cooperation with the Army of the Don. The first division of my Kuban Cossacks in Pokrovsky's Company had received marching-orders for the Manytsch front, simultaneously a division of Terek Cossacks transferred from the Caucasian forces was supposed to take its place. Until these troops arrived, the whole Rostov region, an extremely important area, was left uncovered. There was panic in the great town of Rostov, one of Russia's chief centres of commerce. There was a large Bolshevist element there, which raised its head when it realized that the town had been left empty of troops.

I tried to hasten the arrival of the Cossacks, who were already on the march, and sent an armored car to cover the village of Bataisk, which was some versts from the town on the further bank of the Don. The police gave notice of disturbances in the working-class part of the town, and of the arrival of Bolshevik emissaries. I ordered the arrest of those we proved to be Red agents. The civil administration protested that it was dangerous to do this until the troops arrived, and that it could only add to our difficulties. However, I believed my course of action to be for the best, and that same night I had seventy people thrown into prison, and six of them sent up for court-martial, one of them was an influential lawyer who had compromised himself hopelessly a long time ago. There was a great to-do amongst the disaffected classes. All six were condemned to death and shot within twenty-four hours. Then things quietened down again and remained quiet. General Denikin, who in effect had taken over the command on the Manytsch front, was soon convinced that the troops with which he was operating were insufficient, and he had to use those I had suggested, as I had prophesied to his chief-of-staff. In Manytsch one bitter struggle succeeded another. Twice our troops, under General Chatilov, forced the river, and twice they were beaten back. The bed of the Manytsch was too muddy to get the artillery across the ford, and we could do nothing without it. The situation was also rather worse in the Donetz area, but we held out there in spite of everything.

On April 30th I went to report on our position in the Donetz to the Commander-in-Chief, for it had become critical. I asked him how things were going on the Manytsch front. He told me that in spite of the numerous reinforcements, which included Koutepov's infantry division, Pokrovsky's cavalry troop, Chatilov's division, Greffs' division, Saveliev's Cossack cavalry troop, Zykov's brigade, and a brigade of Cossacks of the Guard, that is to say, an infantry division and seven and a half cavalry divisions altogether, they were making but little headway. And, he added bitterly: "Here we have thirty cavalry regiments—thirty! And they are doing absolutely nothing."

I asked him who was at the head of this mass of cavalry, and was astonished to learn that there was no unity of command. I observed that under these conditions it was difficult to hope for good results. To achieve anything there had to be one mind to coordinate the action of the cavalry.

"You are quite right," said the General, "but no general will submit to the authority of any other, for they are all equal."

I was much struck by the Commander-in-Chief's reply. General Denikin, who appeared to be so strong-willed and inflexible, showed an inexplicable lack of resolution when dealing with his colleagues. He himself was a real soldier, for he was hard on himself, but it seemed that he dared not demand as much from his subordinates. In this instance he could not bring himself to put one general under the orders of another. General Romanovsky was present at one interview, and said to me. "Help us, and the cavalry will achieve unity; all the generals would obey you cheerfully."

I was certain that only coordinated action by the cavalry could end this unlucky campaign which had lasted too long already, and I liked the idea of controlling great masses of cavalry and making them play a leading part. So, although I was still ill, I consented to take over the command. I sent for several officers and my horses, and went to the Manytsch front.

I took stock of the situation from a church tower. The enemy forces were massed in a large village—Veliko-kniageskaia—and on its outskirts, on the northern bank of the river. The thoroughfares on the south and west of the village were defended by trenches. The enemy's artillery was powerful—it was impossible to force a passage. To the east, the Reds had only a very small observation corps, but the river was so shallow there that it was more like a swamp than a watercourse, and so muddy that the artillery could never be got across the ford without sticking fast. And without artillery we could achieve nothing, as we knew from experience.

I decided to improvise a causeway, using the numerous wooden fences to be found in the neighboring villages. They had to be fastened together to form a floor, which could be put down over the mud to act as a magic carpet for the artillery. It had to be held under the water very firmly, otherwise it would rise to the surface; indeed, it needed to be pinned down with heavy weights. I ordered an experiment to be made on a dirty little lake in our rear. The experiment was very successful, and I had a large number of these platforms made.

Eighteen kilometres to the east of the village, I found a suitable spot for the crossing, and gave the necessary orders.

We fixed the attack for May 4th. I reached the spot at nightfall. The regiments arrived one after the other. They were working the whole night long, and at dawn the crossing began. The bare, flat steppes, covered with briny pools, seemed endless. The regiments, which had already crossed the Manytsch and were marching in single file, looked like a gigantic snake crawling across a desert. By midday two cavalry corps and all the artillery had crossed the river, and in the distance our advance-guard was driving the enemy back towards the west. General Chatilov took several trenches and more than one thousand five hundred prisoners that day.

Our bivouac was not pleasant. It was a very cold night, and we had not a stick or a bundle of straw with which to light a fire, nor had we a drop of drinkable water for the men or horses. Nobody slept that night.

The battle began again at dawn. The enemy put up a desperate resistance, but in vain. General Pokrovsky forced them to fall back on their base. His men were occupying the farms where once the great studs which had furnished our cavalry with remounts had been kept. They had been very prosperous farms, but now they were nothing but a heap of ruins. The houses were roofless and windowless, the gardens trampled down, the sheds doorless and full of rusty, broken agricultural implements. An enormous number of dead oxen and horses littered the pastures and polluted the air.

The attack on the whole front was to begin at five o'clock. An unusually high haystack the size of a two-storey house served me as an observation-post. I could see the artillery firing on two sides, and the cavalry divisions taking up their position. Our aircraft was circling over Veliko-kniageskaia. On the left flank, our first division set off at a gallop amidst thundering cheers and disappeared behind a hill. General Pokrovsky's corps was getting into battle-order.

Suddenly I heard guns in our rear. One of General Zykov's orderlies came to tell me that great masses of enemy cavalry had turned our right flank. With the help of my field-glasses I could see the Astrakhan Cossacks of Zykov's division marching to their help, shells were bursting all around them. Suddenly the Cossack ranks broke and turned tail. I leapt into my car, turned to Pokrovsky's corps, and sent a division to meet the Reds, who were driven back. Once more the troops bivouacked on the spot.

The enemy's reinforcements had come up, and could have put us in a very awkward position at any moment. There was only one way of retreat open behind us, and only an inadequate fortress on the right bank of the Manytsch, and I had no fresh reserves.

On the 6th we resumed the offensive. For three days my troops had scarcely slept and had eaten no hot food; the horses had had nothing to drink, both men and horses were exhausted.

But we had to finish the job, cost what it might. I spoke to the men, and I saw that, in spite of their weariness, they were doing their work.

The artillery opened the attack, and I harangued the troops, had the colours unfurled, and drew up the men in battle-array to the sounds of music, as though it had been a parade.

The bugles rang out, the standards floated on the breeze, swords flashed in the sun, a lusty cheer went up, and the mass of cavalry charged, soon to disappear in a whirlwind of dust. The enemy lost many men and horses, the defeated units wavered and began a hurried retreat.

Veliko-kniageskaia, which had held out for so long, was taken. There was no longer any danger of our forces being cut off from Caucasia, and the 10th Red Army was wiped out. In the last three days we had taken fifteen thousand prisoners, fifty-five guns, and one hundred and fifty machine-guns.

Now there was nothing to prevent us from marching on Tsaritsin and then on to the Volga.

The enemy were in flight northwards, blowing up the bridges and destroying the railroads as they went. I ordered Chatilov's company to pursue them.

The next day I entered Veliko-kniageskaia, where Chatilov had already established his Headquarters. Some Circassians who had been caught in the very act of marauding were brought in I had them court-martialed, and two hours later five of them were hanged.

I ordered their bodies to be left on the gallows for a few days, to prove to the troops and the civil population that no excesses would be tolerated.

A little while after, General Denikin arrived. He was overjoyed and embraced me. He had been present at the cavalry attack, and said that he had never, during the whole Civil War, seen artillery fire as brisk as the enemy's had been when they had fired on our charging cavalry.

The troops operating on the Manytsch, to wit, Pokrovsky's cavalry troop, Chatilov's and Saveliev's company of Don Cossacks, the Circassian and the Astrakhan Cossack divisions, the 6th infantry division, and Ulagay's cavalry troop, which was maneuvering in the east, were to form henceforth the Caucasian Army. The troops in the coalfield area of Donetz, under General May-Mayevsky, received the title of the Volunteer Army. My Army was ordered to Tsaritsin and to take it.

"Well," Denikin said to me, "when are you going to win Tsaritsin for us?"

I told him that if everything went according to plan, we would be at the gates of the town in three weeks. The rest depended not on me, but on him. It was impossible to take the town without artillery and infantry. General Denikin promised to send me a Cossack infantry brigade and the necessary artillery. As his train moved out, he smilingly held up three fingers to me—an allusion to the three weeks in which Tsaritsin was to be taken.

After the defeat of the enemy at Manytsch, General Denikin lost his fear of seeing the armies cut off from their base, and concentrated all of his efforts on Kharkov, where the situation had improved somewhat.

I kept my promise. Three weeks later we were at the gates of Tsaritsin. But at what a price! We had traversed three hundred kilometres of salty steppe-land which lacked water and vegetation of any sort; the whole time we had been fighting the enemy, who occupied strongly fortified positions at many points. The nearer we got to the town, the more stubborn was the resistance of the Reds, whose ranks were constantly being reinforced by the arrival of fresh troops. As my cars were "in dock", and, in spite of my entreaties, Headquarters had not sent me any new ones, I did most of the journey on horseback, riding with the fourth troop (Chatilov's).

For days we saw neither houses nor people, nothing but a few signalman's huts, and most of these even were abandoned. Sometimes a convoy of wounded would pass us—hundreds of carts drawn by camels, which scarcely seemed to move, so slow was their pace—and they still had hundreds of kilometres to cover, weeks to travel, before they reached their destination.

The grilling sun beat down on the poor wretches lying there in the carts, which were devoid of hoods and springs; the axles were never oiled, and made an unholy din in consequence. And for days there was not a drop of water to refresh the sufferers.

I remember one night which we spent in the open, on the eve of a bloody battle. It was a beautiful night, the sky was covered with stars, the steppe with tents. I was lying on my cloak, my saddle for a pillow, and I could hear my soldiers laughing and talking, the horses snorting with fear in the mist, and the firing in the distance. I felt I was back in the times when the technique of modern warfare was still unknown—when telegraphs, telephones, motor-cars, lorries, and railways did not exist, when the commander marched with his troops, slept on the ground as they did, and sometimes lacked water to quench his thirst, even as they.

We had kept our promise, but Headquarters had not kept theirs. The promised artillery, infantry, cars, and lorries had not arrived, and they had done nothing to help us put the Velikokniageskaia-Tsaritsin railway in good repair—and it was our only line of communication. I had sent dispatch after dispatch in vain—nothing happened. Headquarters seemed to have forgotten us. All its attention was concentrated on the Kharkov front.

On May 22nd, after General Pokrovsky had won a victory, I telegraphed to the Commander-in-Chief: "it would be criminal not to follow up our success. What we can do cheaply now will cost us huge losses in the future. Courage is not enough. The cavalry can do wonders, but it cannot remove barbed wire. If you do not send me infantry, guns, munitions, and more cars, without which I cannot move about and direct the troops as I should, our success will be but a Pyrrhic victory."

In a dispatch of May 24th, in which I more or less repeated the same thing, I added: "I realize the necessity of continuing operations on other fronts, but I must insist that if the Tsaritsin operations fails or is delayed, all your other operations will come to nothing. You promised me artillery and infantry, and I based my whole campaign on your promise. While I held my command in Caucasia, I never asked you for a single man; today I insist on having what is indispensable. I feel it my duty to tell you the truth quite crudely like this."

Tsaritsin was surrounded by many lines of trenches and four or five lines of barbed wire. A strong artillery force defended the approaches.

On May 29th I summoned a Council of War. I told the generals who composed it that it was unlikely that the infantry and artillery we were expecting would arrive yet awhile, and I asked their advice: should we risk an attack, or merely entrench ourselves and await the arrival of reinforcements? It was unlikely that an immediate attack would succeed, but on the other hand the enemy were receiving reinforcements daily, and making their position more and more secure, so that even if we waited we would have very little more chance of success. Our troops were exhausted by the immense difficulties of their march across the desert, and had been visualizing Tsaritsin as the Promised Land. If we kept them waiting too long now, they would be bitterly disappointed. Moreover, it was quite possible that the enemy would take the offensive. If we were driven back on to the steppe, where there were no means of getting fresh provisions, our plight would indeed be terrible. The Council was unanimously of the opinion that we must attack.

On June 1st our attacking force got through the enemy's lines and took several villages. But after two days of hard fighting, I realized that all our efforts to take the town would be fruitless. The enemy's artillery was too powerful, our casualties were enormous. We had lost five lieutenant-generals, three brigadier-generals, and eleven captains. Our ammunition had run out. We had to abandon the offensive and resume our old position.

On June 4th the enemy took the offensive, supported by all their artillery and fresh reinforcements. I withdrew my troops to within twenty kilometres of the further bank of the River Tchervlennia, and decided to wait there for the promised reinforcements.

The failure of our attack and the number of our casualties caused me intense anxiety, which was all the more acute because I could do nothing. I therefore wrote to General Denikin. I reminded him of the promises he had made me which his General Staff had not fulfilled, I said that since I was only too sure that things would be the same in the future, I could not assume any further responsibility, and requested that, as soon as the Tsaritsin enterprise came to an end, he would appoint someone else in my place. I sent this letter to the Commander-in-Chief by an officer who knew its contents. On the urgent entreaties of General Yusefovitch, however, I stopped the delivery of this letter by telegram. Moreover, on June 4th, Headquarters let me know that they had issued an order to send me an infantry division, five batteries, three armored cars, and six tanks, and in addition the railway was to be put under repair. I ordered the bearer of the letter to bring it back to me.

Meanwhile the Army of the Don and the Volunteer Army were doing better and better. There was rejoicing at Rostov and Ekaterinodar. Headquarters were obsessed with the desire to take Moscow at the earliest possible moment, and forgot that success did not depend solely upon a rapid advance, it was just as necessary to cover our flanks and keep possession of our base.

General May-Mayevsky, who had recently been appointed to the command of the Volunteer Army, was a good officer and knew his job, he got on well with his subordinates and men. If he had not worn a uniform, you would have taken him for a comedian from a little provincial theatre. He was as round as a barrel, and had a chubby face and a bulbous nose. He knew how to make himself pleasant, and success had not robbed him of his hearty manner. But his conduct at his headquarters in Rostov roused the indignation of every honest man. His orgies brought discredit on the Army and on authority in general. The rear of the Army was always badly organized. The generals had almost absolute power and thought themselves satraps.

The troops followed their example and considered everything permissible. Violence and abuse reigned supreme. As I have already said, at the beginning of the Civil War the Cossacks had been anxious to win back their possessions, and yet I had managed to inculcate ideas of lawfulness into my troops. When General Pokrovsky's men had been incorporated in my Army, even they had been forced to give up marauding. If a little firmness had achieved this result with the Cossacks, how much easier it should have been with the regular Army!

As the fresh troops could not possibly arrive until June 11th, I went back to my Headquarters, which were established at Kotelnikovo Station. Naoumenko, the Ataman of the Kuban campaign, joined me there. The question of raising an Army from the autonomous Kuban had again arisen, and there were still misunderstandings between the Commander-in-Chief and the autonomous Kubanian Government. Naoumenko told me that General Denikin and his staff were very annoyed with me. They considered that the tone of my dispatches was inadmissible. "General Wrangel," they said, "does not ask for things, he demands them, he seems to give us orders." Furthermore, they knew that I had not altogether shared their point of view in their misunderstanding with the Rada of the Kuban.

On June 13th the Volunteer Army took Kharkov. The Army of the Don continued its northward march.

The Tsaritsin-Tikhoretskaia railway had been repaired, and the long-expected reinforcements arrived during the night of the 16th. I resumed the initiative. The tanks and the armored cars went first, then the infantry. Once they had destroyed the barbed wire, the cavalry charged. The enemy were driven back on to their last line of trenches.

In the morning we returned to the charge and swept up to the last line of trenches. By the evening our troops were in the town.

The enemy fled towards the north. During these four days of fighting we took two armored cars, one hundred and thirty-one locomotives, ten thousand lorries, two thousand and eighty-five of them loaded with munitions, seventy guns, three hundred machine-guns, forty thousand prisoners, and innumerable cars and carts—an immense amount of spoil.

On the 19th, I entered Tsaritsin and went to the Cathedral, where the *Te Deum* was sung. The archbishop who officiated had been forced to flee the town to escape death, and for weeks had laid in hiding in the suburbs, he had only just come back. The rest of the priests who took part in the service had just been released from prison by our soldiers. During the service the bishop and most of his subordinates wept.

That evening the Commander-in-Chief's train drew into the station. He thanked us and looked at me with a smile. "Has your mood changed? It was not too good."

"Yes, Your Excellency, I have been through some very terrible moments."

In the report which I presented to the Commander-in-Chief, I stressed once again the danger of increasing the length of the front without having the necessary reserves and a well-organized rear. I proposed that we should entrench ourselves on the Tsaritsin-Ekaterinoslav front for the time being, so that the Volga and the Dnieper would be covering our flanks. Then we could detach the troops necessary for operations in the south-east in the direction of Astrakhan, and at the same time concentrate three or four cavalry troops at our centre round about Kharkov.

When the time was ripe these troops could be used nearer Moscow. At the same time the rear had to be organized, the regimental *cadres* enlarged, the reserve forces increased, and new bases established.

General Denikin read my report and then said with a sly look. "I see! You want to be the first man to set foot in Moscow!"

The next day, the 20th, General Denikin attended Divine Service and reviewed the troops. After the parade, he invited General Yusefovitch and myself into his carriage and read us his order in General Romanovsky's presence. My Army was to march on Saratov, and then on to Moscow via Nijni-Novgorod, the Army of the Don, commanded by General Sidorin, was to go to Moscow via Voronege-Riazan, while May-Mayevsky's Army was to advance on Moscow direct from Kharkov via Kursk, Orel, and Tula.

This order, later known as the advance on Moscow, was nothing more nor less than a death-sentence for the Armies of Southern Russia. All the principles of strategy were ignored, there was no choice of a principal direction, no concentration of the bulk of the troops in this direction, and no maneuvering. It merely prescribed a different route to Moscow for each of the Armies.

General Yusefovitch and I were simply bewildered, but General Denikin himself seemed to be delighted with his plan. When we had read it he added merrily—

"Yes, we are going to advance on big lines now. I shall have to use a large-scale map for this campaign!"

As General Yusefovitch had been appointed to the command of an army corps, I asked the Commander-in-Chief to give me Chatilov, whom I had known for a long time, for my new chief-of-staff.

II. - On the Volga

My Army had sustained heavy losses; the long-expected reinforcements had not come from the Kuban. General Denikin had ordered an infantry division and the division of Terek Cossacks to rejoin the Volunteer Army; the troops that remained with me were exhausted after their three hundred kilometre march across the desert and their forty days of incessant fighting. I asked the Commander-in-Chief to grant a few days' delay, to give the troops time to recover.

"Certainly, take fifteen days," was the reply.

I gave the necessary orders, but two days later I received orders to continue the pursuit of the enemy immediately. At once I sent off the 1st corps of Kuban Cossacks, who were less tired than the others, in the direction of Saratov, but they were checked at Kamychin. After the defeat of the Reds at Tsaritsin, the remnants of their 10th Army had fallen back on this town, where numerous reinforcements from Moscow had joined them. Also several divisions of the Siberian Army which was opposing Koltchak had been ordered there. The Red artillery was strong, and was reinforced by the whole Volga fleet.

As the 1st company could not take the position alone, I sent the 4th cavalry corps to join it, whilst I myself went to Ekaterinodar to see about the reinforcements I should have received from the Kuban.

The Commander-in-Chief received me in the presence of General Romanovsky. I told him about the condition of my troops: my Cossack regiments only numbered five to six hundred men, and the reinforcements had not arrived. The General Staff was too large for this small contingent. If the effectives could not be increased, it would be best to discharge some of them, and make my army into a regiment.

The General told me that he could do nothing, and that "the Kuban separatists were shirking their duty" in not sending me fresh troops. General Romanovsky advised me to come to a direct arrangement with the Cossack leaders. I replied somewhat dryly that this was not within my province. I commanded an Army, and to negotiate with the Kuban Government was outside my sphere. The Commander-in-Chief ordered Romanovsky to call a meeting of the Cossack leaders and to confer with them in my presence.

The next day General Romanovsky, the Quartermaster-General, the Ataman Filimonov, his colleague, Naoumenko, and I, met to discuss the question of the Cossack reinforcements from the Kuban. The Ataman Filimonov began by saying that the Cossacks were annoyed because their request for a Kubanian Army of their own had not been granted, and General Denikin's promises on the subject had not been carried out. If their request was granted, the whole country would be satisfied, and the reinforcements would be forthcoming. General Romanovsky replied that the Kuban Government could not produce anyone capable of commanding an autonomous army.

"But we are not asking that," said Naoumenko. "Our troops are nearly all under the command of the Commander-in-Chief of the Caucasian Army, he is not a Cossack by birth, it is true, but he is popular throughout the country. If he remains at the head of our army, the Kuban Government and the troops will be satisfied."

I decided to have done with this eternal question once and for all, for it was getting more and more bitter, so I turned towards Naoumenko and said:

"As Commander-in-Chief of the Caucasian Army, I am not responsible for the Kubanian politics; were I at the head of this autonomous Army, I should be. But the Rada's policy is such that there would be only one course for me to take—order my Army to dissolve it."

Silence fell, and General Romanovsky hastened to close the meeting. It broke up without having come to any decision.

Four days later I went back to Tsaritsin. When we had taken this town it had been in a terrible state. Most of the townsfolk had been massacred by the Reds, and the houses and shops had been looted. There were several epidemics raging, and the mortality was shockingly heavy. It may have been from lack of labor, or perhaps it was sheer carelessness, but I heard from the residents that twelve thousand corpses had been thrown into a gulley. By the spring all these putrefying bodies had poisoned the town. It took quite a week to bury them all. The streets were full of the bodies of dead horses, more than four hundred were cleared away.

And yet gradually this town of the dead came to life once more. People who had been hidden Heaven knows where came out from their retreats; the peasants brought their produce to the market, and the shops opened. The price of provisions fell. I had taken a hand in bringing about this result.

Immediately after we had taken Tsaritsin I had examined the positions on the north of the town and had constructed the necessary fortifications there.

I had sent all the troops I could spare to join those who were already attacking Kamychin, and on July 12th we resumed the offensive. After four days of desperate fighting the town was taken. We took thirteen thousand prisoners, forty-three guns, twelve locomotives, one thousand lorries, and a large stock of munitions.

General Denikin detached the new contingents from my Army to reinforce the Volunteer Army. Headquarters informed me that the 1st company of Don Cossacks and the Terek division were to be taken from me to reinforce the main body of troops. The 7th infantry division and the brigade of "plastounes" which had been promised me were not to arrive until later on, but nevertheless I was to continue the advance on Saratov immediately.

I explained to Headquarters that they were asking the impossible. What had I left without the troops they wanted to take from me, as the infantry would not arrive until after the departure of the other troops? Our losses at Tsaritsin and Kamychin had reduced my effective force to three or four hundred men. The reinforcements from Caucasia had not yet arrived, and we were short of saddles and swords, whilst our horses had succumbed to foot-disease. The Reds in Saratov had received huge reinforcements. The Kuban should have re-equipped my Army, but had not done so on the pretext of financial misunderstandings with Headquarters.

But nothing came of my protest. Headquarters did not withdraw the order, and there was nothing for me to do but obey it. And so I obeyed, fully realizing that, however courageous my troops might be, our efforts could only end in failure.

The troops advanced on Saratov. Tsaritsin was alive once more, the shops, restaurants, and cinemas were open. Unfortunately, as so often happens behind the lines, there were cases of excess and debauchery. I was determined to be ruthless in suppressing them. I learned that a group of officers had been guilty of certain excesses in a restaurant, and I had them court-martialed. A captain was condemned to death. The Civil Governor and the staff officers came to me to beg for mercy for him, but I refused to commute the sentence. He was executed, and his sentence posted up in all the public thoroughfares. Immediately all excesses ceased. We continued to pursue the enemy towards Saratov with great vigor, in spite of the extreme exhaustion of the troops, who were at the end of their tether. I never ceased to bombard Headquarters with telegrams urgently demanding reinforcements.

On July 26th the enemy began an offensive. They lost a large number of men and part of their artillery, but they forced our 4th company to retreat. The next day this company resumed the offensive and routed the Reds, though sustaining heavy losses. In my report I wrote that a few more such apparent successes would compel us to fall back on the defensive for lack of combatants. General Pokrovsky's forces had come to grips with a detachment of the enemy's cavalry, which greatly outnumbered ours. After three days of bloody fighting Boudennyi's Red cavalry was beaten. But here again we suffered heavy losses, especially in generals and superior officers. Our peril became more and more obvious.

The enemy was continually threatening Admiral Koltchak's front. The Reds foresaw their danger if we should occupy Saratov, so they concentrated many divisions there, taking them from the Siberian front. The consequences of General Denikin's strategical errors were now becoming obvious. He had rejected the plan that I had proposed from the very first, after the liberation of Caucasia, and had thrown our troops into the Donetz coalfield area. Suddenly circumstances had forced him to transfer a large number of troops to Tsaritsin, but he was already too late, for Koltchak's Army was in flight by then, and the enemy's entire force was massed against us.

If only we had had enough troops to enable us to reach Saratov, as we had been ordered to do, we might still have done so before the enemy had had a chance to unite all their forces. But, alas, even this was impossible, for we lacked the necessary troops. The only thing that we could do now was to await the promised reinforcements, and when they came resume the offensive. But it was doubtful whether the enemy would give us time for this. I summoned a Council of War. We decided to avoid a definite engagement, should the enemy attack us, and to retreat slowly and piecemeal from every position we held in order to gain time. I gave orders to proceed with the fortification of Tsaritsin, where I wanted the decisive battle with the Reds to take place.

On August 1st the enemy attacked us all along the line, as well as the Army of the Don, which was covering our flank. We retreated slowly, fighting all the time. As our troops could not get back to Tsaritsin immediately, I decided to go to Ekaterinodar and see that the Kuban Government sent supplies for its Cossacks.

I got to Ekaterinodar and explained the situation to the Ataman. I told him that if the Cossack reinforcements and the supplies did not reach me, I could not possibly hold Tsaritsin, and if it fell the Kuban would certainly be invaded again. I repeated the same thing to the Government. The Ataman begged me to explain the situation to the Rada. I consented. The President was to send me word of the time at which the Rada would like to receive me. I warned the Ataman that I had to leave for Headquarters at 1 o'clock p m. the next day.

I waited in vain until twelve midday, when at last Naoumenko arrived with an officer from the President of the Rada. This officer told me that the President had heard by the merest accident that I desired to visit the Rada, and regretted that he could not give me an official invitation without knowing if I really wanted one. I replied that as Commander-in-Chief of the Caucasian Army and guardian of the interests of the Kuban regiments, I was ready to do the Rada the honor of explaining the needs of the Kuban Cossacks to it in person, and that the Ataman and the Government knew this as well as I did. I found it was absolutely useless to deal personally with M. Makarenko (President of the Rada and leader of the Opposition). I added that I was leaving in an hour's time, and that the Cossacks would hear from me how much the President of the Rada cared for their welfare.

The officer returned very shortly and said that the Rada was expecting me. Several members of the Rada accompanied him and invited me to go back with them. I told them that I could not postpone my departure, and half an hour later I left for Tsaritsin.

Things were satisfactory on our fronts and on the Astrakhan front. General Erdeli's troops were advancing, whilst his reconnoitring parties were fifty kilometres from the town. The Volunteer Army was approaching Kursk, Odessa, and Kiev. The Don Cossack cavalry, under General Mamontev, was operating in great masses in the enemy's rear, and was already nearly at Tambov, destroying the railroads, blowing up the munition depots as they went, and sending home the recruits the Reds had mobilized.

They had been proceeding with the fortifications at the Tsaritsin fort. This stronghold was very useful to us, both as a base and as a psychological factor. But it alone was not sufficient, it needed a garrison fresh enough to fight, and strong enough to be effective.

My Army continued to retreat slowly and came to blows with the enemy daily. The effective force of the cavalry regiments was now reduced to one hundred or one hundred and fifty. One of the regiments of the 6th division had been entirely wiped out. The brigade of "plastounes" was now only the size of a battalion. Certain batteries had horses enough for only one or two guns.

Realizing the Army's plight, I ordered the evacuation of the town to begin. Seven trains were to leave every day. The first thing to be hurried off was the war material; then the civil and military administrations were to go, and lastly those civilians who wanted to leave the town and who had entered their names at the town hall to this effect. There was luggage room for each person to take one trunk and no more. An enormous number of people entered their names, and I heard that in defiance of the regulations the trains were being crammed with merchandise, furniture, and all kinds of things.

The General whose duty it was to supervise the evacuation told me that he could do nothing, things were going to the devil. I do not know whether it was ill-will on the part of the administration, or simply inefficiency, but on the first day only four of the seven trains got away, and on the second day only three.

I singled out several Cossacks from my escort and went to the station. A passenger train was just leaving. The carriages were full of pianos, mirrors, and valuable furniture. I had it all thrown out and smashed. Then I discovered a train with locked carriages. The documents said that they were loaded with munitions. I had them opened. They were not full of munitions, but of passengers, mostly Jews, who wanted to get away and take their merchandise with them. They informed me that they had bribed the station-master and two of his colleagues. I had these three employees court-martialed, and they were hanged the same day. The news of their arrest and execution was communicated to all the railway stations, and after that the evacuation proceeded satisfactorily. Eight trains left daily instead of only seven, and when the Reds approached, the town was completely evacuated.

On August 20th, the long-expected reinforcements arrived, i.e. a brigade of Cossack infantry. It occupied parts of Tsaritsin, and was reinforced by a cavalry division, the last of the fresh troops that I had at my disposal. I had had to withdraw them from the left bank of the Volga, thus leaving my right flank uncovered. The majority of my troops, after twenty days' marching and fighting, were retreating towards Tsaritsin with the enemy at their heels. The Soviet Government had given orders that the town was to be taken at all costs.

At the first encounter, our regiment at Saratov, made up for the most part of Red deserters, went over to the enemy, who were occupying our first line of trenches. The 4th division of Kuban Cossacks who were in reserve learned accidentally that things were going badly, and without waiting for orders they saddled their horses, galloped to the scene of battle, they threw themselves upon the enemy, and routed them. This charge cost the Reds dearly. Our soldiers performed prodigies of valor; no one would have imagined that these men had just accomplished a two hundred kilometres' march during which they had lacked all necessaries, and were now dropping with fatigue.

The position that the Saratov regiment had abandoned was occupied by a battalion of Cossack infantry. During the battle I had left town and had been present at the cavalry charge. I was informed that a regiment of Red marines, covered by their fleet's artillery, was attacking one of the sections of our positions where the defences were still incomplete. The marines had already made themselves masters of the right flank of our trenches in one part of the suburbs. I ordered the grenadiers to attack the enemy's flank, the 4th Kuban division to attack once more, and my escort (because I had no other forces at my disposal) to occupy the northern quarter of the town to prevent the Reds entering that way, whilst I went back to Tsaritsin.

The streets were full of wounded, ambulance-cars, and lorries. The townsfolk had quitted the town in a panic. Outside Staff Headquarters, they were loading the telephone and telegraph apparatus on to two motor-lorries. My horses were waiting for us. The train which was to take the General Staff away was in the station.

I sent the train on to the next station and ordered the cars to cross the bridge and wait for us on the far side. Then General Chatilov and I, followed by several officers, rode on horseback to the northern part of the town. If there was to be a retreat, I wanted to be with the troops.

A shell fell quite near us and set fire to one of the railway buildings. Another fell on a wooden house and soon reduced it to a blazing furnace. Some members of my escort had preceded us and were already fighting.

We emerged from the town; night had fallen and everything seemed quiet.

"It looks as though we are still holding out," said Chatilov; "we do not seem to have encountered anybody."

"Yes, our counter-attack seems to have succeeded."

By the time we got to a village it was almost dark. One house was lighted up, and saddled horses were waiting outside. It was our 1st corps' General Staff; they had just received news from our right flank. Everything was proceeding according to plan; the Kuban 4th division had attacked a second time, as I had ordered them to. The Cossacks, still drunk with their previous success, had done wonders; they had annihilated a regiment of marines. My escort had driven the enemy out of the suburbs. The grenadiers too had done their work and repulsed the Reds.

When we got back to the town there was not a soul to be seen. Dispatches from the other generals were waiting for us. The enemy were beaten at every point with heavy losses; but they had not lost hope. At dawn on the 24th they returned to the attack, but were again unsuccessful. In a three-day-long battle we utterly routed the 10th and 11th Red Armies, took eighteen thousand prisoners, thirty-one guns, and one hundred and sixty machine-guns.

And yet the Reds made two further attempts to take Tsaritsin. After six weeks of bloody warfare the enemy's Armies were beaten and their spirit broken. The Caucasian Army, rested and reinforced, had become powerful again after so many victories. Tsaritsin was not threatened again for a long while. On October 4th our Army resumed the offensive and advanced fifty kilometres to the north of the town.

The enemy were too demoralized to be a danger to us on our front for the moment, but our numbers were too small for us to be able to dream of marching on Saratov, especially as General Erdeli's troops were retreating in the Astrakhan area, on our right flank.

I asked Supreme Headquarters for fresh orders countermanding the route prescribed by the advance on Moscow. In reply, General Romanovsky insisted on my resuming the offensive. I tried to answer him, but he appeared to take very little notice of my arguments. Obviously Supreme Headquarters had no grasp of the real situation. I obtained leave from the Commander-in-Chief to go to Taganrog[1] and make my report to him in person.

I inquired at Supreme Headquarters if the advance on Moscow was still part of their plan. I found that it was, and though I did my best to prove to them that it was out of the question, General Romanovsky insisted on it. I was heartily sick of the war, and said that since I could not do the impossible, I must request him to replace me with someone more capable.

"You know as well as I do," he replied, "that you are the only man who can do it."

General Denikin's Army continued its rapid march towards Moscow. It took Kiev, Kursk, and Orel. Our cavalry was at the gates of Voronege. All Southern Russia, with its wealth of provisions of all kinds, was in General Denikin's power, and we heard of new successes daily. But it had been clear to me for a long time, and I had not hidden my opinion from the Commander-in-Chief, that we were building on sand, we had bitten off far more than we could chew. Our front was too long in comparison with the number of our forces, we had no organized bases and no strongholds in our rear.

The enemy, on the contrary, adhered strictly to the principle of strategy. Although they had repulsed my Army at Tsaritsin, they realized that three months of heavy fighting had weakened them, so that they could not resume the offensive immediately. Consequently the Red Command was now concentrating its forces on the junction of the Volunteer Army and the Army of the Don. The Commander-in-Chief had no troops with which to oppose this new enemy force. Risings were breaking out in the interior, rebels under the command of the brigand Makhno were sacking the towns and looting the trains and commissariat depots. Disorder was at its height in the country. The local authorities had no idea how to make themselves respected; abuse of authority was the order of the day; the agrarian question was more bitter than

[1] A town in the Don district, to which Headquarters was transferred from Ekaterinodar.

ever. The Government itself knew only too well what it wanted to do about it. Its underpaid representatives were often dishonest.

Relations with the Cossack organizations, especially with the Kuban, had not grown more cordial since Headquarters had left Ekaterinodar for Taganrog, the Rada had become more demagogic than ever, and was putting up a fierce opposition to the Commander-in-Chief.

In spite of all our apparent successes, I thought the future looked far from rosy. I learnt that there was a rumor afloat in political circles that I was in open opposition to General Denikin on military and political questions, and that public opinion was backing me as his successor in the near future. I hardly knew any influential people in so-called "political spheres," and, furthermore, I had not left the Army for months, except to go to Headquarters, so I took the rumors to be mere idle tittle-tattle.

CHAPTER VI

THE REVOLT IN KUBAN

I reached Rostov in the evening, and as I had to spend the night there, I went to the theatre. I took a screened box in the second tier so that the audience should not see me. It was a very fashionable gathering. The ladies in full evening dress and the soldiers in brand new uniforms made the Civil War seem like a bad dream.

When the interval was over, the lights went out, but the curtain did not go up. One of the actors appeared before the footlights and said to the audience: "Whilst we are here, laughing and singing, our brothers are fighting for the honor of Russia—One and Indivisible, and for our safety. We owe our lives, our peace and quiet, and our welfare to these brave men and to their famous generals. Ladies and gentlemen, one of these men, the hero of Caucasia and Tsaritsin, is in our midst tonight. Give him a cheer!" A spotlight lit up my box, and the audience cheered me.

We left the theatre before the end of the play and went to have supper at the Palace. But another ovation was awaiting me there. I took refuge in an adjoining room, which was immediately invaded by a crowd of people I knew, and some complete strangers as well, who came, glass in hand, to drink with me.

Amongst other questions I was asked: "What are your relations with General Denikin? Is it true that you have broken completely with the Commander-in-Chief?"

An invisible hand was fostering intrigues behind the scenes and sowing the seeds of doubt and confusion in all minds.

As soon as I could get away I hurried off to the railway station, hid myself in my carriage, and went to sleep without having had any supper.

I arrived at Taganrog the next morning and presented myself to the Commander-in-Chief. He received me in the presence of his chief-of-staff. He was very pleasant, but it was obvious that he had something against me, and though he tried to be as cordial as usual, he was very much on his guard. I made my report and asked for orders. Romanovsky insisted on the offensive on Saratov, I urged the impossibility of this move. Finally they authorized me to limit myself to defensive action at Tsaritsin, and the Commander-in-Chief invited me to dine with him.

I met several young officers from the Military Academy at the General Staff who were old friends of mine. I could see that Denikin was losing prestige amongst them. I heard nothing but "Can you not make him understand?" and "Can you not explain to him . . ?"

After dinner I had a two hours' tête-à-tête with Denikin. In his opinion everything was going splendidly. The possibility of a sudden change in our luck seemed to him to be out of the question. He thought the taking of Moscow was only a question of time, and that the demoralized and weakened enemy could not make a stand against us. He added smilingly, indicating the map:

"Even General R. is advancing with giant strides, and goodness knows what troops he has! Lord knows what he is fighting with!"

At this point his aide-de-camp brought him a telegram. "It is from General Dragomirov," said Denikin when he had read it. "He says that the General Staff of the Red Army which he has been attacking want to surrender. But General Dragomirov is demanding that this Army should first attack the flank of the other Red Army which is stationed close by."

I drew his attention to the movements of the brigand Makhno and his rebels, for they were threatening our rear.

"Oh, that is not serious, we will finish him off in the twinkling of an eye."

As I listened to him talking, my mind filled with doubt and apprehension.

The General was not such an optimist about the political situation. He railed against the English, who, he said, were playing a double game, and against our neighbors the Georgians and the Poles, adding, "I have decided to break off all negotiations with them. I have informed them that they will get nothing out of us, not so much as an inch of Russian territory."

But he was even more exasperated with the "Separatists", as he still called the autonomous Cossacks, especially those in the Kuban. It is true that the demagogues in the Rada had been getting more and more aggressive and were in open opposition to General Denikin, but I still thought that it would be a simple matter to come to an understanding with the Kuban as a whole. The majority of the Cossacks were not in sympathy with the Rada, and a little firmness was all that was necessary to deprive the brawlers of the assembly of their leadership, then we could treat with the Kuban on an equitable basis on the subject, of their autonomy.

I gave the General my opinion quite frankly, and added that, cost what it might, we must settle the question, or these misunderstandings would have disastrous consequences for us. The Rada would become more united. We had got to seize this present opportunity for solving the problem.

"Oh, quite—but how?"

"We must respect, the Kuban's right to autonomy, and yet concentrate the executive power in the hands of the Ataman and his Government, which will be responsible only to the local Rada. One of the deputies could propose this in the Rada, and I am certain that the majority would agree to it. As, however, the extreme Left could make capital by stirring up trouble, I suggest that under some pretext or another the garrison at Ekaterinodar should be reinforced with thoroughly reliable troops."

The General was thoughtful for a moment, then holding out his hand to me he said, "I give you *carte blanche*."

The same day I went to the Kuban.

Ataman Filimonov, who was very popular with the Cossacks, had suffered more than anyone else at the hands of the extreme Left in the Rada. But he was too cautious and weak-willed to dare to stand up to them, so I did not tell him about my plans, but went to his colleague, General Naoumenko. He viewed my scheme with especial favor because the Left, under the leadership of President Makarenko, were working their hardest to make a definite breach with us. We were to prepare information concerning the negotiations of the Separatists with the Greens, who were still occupying the Georgian frontier.

I took the necessary measures and gave General Pokrovsky, who was in command of the place, ad hoc instructions. Then I went back to Tsaritsin to select a brigade to go to Ekaterinodar for the opening of the Rada. I wrote to General Pokrovsky on October 21st, and urged him once again not to resort to force unless it became absolutely necessary.

Meanwhile Headquarters' bad strategy was beginning to bear fruit. As I had foreseen, the enemy had concentrated their troops at the junction of the Army of the Don and the Voronege-Lisky front on October 18th. I had received a telegram from Romanovsky saying that the enemy had abandoned all hope of getting through our front line and had concentrated enormous forces on the flanks of the Volunteer Army, and we had got to do something about it quickly. "Could you spare us some of your Cossacks, or, better still, resume a general offensive in the north-east?"

I answered that, as I had explained to him many a time, my Army could not possibly begin an offensive, that it would be of very little use to send a few regiments as he had suggested, and that my advice was to take drastic measures, leave a mixed force to defend Tsaritsin, and send all the rest of the troops to reinforce the Volunteer Army.

But Headquarters would not agree, and kept on with their half-measures, taking only two divisions.

October 24th was the opening day of the session of the local Rada of the Kuban. I sent a telegram of welcome to the President. The next day I was just getting ready to go to Ekaterinodar when I received a most unexpected telegram from Denikin, it read as follows—

> In July the Kuban Government concluded an alliance treaty with the Medjilis (a mountain tribe), which is equivalent to treason to Russia. The Kuban Armies were to be put at the disposal of the Medjilis This treaty was signed by Bytch, Savitsky, Kalabukhov, and

> Namitokov. Order the arrest of any of these traitors you can find, and have them court-martialed for treason— *Taganrog*, October 25, 1919 DENIKIN

One of the men mentioned in the telegram, Kalabukhov, was a member of the Rada, as everyone knew, and was in Ekaterinodar. Denikin ought to have known that the arrest of this man could be no light matter, nor could it be done without the sanction of the Rada. A fresh collision between the Commander-in-Chief and the Kubanian Government was inevitable, and obviously it was no good talking amicably about revising the constitution with this conflict imminent.

General Denikin had promised me complete freedom of action, had given me *carte blanche*, to use his own expression, and here he was confronting me with an accomplished fact in the shape of this telegram!

Nevertheless, I went to Ekaterinodar to decide on the spot what to do. I remained in the train and requested Generals Naoumenko and Pokrovsky to come into my carriage. I learnt from them that General Denikin's telegram had been like a match to gunpowder. Ataman, Government, and Rada were all furious. The local Rada, which had just been convoked, had elected Makarenko president by way of demonstration, and had ordered the formation of a special regiment to guard the Rada. General Pokrovsky urged me to make a *coup d'état*, dissolve the Rada, arrest the miscreants, and have them shot.

I absolutely forbade him to attempt any such measure, and went over to the spas to gain time and take a few necessary measures. I detailed the situation to Denikin, and begged him to tell me specifically what he wanted.

On October 30th all the commanders of the Army as well as the Ataman received a circular telegram from the Rada and the Kuban Government denying the alliance which they were supposed to have concluded with the Medjilis. The accused had not had full powers of action, and the Kuban Government itself was ignorant of the fact that any such treaty had been arranged with the Medjilis. If those implicated had really exceeded their authority, they were answerable to the Rada, who alone could judge them; a representative of the Rada could submit only to its judgment. Thus General Denikin's order was illegal and constituted an offence against the constitution. The Kuban Government demanded the revocation of the order.

The same day I received a formal order from General Denikin: I was to adhere strictly to his telegram. Therefore I ordered General Pokrovsky to have Kalabukhov and the chief offenders arrested and court-martialed.

The meeting of the Rada had been a stormy one. President Makarenko's speech had contained the sentence. "There is not a single general with so much as a grain of honor in his character in command of the Kuban Cossack regiments." His words roused even the Assembly itself to indignation; I took the opportunity to telegraph to the Ataman Filimonov, who was urging me to address the Rada, the following message—

> The insulting speech which the President of the Rada has made in the Assembly concerning all the generals, in the presence of members whom the Commander-in-Chief regards as traitors, prevents me from accepting your invitation. It would accord neither with my personal dignity nor with the dignity of the Army of which I have the honor to be the chief.

I ordered this telegram to be published in the newspapers, and told General Pokrovsky to carry out the Commander-in-Chief's orders—that is to say, to have the culprits arrested and tried. On November 6th General Pokrovsky informed me that the Rada had handed Kalabukhov over to him. General Pokrovsky had occupied the environs of the building in which the Rada was sitting, cheered on by the Cossacks, and had proceeded to disarm the guard and arrest the chief offenders. The Rada had sent a deputation to the Commander-in-Chief to offer him a polite apology, and Makarenko had fled.

That evening I left for Ekaterinodar. I was welcomed at the station by the Ataman, his colleague, the members of the General Staff, General Pokrovsky, and numerous deputations. The Cossacks of the Guard formed a platoon of honor. I anticipated that this solemn reception would have a salutary effect on the members of the Rada. Kalabukhov had already been condemned by the court-martial, and General Pokrovsky had ratified the death-sentence, which had been carried out at dawn. The other prisoners had not yet come up for judgment. The Rada had interceded for them, sending a delegation to the Commander-in-Chief.

After an interview with General Pokrovsky, I went to the Rada, which was already in session. In the speech which I intended to make I had decided to avoid the political side of the question as much as I could, because I did not entirely share the opinion of Headquarters on the Kubanian question.

As I entered the Chamber, the Ataman welcomed me, and ended his speech by begging me to release all the deputies who had been arrested, so that they might be judged by the Rada itself.

From the tribunal I made a long speech, dwelling on the great exploits of the Kuban Cossacks, the hardships they were enduring because certain demagogues were cutting off supplies for political reasons, and the terrible condition the country would be in if the Reds should return. In conclusion I said: "Gentlemen, politics are none of my business. I am only a soldier, but I know where the trouble lies. The party spirit of a few wretched individuals prevents the Ataman, the Rada, and each one of you from doing all that you want to do for your brothers and sons. In spite of all your goodwill, your hands are tied, and you can do nothing. Brothers-in-arms, from the day when your Ataman and his Government are masters, instead of these brawlers, your children will want for nothing. I am leaving for the front—can I say to my splendid men that their fathers and brothers, the members of the local Rada, are coming to their rescue like one man?"

The Assembly answered me with cries of "Yes, tell them that!" and with cheers. I went back to my train. A delegation from the Rada came to me there to intercede afresh for the prisoners.

Once again I made flattering remarks about the Kuban Cossacks, then mentioned casually that if we could be sure that the Ataman and the Rada could really be of some help to the troops, we would be only too happy to forget the past. "The Ataman and the Government have given proof enough of their goodwill, but can they do anything?"

They began to discuss the question I had propounded there and then, and changes in certain clauses of the constitution were worked out so that they could be proposed in the Rada the next day. Finally, we achieved our object—the constitution was revised, and power passed to the Ataman.

I telegraphed to General Denikin that I had promised to spare the lives of those members of the Rada who were under arrest.

Ataman Filimonov, who had proved to be very weak, resigned. General Ouspensky was elected in his stead. My mission being finished, I went back to Taganrog.

The situation had grown much worse since my last visit to Headquarters. The enemy's cavalry had penetrated our front line at the junction of the Army of the Don and the Volunteer Army, and was now threatening the rear of the latter. Orel and Kursk had been abandoned, and the front was rapidly drawing in on Kharkov. Further back, the province of Ekaterinoslav was a prey to risings. The people's discontent grew with our reverses. General Youdenitch's offensive on Petrograd had petered out, and the fragments of his Army were falling back towards Esthonia. In Siberia, Koltchak's beaten Army was in rapid retreat. The storm was brewing. . . .

I made my report to the Commander-in-Chief and asked his permission to reopen the strategical question. Once again I insisted on the necessity of sending not two regiments but all I could spare to reinforce the Volunteer Army.

At last the General told me to wait for him at Rostov, as he would be there shortly, and would then discuss the question with me again.

My stay in Rostov was a very painful business. People there were acutely dissatisfied with Denikin, and very uneasy about the state of May-Mayevsky's Volunteer Army, which was completely discredited. As is usual in such cases, as one man was more and more discredited, another became dearer and dearer to the people. Unfortunately, this other was myself. When I went into a house people crowded round the door; in the restaurants they prevented me from eating; morning or evening. I was greeted with the same ovations, and always heard the same questions: "Have you been appointed as May-Mayevsky's successor yet?"

"When are you going to take the situation in hand?"

"You are the only man we can rely on."

Therefore there was a great deal of gossip going about, and the mischief-makers certainly profited from it to make things difficult for me with Denikin.

On November 11th I received a letter from the Commander-in-Chief. He wrote that, after ripe reflection, he had decided that he could not agree with my strategical proposals.

On the same day General Chatilov let me know that the enemy were resuming the initiative on the left bank of the Volga, and Denikin sent me back to Ekaterinodar, where I had to see the new Ataman. From there I went to my Headquarters. But I had scarcely arrived before a telegram recalled me to Taganrog.

On the other fronts, things had gone from bad to worse. The Armies were in rapid retreat all along the line. Already there was fighting near Kharkov. The concentration of cavalry which I had proposed a few days earlier was no longer possible.

The disaster that I had foreseen for so long seemed to be upon us at last.

CHAPTER VII

DISASTER

I. - The Retreat from Kharkov to Rostov

I went to Taganrog on November although I was still ill after a violent attack of fever. I went straight from the station to the Commander-in-Chief, who said abruptly.

"I beg you to take the command of the Volunteer Army."

I replied that I now doubted whether I should be of any use in this position. Everything that I had suggested hitherto must now go by the board. We could not even count on holding Kharkov, the crux of our strategical position.

He interrupted me. "I see what you mean quite clearly. But the loss of Kharkov will not injure your reputation."

I told him somewhat dryly that I was not thinking about my reputation, for it did not need safeguarding, but about doing my job. I did not want to undertake what I believed was an impossible task.

"Your refusal," said Romanovsky, "puts the Commander-in-Chief in a dilemma. We are going to concentrate all the cavalry of the Volunteer Army and the Army of the Don in the Kupiansk area, and nobody but you can take the command. You are under a moral obligation to serve Russia."

I asked for time before giving a definite answer.

I returned to my train and found Chatilov, my chief-of-staff, who had already received all the necessary information from Headquarters. We set about studying the situation. It was indeed desperate. Our front was two thousand kilometres long, beginning on the Volga and ending at Odessa. Our effective forces, including the Cossacks, numbered one hundred thousand men, while there were thirty thousand more at the depot. The Red forces numbered one hundred and eighty thousand, and they had huge reserves. The Volunteer Army's infantry numbered only two thousand six hundred, and its cavalry was reduced to a thousand men. These had to face fifty-one thousand foot and seven thousand horse.

The Supreme General Staff was basing all its hopes on the concentration of cavalry at Kupiansk. The Terek and the Kuban regiments there had suffered very heavily, but the Don regiments were still intact and well mounted.

The ill-fated advance on Moscow was still going on, and was tying the hands of the High Command. Peasant revolts were raging behind the lines in the Governments of Ekaterinoslav, Poltava, and Kharkov, and Makhno and his bands were molesting the troops.

General Chatilov agreed with me that the situation was hopeless.

The next day General Romanovsky, accompanied by the Quartermaster-General, returned to the charge. He said: "General May-Mayevsky cannot hold out any longer: he has completely lost his head . . ."

I interrupted him: "Everyone knew that a long time ago—except Supreme Headquarters! I warned you of the danger a hundred times when there was still time to avert it, but every time you turned a deaf ear. And now that the danger has materialized, you expect me to save you'"

"Let us forget the past, General," said Romanovsky. "Let us think only of the future. Make this sacrifice for Russia."

"If I do, it must be on my own terms I reserve the right to choose my colleagues, especially my chief-of-staff."

The General agreed to everything I said.

The following day I presented myself to the Commander-in-Chief. As I left him I asked him who was going to take my place as commander of the Caucasian Army.

"General Pokrovsky. What do you think of him?" he replied.

"He is very brave and very intelligent," I said, "but he has not the necessary qualities for the commander of an Army."

The General smiled. "Once we have taken his cavalry away from him his Army will be no larger than a company. Only since you are taking Chatilov with you, I do not know who to give him for his chief-of-staff. What do you think about General Siegel?"

"An excellent man, by all accounts."

"Honest?"

"Of course . . if he was not, I should not have kept him as quartermaster."

"Splendid, then he will not let General Pokrovsky do too much pilfering."

I began to lose all understanding of my chief's mentality.

On November 25th I left for Kharkov, taking a few officers with me in addition to my chief-of-staff.

The further north we went the greater the general confusion seemed to be. The railway stations were choked with trains evacuating infinite numbers of refugees, including many perfectly able-bodied soldiers.

These trains were full of the belongings of different regiments. I saw sentinels on guard before one train. I saw some officers in a Pullman car. I sent one of my aides-de-camp to ask what regiment they belonged to. He discovered that nearly every regiment had its trains on the railway. All the troops were living on the population, often requisitioning far more than they needed, and selling the surplus. In addition, some of these regiments had two hundred carriages reserved for the transport of their baggage.

The stations were swarming with refugees, mostly women and children—some ill, some starving, some in the last straits.

May-Mayevsky's train passed ours; he had already left the Army.

In one of the stations we found several ambulance-trains which had been there for days awaiting an opportunity to move on. Not far from the station there was a hospital, destitute of staff, drugs, and nurses, in it were several dozen wounded, utterly destitute and literally dying of hunger. A few of them had dragged themselves into the street in search of a scrap of bread. My arrival became known, and two of these poor wretches crawled over to my carriage and implored me to help them. They told me that one of the officers there had just hanged himself in despair.

At the principal points on the railway I left bands of soldiers with generals or colonels with plenary powers at their head. They were to search all the trains going to the front, seize stolen objects, send back deserters to their regiments, and shoot recalcitrants and marauders. Staff-officers were to supervise the regular running of the trains.

The dispatches from the cavalry generals were hopeless. They can be summed up in the words: "For the moment it is impossible for the cavalry to fight."

My dispatch to the Commander-in-Chief, which I quote in full, gives a more or less complete picture of the situation at the seat of war.

DISPATCH TO THE COMMANDER-IN-CHIEF

YOUZOVKA NO 010464. *December* 9, 1919

I arrived here November 26th, and having acquainted myself with the situation along the principal section of the front, I have the honor to make the following communication to you—

Our disadvantageous position at the present time has two principal causes—

1. A strategy diametrically opposed to the rudiments of the art of warfare
2. Complete disorganization behind-the-lines

In my dispatch No 82, of April 4, 1919, I felt it my duty, whilst insisting on the advance on Tsaritsin, to draw your attention to the impossibility of simultaneous action in several directions whilst we lacked the necessary forces. After we had taken Tsaritsin, General Yusefovitch and I sent you two dispatches in which we indicated the necessity of occupying the short Tsaritsin-Ekaterinoslav front, which is defended on both its flanks by large rivers, and of concentrating three or four cavalry corps in the Kharkov area for operations along the shortest route to Moscow.

This plan, to quote your own remark at our interview in Tsaritsin, was only dictated by "my desire to be the first man to enter Moscow."

When the enemy recently concentrated considerable forces near Orel, and began to put pressure on the Volunteer Army, General Romanovsky asked me, on October 17th, for some troops to reinforce our front line.

I telegraphed on October 18th that "In view of the reduction in the effective force of the cavalry, the problem could not be solved by sending one or two troops," and suggested a radical measure—"the sending of three and a half Kuban divisions."

My suggestion was turned down, and a hybrid measure was adopted only two divisions were taken from the Caucasian Army. Later events compelled a return to the measure I had suggested, three and a half divisions have now been taken from the Caucasian Army, but the time that has been lost is irreparable.

We wanted to do too much and make ourselves master of every position at once, and we have succeeded only in weakening ourselves and so becoming powerless.

The Bolshevists, on the contrary, have held firmly to the principle of the concentration of forces and the launching of operations against our strongest point. When the Caucasian Array's advance on Saratov threatened the Bolshevists' eastern front the Red Command let our troops advance on Kursk and Orel with perfect equanimity, inexorably following the plan of concentration at Saratov, followed by a great mass-attack which would shatter the Caucasian Army and throw it back to the south, weakened as it was by a thousand-kilometre march and the sending of some troops to other fronts.

It was only when the remains of the Caucasian Army retreated to Tsaritsin, powerless now to undertake a fresh offensive, that the Red Command, uniting its forces for the defence of Moscow, began operations against the Volunteer Army which was advancing without reserves along an enormously long front, and turned it back.

In spite of the transport crisis and other difficulties, the Red Command have carried out the principle of the concentration of forces in its entirety

We have been advancing continuously, but have taken no steps to consolidate our possession of the immense territories we have conquered.

We have made mistakes from the Sea of Azov to Orel, we have not a single fortified position nor a point of attack. Therefore, if we have to retreat, we shall have not a single place on which to fall back.

The continual advance has reduced the Army's effective force. The rear has become too vast. Disorganization is all the greater because of the re-equipment system which Supreme Headquarters have adopted, they have turned over this duty to the troops and take no share in it themselves.

Headquarters ought to provide and distribute all necessaries, making use of all the spoils of war for this purpose.

The war is becoming to some a means of growing rich, re-equipment has degenerated into pillage and peculation.

Each unit strives to secure as much as possible for itself, and seizes everything that comes to hand. What cannot be used on the spot is sent back to the interior and sold at a profit. The rolling-stock belonging to the troops has taken on enormous dimensions—some regiments have two hundred carriages in their wake. A considerable number of troops have retreated to the interior, and many officers are away on prolonged missions, busy selling and exchanging loot, etc.

The Army is absolutely demoralized, and is fast becoming a collection of tradesmen and profiteers.

All those employed on re-equipment work—that is to say, nearly all the officers—have enormous sums of money in their possession, as a result, there has been an outbreak of debauchery, gambling, and wild orgies. Unfortunately, several highly placed officers have set the example of costly banquets and have spent money lavishly, for all the Army to see.

Our badly organized police and counter-espionage systems are a great help to the Bolshevist agitators in their subversive work behind-the-lines. Each of these two systems works independently of the other, the officials are both underpaid and unsuitable.

As a result of the inadequacy of their salaries, the most indispensable of the railway officials quitted their posts when the Bolshevists arrived and went over to the enemy.

The population greeted our Army with wild enthusiasm, they have all suffered from the Bolshevists, and only want to be allowed to live in peace, and yet they have to endure the horrors of pillage, violence, and despotism all over again. Result: confusion at the front and risings in the interior.

When I arrived here, Kharkov had already been abandoned by the General Staff, and the Army was in full retreat.

The evacuation has been conducted disastrously, without plan or order. None of the institutions were given directions concerning the route they were to take, nor even concerning their destination. Everybody merely wandered off anyhow. I found the railroads blocked by trains and abandoned ambulances without any staff, but full of sick and wounded who had eaten nothing for three days. When I reached Slaviansk a wounded officer had just hanged himself rather than endure the tortures of starvation. Crowds of refugees—mostly officers' families—are cramming themselves into all the trains and stations; no steps are being taken to evacuate them, and they are literally dying of cold and hunger. . . .

On the road between Zmiev and Izioum, behind-the-lines, local bands are destroying the railroads, molesting the troops, and robbing the ambulances and luggage-vans.

I find that our forces have diminished, the 1st Corps has about two thousand six hundred men, the 5th, one thousand and fifteen cavalrymen, the Poltava group musters one hundred foot and two hundred horse, the cavalry troop is about three thousand five hundred strong. Total: three thousand six hundred foot, four thousand seven hundred horse. The Kuban Corps is a mere brigade, Kornilov's regiments are only battalions. Markov's two regiments and the "Special" brigade have only their *cadres* left, and are out of action. Of Drosdovsky's division, only three companies are left. The troops refuse to use the tanks because they are afraid of losing them. The artillery is no longer of any use.

The enemy have fifty-one thousand foot, seven thousand horse, and more than two hundred and six guns.

Behind-the-lines we have only the remains of Alexeiev's division, three hundred men all told.

The Army has been on the march for months, without respite or rest, and is utterly exhausted. The horses have developed foot-disease, therefore we have often been forced to discard guns and equipment.

The condition of the cavalry is simply lamentable. The horses have not been shod for a long while, and have nearly all gone lame, whilst many of them are ill from exhaustion. Most of the units are out of action, as their commanders can witness.

The bitter truth is that there is no longer an Army. Measures are being taken to restore order to the interior, bases are being organized, all the available contingents are being mobilized, but all these measures have come too late, and it will take a long time to create a new Army.

The enemy realize this, and are doing their utmost to exploit their successes in every possible way.

We must have the courage to see things as they are, to look the situation squarely in the face, and be ready for fresh ordeals.

I consider it indispensable—

1. To adhere to a definite plan—that is to say, to choose one principal direction in which to concentrate our forces, and to be ready to abandon part of the occupied area if it should be necessary.

2. To evacuate Rostov and Taganrog at once.

3. To choose bases behind-the-lines and fortify them.

4. To cut down the over-large General Staffs and send the surplus and useless personnel to the front.

5. To provide the necessaries of life for the families of officers and employees who cannot do their work properly until they know that their wives and children are safely out of misery and danger, and to organize colonies immediately for the families of officers and officials, so that these families can be provided with food and shelter. Arrangements must be made to transport them to a place of safety in case of danger.

6. To take measures, ruthless if necessary, to put down marauding, drunkenness, and every kind of abuse, and to begin with the higher ranks, whose bad example is corrupting the troops, whatever their military worth may be.

7. To provide reinforcements of men and horses. To re-equip the cavalry, or this branch of the Army will be worthless. I have written many dispatches on this last point, but all in vain, the matter is extremely urgent. The enemy are using all their resources to create large cavalry units. Our cavalry was established and recruited without any kind of system, and it will soon fall to pieces altogether.

8. To put the counter-espionage organization and the police force in order, to amalgamate them, and to furnish them with sufficient credits.

9. To put the railways under military control, and to subordinate the head officials to the chief of Military Communications. At the same time to guarantee a regular living wage to the employees.

To sum up, unless the above measures are put into force, it is impossible to improve our situation. Moreover, unless they can be put in hand immediately, I must request you to transfer the command of the Volunteer Army to someone else, for without them I can accomplish nothing.

LIEUT-GENERAL WRANGEL
CHATILOV, *Chief-of-Staff*

I delivered this dispatch to the Commander-in-Chief myself, and sent a copy of it to his two colleagues, Generals Loukomsky and Romanovsky, begging them to urge as swift a decision as possible. General Denikin crossed over to the light and began to read it. When he had done so, he put it down on the table without a word, and looked at us despairingly. Then he said dully "All the same, we must go on with it."

"Of course, Your Excellency, and do our utmost to win the upper hand. But before we do anything else, we must come to a decision. The enemy are operating between the Volunteer Army and the Army of the Don, and want to drive me down to the sea. Our cavalry is no longer capable of fighting. If you order us to retreat to Rostov and join the Army of the Don, we shall have to retreat with the enemy striking blows at our flanks the whole time. If, on the other hand, we retreat into the Crimea, where we still have some troops . . ."

The General broke in. "I have been thinking it over for a long time and I must follow the dictates of my conscience. I have not the moral right to abandon the Cossacks to their fate. We must retreat together."

He asked a few unimportant questions and then dismissed us.

Chatilov and I walked along in silence.

"What is your opinion?" I asked him.

Chatilov shrugged his shoulders. "They have lost their heads—they are no good for anything now."

I could not forget the tragic expression on Denikin's face as he read my report. He had to watch the work into which he had put his whole strength collapse in an instant. It was certainly terrible for him. If he was to look the calamity in the face and still keep his sanity, he must know that he was not bearing this burden which fate had thrust upon him alone. It was essential that he should have the moral support of his closest colleagues. So I wrote to him—

YOUR EXCELLENCY,

At this moment, when luck is against us, when the ship which you are piloting between the rocks and the storm is in danger of submersion by the foul Red waves, I feel morally obliged to tell you that I understand what you must be suffering. If at this crucial moment it lightens the load with which circumstances have burdened you to know that you are not alone, please believe that I, who have followed you almost from the beginning, will continue to share your joys and sorrows, and will do everything within my power to help you.

P. WRANGEL.

December 10, 1919

Some days later the General wrote to me—

December 13, 1919

Your letter touched me very deeply. Your collaboration and your sentiments lead me to hope that our luck will turn; I know that it will turn. Your heart's cry has found an echo in mine, and I wish you luck and success.

DENIKIN.

P S —Some of your proposals have been carried out, the rest are in hand.

But at the same time I learnt that nothing had been done about the evacuation of Rostov and Taganrog.

Furthermore, on the same day that I received the Commander-in-Chief's friendly letter, I also received a circular telegram which he had addressed to all the generals of the Army. It said that certain generals had allowed themselves to express their own opinions in their dispatches in an inadmissible manner, threatening to leave the service if their advice was not followed. In consequence the Commander-in-Chief demanded obedience and forbade any future statement of conditions.

Supreme Headquarters' new instructions ordered the chief of the Army of the Don and myself to concentrate as strong a force as possible on the junction of our flanks and to attack the enemy's cavalry.

I spoke to General Sidorin, commander of the Army of the Don, as soon as I received these new orders I said to him: "My troops—and I have practically none left—are in such a condition that I cannot possibly resume the offensive in concert with you. I am not even sure that I can manage to effect a junction with your Army, as I have been ordered to do, unless you can give me a helping hand."

"Yes, Supreme Headquarters have evidently failed to grasp the situation," said Sidorin. "I have petitioned them in vain, but have received no explicit reply. Only yesterday my chief-of-staff asked General Romanovsky for information, and he answered: "When the commander of your Army sees the commander of the Volunteer Army the two of them will be able to concoct something."

As I had to go to Rostov shortly, I arranged with Sidorin that he should come and meet me there; I also said that I wanted the commander of the Caucasian Army to come along and help us settle certain questions. I informed General Romanovsky of this by telegram, so that the Commander-in-Chief could authorize the commander of the Caucasian Army to go to Rostov for a few hours.

His reply was a circular letter addressed to all the generals of the Army, running as follows—

> The Commander-in-Chief cannot permit the generals of the Armies to treat directly with one another, and forbids them to leave their Armies in future without his express permission.

The front was drawing nearer and nearer to Rostov, and there was keen anxiety in the town. There were open complaints against the Commander-in-Chief. He was accused of having been responsible for the catastrophe, the malcontents shouted that he must be overthrown.

As all such remarks invariably found their way to Denikin, I attributed the circular telegram to them, and decided to have a frank discussion with him. I went to Taganrog. The Commander-in-Chief received me alone, without even his chief-of-staff. After I had made my report, he told me that he had decided to reduce the Volunteer Army to a single corps once its junction with the Army of the Don was accomplished. To avoid offending the Cossacks, he would be compelled to give the command of these troops to Sidorin, chief of the Army of the Don.

As he attempted to be more explicit, needless though this was, for I thought he was perfectly right, I told him that I shared his opinion completely, and in the circumstances I was ready to take any post he liked. "If I cannot be useful to the Army, perhaps I could go into the rear, or abroad."

"No, no—we need you here."

"Your Excellency," I said, "may I speak quite frankly to you? I believe that I no longer enjoy your confidence. Dare I ask the reason?"

"What do you mean?" he asked. "You are quite mistaken. I have always had the greatest confidence in you. But you have not reciprocated it. You have done everything you could to poison our relations. You have written to me in such a way that I have had to hide your dispatches from my colleagues. Have I ever been anything but correct in my dealings with you?"

"Your Excellency, you are forgetting your last circular telegram forbidding the Army chiefs to make arrangements with one another. How can you explain that, except by a lack of confidence in their loyalty? As to my dispatches, they were absolutely necessary under the circumstances. I could not possibly have acted in a way which would have injured my troops."

The General got up.

"Let us say no more about it." He held out his hand. But I knew that we had not come to terms, and that our interview had been fruitless. He merely wanted to put an end to a disagreeable conversation.

In the middle of December, after a march of three hundred kilometres, during which the enemy was on our flank the whole time, we at last effected our junction with the Army of the Don. We had carried out our orders and made an extraordinarily difficult retreat of which any Army would have been proud.

Once the junction of the Armies was effected, my task was finished, so on December 19th, late at night, I reached Taganrog. The depots were on fire, the station full of refugees. Headquarters had left in great haste without waiting for the completion of the evacuation, which had been begun too late. The townsfolk, in a panic, were fleeing in carts and on foot.

An English officer found me. He told me that Supreme Headquarters had broken their promise and left without taking with them the staff and archives of the English Mission. I suggested taking the Mission in my train, but there was no room for all the archives, and the Mission felt they had no right to abandon them. I promised to send them a train from Rostov, and I did so.

I found the Commander-in-Chiefs train at Rostov, the Commander of the Army of the Don and the Ataman of Kuban were also there. The Commander-in-Chief invited us into his carriage.

We had not been there a moment when the English General Holman was announced. He was asked to come in. He told us that he had just received a telegram from his Government which declared that it was ready to help with the evacuation and give its protection to the families of military men, the sick and the wounded.

When he had gone, the Commander-in-Chief acquainted us with the situation and gave us our orders.

The troops were to be concentrated in a fortified place chosen for the purpose. He added that since the fortifications were merely sketched out, their value was purely psychological. The Volunteer Army was henceforth to be an army corps incorporated in Sidorin's Army. I was to go to Kuban and the Terek to try and raise some troops.

I asked General Denikin's permission to take General Chatilov with me, and he gave it. I prepared to leave the next day. I was assailed on all sides throughout that day. The town was in a state of panic. Some people begged me to take them with me, others wanted to know why I was giving up my command, others again complained of Supreme Headquarters.

Rumors of sedition reached the Commander-in-Chief, and he, believing them, had the "Intelligence Department's" documents seized and several of its employees arrested. One of the officers denounced General Loukomsky, adjutant to the Commander-in-Chief, asserting that he was at the head of the conspiracy against Denikin. It was soon proved that all these fears were absolutely unfounded, but, nevertheless, the informer remained at his post—a confidential one—under Romanovsky.

At this moment of imminent peril, Denikin continued to busy himself with purely theoretical questions. On December 11th he issued the following programme—

1. Russia—One and Indivisible! Protection of religion. Re-establishment of order. Increase in the productive powers of the country and reorganization of national economy. Greater productivity of labor.
2. War to the death with Bolshevism.
3. A military dictatorship. This Government will ignore the demands of all political parties, and will crush any resistance to its authority be it from Right or Left. The nature of the Government can only be decided later by the people themselves. We must act in accordance with the people. A complete agreement with the Cossacks without injury to the sovereignty of Russia. Rallying of Transcaucasia to Russia.
4. Foreign policy will be national—Russian first and foremost. Although the Allies are wavering, we must continue to move with them. Any other grouping is morally censurable and impossible of realization.
5. Slav solidarity, but not an inch of Russian territory to win help.

A Cabinet was constituted on December 17th. It consisted of eight members, including the President, a Minister of War and the Admiralty, and Ministers of Finance, the Interior, Commerce, Justice, Transport, and Supplies. The Minister for Foreign Affairs and the Comptroller-General were not in the Cabinet, but were directly dependent on the Commander-in-Chief.

A Consultative Committee for legislative questions was also set up.

II. With the Army in its Last Days

When I reached Ekaterinodar with Chatilov, I found that the object of my mission was already well known. The Cossacks were well-disposed towards me, but Naoumenko told me that the Opposition were making themselves heard. The struggle between the Kuban Separatists and Supreme Headquarters had begun again.

On January 2nd a meeting of the Supreme Union of Cossacks was to take place. The Union consisted of one hundred and fifty representatives from the Don, the Kuban, and the Terek, and it was meeting to draw up a constitution for a federated Cossack State.

I was disagreeably surprised to meet General Chkouro in the Kuban, and to discover that he was there on the same mission as I. The Commander-in-Chief had also sent him to raise fresh troops. He was accompanied by a staff-officer assigned to him by Supreme Headquarters and a few aides-de-camp and orderly officers, including two agents from the Intelligence Department who General Romanovsky had tried to foist on me, but for whom I had no use. I soon learnt that these two creatures had been secretly entrusted with the task of informing Headquarters of my actions and movements. They went about telling all those who cared to listen that I was hoping to make a *coup d'état* and re-establish the monarchy, and that I was an enemy of the Allies and a partisan of Germany.

Under these conditions I could not possibly accomplish my mission. Therefore I restricted myself to collecting the necessary materials, and having done this, made for Headquarters, fully determined to insist on my recall.

At one of the stations I received a circular telegram. It stated that General Chatilov, chief-of-staff of the Volunteer Army, had illegally quitted his post to go into the rear with General Wrangel; the Commander-in-Chief therefore gave orders for proceedings to be taken against him.

I received the same telegram at every station.

The charge was absolutely false. Chatilov had been authorized to go with me by Denikin himself, in the presence of General Romanovsky.

I came up with Denikin's train after leaving Rostov, where we were already at grips with the enemy.

I made a verbal report to the Commander-in-Chief on the Caucasian situation. I told him that the Cossacks were not altogether to be trusted, and that it would be much wiser to concentrate all the troops we still had on the eastern front, and then try to come to an agreement with the Poles, and, if possible, with Serbia and Bulgaria. Also, it was absolutely necessary to hold New Russia,[1] cost what it might.

---

[1] New Russia is the name of the region to the north of the Black Sea which was annexed by Russia in the reign of Catherine II—TRANSLATOR.

When I had finished, I gave him a written report, which repeated what I had already said briefly in greater detail. The General had listened to me in silence, and he read the report too without saying a word.

I told him that in the circumstances which I had just explained to him, it was impossible for me to perform the task he had entrusted to me.

He was still silent.

"Then you would undoubtedly refuse the command of the Kubanian troops," asked Romanovsky.

"Yes," I replied, "for I should not be able to succeed. But I am ready to do my utmost anywhere where I can be useful, either in the Army or in the rear. I should particularly like to go to the Novorossiisk district if the Commander-in-Chief intends to fortify it. I think it is urgently necessary to do so."

"Certainly not," said Denikin "To fortify the town now would be to admit the possibility of disaster. It would cause a panic."

I saw that it was useless to argue. General Chatilov brought out the circular telegram of which I have already spoken, read it, and said in a voice which he forced himself to control: "Dare I ask you what this telegram means?"

Silence.

I lost my temper. "It means that intrigues are still flourishing—that is all. . . ."

Romanovsky mumbled that there had been a misunderstanding.

The Commander-in-Chief bade us good-bye.

"Your Excellency," said Romanovsky, "will you allow General Wrangel to remain for a moment?"

When Chatilov had gone, he said. "Were you alluding to me when you spoke of intrigues?"

"You ought to know me well enough to realize that if I had been, I would not have hesitated to accuse you to your face. But I do not know their source, and I do not want to, I merely state facts, and that is enough. Do you want further proof? Think of the telegram concerning my interview with Sidorin and Pokrovsky."

"Admit," said Denikin, "that in the present case you are wrong as well as right."

He got up and held out his hand. I saluted and left him.

Shortly afterwards General Romanovsky came to tell me that the Commander-in-Chief had decided that he must fortify Novorossiisk after all, and that he wanted me to do the job. We went to see Denikin together, and in his presence the Chief-of-Staff repeated what he had already said to me. I asked permission to take Chatilov and some officers of my former General Staff with me.

"I do not suppose the Commander-in-Chief has any objection," said Romanovsky.

Denikin made a gesture of assent. Throughout the interview he said not a word. It was the last interview I ever had with him.

I left the next day. I reached Novorossiisk on New Year's Eve (December 29, 1919). An icy wind was blowing, as it always does at this time of the year. The town had no fuel whatsoever, the station and sheds were crowded with numbers of refugees, who were shelterless and exhausted by fatigue and privations. There was a widespread epidemic of typhus, and a shockingly high rate of mortality. Every train took away a fresh load of sick and dead, they were also heaped on to carts and lorries. It made me shudder to see these vehicles full of the dead and dying, with their arms and legs hanging over the sides.

General Loukomsky, who was acting as chief of the Cabinet, was already in Novorossiisk, together with the other members of the Government. The administration of the town was in the hands of a military governor and the commandant of the fort; they were often at loggerheads, which all added to the confusion.

With the cooperation of Loukomsky, we set about fortifying the place and drawing up a plan for its evacuation. The colonel in charge of the English Mission gave us all the help he could with the evacuation. He introduced me to a member of Parliament called MacKinder, who came to see me one day. He asked my permission to speak quite plainly. He showed me a telegram he had received from London, notifying him that Warsaw was talking of a *coup d'état* to overthrow Denikin, the same rumors named me as his successor. The English Government had charged him to find out the truth of the matter.

I thanked him for the confidence with which he had honored me, and told him that these rumors had arisen because certain people who wanted to sow discord at any cost, had been spreading them abroad for a long time. Sometimes, it is true, I did not share the Commander-in-Chief's opinions, but that was on strategical questions rather than on political matters, and since I was under his orders of my own free will, I would never, in any contingency whatsoever, act against him.

MacKinder asked me if he might communicate my reply to his Government? I authorized him to do so.

The same day I sent General Denikin an official account of my interview with MacKinder, together with my answer to his questions. He did not reply.

A few days later General Loukomsky was appointed Governor-General of Novorossiisk. This appointment released me from my task.

The struggle between the Commander-in-Chief and the Cossacks was still going on. A new and recently elected Rada had repealed the laws passed in November and elected General Bukretov as Ataman, he was in open opposition to Supreme Headquarters. This Rada would recognize Denikin only as chief of the troops. It was obvious that we should soon be compelled to leave the Kuban.

In the Crimea, as in New Russia, our affairs were going far from brilliantly, and authority was for the most part in the wrong hands. General Slachtchov was a very brave and a very energetic man, but he was a slave to morphia and a confirmed drunkard, and quite incapable of holding a responsible position, however small it might be. General Schilling, commander of the troops in New Russia, had no authority over the troops, public opinion was clamoring for his dismissal and my appointment in his place.

General Loukomsky asked me if I would consent to take this command. I told him that I would take any command in which I could be of some use. He communicated my answer to the Commander-in-Chief, but Denikin refused to appoint me.

Shortly afterwards I received a telegram from General Schilling suggesting that I should act as his adjutant. I did not reply directly, but sent on the telegram to General Loukomsky, adding that, on the whole, I was ready to agree if Denikin gave his authorization, but that I wanted to make sure of this first.

The Commander-in-Chief gave his consent. I arranged to leave on the first boat, which was sailing on January 27th. But in the meantime we learnt that our troops were already in retreat in New Russia and the Crimea.

General Holman showed me a telegram he had just received saying that Odessa would be in the hands of the Reds in a few hours.

That evening General Romanovsky telegraphed me that it was useless for me to join Schilling at Odessa, because, since the town had fallen, the post of adjutant to the commander of the forces had been suppressed. Another telegram from General Denikin cancelled my nomination to the post of commander of the Crimean troops.

Realizing that the Supreme General Staff most emphatically did not want me, I sent in my resignation on January 27th. General Chatilov followed my example. I left for Yalta, where I had a villa.

As we entered Sebastopol, the Admiral of the Fleet's launch challenged us, and his chief-of-staff, Admiral Bubnov, came on board. He had come to request me to accompany him to the Admiral's quarters, where I would find General Schilling, who had arrived the evening before and wanted to see me.

He told me that the evacuation of Odessa had been a veritable nightmare. No measures had been taken to maintain even a semblance of order. In the port the refugees were killing one another and committing suicide in despair. The section of our Army commanded by General Bredov had not been able to embark and was trying to get through to Rumania.

According to him, all the troops were indignant at Schilling's behaviour, and Slachtchov was powerless to calm them. The Crimea was on the verge of complete disaster.

The downfall was now very close at hand. The peninsula was full of fugitives and the debris of various regiments. The governor and the commander of the fortress of Sebastopol had lost their heads. Powerful hostile elements were trying to stir up the people. A certain Captain Orlov, at the head of a fairly large band, had declared war on the local authorities, and had adopted as his slogan—

We must put the interior in order before we can beat the Bolshevists.

Orlov had suddenly seized the town of Simferopol and imprisoned the chief-of-staff of the Crimean Army and the commandant of the fortress of Sebastopol. The civil governor was powerless and had done nothing.

Slachtchov had ousted Orlov from Simferopol, and in consequence he had withdrawn into the mountains, whence he was advancing on the town of Yalta. He found many supporters in the country.

Thanks to Slachtchov, we were still holding the isthmus of Perekop, which joins the Crimean peninsula to Taurida in the north, but it was obvious that we could not continue to hold it for long. We had suffered heavy losses, and had come to the end of our ammunition.

My first impression of Schilling was a good one. He was a big, well-built man with a frank expression. He said "General, I want to speak to you, not in my capacity of general and commander of this place, but as one officer of the Guard to another. You probably know what has been happening in Odessa. I shall never be forgiven. I only arrived here today, but I have already realized that they are hostile to me here too. Thus I cannot possibly remain at the head of the troops. I am ready to give up my command to you."

I replied that I had already been nominated for the post, but that the Commander-in-Chief had vetoed my appointment, and that, furthermore, I had sent in my papers and was expecting my discharge at any moment.

As Schilling and Nenukov (the Admiral of the Fleet) insisted, I added that, even were I appointed, it was obvious that my relations with Denikin would inevitably lead to friction, which would imperil the whole campaign.

I found General May-Mayevsky at my hotel. He told me that the first general order in which I had announced my appointment to the Volunteer Army had distressed him very deeply.

"Why, General, there was not a single word in it to which you could take exception."

"You declared quite clearly and openly that you intended to be merciless towards drunkards and marauders. You will agree that this was aimed at me."

And as I failed to understand, he tried to be more explicit.

"You see, in war-time you must leave no stone unturned and neglect no means by which you may achieve your ends. If you insist on the officers and men living like ascetics, they will not fight much longer."

I was highly indignant.

"Well, then, General," he said, "what is the whole difference between the Bolshevists and ourselves?"

He answered his own question without pausing, and he thought his answer irrefutable.

"Is not the whole difference simply that the Bolshevists have not scrupled about their means, and therefore have gained the upper hand?"

The next day I met Schilling again. He seemed to be very confused, and told me he had decided that his fears had been groundless and that the troops were not hostile to him after all. I assured him that I would forget that we had ever had our conversation of the previous evening.

A few days later I received a telegram from General Schilling announcing that the fortress of Sebastopol had been declared in a state of siege. An hour later came a second telegram with duplicate copies for all the authorities. It begged me to take command of the Aluchta, Bakhtchigaray, and Sebastopol areas, and warned the local authorities that in future they were to take orders from no one but me.

I telegraphed to General Schilling immediately, saying that in the circumstances it was dangerous to divide the command, and that I could not assent to his proposition nor take any command without the consent of the Commander-in-Chief. I begged him to cancel the instructions he had given to the authorities.

The same day Captain Orlov published a proclamation—

> To officers, Cossacks, soldiers, and sailors! The whole of the numerous garrison of Yalta has come over to my side, including a company of several hundred men, complete with artillery and machine-guns. General Schilling wants to negotiate with me, but I will not enter into any discussion with this man until he has brought to life again all those men whose deaths he caused in Odessa. I hear that our new leader, General Wrangel, is in the Crimea. He is the only man with whom we can and will negotiate! He is the man in whom we all have complete faith, he will sacrifice everything in the struggle against the Bolshevists and those who are corrupting the interior. Long live General Wrangel—the strong man with the mighty soul!

I immediately sent the following telegram to Captain Orlov, and duplicates to Schilling and the local authorities, urging them to publish it in the newspapers—

> I have noted the proclamation in which you declare that you submit to my authority, although actually I am holding no command

> whatsoever. Until recently, the Army has been invincible solely because it knew how to obey its leaders blindly. Having forgotten its oath of loyalty, it has come to Civil War. We have renewed the struggle of our own free will, and of our own free will, which is equivalent to an oath, we have put ourselves under the orders of our superiors. Neither you nor I have the right to be disloyal to them. Speaking as an old soldier who has served his country loyally all his life, I earnestly beg you to put an end to your rebellion and submit to your immediate superiors.

I heard that General Schilling, the Commander-in-Chief's adjutant, General Loukomsky, the commandant of the fleet, and many others had written repeatedly to Denikin, begging him again and again to appoint me as Schilling's successor, but all in vain. The Commander-in-Chief was determined not to give his assent. . . .

The official newspaper of February 8th published a general order to the effect, that Generals Loukomsky, Wrangel, and Chatilov had been cashiered at their own request. Admiral Nenukov, the Commander of the Fleet, and Admiral Bubnov, his chief-of-staff, were also cashiered very suddenly. Then Denikin issued an order to General Schilling to arrest all those who had inspired Captain Orlov's revolt, "whatever their position or rank might be." Supreme Headquarters had these two orders posted up side by side.

Finally, the captain of the English guardship sent me a wireless message from General Holman, worded thus—

FROM R.A., SECOND IN COMMAND TO MARLBOROUGH

W.I.T. Cipher.

> Inform Wrangel destroyer will bring him to Novorossiisk at once. Following from Holman. Holman guarantees his safety, and will endeavor to arrange meeting between him and Denikin, but he should not come unless he is prepared to abide by Denikin's final decision regarding his future movements. Wrangel should understand the whole future of Russia is at stake. He must be prepared to state publicly his adherence to Denikin's new democratic policy, and sternly discountenance reactionaries now using his name. Holman trusting to his loyalty as enough for length of coming to Novorossiisk. If Wrangel desires, send him destroyer to arrive tomorrow, Wednesday. Inform me time of arrival as soon as possible.

By this time I was incapable of understanding anything of anybody. I requested Chatilov to go to Holman, thank him on my behalf, and tell him that since I had committed no crime, I had no need of guarantees of safe-conduct, and that I considered it absolutely useless to vindicate myself to Denikin.

Chatilov departed, but returned the next day to tell me that Admiral Seymour, the Commander of the English Fleet, had told him that General Denikin was demanding, via Holman, that I leave Russian territory immediately.

I wrote Denikin a letter. Written as it was in anger, it contained personal allusions here and there, but it gave an accurate history of our misunderstandings. I recalled to him, quoting documentary evidence, the many occasions on which I had warned him of the danger of his irresolute policy and the inevitable consequences of his faulty strategy. I had more than once extricated him from the morass into which his unfortunate opinions had landed him. I wrote that if catastrophe was upon us today, it was not I but he who was the sole culprit. Since I had left the service, I was no longer constrained to obey him, and he was powerless to force me to do so; but nevertheless, since he imagined that my presence would prevent him from accomplishing his work, I consented to leave Russia of my own free will.

I sent copies of this letter to Holman and to all those whom Denikin had dismissed because he had realized that they were my supporters.

Chatilov and I left for Constantinople to join my family.

III. - In Exile

I had never been to Constantinople before, and I was dazzled by its beauty. I spent the days rambling through the town and its suburbs. The English had offered hospitality to my family on the Island of Prinkipo, so Chatilov and I went to the Russian Embassy, where our military agent put his study at my disposal. The great rooms in the Embassy were full of refugees who had come to obtain visas, or ask for help and protection. Most of them were absolutely penniless. Americans, Englishmen, Frenchmen, and Italians had all come to the rescue and provided food and shelter for them. We also were penniless, but I managed to obtain a loan from the bank. I did not wish to impose on the generosity of our Allies any longer than was necessary, so once I had obtained the loan, I decided to go to Serbia.

An incessant stream of refugees was arriving from Novorossiisk. They said that life there was one long hell. The latest-comers told us that the town was crowded with troops and refugees, the enemy were shelling the harbor, which was full of the unhappy wretches who had leapt into the water in a panic, only to die there.

The Commander-in-Chief was completely discredited. He had been forced to dismiss Romanovsky, his chief-of-staff, to appease the public anger, he had replaced him by General Makhrov. He had been forced to protect himself with English troops, and on March 14th had boarded a torpedo-boat bound for the Crimea. He had been able to evacuate only the Volunteer troops, one Kubanian brigade and some of the troops from the Don. The rest of the Kubanian Army and the Army of the Don had been abandoned, and was retreating to Tuapse along the coast.

The day before our departure for Belgrade, the English High Commissioner, Admiral de Robeck, had invited me to lunch. As I was on my way, I received a wireless message from General Holman. It stated that Denikin had decided to give up his command and had summoned a Military Council at Sebastopol to elect a new Commander-in-Chief. He requested me to go there and take part in it. This telegram seemed just a little strange to me. I had been dismissed, Denikin had only recently demanded my exile, and here he was summoning me to take part in the election of the Commander-in-Chief of an Army of which I was no longer a member! I could not understand it.

I did not learn till later that the dismissal of Romanovsky had not saved the situation, and that public opinion was demanding Denikin's resignation also. He had only two alternatives, either to enter into an open struggle against the generals and superior officers, or to resign. General Denikin preferred the second course.

We lunched on board the *Ajax*. I could scarcely keep up the conversation, the telegram so haunted me. I had no doubt at all that disaster was inevitable, and that there was no longer an Army. If I returned to the Crimea, I should never come back, and yet I told myself that it was my duty to share the fate of my comrades-in-arms, and to tread the road to Calvary to the end.

After lunch, the Admiral invited General Milne, Commander of the Army of Occupation, and myself into his study.

"I sent you a wireless message from General Holman," he said. "If you wish to go to Sebastopol, one of our ships is at your service. I am very well informed on the Crimean situation, and I know beyond a doubt that you will be called upon to succeed Denikin. I also know the state of the Army and the hopelessness of the cause, I doubt whether anyone can save it. I have just received a telegram from the English Government, it aggravates the situation considerably. It is addressed to General Denikin, but I cannot conceal its contents from you. I do not want to deal treacherously with you. If you do not learn its contents here and now, it will be too late. Read this before making your decision."

He handed me the following note addressed to General Denikin—

SECRET

The British High Commissioner in Constantinople has been ordered by his Government to make the following communication to General Denikin—

The Supreme Council (of the Allies) is of the opinion that, on the whole, the prolongation of the Russian Civil War is the most disturbing factor in the present European situation.

His Britannic Majesty's Government wishes to suggest to General Denikin that, in view of the present situation, an arrangement with the Soviet Government for an amnesty for the Crimean population in general, and the Volunteer Army in particular, would be in the best interests of all concerned.

The British Government is absolutely convinced that the abandonment of this unequal struggle will be the best thing for Russia, and will therefore take upon itself the task of making this arrangement, once it has General Denikin's consent. Furthermore, it offers him and his principal supporters hospitality and a refuge in Great Britain.

The British Government has, in the past, given him a large amount of assistance, and this is the only reason why he has been able to continue the struggle up to the present, therefore they feel justified in hoping that he will accept their proposal. If, however, General Denikin should feel it his duty to refuse, and to continue a manifestly hopeless struggle, the British Government will find itself obliged to renounce all responsibility for his actions, and to cease to furnish him with any help or subvention of any kind from that time on.

BRITISH HIGH COMMISSION.

CONSTANTINOPLE,
April 2, 1920.

England's refusal to give us any help in the future robbed us of our last hope. But I had made up my mind.

"Thank you for having warned me, Admiral," I said. "Until this moment I was still hesitating, but now I have no doubts. If I am chosen, it is my duty to accept the command."

Admiral de Robeck, obviously much moved, wrung my hand. I decided to leave the same evening, so went to say goodbye to my family.

Once again I must take the opportunity to mention my wife's moral courage. She was certain that I was going to my doom and that we should never meet again, but she made no effort to detain me; she said only that duty was the most important thing in the world.

Chatilov was overcome with dismay when he heard of my decision. "You know that it is an impossible fight: the Army will either be killed off to the last man, or it will capitulate. You will be dishonored forever afterwards. You have already lost everything except your spotless reputation, it would be madness to lose that too."

But when he saw that my decision was unalterable, he told me that he was coming with me.

We boarded the man-of-war *Emperor of India* on March 21st and sailed for the Crimea, where, it seemed, the epilogue of the struggle was to take place.

The next day this same man-of-war was to put in at Feodossia to take General Denikin on board; he was leaving for Constantinople without even having bid his troops farewell.

The man had been most courageous and quite indifferent to danger in the old days of the Great War, but he had gradually become an altogether different person. He arrived unexpectedly in Constantinople, where his wife was awaiting him, and he and General Romanovsky went straight to the Russian Embassy. Whilst he was talking to our military agent, General Agapeiev, Romanovsky waited for him in an adjoining room. When someone went into this room he found that Romanovsky had been assassinated. Nobody had heard the shot, but an officer and a Sister of Mercy had been seen hurrying down the staircase.

General Denikin's wife, distracted with fear, begged General Holman, who had just arrived, to send some English soldiers to the Embassy to guard her husband. Our military agent urged Denikin to prevent our Embassy from being occupied by a foreign guard, but in vain. The Embassy was occupied and the doors guarded by sentinels. At the Mass for the Dead, which was said that evening, Denikin was present, surrounded by English soldiers.

The next day, without paying his last respects to his friend, he left for England.

BELGRADE, *July* 31, 1922.

Part II

On the Last Strip of Native Soil

CHAPTER VIII

THE CHANGE OF POWER

On March 22, 1920, the *Emperor of India* dropped anchor in the Sebastopol roadstead. It was a radiant spring day. The blue sky was reflected in the calm sea, and Sebastopol, bathed in sunshine, lay white and glittering on the hills that surround the bay. People were moving busily about the quays in all directions, many small sailing and rowing boats were crossing the bay. The atmosphere was so normal that it was quite impossible to realize that this beautiful town was on the verge of ruin, that in a few days perhaps, the Red waves would submerge it, and Red agents execute bloody reprisals there.

A large ship's boat flying the St. Andrew's flag came alongside; an officer climbed the ladder on to the bridge. He told me that he had been sent to me by the commandant of the Fleet, and that a suite had been reserved for me on the cruiser *General Kornilov*. I ordered my luggage to be trans-shipped to the cruiser, and decided to go ashore at once and see General A. M. Dragomirov, the president of the Military Council. According to the officer who had come to meet me, a meeting of the Council had begun at midday in the Grand Palace, where the commandant of the Fleet had his quarters. General Dragomirov was there also.

The first acquaintance I met after landing was General Ulagay, commander of the Caucasian Army. This Army, composed of Kuban and Terek Cossacks and some of the Don Cossacks, had not been able to embark, and was retreating along the shores of the Black Sea on the Sotchy and Tuapse road. An enormous crowd of refugees was following it. General Ulagay said that the number of Kubanians and refugees amounted to forty thousand, in addition there were twenty thousand Don Cossacks. The units were utterly demoralized, and there was little use in hoping that they would put up any serious resistance to the enemy. Officers as well as Cossacks showed great hostility towards the "Volunteers." They reproached General Denikin and the "Volunteer regiments" for having seized all the ships and escaped from the Crimea, abandoning the Cossacks to their fate.

The Cossacks were retreating across a mountainous country where communications were very primitive, they were being pursued by "Comrade" Boudennyi and his cavalry force, which was inferior in numbers to ours, but greatly heartened by its victory. The Kuban and Don units had abandoned most of their transport, the necessary provisions were unobtainable as they went along, and both men and horses were weak from hunger. It was still very early spring, and the grass had only just begun to come up, so that the horses had to eat withered leaves and gnaw the bark of trees. The Cossacks had confiscated the people's last reserves of food, and were living on horse-flesh and the maize which had been gathered in at the last harvest.

General Ulagay had left his army near Sotchy. Recently, disputes had broken out amongst members of the Kuban Rada. The number of voices clamoring for negotiations with the Bolshevists was increasing, others proposed that Georgia should be asked for help. General Bukretov, the Ataman of the Kuban, and the engineer Ivanis, President of the Kuban Government, had started for the Crimea.

I asked Ulagay: "Does our numerical superiority entitle us to hope for at least a partial success—say the recapture of Novorossiisk—which would make a revictualling possible? Once we have re-established and re-organized our forces there, could we not attempt to take the initiative out of the enemy's hands?"

But General Ulagay answered me with a discouraging gesture, "We cannot do anything, the Cossacks will not fight, the regiments have completely lost their nerve."

Then I realized clearly that the situation was hopeless. The officers had lost their nerve as well as the Cossacks, and we could not rely on the Cossacks to continue the struggle.

Nearly twenty-five thousand Volunteers and ten thousand Don Cossacks, including those from behind-the-lines, had been sent down into the Crimea. The Cossacks had arrived without horses and even without arms. Whilst they were landing they had actually thrown away most of their rifles. The regiments were absolutely demoralized, they were in such a condition that General Denikin had agreed with General Bogarevsky, the Ataman of the Don, and General Sidorin, Commander of the Don Army, to drop his plan of entrusting the defence of the Kertch Straits and the shore of the Sea of Azov to the Don units, he decided instead to reimbark them immediately and transport them to the Eupatona area, first confiscating the last of their arms.

The Volunteer regiments had arrived in a similar condition of complete disorganization, the cavalry had no horses, and all the units lacked transport, artillery, and machine-guns. The men were in rags, and felt very bitter, for the most part they refused to obey their officers any longer. Under these conditions, the contingent from the Volunteer Army no longer constituted an effective fighting force.

The front was being held by General Slachtchov's units, which had been amalgamated, and now formed the Crimean Corps. This Corps consisted of innumerable remnants of other military units and also of embryonic ones—general staffs and regiments-of-the-line. There were quite fifty infantry and cavalry units, and not more than five thousand five hundred combatants (three thousand bayonets and two thousand sabres) The enemy had the 13th Soviet Army on General Slachtchov's front, and its effective force was about six thousand bayonets and three thousand sabres. Under these conditions General Slachtchov's forces were sufficient to defend the isthmuses; but the disparities in the make-up of the various units and their lack of preparation, as well as the enemy's gradual flow of reinforcements which our scouts reported, made our position less secure than it at first sight appeared.

I found General Dragomirov at the Grand Palace. The meeting of the Military Council was due to begin in an hour's time, so he hastened to tell me of the most recent events.

There had been too many people at the Conference which had met the evening before. In spite of all General Dragomirov's efforts, it had failed to come to a definite decision. A large number of the participants had refused on principle to discuss the question of the election of a successor to the Commander-in-Chief, for they considered it inadmissible to introduce the electoral principle into the Army, and thought that General Denikin himself should appoint his successor.

General Slachtchov withdrew from the Conference and left Sebastopol, on the pretext that his presence was needed at the front, and the representatives of the Crimean Corps left with him. After the Conference, General Dragomirov communicated the results of the first meeting to General Denikin, who was at Feodossia, and told him of the views which had been expressed. But General Denikin categorically refused to appoint a successor, and repeated his demand that the Military Council should choose a new Commander-in-Chief.

I personally considered it absolutely inadmissible that a new Commander-in-Chief should be elected by his future subordinates, and a nomination by General Denikin seemed to me to be the only right way of securing the succession. I told General Dragomirov of the English Ultimatum that I had brought.

"What with the information I received at Constantinople, and the news I heard from General Ulagay, and the Allies' decision to give us no further help, I see no possibility of continuing the struggle," I told him. "I have come here because I cannot refuse to share with the Army what are, perhaps, its last hours, and if fate calls me to the leadership of the Army, I will accept the ordeal. But I do not think that General Denikin has the moral right to abandon the work which has been entrusted to him. It is his duty to finish his work and to take full responsibility for whatever happens."

"The Commander-in-Chief has definitely decided to resign. I am sure he will not change his mind," answered General Dragomirov.[1]

---

[1] On March 20, 1920, General Denikin wrote to General Dragomirov—

(continued next page)

The adjoining room, in which the meeting was to be held, was gradually filling up. Noises, voices, and the trampling of many feet could be heard. An aide-de-camp had brought in some papers and left the door ajar, and I could make out a crowd of several dozen men or more.

"That's not a Military Council, Your Excellency, it's a Soviet," I said. "I do not think it will be possible to hide the new facts from the Conference, and they radically transform the whole situation."

I mentioned the English Note. "The new Commander-in-Chief, whoever he may be, ought to know exactly what his comrades-in-arms expect of him under the circumstances, they in their turn ought to know what their new chief can promise them. It is impossible to discuss the issues in such a large meeting, and in one composed so largely of young boys. There are regimental commanders here who in normal times would scarcely be lieutenants. I think we ought to weed out from the Council all those below the rank of Army Corps Commander or its equivalent."

General Dragomirov agreed willingly. He dismissed all the members of the Council I suggested, and requested the superior officers to come into his study. The news of the English Ultimatum alarmed everybody, all realized its gravity to the full, and became gloomy and silent. General Dragomirov announced that General Denikin was still insisting on the election of his successor. But all the members of the Council still considered this course to be inadmissible.

The president of the meeting proposed the following compromise—

COMMANDER-IN-CHIEF OF THE SOUTH RUSSIAN ARMY

FEODOSSIA　　　　NO 145　　　　*March* 20, 1920

My Dear Abram Mikhailovitch

For three troubled years of Russian history, I have been foremost in the struggle, devoting to it all my strength, and bearing the heavy burden of power, as destiny decreed.

God has not given my troops victory. Faith in the Army's vitality and in its historic mission is still alive, but the intimate ties binding the Chief to his men are broken, and I have no longer the strength to command them.

I order the Military Council to elect a suitable man to whom I can delegate my power and my command.

Yours truly,
A. DENIKIN.

> The superior officers should meet in unofficial conference, discuss their views, and suggest the man whom they thought most capable of doing what was to be done, General Dragomirov should then report their decision to General Denikin, emphasizing, however, that the opinion of the members of this meeting did not bind the Commander-in-Chief in any way, and suggesting once again that General Denikin should promulgate an edict appointing his successor.

I asked permission to speak, and explained once again what I had already told General Dragomirov: under the present conditions I could not see any hope of a successful struggle. The English Ultimatum had destroyed our last hope. We had now to drain the bitter cup to the dregs. In these circumstances General Denikin had no right to leave the Army. My words were received in icy silence, and I saw clearly that the question of General Denikin's resignation was already regarded as settled by all present as well as by the General himself.

"And even if General Denikin leaves the Army," I continued, "and the heavy cross falls to one of us, that man ought to know exactly what his electors expect of him before he accepts the post. I repeat that I do not think that the new Commander-in-Chief can possibly promise a victorious issue. The most we can demand of him is that he keeps unstained the honor of the Russian flag which has been entrusted to the Army. It is true that I am not so well acquainted with the general situation as everybody here, and maybe I exaggerate its hopelessness. But I believe that it is essential to be clear on the question before we do anything else." No one said a word.

At last General Makhrov began to speak, saying that although there seemed to be no way of escape from our situation, we ought to continue the struggle, "as long as we have a hundred-to-one chance, we ought not to lay down our arms."

"Yes, Peter Semenovitch, you would be right," General Chatilov answered, "if we had even one chance . . . but I think the enemy has not only ninety-nine chances, but ninety-nine, and then nine more."

General Makhrov had no answer ready. I had no doubt that the members of the Conference would choose me. The die was cast, I had said my say, the rest did not depend on me. I pleaded fatigue, and asked General Dragomirov's permission to leave the meeting.

My heart was unbearably heavy, and I wanted to be alone so that I could think clearly. I left the Palace and went for a stroll in the town, seeking solitude. I reached the famous boulevard, and paced its deserted walks for a long time. I could not lose my feeling of intolerable oppression, and began to feel that the only cure for my mental anguish would be the comfort of unburdening my soul of all that tormented it to a sympathetic listener.

Then I remembered a visit I had paid to Mgr. Benjamin, Bishop of Sebastopol, when I had been passing through the town on the eve of the evacuation of our native territory. I had been suffering deeply then also, and I had enjoyed a cordial conversation with Mgr. Benjamin, imbued with sincere mutual sympathy, which had eased my mind considerably, I decided to go and see him now. He had already heard of my arrival and seemed pleased to see me.

"You did right in coming here. God has inspired you, it was your duty, he said. "I know how terrible it will be for you, I know the weight of the burden you are assuming. But you have no right to refuse the task. You must sacrifice yourself for the Army which is so near to your heart and to Russia's. Divine Providence has chosen you out, working through men who believe in you and are ready to put their fate in your hands. Before you arrived here, and immediately after General Dragomirov had called the Military Council, many Russian men wrote to him nominating you—Orthodox clergy, Catholics, Mussulmen, and political and social organizations. Wait a moment, here are copies of two such petitions."

Mgr. Benjamin turned over the papers spread out on the table and passed me two. Whilst I was reading them, the Bishop went into an adjoining room and brought back an antique image of the Holy Virgin, framed in gold and adorned with pearls. He came over to me.

"I made up my mind to bless you with this Image as soon as you should arrive here for your new venture."

I knelt, and the Bishop blessed me. A great weight fell from my heart. My mind was once more at rest, and, resolving to submit to fate calmly, I went back to the Grand Palace.

The Conference had been over for some time. The next meeting had been fixed for six o'clock that evening. The superior officers had elected me unanimously as General Denikin's successor. General Dragomirov had informed the Commander-in-Chief of the result of the Conference.

Admiral Guerassimov, the commandant of the Fleet, invited me to lunch. I questioned him as to our tonnage, and the reserves of coal and oil which the ships would need in case of a forced evacuation. His answers were most unsatisfactory. There was enough tonnage in the Crimean ports, but not a ship could put out to sea. So far from there being reserves of coal and oil, the ships had no supplies at all. Nor was there any possibility of lighting up the warships with electricity.

"Perhaps you will not believe me," added Admiral Guerassimov, "but we cannot even put the tugs under steam to conduct ships into the roadstead. If, God forbid, there should be a disaster at the front, no one will be able to escape."

At six o'clock, the Council of Superior Officers met again under the presidency of General Dragomirov. I announced that I knew they had chosen me as General Denikin's successor; that the trust which my comrades-in-arms had put in me in these terrible times put me under a twofold obligation. I must justify that trust to them and to myself. Before I consented, I wanted to make sure that I was able to do what was expected of me, as I had already pointed out, I had no right to promise them victory under such conditions as then prevailed—indeed, victory was impossible. I could promise them only one thing: that I would not lower our colors before the enemy, we would perish first. I promised to keep the honor of the Russian flag intact, until the end.

"The English have decided to withdraw from the game," I said. "If we reject their mediation, our refusal will give them a pretext for washing their hands of us and withdrawing altogether. I will most certainly never countenance negotiations between ourselves and the Bolshevists. But I think the most important thing is to avoid giving England an opportunity to leave us in the lurch. We must throw the odium of these negotiations upon England, and prolong them until we have attended to our fortifications, put the Army and the rear in order, and secured coal and oil for the Fleet in case of an evacuation. . . If you approve of my ideas, will you formulate in a special resolution the tasks you wish to delegate to the new Commander-in-Chief."

I suggested that it should be drawn up there and then, so General Chatilov took it down at my dictation.

> At the Conference of Superior Officers, originally the Military Council, which met at Sebastopol on March 22, 1920, by order of the Commander-in-Chief, to elect a successor to General Denikin, Cavalry General Dragomirov, the President of the Council, read the British Government's Ultimatum to General Denikin, this urges him to cease the unequal and hopeless fight, promising him that if he does so the Government of Great Britain will propose to the Soviet Government that an amnesty be concluded for the Crimean population, with special reference to the South Russian troops, but it states categorically that if General Denikin refuses, the British Government will give him no support or help of any kind.
>
> Therefore the Conference has expressed a wish that the Commander-in-Chief should appoint General Wrangel in his place. Once he has accepted the Supreme Command, he will negotiate with the Allies to secure the safety of all those who have fought against the Bolshevists, and to make the most favorable terms he can for those individual members of the Armed Forces of South Russia who do not consider it advisable to trust to the Soviet Government's guarantee of security.

> I have the right to expect (I concluded) that you will all sign this resolution, at all events those clauses with which you agree, and thus share with me the heavy responsibility to the Russian people which I have accepted at your request. I am perfectly aware of the weight of this responsibility, and I beg you to reconsider the whole matter just once more.

I left the Council Chamber and went into an ante-room. Ten, fifteen, twenty minutes went by, and still the discussion continued. Every now and then I could hear snatches of animated conversation—they were arguing. At last the door opened. General Koutepov, the commander of the Volunteer Company, came in.

"Will you come in, Your Excellency?' We can decide nothing without you," he said.

"But what is there to decide?" I asked.

"Well, whilst admitting that no one can make a decision for anybody else, there are some members who will not sign," he answered.

"Who are they?" I questioned.

"General Turbin and General Ulagay."

I hardly knew General Turbin, the commandant of the fortress, but the gallant and noble General Ulagay was very well known to me. I did not suspect him of lack of civic courage; I had to find some other reason to explain his attitude. I went back to the Council Chamber.

"Gentlemen, you still seem to have some doubts. It is absolutely necessary to clear them up, because our decision will be of no value at all unless we are unanimous," I said.

General Ulagay began to explain his point of view. No one could object to the proposed decision, but he felt that, by making a resolution signed by all the members of the Council the condition of my consent, I was showing a lack of confidence in my colleagues. He was certain that not one of them would go back on his spoken word, and therefore there was no need for their pledge in writing.

"I am astonished," I said, "to hear such words from General Ulagay. From him of all people! It seems to me that we have fought side by side often enough and had opportunity enough in other ways to prove one another's worth. I will not admit that there is the slightest suspicion of distrust between us two. For myself, I have no need of written confirmation of the spoken word of any member of this Council. But nobody knows what will happen to us in the near future. Each one of us, and myself especially, will have to account to Russia of the future, the Russian people, and all those whom we hold dear."

General Ulagay immediately said that he was willing to sign. General Turbin said nothing. Each went in turn to the table and signed.

I was the last to sign:

> I have shared the honor of its victories with the Army, and cannot refuse to drink the cup of humiliation with it now. Drawing strength from the trust which my comrades-in-arms place in me, I consent to accept the post of Commander-in-Chief.
>
> Lieutenant-General Baron P. Wrangel
>
> *March* 22, 1920

As I was signing this, General Dragomirov was called to the telephone to speak to General Denikin, who asked if I had been informed of the new political situation and the decisions of the Conference of that morning. On being told that I had, General Denikin announced that he had issued the edict appointing me his successor.

This edict ran as follows—

EDICT OF THE COMMANDER-IN-CHIEF OF THE ARMED FORCES OF SOUTH RUSSIA

FEODOSSIA. No 2899 *March* 22, 1920

1. Lieutenant-General Baron Wrangel is hereby appointed Commander-in-Chief of the Armed Forces of South Russia.

2. Sincere greetings to all those who have followed me loyally in the terrible struggle. God save Russia and grant victory to the Army!

LIEUT-GEN. DENIKIN.

We went into the chamber where all the members of the Conference had assembled, and General Dragomirov announced that I would speak.

I began to speak, and immediately felt a lump rising in my throat. I was deeply moved by the affecting yet cheerful welcome which my comrades-in-arms gave me. I felt that amid their pitiful calamities, their shattered hopes, their sufferings and privations, they turned to me for help and support. The news that I had for them could only be a fresh blow.

What was waiting for them all in the only too near future? What was awaiting our followers who were sacrificing their personal interests, their health, their very life for this struggle for the freedom and welfare of their country? What was awaiting the tens of thousands of Russian citizens who, blinded with terror, had taken refuge here, under the protection of the bayonets of our Army?

Would these great sacrifices lead to nothing? Had all these tears and all this blood been shed in vain? Would this shining page of Russian history be expunged without leaving a trace—this story of the battle her finest sons were waging against the noxious exhalations of the Russian conflagration, the torrents of blood, and the ruin and shame of their country?

With an effort I mastered the emotion which was tearing at my throat, and finished my address.

I stayed behind with Generals Dragomirov and Chatilov, for I had decided to answer the British Government's Note immediately. I sent for A. A. Neratov, the Chancellor of the Foreign Office, but as he was ill, B. A. Tatichtchev came instead I began to dictate to Chatilov our answer to England. Tatichtchev soon arrived, and I signed the note straight away—

TELEGRAM FROM GENERAL WRANGEL TO ADMIRAL DE ROBECK AT CONSTANTINOPLE

SENT FROM SEBASTOPOL MARCH 22-APRIL 4, 1920

General Denikin has issued a General Order appointing me Commander-in-Chief of the Armed Forces of South Russia, and I have already entered upon my duties. The British Government's categorical demand that we cease fighting makes it impossible for my Army to continue. I put upon the British Government all the moral responsibility for the consequences of the decision they have made. I do not admit the absolute possibility of direct negotiations with the enemy, but I leave the fate of the Army, the Navy, the population of the occupied territory, and all those who have actually fought on our side, to the good offices of the British Government. I consider that those who have deprived the Armies of South Russia of their support at the most critical moment, even though these Armies have in the past shown constant loyalty to the Allied cause, are in honor bound to ensure the inviolability of every member of the armed forces, of the population in the occupied legions, of the refugees who wish to return to Russia, and of all those who have fought the Bolshevists and are now in the Soviet prisons of Russia. I have the right to ask my subordinates to sacrifice their lives for the safety of their country, but I cannot ask them to accept an amnesty from the enemy and profit by it, if they consider it dishonorable. Therefore it is absolutely necessary that the British Government should be prepared to offer a refuge outside Russia to the Commander-in-Chief and his principal colleagues, and also to all those who prefer expatriation to the clemency of the enemy. I am ready to accept the simplest living-conditions for these people once

> they are abroad, in order to ensure that only those whose sentiments prevent them from accepting the amnesty will take advantage of the opportunity. It is understood that I give myself first place amongst the above. It is necessary that the armistice question be settled as soon as possible, so that work may be put in hand immediately by the agents of the English Command attached to my General Staff. The Crimea must not be handed over to the Soviet Command for at least two months from the time when the negotiations are completed, in order that the operations connected with the cessation of fighting, and the liquidation of the administrative, military, and civil organs, may be accomplished peacefully. During this period the Allies must continue to furnish the Army and the population of the occupied region with everything that is necessary for them.
>
> WRANGEL.

I was preparing to return to the cruiser *General Kornilov*, when I was handed a telegram from General Slachtchov. It said that he thought I was in danger in Sebastopol, and asked me to authorize him to come over with an armored car and a detachment of his troops to safeguard my person. I ordered an answer to be sent saying that I had no need of a guard, and that I considered it superfluous to send an armored car or a detachment of troops, but that I would always be very pleased to see General Slachtchov himself. Late that night I returned to my suite aboard the *General Kornilov.*

Dawn had scarcely come before the unaccustomed sounds of the matutinal sweeping of the decks awoke me. The chains grated, the scrapers crackled, the water thrown up by the pumps plashed, the metal bulkheads echoed with the footsteps of the sweepers. I could not fall asleep again, for my mind was tormented by irritating, worrying thoughts, so I got up and dressed, and sat down at a table to write out an order to the troops.

What could I say to them to revive their flagging spirits? The difficulty and apparent hopelessness of our situation was equally well known to officers and men. This day or the next they would hear that the Allies had abandoned us. Would not this fresh blow weaken the courage of the men who were defending with their lives the last strip of their native soil? The troops knew that I had never withheld the truth from them, and therefore they always believed me. I could not on this occasion, any more than at former times, give them false hopes. I could only promise them that I would do my duty and ask them to follow my example.

EDICT OF THE COMMANDER-IN-CHIEF OF THE ARMED FORCES OF SOUTH RUSSIA

SEBASTOPOL. No 2900 *March* 22, 1920

By Order No 2899 of March 22nd, General Denikin has appointed me his successor. Fully conscious of my responsibility to my country, I now stand at the head of the Armed Forces of South Russia. I will do my utmost to extricate the Army and Navy from its present difficult situation in an honorable way.

I call upon all the loyal sons of Russia to help me with their entire strength, so that I may do my duty. Knowing our gallant land- and sea-forces as I do, for I have shared their triumphs and sufferings, I feel sure that the Army will bar the entrances to the Crimea, while the Fleet defends its shores.

Our success depends on this. Let us set to work and trust in God.

LIEUT.-GEN. BARON WRANGEL

General Chatilov came on board. He had not slept any better than I. He had sat up far into the night with General Makhrov, the chief-of-staff, familiarizing himself with the essential facts of our situation.

Governmental machinery was almost non-existent. When General Denikin had arrived in the Crimea he had applied to M. V. Bernatzky, the ex-Minister of Finance, and entrusted him with the task of forming a new "ministerial cabinet." With the exception of Bernatzky, who was at Feodossia, and Neratov, the chief of the department for foreign affairs, who was ill, all the chiefs of the civil branches of the administration and most of their more important colleagues had gone away. At the head of what remained of the important departments, only very secondary officials were to be found; though they still had very large staffs, they had been deprived of their premises, and were going about dragging round with them the remains of their scattered documents.

When the branches of the administration and the different institutions had been liquidated and disbanded, General Denikin had promised four months' wages to all those who had been dismissed. Furthermore, enormous sums had been disbursed as "evacuation subsidies."

The tiny Crimea, completely lacking in natural resources, had been compelled to board, feed, and subsidize the Army as well as the excessively large organizations behind-the-lines, month after month.

The inefficient financial policy, General Denikin's obstinate refusal to use the enormous natural wealth of South Russia to attract foreign capital, and the inadequacy of the tax-collecting machinery, all led to a financial system which was summarized by its policy of issuing paper money. Even these issues, coming one after another, could not supply the demand for money, which became more and more pressing as the paper money depreciated. At the time of the retreat from the Crimea, three or four paper-money printers' offices had been partially evacuated and were no longer working, as essential parts of their plant had been lost. Those which were still at Feodossia could not turn out the requisite quantity of paper money. The loss of the South Russian territories and the departure of the Allies endangered the disposal of such sums as we had in the banks, or deposited with our financial agents abroad, insignificant though they were, and our numerous creditors were already claiming them.

The Army had more than one hundred and fifty thousand mouths to feed, of which scarcely one-sixth could be considered as combatants, the rest were the wounded, the sick, all kinds of invalids, the pupils at the important and less important military schools, a large number of reservists of different ranks—most of them old men—and the employees at many institutions behind-the-lines.

The Crimea is devoid of local resources, and in normal times lives at the expense of fertile Northern Taurida; now, with this increase in its population, and with its economic machinery disorganized by long years of international and civil war, it could feed neither its own population nor the Army. There was a dearth of bread already in the south coast towns—Sebastopol, Yalta, and Feodossia, owing to the difficulties of transport. The price of bread was rising higher and higher, and the most necessary fatty substances were lacking. There was no coal, and not only the fleet but also the railway was threatened with a lack of fuel.

Enormous stocks of clothing and munitions had been abandoned in South Russia, and we had nothing with which to re-equip the Army, which lacked clothing and arms. We had only just enough rifles, and we lacked machine-guns and artillery altogether. Nearly all the tanks, armoured cars, and aeroplanes had been abandoned or had fallen into the hands of the enemy. The few that we had been able to keep could not be used for lack of petrol. Our stock of munitions for firearms, especially for the artillery, would only last for a very short time.

There was no harness for the artillery we had, the cavalry had no horses, the only mounted unit was General Morozov's second cavalry division, which was a part of General Slachtchov's Army Corps, it had managed to reach the Crimea by road from the north. Except for this contingent, all the troops concentrated in the Crimea had lost the whole of their transport. The Crimea was poor in horses, and could not supply remounts, especially since the field-work season was just beginning.

The troops were completely out of hand, for the confused retreat had been going on for several months. Drunkenness, abuse of authority, pillaging, and even assassination had become frequent at the centres where the units were stationed.

Dissoluteness had also affected the Higher Command. They interfered in politics, intrigued, and mixed in undignified quarrels. The atmosphere was highly favorable to adventurers of all kinds, both on a petty and a large scale.

The High Command of the Don troops also left much to be desired. General Sidorin, the commander of the Army, and his chief-of-staff, General Keltchevsky, had definitely broken with the Volunteers, and were leaders of a separate Cossack policy, seeking support from the Cossack "democracy."

General Slachtchov, formerly omnipotent master of the Crimea, had remained at the head of his Army Corps after its Headquarters had been transferred to Feodossia. General Schilling had been put at the disposal of the Commander-in-Chief. General Slachtchov, excellent and energetic officer as he was, showed himself well able to cope with his mixed, disparate units. With only a handful of men, and in the midst of disaster, he had held the Crimea, but his complete independence, the absence of all control, and the impossibility of his being called to account for his actions, had turned his head. He had an unbalanced temperament and a rather weak nature, and fell an easy prey to the basest flatteries, he was a bad judge of men, and, moreover, had an unhealthy taste for drink and drugs. He had lost all sense of propriety in the general atmosphere of dissoluteness. No longer content with the role of military leader, he thrust himself into an influential position in general politics, inundating Headquarters with different projects and demands, each more absurd than the last; he insisted on the discharge of a whole list of officers, demanding that the profession be opened to other more suitable men.

The internal administrative machinery was in a state of complete decay, it had evolved from a personal dictatorship to a democratic government, which left the Commander-in-Chief the direction of only the Armed Forces; thus General Denikin had jumbled up all the cards in his political game. If firm and accurate orders had been lacking only recently, there had always been an absence of undivided and determined control in internal politics. Parallel with the civil administration, the political section of the General Staff presided over by the second Quartermaster-General, formulated a policy according to its ideas. This duplication of authority led to inevitable contradictions. Mistakes in the appointment of local representatives of the central authority still further accentuated the muddles, and exposed the impotence of the governmental machinery.

The feeling amongst the Tartar population was favorable to us on the whole. It is true that the Tartars did not want to join the Army, and eluded mobilization by every means in their power, but up till now the rural population had shown no hostile tendencies. The feeling in the towns, especially in the ports, with their industrial population, gave no cause for alarm on the whole, although the influence of Socialist revolutionaries, who had succeeded in getting into the municipalities in large numbers, thanks to the new democratic electoral law, had caused some trouble in the neighboring port of Sebastopol. The General Staff had been informed that a strike was brewing.

Captain Orlov, who had escaped into the mountains with some companions, had been joined by several dozen deserters who were hiding themselves in the mountain villages. He made several appearances on the high road to Simferopol, attacking travellers and solitary policemen. But he did not undertake any larger enterprises. When the Army reached the Crimea, Orlov's command was augmented by unscrupulous adventurers, greedy for gain, one such was Captain Makarov, personal aide-de-camp to General May-Mayevsky. We heard that Bolshevist agents were supplying Orlov's and Makarov's bands with arms and money.

Future conditions of work seemed difficult, almost hopeless. Not only had we to build up everything from the depths of ruin, but we had also to discharge old obligations.

General Chatilov had found time to see General Makhrov, the new chief-of-staff. I knew him very well, he had been chief of the Military Communications Department in the Caucasian Army for a long time. He was a very gifted staff-officer, serious and well educated.

I believed that any change of personnel, especially in these days of general disintegration, could do nothing but harm. The changes which were unavoidable had to be made gradually, as the work went on, and as imperceptibly as possible.

The recent relations between General Denikin and myself obliged me to behave with the most careful correctness towards all his old colleagues who were now working with me. I had explained all this to General Chatilov, requesting him to have a friendly chat with General Makhrov and tell him of my suggestions and ideas for the future work of the General Staff.

This work took an enormous amount of my energy, and meant personal activity in the rear as well as at the front. In these trying days the personal prestige of the Commander-in-Chief was of the greatest importance. One of my predecessor's biggest mistakes had been his gradual dropping of all direct contact with the troops. I suggested to Chatilov that he take the post of adjutant, so that he could fill my place at Sebastopol during my visits to the front.

General Makhrov's report confirmed what General Chatilov had told me.

The strategic situation was as follows: relations between the Bolshevists and the Poles had become seriously strained, and the reopening of hostilities on the Polish front could be expected any day. After the collapse of General Denikin's Army the Reds had thrown every available unit on to the Polish front, except for an inconsiderable number of troops which were pursuing the demoralized fragments of the Cossack troops; the Cossacks had lost their fighting spirit, and were retreating towards the Black Sea.

On the Crimean front. General Slachtchov's units were faced with the 13th Soviet Army's six thousand bayonets and three thousand sabres. The enemy were continuing to fortify their positions and strengthen them with artillery. It seemed as if the Red Command's strategical plan envisaged a widespread offensive on the Polish front and defensive action on ours.

Our troops were holding very vulnerable positions which did not lend themselves to an active defensive. During the summer season, the Sivache would become fordable in its middle reaches, and we could easily be circumvented. It was imperative to advance and seize the mouths of the Salkovo and Perekop passes.

General Makhrov proposed to use the least demoralized regiments of the Volunteer Corps for the projected operation. He planned to bear down on both the enemy's flanks and deliver a frontal attack, whilst troops which were still to be disembarked were to surround the enemy from the rear. I suggested to General Makhrov that he should elaborate every detail of the operation with the commandant of the Fleet, and at the same time get into touch with our naval base at Constantinople, so that the necessary fuel might be delivered immediately. I gave instructions for the planning of our future line of defence, and the making of all the calculations necessary for the organization of fortifications along it.

Simultaneously the foundations of the fortifications at the northern approaches to Sebastopol were laid, they were to cover the port and our main base.

I gave instructions that the work of lifting, classifying, and registering all the abandoned material in the Crimea should be proceeded with immediately and completed speedily, and that the workshops and depots should be put in order as far as possible. I decided to put the work of re-equipping the Army and the urban population of the Crimea into the same hands in order to avoid interdepartmental friction and ensure the most economical use of the meager local resources in the general interest. I appointed General Viltchevsky chief of the Commissariat, he had held a similar post in the Caucasian Army, and I knew him to be honest, incorruptible, energetic, and strong-minded.

We had to combine an infinitely large number of military units into compact formations, reduce the General Staffs, and reinforce the ranks of the regiments with new combatants, giving some sort of regular organization to the whole Army I formulated a scheme for reducing the troops to three Army Corps—one under General Koutepov, to be composed of the units of the old Volunteer Corps, Kornilov's, Makhrov's, and Drosdovsky's divisions, and General Slachtchov's Army Corps, in which the numerous units had been reduced to two infantry divisions—the 13th and the 34th. The *cadres* made part of this Corps, and the Don Cossack units had been combined with the

Don Army Corps. The regular cavalry units had been reduced to six regiments

Although I was preparing to continue the struggle, I felt it was absolutely necessary to safeguard the Army against disaster. I urged General Makhrov to elaborate a plan of evacuation as soon as possible, in cooperation with the Commander of the Fleet's General Staff, to decide which ports the troops should make for in case of an embarkation, and to take measures for the concentration of the necessary tonnage in the ports and the procuring of reserves of coal and oil. So long as the fleet lacked coal and oil, we were in danger of a catastrophe.

The provisioning of the Crimea with fuel, as with everything else, was done from Constantinople, for the resident High Commissioners, the direct representatives of their Government's policies in the Near East and South Russia, were there. I told General Chatilov to go at once to Constantinople and settle the measures for the provisioning of the Crimea with our military agent there, as well as to discuss other matters of a most pressing nature.

General Chatilov saw Admiral de Robeck, the British High Commissioner, and General Mine, the commander of the English Army of Occupation. Chatilov led the discussion round to my answer to the Ultimatum, and did his utmost to prevent the English from "backing out" of their part in the negotiations with the Bolshevists, and to ensure our gaining as much time as possible.

General Slachtchov arrived at Sebastopol. His eccentric uniform, his bursts of nervous laughter, and his confused and abrupt way of talking, created a very bad impression. I expressed my admiration at the way in which he had accomplished his difficult task of defending the Crimea, and told him I was sure that the gallantry of his troops would make it possible for me to reorganize the Army and put the rear in order. Then I told him of the Military Council's decisions. He replied that he was in full agreement with the decisions, and begged me to believe that his troops would do their duty. He thought there was a possibility of an offensive from the enemy within the next few days. In a few words I told him of the projected plan for seizing the outlets from the Crimea. General Slachtchov then broached general political questions. He thought that the Army and the populace should be informed of the new Commander-in-Chief's ideas regarding domestic and foreign policy as soon as possible.

The vacillating policy of the last phase of Denikin's rule, lacking continuity, and undermined by the intensive propaganda of hostile groups, had confused and bewildered everybody. Now we had to give clear and definite answers to the most searching questions, and snatch away our enemies' trump cards. Otherwise we could not restore the troops' lost faith in the justice of our cause, nor could we win back the confidence of the populace. I could make no answer to him.

I returned to the cruiser *General Kornilov* and that evening received a deputation from the clergy and the political groups.

The deputation greeted me very warmly, and expressed their belief that the Russian flag was now in capable hands. I thanked them and emphasized the value I set on their moral support in such trying times. "You realize our situation, you know the weight of the burden which has fallen upon me, you have probably heard of the fresh blow our erstwhile Allies have dealt us. In these circumstances it would be dishonorable for me to promise you victory. All I can do is to promise to save you from this dilemma without loss of honor," I told them.

Immediately afterwards I interviewed certain members of the deputation separately. They raised nearly all the questions which everyone had nearest at heart: the peasant problem, which, together with the agrarian problem, had become a burning question and a powerful plank in the enemies' propaganda, the acute question of the relations between the South Russian Powers and the other new states which had been set up on Russian territory, the relations between the Supreme Command and the Cossack Governments, and finally the position of the Eastern Powers, and particularly the possibility of German support now that the Entente had abandoned our cause. All these questions were causing great anxiety to the Army and to society. My answers seemed to meet with eager approval, and my audience insisted on the necessity of circulating my views amongst as wide a circle of the populace as possible.

The next day I received a visit from representatives of the Allied Military Missions. During my interview with General Mangin, chief of the French Mission, I discovered that he did not yet know about the English Ultimatum.

On March 25th, a solemn *Te Deum* was followed by a review of the troops in Nahimov Square. After Mass had been celebrated in the Cathedral, a religious procession, headed by Bishop Benjamin, wound its way to the Nahimov Square, accompanied by the pealing of bells. On the way it was joined by processions coming from other churches. The troops were deployed all along Ekaterinskaia Street and round the square. An altar had been set up in front of Admiral Nahinov's monument. By it stood a group of well-known people and representatives from the Allied Missions. The surrounding windows, balconies, and even roofs, were crowded with onlookers. The day was sunny and calm, the blue sky was reflected in the still bay as in a mirror. The hymns poured out into the silence in wave after wave of sweet sound; not a flame of one of those innumerable tapers stirred; the smoke floated up from the incense in translucent clouds. After the religious service, Bishop Benjamin read the Senate's edict which had arrived the night before, and which enjoined the whole population to unite under the new Commander-in-Chief.

The Bishop then mounted another step or two and spoke:

"Listen, people of Russia, listen, Russian soldiers, listen representatives of our Allies, and listen also you Bolshevists are hiding in the crowd there!" So began Mgr. Benjamin's address, and his voice penetrated to the further corner of the great square. He spoke of the cruel sufferings which God had visited on our country, that it might atone for the sins of all classes of the Russian people, of the gallant deeds of those who had kept the flag flying during the years of shame and disaster, of the path of sorrow which the Russian Army had already been treading for the last few years.

"This path is a thorny one, and its end has not yet been reached. We have just been enduring terrible trials, perhaps the near future is preparing fresh ones for us. But faith can work miracles, those who have faith, those who march courageously along the road which conscience dictates without losing their honor, will conquer. A month ago the Russian Army was driven back on to the sea at Novorossiisk in a dying condition, perhaps two months hence it will have taken on a new lease of life, and will go forth and conquer the enemy."

This speech was delivered with admirable force and enthusiasm, and made a profound impression on its hearers.

After the troops had been sprinkled with Holy Water, the regiments were massed in the square. I, too, mounted the steps of Nahimov's monument and addressed the troops. Having in a few words drawn a gloomy picture of our position, I said that I had assumed the leadership of the Army without hesitation or fear. I trusted in God, who would not let the righteous cause perish, and would give me judgment and strength enough to help the Army out of this difficult situation. I knew the wonderful gallantry of the troops, and I firmly believed that they would help me to do my duty to our country, I had faith that the bright day of Russia's resurrection would yet dawn.

The troops marched past. Their uniforms were old, and bad weather had played havoc with them, their boots were worn out and patched, their faces haggard and cadaverous. But their eyes sparkled merrily and their heels tapped the ground with a firm tread. They were remembering the recent deeds of their martyred heroes, and a comforting feeling was awaking in the depths of their hearts: "Everything is not yet lost—we can still hold on!"

The following day I moved from the cruiser *General Kornilov* into the residence which had been prepared for me in the town, it was called the Little Palace, and was a tiny bungalow with a minute garden, originally built for the High Admiral of the Russian Fleet, Grand Duke Alexis Alexandrovitch.

The superior officers had separated after the Military Council of March 22nd. General Ulagay had rejoined his army, General Sidorin had gone to Eupatona, where the Don regiments were stationed, General Koutepov had gone to Simferopol. The reorganization of the Crimean, the Don, and the Volunteer Army Corps was well in hand, the equipment had been inventoried, and the troops were falling back into some kind of order.

My General Staff, in concert with the Commander of the Fleet, had elaborated a detailed plan for the projected operation which was to win the Crimean passes for us. We were only awaiting the arrival of assignments of coal from Constantinople to launch the attack. For this operation we intended to use General Slachtchov's Army Corps, units from the Volunteer Corps, Drosdovsky's men, and Alexeiev's. When the campaign was over I wanted to concentrate the Volunteers in the north-west part of the peninsula, and entrust the defence of the Perekop isthmus to them, whilst the Crimean contingent could be concentrated further east, to defend the Salkovo and Guenitchesk Passes. Ranged along the railway to defend a much-reduced front, it could rest and reorganize quite peacefully.

M. Perlik, the Governor of the Crimea, came from Simferopol. He was very uneasy about the provisioning of the town. Owing to the disorganization of the railways, the transport of corn from the northern agricultural part of the peninsula to the coast towns had ceased; the appearance of a large number of troops and refugees in the Crimea had made the question still more acute. There was also a dearth of other necessary foods—meat, tea, and sugar were lacking. The excessive and disorderly requisitioning by the troops had completed the economic disruption and infuriated the population. We had to take immediate steps to put an end to this state of things.

When the Army had arrived in the Crimea, the Bolshevist agents had redoubled their activity. They worked especially amongst the peasant population. The agrarian question was not quite so acute in the Crimea as elsewhere in Russia, but agitation based on the claim for land fell on very fertile soil there, especially in the northern agricultural districts. The agrarian question was particularly acute in Northern Taurida, with its large villages and its great landed estates. We heard that the propaganda against us had been very successful with the peasants of that district. The Governor of the province attached exceptional importance to the information the population had received concerning the Government's intentions with regard to the agrarian question.

General Denikin had hesitated to the last to cut the Gordian knot, and the question had not got beyond the stage of interminable discussions in the different commissions. The groups which were hostile to us had seized on the agrarian question for propaganda purposes, and an unhealthy atmosphere enveloped this complex problem, even the sympathetic groups and the well-intentioned organs of the Press were quite bewildered.

The Crimean Press consisted of a certain number of daily papers. The Sebastopol newspapers set the tone. There was Burnakin's *Vetcherneie Slovo*, a boulevard paper of a monarchist complexion, the *Youg Rossu*, directed by Arcadius Avertchenko, which was moderate in tone, and the *Krymsky Vestnik* a Jewish Radical newspaper. There was not a serious national paper.

The censorship left much to be desired, its functions were nearly always discharged by assiduous officers who had neither the knowledge nor the requisite breadth of view for the work. Quite often absolutely harmless articles were censored, they had had the misfortune to arouse the suspicions of the censor simply because he had not understood them, whilst very provocative paragraphs often appeared in the daily columns. Sometimes it would be stated "on good authority" that so-and-so, a very unpopular man because of his earlier activities, had been appointed to an important post, sometimes a "reform in the Army—the suppression of officers' epaulettes," or the like—would be prognosticated.

Such news produced a very painful effect, considering the prevailing atmosphere of nervous tension. Lately the Press had been discussing the shackles of censorship in a very heated manner, claiming "freedom of the Press" and such-like things. The uproar had become intolerable. So I invited the directors of three of the papers to Sebastopol. I offered them some tea, and expressed my pleasure at entertaining representatives of the local Press which stood so close to the Government, and whose voice had the ear of the whole provincial Press:

> Gentlemen, my former activities are known to some of you, and you know that I have always been the friend of the Press. I attach exceptional importance to the printed word nowadays, when no sedition of the country or of the populace can remain outside politics. I respect the opinion of others, and have no intention of restricting the freedom of the Press, whatever its views may be, provided, of course, that they do not favor our enemies. At the same time, I must draw your attention to the fact that we are living in exceptional times. We are, indeed, living in a besieged fortress, not only does the enemy threaten us on the north, we have also to keep a strict watch all along the shore, to prevent him landing his troops, in these conditions we cannot dispense with the censor. Even in the freest countries a most strict censorship is always imposed at the seat of military operations, how much more necessary is it in a besieged fortress! This censorship cannot confine itself to purely military questions, because in time of war, especially Civil War, ideas are weapons of war as much as guns and rifles, and military and civil censorship cannot be separated.
>
> I do not question your patriotism, gentlemen, and would be only too happy to free you from the restrictions which are hindering your work. At the same time I am responsible for the cause of which I am the leader, and I have to take measures to protect the Army and the populace who are under its care against anything which might threaten their safety. I suggest that you choose one of two courses,

> either adhere to the present system if I promise you that I will do all I can to improve the censorship and find competent censors, or, abolish the censorship and put all the responsibility on the directors, who will be answerable before the judiciary. In the event of the publication of articles or paragraphs prejudicial to our cause, they would come under the code of military justice, which applies to crimes of a military nature. I ought to point out to you that according to war-time regulations, acts prejudicial to us or favorable to the enemy are liable to very severe punishment, even to the death-penalty. Think over my suggestion, gentlemen, and then let me know your answer.

The director of the *Krymsky Vestnik* was the first to speak. He hastened to declare that, taking into consideration the exceptional difficulties of the moment and all the arguments that I had put forward, he was ready to admit that the suppression of the censorship could not be considered at present. The representative of the *Youg Rossu* endorsed his opinion. Burnakin was the only one to declare that he was ready to assume full responsibility for his paper. After this interview, the question of the suppression or the censorship was not raised again in the Press.

I decided to entrust the administration of foreign affairs to P. B. Struve, a member of the Academy. Until now the position of director of foreign affairs had been nominally held by S. D. Sazonov, who was living in Paris, being so far from the struggle, he could not possibly ascertain the facts of the new situation and adapt himself to new working conditions. He could only resign himself to the fact that the position of Russia's representative had changed, and with great dignity he withdrew more and more from action of any kind. His presence in Paris became purposeless, especially as it was undoubtedly the duty of the director of foreign policy to be at the centre of government.

With the departure of S. D. Sazonov, there was no longer any reason for the continued existence of the political delegation of which he was part, which was stationed in Paris. At the head of this delegation was Prince G. E. Lvov, ex-president of the Provisional Government, and it included well-known statesmen, who sent out protests, memoranda, etc., on different problems of our foreign policy, but had no real importance. I telegraphed to our Ambassador in Paris that henceforth all communications would take place only through him. From that day on, the political members of the delegation went into opposition to the Supreme Command, and took every opportunity to discredit in foreign circles the cause which we were maintaining with such great difficulty.

On March 29th I promulgated a statute for the administration of the territories occupied by the Armed Forces of South Russia, the Regent and

Commander-in-Chief was to exercise the fullest civil and military powers, without any limitations whatsoever. The Cossack territories were to keep their internal autonomy, but the Cossack troops were to be subject to the Commander-in-Chief. From this time on, the Commander-in-Chief had full authority over the Cossack troops; a term was put to the existence of separate regulations for different troops in the same army. This Act stated the principle of dictatorship clearly and openly for the first time.

CHAPTER IX

EARLY PROGRESS

Although I had adopted a series of measures for putting the Army in order and for reorganization behind the front, I had not forgotten how necessary it was to provide for an evacuation in case of misfortune, and I was continually begging for fresh consignments of coal to be sent from Constantinople.

If we should be forced to leave our native soil, we would not be able to count on the sympathy of other countries, probably not one of them would offer us a refuge. The Slav countries alone, especially Serbia, who owed everything to Greater Russia, might prove exceptions. I wrote to Prince Alexander of Serbia asking for shelter and protection should the worst happen. I wrote that I was doing my utmost to save the last shred of my country from Red domination, that I was trying to believe that God would help me, but that I had to be prepared for the worst.

It was nearly Easter. How different it was from the same season in former years. Spring was at its height and the churches were full, but there was not that air of gay expectancy which is customary on the eve of a festival. Prices were rising rapidly, and there was a food-shortage, everyone was living in fear of a terrible future. On Good Friday I went to Confession, and the next day to Communion. After midnight Mass in the Cathedral, I had a meal in the officers' mess of the Cossack regiment of the Guard, which was garrisoned at Sebastopol. It was one of the reduced regiments which had kept its old officers, most of those who were now commanding Sotnias[1] had commanded much smaller units during the Great War.

On March 31st a fierce engagement took place in the Perekop area. The Reds had concentrated nearly three thousand cavalry and had attempted to launch an offensive, but our counter-attack had thrown them back. On April 1st, our right flank detachment, which was to draw off the Red reserves, disembarked without incident near the village of Kirillovka, forty versts to the north-east of Guenitchesk. But whilst it was advancing to join us in the Guenitchesk area, the Reds attacked and repulsed it, inflicting heavy losses.

However, our units captured the southern suburb of Guenitchesk the next day, and simultaneously our left flank troops disembarked near Khorly. The landing took place under difficult conditions. The Reds were holding Khorly with two regiments well equipped with rifles and four pieces of

[1] A Sotnia is a unit of one hundred Cossacks—TRANSLATOR

artillery, these had been installed expressly for the purpose of bombarding the only canal we held which ran into the seaport. Nevertheless, our troops overcame all difficulties, thanks to the help of the sailors.

The following day our right flank units made a second effort to advance, and simultaneously the right flank units of the Crimean contingent, led by the gallant General Angouladze, attacked the Sivache Station and captured it. The Sivache bridge, which had been damaged by the enemy, was quickly repaired, and our units continued to advance. Supported by armored cars, they occupied Tchongar Station which had been fortified by the enemy. A fierce battle was waged in the Perekop zone on April 3rd, and lasted the whole day. Our troops repulsed every attack the enemy made. On the same day our left flank troops, following up the offensive, seized four of the enemies' guns and all their equipment. The troops had fought brilliantly, for they had been surrounded by the enemy and had been very short of ammunition.

On the evening of the 3rd I left for the front, and late the next morning arrived at Taganache Station. There I joined General Slachtchov, and motored with him to join our troops who were advancing on Djimbuluk Station. Bishop Benjamin was with us, for he wished to accompany me. Our forces were attacking, supported by fire from an armoured car. The enemy had withdrawn, but were bombarding our lines. Our skirmishers were lying low on the plain. The enemy's shells had thrown up fountains of liquid black mud. I got out of the car and walked down the ranks of the sharpshooters, greeting the men and thanking them for the fine work they had done the previous evening. Bishop Benjamin, cross in hand, blessed the skirmishers. General Angouladze, the divisional commander, put himself at the head of the skirmishers and led the attack..

They soon captured Djimbuluk Station, which had been fortified by the Reds. The enemy abandoned the Tchongar peninsula in disorder, and retreated, pursued by our units. I visited our reserve troops and then returned to Djankoie Station, motoring to Perekop from there. The next morning General Angouladze's command captured Salkovo Station.

Meanwhile our left flank had continued its advance, repulsed the enemy's cavalry attack, broken through the Red front south of Preobrajenka, and rejoined our forces at Perekop, bringing with them all the wounded, and the trophies they had wrested from the enemy. During the fight General Vitkovsky, commander of the left wing units, had had two horses killed under him, and we had taken six big guns and sixty machine-guns.

The task I had set the troops was accomplished, the repercussions on the morale of the troops were more important than the actual successes. These last battles had shown that the Army still retained its old invincible spirit, and whilst that was still alive all was not lost.

Word had reached Sebastopol that hostilities had begun again on the Polish front. The Polish troops had taken up the offensive and forced the Reds to give ground. Our military situation, which had been so difficult a little while ago, was now a trifle easier. We hoped that the enemy would concentrate on the advancing Poles and give us a respite, which we could use profitably in many ways.

The troops were ordered to proceed at once with the fortification of the positions they had conquered, at the same time they were to begin preparing fortified lines in the rear.

On my way back to Sebastopol I stopped at Simferopol for an hour or so and received several visitors in my carriage, including M. Ratimov, director of a daily newspaper, the *Eupatorusky Vestnik*, who had requested a personal interview with me. He asked that the Supreme Command should support his newspaper, which was entirely sympathetic to the Army. He was in a very difficult position in Eupatona: the General Staff of the Don Army Corps would not support his publication, for it published its own paper, the *Donskoy Vestnik*, and regarded M. Ratimov's paper as its rival and opponent. The views of the Don paper were frankly hostile to the Supreme Command. To support his statements, M. Ratimov presented me with a whole series of copies of the *Donskoy Vestnik*. I ran through them and was absolutely staggered. I knew perfectly well that this paper was produced by the commander of the Don Army Corps and his chief-of-staff. Its director was Count du Chayla, chief of the Cossack squadron, and I had heard very unfavorable reports of him. He had taken part in the political disturbances in the Don which had been directed against the Supreme Command.

That there was a spirit of opposition at work amongst the officers of the Don Army I knew quite well, but what I now saw exceeded all my apprehensions.

In a series of articles in this official paper, inadmissible attempts were made to rouse the hostility of the Cossacks against the Volunteers, and to excite them against the generals and high dignitaries, the idea of the secession of the Cossack districts from Russia was also broached. I really did not know which to admire more—the utter vileness of the treason of these men who were at the head of the Don troops, or the coolness of their work, open and undisguised as it was. I suggested to M. Ratimov that he should come with me to Sebastopol.

As soon as we arrived I sent for General Bogarevsky, the Ataman of the Don, and gave him the copies or the *Donskoy Vestnik* that I had received from M. Ratimov. I suggested that he should see M. Ratimov himself. I left the two of them together and went into my study. Thereupon I drew up a general order enjoining Lieutenant-General Sidorin to delegate his work to General Abramov, dismissing Lieutenant-General Keltchevsky, the chief-of-staff, and summoning Count du Chayla, the editor of the political section and the director of the paper, before a military tribunal. The police-magistrate for important cases received an order to try this case immediately, and to conduct an inquiry so that we might discover the names of any others who were also guilty, that they too could be tried.

After I had drawn up this order I went back to General Bogarevsky, he was standing by the window reading a copy of the *Donskoy Vestnik*. He looked very baffled and sheepish I showed him my general order.

"Have you anything to add?"

"No—of course not," muttered the Ataman in strangled tones, and with a visible effort.

I immediately signed the order and gave it to my aide-de-camp, who saw to its execution.

The inquiry revealed that Generals Sidorin and Keltchevsky were the ringleaders. Count du Chayla had played only a minor part; he attempted to commit suicide when he was arrested, and wounded himself very seriously. General Sidorin tried to win the support of the officers of the Don Command, but with no response.

I studied the report of the inquiry and ordered Sidorin, Keltchevsky, and du Chayla to be indicted before a military tribunal, of which General Dragomirov was president. The tribunal sentenced the two Generals to hard labor, I commuted the sentence to dismissal from the service and prohibition to wear uniform.

As Count du Chayla was in hospital recovering from his self-inflicted wounds, his trial was conducted separately, and did not come up before the tribunal until much later. The tribunal took into consideration the fact, that Count du Chayla was only a common adventurer and a minor accomplice, and since I had seen fit to reduce the sentence of the principal offenders, they acquitted him. He went abroad, and continued his policy of hostility to the Army even after we had evacuated our native territory.

A vigorous blow had put an end to the machinations of the Don Command, and the intriguing and lying of the dissatisfied generals ceased, they felt that they could no longer fish in troubled waters with impunity. Most of these gentlemen left the Crimea with all speed, and that was that! But General Slachtchov could not calm down again. He noticed that I carefully avoided discussing with him questions which had no connection with his command, so began to bombard me with his incoherent dispatches.

In Simferopol, General Koutepov was keeping order amongst his troops with an iron hand, the court-martial was ruthless in its sentences, and all pillagers and deserters were executed. Local Liberal clubs, led by M. Oussov, the Mayor of Simferopol, were in violent opposition to General Koutepov. M. Oussov sent him protests against capital punishment, etc., in the name of the whole group. I invited the Mayor to come to Sebastopol the next day. The Liberal Press announced his departure and hinted that the Commander-in-Chief's invitation to the Mayor foreshadowed changes in the military administration, and that the Supreme Command evidently intended to proceed against certain administrators who had exceeded their authority.

The Mayor came into my study with an air of victory, but when he saw that I neither held out my hand to him nor asked him to sit down, he seemed disconcerted.

"I know all about your disagreement with General Koutepov, who is merely carrying out my orders," I told him. "I am not going to discuss with you who is in the right, or which of us two has given orders. I am responsible to the Army and the people, and I follow the dictates of my mind and conscience. I am quite sure that were you in my place you would act quite differently, but as it happens, destiny has given me and not you the direction of the Russian Cause, and I will do my duty as I see it. Furthermore I will stop at nothing in the accomplishment of my duty, and will not hesitate to cut down anyone who tries to stop me. You protest because General Koutepov has hanged a score or so of men who were a danger to the Army and our cause. I warn you that should the necessity arise I would not hesitate to increase the number by one, and that one would be yourself."

The Mayor left my study, obviously crushed. The next day the newspapers said that the Mayor of Simferopol had come back from Sebastopol, but that he refused to give any details of his interview with the Commander-in-Chief. A few days later the same papers announced that M. Oussov was seriously ill and had resigned his mayoralty.

General Ulagay had come over to Sebastopol again from the Caucasian front, with him was General Starikov, the commander of the Don Army Corps. All General Ulagay's attempts to launch an offensive had been so much trouble wasted. The Cossacks would not fight any more. Discord was rife between the Kuban Government, the Rada and the commanders of the Kuban and Don troops. Generals Ulagay and Starikov were insisting on the transfer of Cossacks from the Kuban into the Crimea, but General Bukretov, the Ataman of the Kuban, refused to give his consent.

I called a conference, consisting of the Atamans of the Don, Kuban, and Terek, Generals Ulagay, Starikov, Chatilov, and Makhrov, and the Commander of the Fleet. Ulagay and Starikov repeated their statements. The Atamans of the Don and Terek supported them, but General Bukretov again declared that he considered the transfer to be undesirable, and that in his capacity of Ataman he felt that he must consult all the Cossacks on the subject.

I replied that it was unthinkable that the Cossacks should be allowed to discuss their officers' orders. General Bukretov countered with "And I, as their Ataman, cannot allow them to be transferred to the Crimea, the Volunteer Army has always been a stepmother to them. I cannot see any reason for doing it. It is not true that the Cossacks will not fight, it is only their superiors, Generals Ulagay, Chkouro, Naoumenko, Babiev, and others who will not fight."

"If that is so, let General Bukretov command the Army himself!" General Ulagay burst out. I silenced him and spoke to Bukretov.

"You are accusing the superior officers of lacking the will to fight. I have known them for a long time, and I cannot believe you. But your remarks have convinced me that the Supreme Command cannot be exercising the necessary authority over the Cossacks in view of the attitude of the Ataman, the Government, and the Rada. You have assured us that the Cossacks are ready to fight under new officers. I am delighted to hear it! Take the Command of the Caucasian Army yourself and go and fight the Bolshevists!"

"Oh, no, I will not accept the Command myself," he cried.

"Well, then, we have nothing further to discuss," I said. "You refuse to shoulder your responsibilities, and I cannot tolerate irresponsible persons inciting the Cossacks against the Command. Get out, but do not leave the Crimea."

I turned to Admiral Guerassimov. "Please see that no vessel leaving the Crimea takes General Bukretov on board."

General Bukretov hurried out. Everyone present seemed somewhat confused. Generals Bogarevsky and Vdovenko tried to persuade me to revoke my decision.

"The Ataman's person is inviolable," said General Bogarevsky. "You, in cooperation with the Atamans, have just promulgated an edict confirming the autonomous rights of the Cossacks, the sequestration of General Bukretov will make a very bad impression on them." General Chatdov also tried to persuade me, but I held firmly to my own view.

"I cannot allow General Bukretov to go back to the Army and continue his propaganda. I do not believe him for a moment when he says that the Cossacks want to fight, but he is responsible for all that has just happened," I replied.

At last General Chatilov suggested that he should go to General Bukretov's house and have a private talk with him.

A half an hour later General Chatilov came back and announced that General Bukretov had consented to accept the command of the Army. I requested him to go back again and tell the Ataman that I regretted our little misunderstanding and begged him to rejoin the Conference. General Bukretov came back.

"I am very pleased that you have reconsidered your decision and are ready to take upon yourself this heavy responsibility. Let us forget all our misunderstandings," I said to him, my hand outstretched.

I signed the order appointing General Bukretov commander of the Army straight away, and put Generals Ulagay, Chkouro, Naoumenko, and Babiev at his disposal.

On April 9th I presided over my first Council of the chief administrative officials. It was being borne in upon me more and more strongly that the men at the head of the different branches of the administration were not capable of performing the gigantic task which destiny had thrust upon them. The whole civil and economic life of the country was disorganized. All its fundamentals had to be recreated, not merely reconstructed, but actually recreated in the strictest sense of the word, when all the new political and economical conditions were taken into account. Only men with the widest knowledge, the greatest administrative experience, and quite unusual political adaptability could have coped with the problems of the moment, and it was difficult to find men with both the last two qualities. The most experienced administrators had acquired their tact and knowledge of affairs in the service of the old Russian bureaucracy with all its traditions, and from these traditions they could not free themselves. They could not do any good work unless they had stable, complete administrative machinery, which was entirely lacking during the Civil War. It was inevitable that they should apply all the negative characteristics of the old bureaucracy to their work; they did not know how to estimate the real needs of the population, and complicated all their actions with the inevitable Red Tape. They were slow, as are all bureaucracies, and set great store by out-of-date procedure. Creative work inventing its own forms was a necessity in a period of revolutionary upheaval, and this was beyond their powers. But the colleagues General Denikin had chosen from Liberal circles were even less able to cope with their work than ex-Imperialists. They were for the most part men of words and not of action, members of the Intelligentzia who showed themselves to be incapable of action even in the political battlefield. They were incapable of any creative work, for they had neither the necessary knowledge nor the bureaucratic experience.

I realized quite clearly that under the abnormally difficult conditions which then prevailed, only a statesman of uncommon ability could cope with the gigantic task awaiting us in the Crimea. I was convinced that the only man great enough for the task was M. A. V. Krivochein.

I had known him personally for a long time. All Russia had recognized his statesmanlike work years ago. He had a masterful character and an extraordinary capacity for work, and during his long career had studied the most diverse branches of the administration. He had served in the Ministry of the Interior in the department which dealt with the affairs of the Zemstvos, and there had gained a deep knowledge of the peasant question. He had been in the State Agrarian Bank, and was ex-chief of the Emigration Department, an annexe to the Ministry of Finance. In this last capacity he had given a strong impetus to the activities of the Peasant Bank, and had put it on the way to creating small peasant proprietors. For six years he had been Minister of Agriculture and P. A. Stolypin's most intimate colleague, and had earned out his agrarian reforms for him. He owed his high position in the bureaucracy entirely to himself and his personal qualities, he occupied an exceptionally high position in administrative spheres, and at the same time wielded unusual authority in the political circles of society. A distinguished administrator himself, he had the knack of always choosing good colleagues, many of them filled important posts in different branches of the administration after they had been trained under him.

He was an exceptionally learned man, very cultured and broad-minded, with dearly formulated and well-defined opinions. He was tolerant too, and had the rare gift of being able to see other people's point of view, he could win over his hearer by avoiding, with the most consummate tact, every topic that might offend him. By reason of his early work, he belonged to the older school or statesmen, and obviously was not one of those who were ready to throw in their lot with the Revolution, although he clearly realized the necessity of reckoning with it. He knew how to adapt himself to the new conditions of work which required continual changes, and did not admit of any conventional routine.

I realized what enormous sacrifices M. Krivochein would have to make if he consented to share my heavy load with me, but, knowing him, I hoped that he would consent, an ardent patriot and a man with a sense of duty would make this sacrifice for his country.

N. M. Kotharevsky left for Paris on April 9th, taking my letter to M. Krivochein.

The early progress of the new regime did something to reassure the population, for energetic steps had been taken to re-establish order in the interior, and there had been a victory at the front recently. But the real situation was still unknown. Enemy propaganda was having its effect. In the many interviews I had with representatives of the civil and military powers and with politicians, I noticed that each one expected pronouncements from the new rulers on all the burning questions of the day: the agrarian question, our relations with the Cossacks, the new states on Russian territory, and Western Europe. Admiral MacCully, the chief of the American Mission, who was very well disposed towards us, and also General Mangin, chief of the French Mission, both pointed out to me the necessity for making my opinions public, in order to guard against the suggestive rumors which were being circulated in foreign circles about the change of power.

I bowed to public opinion, invited Press representatives to call on me, and expressed the following views to them on the problems of the moment—

> After six days of hard fighting, we have taken the Crimean Passes and have entrenched our position.

The Army is being reorganized with all speed, and is falling into some sort of order again after the ordeals it has suffered. In the very near future I am going to introduce a whole series of organization-measures which should eliminate some of the defects which make the administration of the Army so difficult. A series of measures for raising the moral tone of the Army have already been put into force. Tribunals of honor with wide powers have been set up for the officers in the units, they can even degrade superior officers.

Simultaneously with the above measures, we will attempt to settle the most urgent questions affecting national life.

Three years of anarchy combined with the frequent changes of Government have complicated the problems of industrial and economic life, and they cannot be settled at one blow, each new Government adopted a programme likely to capture the sympathies of the population by seductive promises which nobody could possibly fulfill.

The agrarian question is a case in point. I am endeavoring to settle the most vital questions, and yet remain within the bounds of possibility.

The essential task before the authorities is the creation of a rule of law for the people of that part of South Russia which is occupied by my troops, so that they can subsequently fulfil their promises in the most comprehensive way.

I am preparing measures which will enable the workers on the land to obtain as large a plot of ground as possible in individual ownership. The future of Russian agriculture belongs to the small peasant proprietor, big landed estates have had their day. The improvement of the material welfare of the workers and the satisfaction of their industrial needs is one of our principal cares.

Let us now turn to the causes of our failure, they are many. They can be summed up by saying that strategy was sacrificed to a policy, and, what is more, to a worthless policy.

Instead of uniting all the forces fighting Bolshevist Communism and evolving one policy for them—"a Russian policy"—free from all party spirit, a partisan "Voluntarist" policy was adopted, whose directors were the enemies of Russia in everything that did not bear the mark of "Voluntarism."

They fought the Bolshevists, it is true, they also fought the Ukrainians, the Georgians, and the Azerbeidjanians, it needed very little to set them fighting the Cossacks, who made up half our Army, and who had declared their indissoluble union with the regular troops by the blood they had shed on the field of honor. In short, having proclaimed the principle of Greater Russia, One and

Indivisible, they proceeded to disrupt all the Russian anti-Bolshevist forces and to divide Russia up into a chaos of impromptu states fighting one against the other.

I visualize quite another way of resurrection for Russia. A few days ago, I signed an agreement with representatives of all the Cossack troops, defining the conditions which are to govern our relations with one another. The Cossack States are to keep their autonomy in internal affairs, but their armed forces are to be subordinate to us on certain conditions.

Outside the Cossack States, I have assumed full and unlimited civil and military power. In questions of internal policy I intend to rely largely on the cooperation of public opinion

We are within a besieged fortress, and only a strong and united power can save the situation. The prime necessity is that of fighting the enemy, we have no time for party warfare.

When the spectre of Bolshevism, which threatens us all, is laid, popular wisdom will find a political formula which will satisfy all classes of the population, but until the struggle is over, all parties must be as one, and do the necessary work without any partisan spirit. The strictly simplified administrative machinery that I am setting up contains no party men—only workers. I recognize neither monarchists nor republicans, but only clever men and hard workers.

I hold the same opinion on the question of "orientations." Make agreements with whoever you like, but my watchword is, "For Russia!"

As for the German "orientation" of which people have been writing and talking for the last few weeks, I cannot take it seriously. Germany is exhausted after the War, and absorbed in her home affairs, it is obvious that she cannot give effective support to any other country.

It is not by a triumphal march from the Crimea to Moscow that Russia can be freed, but by the creation, on no matter how small a fragment of Russian soil, of such a Government with such conditions of life that the Russian people now groaning under the Red yoke will inevitably submit to its attractions.

On April 11th I appointed a Commission to study the agrarian question, its president was Senator Glinka, the ex-director of the Emigration Bureau, and one of A. V. Krivochein's most intimate colleagues.

I realized that the agrarian question could not be settled satisfactorily if it were treated as one problem, for Russia is so immense, and its ethnographical and economic variations so many, moreover, dissolution and anarchy had ruined the economic life of the country and falsified all legal relations. Any decision would provoke much discontent, and we would have to correct our errors later, in the light of experience. But present conditions of life forbade us to delay any longer—the Gordian knot had to be cut. The question had to be settled for an important psychological reason: we had to tear the enemy's principal weapon of propaganda from him, kindle the imagination of the Army and the populace, and make a favorable impression on foreign opinion.

From the first moment I set foot in the Crimea I realized how necessary it was to re-establish the bare elements of normal justice, for all such ideas had been badly shaken during the years of Civil War

The absence of a strong, legal government and of a law-abiding spirit was one of the principal causes of the dissolution of General Denikin's Army. The troops had become demoralized, the supreme military jurisdiction under the Attorney-General for the Army and Navy was powerless. One of the Commander-in-Chief's edicts gave the immediate superior of an offender the right to institute criminal proceedings against him and try him. The Army Corps tribunals, composed of competent jurists, were almost at a standstill, quite half the total number of cases were never heard at all except in the courts-martial, which were absolutely dependent on the military leaders. These courts-martial became the most active dispensers of justice, and composed as they were of men who for the most part lacked the most rudimentary knowledge of the law, they often committed the grossest errors which were irreparable, and which undermined the very foundations of the idea of justice and legality. Thus the good name of Justice was compromised.

My order of April 6th decreed that henceforth judicial proceedings should depend not on the goodwill of the military authorities, but on the attorney, who was to present the indictment to a competent tribunal, at the same time informing the accused's immediate superior, so that he could issue the necessary order.

Parallel to other measures for the stamping out of pillaging and brigandage, an order of April 14th set up special commissions with military jurisdiction for the commanders of garrisons and fortresses, and later on for the general staffs of Army Corps, divisions, and isolated brigades. These commissions, consisting of a president and five members, were selected as far as possible from men who had had a special legal education, the secretary had to be one of these. They were directly subordinate to the Attorney-General. Cases of murder, pillaging, theft, illegal requisitioning, and any other illegal action against the inhabitants of the area, if committed by a soldier, all came within their competence.

The geographical limits of each commission's authority were the boundaries of the district, or alternatively it took cognizance of crimes committed by any member of a particular military formation. A little later, the better to guarantee the interests of the civil population, representatives of the peasants were also put on the commissions. Every volost (district) was entitled to two representatives with deliberative powers and the right to be present at judicial inquiries, the chief commission had to record in a special *proces-verbal* all the opinions expressed by the representatives of the volost, and act on them if they were not contrary to the law and could be executed without prejudice to the inquiry.

The trial was conducted by one of the members of the commission, who had the powers of a police-court magistrate, but was not bound to observe all the formalities that the law had provided for judicial proceedings of earlier days.

It is true that this arrangement led to a certain amount of confusion between the functions of the attorney and the judge, but this was inevitable owing to the conditions under which the commissions worked: they had to have full powers and independence to ensure quick and decisive action. Nevertheless, the member of the commission who had conducted the examination did not have a voice in the final verdict. As for procedure, the special commissions had to adopt the system on which the courts-martial worked. The verdicts had to be ratified by competent military chiefs, if these did not agree with the verdict, the case passed to the Army Corps tribunal, or to that of the military district.

Throughout the whole period of the struggle in the Crimea, these commissions with military jurisdiction rendered invaluable services to the Government in its campaign against the various abuses which were corrupting the Army. Pillaging by the troops ceased almost entirely. Besides the testimonial of numerous impartial witnesses, I also received a whole series of resolutions adopted by village assemblies, thanking me for having set up these commissions which had delivered the people from extortion and pillaging; these bore witness to the utility of the commissions better than any words of mine can do. Even the section of the Crimean Press which had denounced the commissions at first finally recognized their usefulness.

Other edicts excluded cases against minors between the ages of ten and seventeen from the competence of the courts-martial, and prohibited public executions. In view of the prevailing callousness, public executions no longer served to intimidate, they merely aggravated the existing state of moral apathy.

Our political position was still uncertain. On April 6th-19th Admiral Seymour sent me the following Note—

> The Admiralty begs to inform you that on Saturday, April 17th, Lord Curzon sent a telegram to M. Chicherin saying that although the Armed Forces of South Russia have been defeated, they cannot be allowed to go on to disaster, and that should M. Chicherin not reply without delay that he is at least ready to accept Lord Curzon's mediation and suspend all further offensive action in the south, His

> Majesty's Government will be obliged to order His Majesty's Fleet to take all necessary steps for the protection of the Crimean Army and the prevention of the invasion of their place of retreat by the Soviet forces.

At the same time General Mangin, chief of the French Mission, wrote to Struve—

> As a result of our conversation of today, I have the honor to enclose an extract from the telegram from the Minister of Marine of the French Republic, which I have already sent to General Baron Wrangel—
>
> "The French Government will act in concert with the British Government in supporting General Wrangel with material help, so that he will not be forced to make an armistice with the Soviet on their conditions, but will be in a position to make a proper treaty on behalf of his Army."

On April 11-24th Neiatov, our diplomatic representative at Constantinople, telegraphed—

> According to a Bolshevist radiogram, Curzon has sent an ultimatum to Moscow, an armistice is to be signed with the Volunteer Army, and if hostilities continue, he threatens intervention by the English Fleet. Chicherin has agreed to begin peace negotiations immediately.

But five days later, General Percy, Head of the English Mission, sent me the following Note—

> BRITISH MILITARY MISSION'S HEADQUARTERS
>
> SEBASTOPOL,
>
> *April* 29, 1920
>
> YOUR EXCELLENCY,
>
> General Milne, Commander-in-Chief of the Black Sea Army, charges me to communicate to you the following message from Lord Curzon to Admiral de Robeck, High Commissioner—
>
> "The answers that we have received from M. Chicherin in reference to our attempts to make terms for General Wrangel's Crimean Forces have not been encouraging up to now. Instead of stating the Soviet's conditions, as we asked him to do, Chicherin is trying to obtain further political concessions which we cannot grant him. Therefore we are powerless for the moment to obtain what General Wrangel demands. Should we be unable to make terms for

him, as seems probable, the only alternative is for him to do what he can for himself. Should General Wrangel prolong the struggle, it can have only one result, and we cannot encourage it by subsidies in money or kind."

BRIGADIER-GENERAL PERCY,
Chief of the British Military Mission

TO HIS EXCELLENCY THE COMMANDER-IN-CHIEF
OF THE ARMED FORCES OF SOUTH RUSSIA

In the meantime, negotiations between the Poles and the Bolshevists had been broken off, and the Polish troops had launched an offensive and thrust back the Reds all along the front, therefore they hastily concentrated all their forces on the western front. The fall of the Crimea would leave the Red Command free to concentrate all their efforts against the Poles. France, who invariably supported Poland, had naturally realized this, therefore the French Government would not sympathize with the new English policy. On my initiative, Struve telegraphed to our Ambassador in Paris, V. A. Maklakov, and asked him to sound the French Government as to their intentions.

Maklakov telegraphed on April 18th-May 1st—

> French Government hostile to Entente with Bolshevists, will not use any pressure to secure capitulation of Crimea. Will not participate in any mediation aiming at this, even if others undertake it. Sympathizes with idea of defending Crimea and the Tauric Province. French Government considers Bolshevism to be Russia's principal enemy, and therefore sympathizes with Polish offensive. Will not countenance idea of a camouflaged annexation of the Dnieper area. If a Ukrainian Government is set up, will only recognize it *de facto.*

I answered the British Government's Note of April 16-29th by a letter to General Percy on April 16th-May 2nd—

> On April 2nd the British Government invited General Denikin to end the Civil War, warning him that if he did not comply they would withdraw their support from the Armed Forces of South Russia
>
> I had become Commander-in-Chief by then, so I informed the British Government that since I had no choice but to obey their demand, I surrendered the Army, the Navy, and the population of South Russia to the good offices of His Britannic Majesty's

Government. I believed we could trust them implicitly to regard it as a question of honor to save all those who did not wish to accept the enemy's mercy. I indicated at the same time that it was absolutely impossible for us to negotiate directly with the enemy.

Lord Curzon's communication to M. Chicherin, which Admiral Seymour sent on to me, contains an explicit declaration that should the Soviet Government refuse to accept English mediation, or should there be a fresh offensive on the southern front, the British Government will order its ships to protect my Army and avert a Soviet invasion of the refuge which the Armed Forces of South Russia have found in the Crimea.

In your letter of April 29th you communicated to me the gist of Lord Curzon's message to the British High Commissioner at Constantinople. It seems that M. Chicherin has brought forward certain political claims which are unacceptable, and that therefore the British Government has decided that the only possible course still open is for me to try and obtain for myself the conditions I want from the Soviet Government.

I cannot believe that the British Government now intends to renounce the role of mediator which it assumed on learning that I could not possibly enter into direct negotiations with the enemy.

I realize the difficulties of the situation in which the Kubanian troops now find themselves, isolated as they are along the shores of the Caucasian, and I have authorized Ataman General Bukretov to negotiate for himself, releasing him from the obligation which binds him in his capacity of Ataman to enter into no separate negotiation or arrangement. General Bukretov, forced to open negotiations with the Bolshevists under peculiarly unfavorable conditions, has asked me today to send him transport enough for at least ten thousand men, so that he will be in a position to transfer those who refuse to yield to the Soviet power to the Crimea. I am arranging to do as he asks.

This incident is one more proof that neither amnesty nor promise of any kind will bring peace to Bolshevist Russia if the people themselves are not willing to tolerate the Bolshevist rule. The popular insurrection in the upper Don in the April of last year in which forty thousand Cossacks took part, and which was headed exclusively by non-commissioned officers except for just one Cossack officer of higher rank, and the rising which has just begun in Eisk and Timochevka on territory recently occupied by the Bolshevists, just at the moment when the Ataman and the Kuban Government are opening negotiations, are also witnesses.

> The sole method of saving Russia from permanent anarchy is to preserve a healthy nucleus around which all the movements which have broken away from the tyranny of Bolshevism by brute force can group themselves. Russia cannot be saved from the danger which threatens to engulf her and all Europe by another march on Moscow, but by the union of all the popular anti-Communist forces. Hence the integrity of the territory occupied by the Armed Forces of South Russia, as well as of the Cossack territories, is a fundamental necessity if we are to attain the goal that the Allies have set up—the goal that is really incumbent upon the whole civilized world, i.e. the ending of the Civil War and of Russian anarchy.
>
> To facilitate the British Government's negotiations with the Soviet, I propose to send special delegates to London—men who understand the present situation in my territories and the Cossack States, and who know my intentions.
>
> Finally, I think I ought to point out to the British Government, as well as to all the Powers of the Entente, the danger which they themselves run from the situation they have created by their decision to deprive me and my Army of all support at this critical moment. This decision was not made as a result of any action of mine. Their action is equivalent to a victory for the Soviet Powers and a capitulation to Communism, and it will of necessity influence the feelings of the Russian people who will not compromise with the Soviets, towards the Allies in future.
>
> Will you be good enough to transmit this to His Britannic Majesty's Government.

In mid-April, the Bolsheviks resumed the offensive in Caucasia and occupied Sotchy. General Morozov, the commander of the Kubanian Army, and some members of the Rada began to negotiate with the Bolshevists with General Bukretov's consent.

When I heard this, I ordered all our available tonnage to be sent to the port of Adler, and sent an urgent petition to Admiral de Robeck for the cooperation of the English Fleet. General Chkouro was just leaving for Adler too, so I entrusted him with the task of commanding those troops which should refuse to negotiate with the Bolshevists and of transferring them to the Crimea. The embarkation was effected by means of rowing-boats, under the most difficult conditions, the men were put on to Russian transport-ships and English men-of-war. Horses, big guns, and machine-guns had to be abandoned. Only the Don Cossacks had reached the Crimea after the evacuation of Novorossiisk. This time I ordered the Kubanian Cossacks to be embarked first. General Bukretov and Morozov and members of the Kubanian Government and Rada had persuaded officers and Cossacks that the Crimea was an ambush, and that within a few days all the units of the Army there would be forced to capitulate.

The embarkation was finished on April 19th, and the ships sailed for the Crimea. Many of the Kubanian Cossacks did capitulate, a small minority took refuge in the mountains, and the rest embarked, as the majority of the Don regiments and the brigade of Terek and Astrakhan Cossacks had done.

General Bukretov himself resigned his Atamanship, giving up his insignia to the President of the Government, in accordance with the laws of the constitution. The President, the engineer Ivanis, fled to Georgia. He was followed by the Separatist members of the Kuban Rada, who took part of the regional funds with them.

On April 21st the troops who had been evacuated from the Caucasian coast reached Feodossia. I went over there the next day to review the regiments and chat with the officers. Most of the officers and Cossacks were my old comrades-in-arms who had fought under my command in Northern Caucasia, before Tsaritsin. Only the most tenacious fighters had been sent to the Crimea, those who had lost their faith or their courage had remained on the coasts of Caucasia. Everyone who had just arrived was furious at the treason of the Ataman and the Separatist members of the Rada. I felt sure that the Cossack regiments, purged of traitors and cowards, freed from the disintegrating influence of demagogues in the Rada, trusting to energetic officers, and rested and re-equipped with all they needed, would once more become those admirable units which had fought the enemy so grimly in Northern Caucasia and on the Don.

The Don regiments were sent to Eupatona to join up with the Don Army Corps. The Kubanian units were reduced to one division, and the Terek and Astrakhan brigade was attached to it. I put gallant General Babiev at its head.

Babiev was one of the most brilliant cavalry generals in South Russia. He was brave and exceptionally high-spirited, and had a rare instinct for commanding cavalry. He was himself a first-class horseman, a *djignite*, to use the Caucasian term, and was adored by the officers and Cossacks. He had always been victorious whether he was commanding a regiment, a brigade, or a division. His cavalry charges always threw the enemy's ranks into confusion. During the Great War and the Civil War, General Babiev, who was always to be found in the most dangerous places, had been wounded nineteen times. His right arm was shorter than the other, but in spite of all his wounds he had kept his irrepressible spirits. An ardent Russian patriot, he was highly indignant at the anti-national intrigues of the Cossack Separatists. I could set my mind at rest about the units he was commanding.

Some days before my journey to Feodossia I had inspected the regiments of the Don Army Corps at Eupatoria. General Abramov was now at their head, he was an extremely brave man and incorruptibly honest, a very resolute leader, and an exceptionally tactful one. By birth he was a Don

Cossack, by education a staff-officer. Before the Revolution he had commanded a division of regiments-of-the-line, and for a long time had been quartermaster-general to one of the armies. He had also commanded a brigade of Cossacks-of-the-Guard in South Russia, where he was deservedly held in high esteem. Now at the head of an Army Corps, he was rooting out all the germs of disorder with a firm hand. He had discharged quite a number of superior officers and improved the morale of officers and Cossacks. I had no doubt that in a very short time he would restore the Army Corps to order and make it fit for battle.

On this same journey I went from Eupatona to the front, where the units of the Crimean and Volunteer Army Corps were stationed. The regrouping which I had initiated had been carried out. The Crimean Army Corps was arranged in echelons along the railway in the Salkovo district, the Volunteers were occupying the fort below Perekop The students from the military schools who had fought in the ranks of General Slachtchov's troops had been separated out, and it was made possible for these young men, some of them still almost children, whose lives were so precious to Russia, to continue their studies The front-line units who had had time to rest, clean up, and fit themselves out, seemed cheerful and confident. Fortifications were going forward rapidly, trenches were being dug, machine-gun emplacements constructed, and barbed-wire entanglements put up. Behind the lines similar work was being done just as actively, and strategical railroads were being constructed with feverish haste.

Discipline was much better, especially in the big towns. I insisted relentlessly that all the garrison officers should take the most energetic measures to put down disorders and slackness amongst the soldiers behind-the-lines. I gave orders that all those who were fit to fight were not to leave their units without real justification, and that all the wounded who had quite recovered were to leave hospital and return to the front immediately. I also insisted on the observation of the rules concerning uniform.

On April 28th I issued an edict, changing the name of the Volunteer Army to that of the Russian Army. The Army Corps were to be known by numbers, and the Cossack troops by the name of the district from which they came.

The name "Volunteer" had been extended from the Army to include the policy of those who directed it. It no longer meant certain military units, it had become the common name for the whole movement of which General Denikin had been the leader. The "Volunteerist" party, Press, and Powers had become current terms.

Glorious though it had been in the past, associated as it was with the early progress and heroic struggles of Generals Alexeiev and Kornilov, the term "Volunteerism," which had been so dear to all participants in the struggle, had with time lost its old attraction. It had been discredited in public opinion and even in the Army because of the policy of General Denikin and his closest colleagues, the contemptible behavior of criminal elements which had infested the Army, and the fatal conflict between the "Volunteerist" High Command and the Cossacks. Of the two armies fighting in Russia, the right to the name "The Russian Army" belonged to the one composed of men who had remained loyal to the national flag, sacrificing everything for the welfare and honor of their country. Obviously the name "Russian Army" could not be given to troops whose leaders had replaced the Russian tricolour with the Red flag, and the very name of Russia with the name International.

It is true that there were also many honest Russians in the ranks of the Red Army, which was not as it had been two years previously. During the struggle in Northern Caucasia the Bolshevist troops had consisted of all the shady characters which the eddy of the Revolution had thrown up from the lowest social strata. They were the very worst elements which has demoralized and disintegrated the Russian Army. Such a foe deserved no mercy. But in the later stages of the struggle both sides had been forced to use conscription, after that, the same elements were to be found in both armies, their presence in one or the other depended largely on chance geographical circumstances.

My predecessor had not reckoned with this factor. His narrow and uncompromising policy had persecuted not only all those whose ideas differed from his own, but also everyone who had dealings of any kind with hostile organizations, or even with organizations not sufficiently favorable to the volunteer cause. He had hunted down not only those who had been in touch with the Bolshevists in some way or another, perhaps against their will, but also anyone who had been connected with the Ukraine, the Georgian Republic, and so on. This insane and cruel policy provoked a reaction, alienated those who had been ready to become our allies, and turned into enemies those who had sought our friendship. We had not brought pardon and peace with us, but the cruel sword of vengeance. An incredible number of officers who had welcomed us as their liberators came under our command only to fall a prey to our suspicion, and to languish under interminable inquiries. The same relationship had been established with the civil population in the recently occupied territories. Everyone became suspect, were their crime no greater than that of having sold to the Reds, of their own free will, means of transport for the conveyance of food, or of having accepted a post as clerk in a food cooperative centre or a telegraph bureau because they were dying of hunger.

By an edict of April 29th I freed all the officers and soldiers who had given themselves up and come over to our side before or during the struggle, from every kind of proceeding and service-restriction, as well as all those who had served previously in the Soviet Army, and who had, therefore, already undergone punishment and service-restrictions after the territory had been occupied by the Armed Forces of South Russia of their own free will; they were all reinstated in the ranks and privileges they had held on December 1, 1917. At the same time, all the officers and soldiers who had served the new States, Ukraine and Georgia, and who had undergone punishment and restrictions on that account, were exempt from all further punishment or service-restrictions.

By an edict of June 8th these concessions were also extended to the staffs of institutions and the civil administration.

At the end of May, I addressed the following appeal to the officers of the Red Army—

> Officers of the Red Army! I, General Wrangel, have taken over the command of the remains of the Russian Army. Not Red—but Russian! The Army which, not long ago, was still powerful and terrible to its enemies, and in the ranks of which many of you served.
>
> Russian officers have always served their country loyally and courageously, they have died that she might be happy. They are part of one united family. Three years ago the Russian Army forgot its duty and opened the gates to the enemy, and the frenzied people began to burn and pillage their own native land.
>
> Now our Mother Russia lies before us—ruined, dishonored, and covered with the blood of fratricidal warfare.
>
> For three terrible years those officers who remained loyal to their sacred traditions have been treading the path to Calvary to save the honor and welfare of the country whose own sons have brought shame upon her. These blind, unconscious sons were under your command, one-time officers of the invincible Russian Army!
>
> What has led you to follow this shameful course? What is it that has brought you to raise your hand against your old comrades-in-arms, your regimental colleagues?
>
> I have spoken to many of your number who have left the Red Army of their own free will. They all tell that mortal terror, hunger, and fear for the future impelled them to serve the Red scoundrels. Few men are capable of greatness of soul and total self-abnegation. Many of them tell me that at the bottom of their hearts they feel that they have fallen very low, but their fear of reprisals prevents them from coming over to us.
>
> I like to think that amongst you Red officers there are still some honest men in whose hearts love of country is not dead.
>
> I call upon you to join us, so that you may atone for your shame and once more join the ranks of the Russian Army—the true Russian Army.
>
> I, General Wrangel, Commander-in-Chief at this moment, give you the word of an old officer who has given the best years of his

life to his country, that I will forget the past and give you an opportunity to atone for your errors.

Regent and Commander-in-Chief of the Armed Forces of South Russia
GENERAL WRANGEL

I ordered this proclamation to be distributed as widely as possible amongst the enemy; it was conveyed across the frontier by our agents, and dropped from aeroplanes as though it were a tract.

The difficulties of the agents of the military and civil administration worried me very much. The ever-increasing cost of living caused them much suffering, especially if they had families. I issued successive orders increasing their rations and providing help for the families of those who had died or been taken prisoner or abandoned during the evacuation of Odessa and Novorossiisk.

Simultaneously I began to reduce the staff of officials which had swollen to impossibly high numbers, take steps to get a bigger yield from the revenue, and raise the Customs duties and other taxes.

But the trouble still continued to fall. The little territory of the Crimea could not possibly feed the Army, there were no exports, and consumption exceeded production. M. Bernatzky, Minister of Finance, was quite right when he said that only a foreign loan could bolster up the rouble, but under the prevailing conditions we could not be sure of getting a loan.

As the cost of living rose, things grew difficult for the urban population, especially the workmen. The hostile elements in our midst profited from this at once, and for some days past a certain amount of excitement had been noticeable amongst the factory hands of Sebastopol; they were organizing a strike. If this materialized, we would be in a dreadful position; the factories were doing urgently necessary work, repairing artillery and machine-guns, and preparing aircraft bombs and equipment for the fortifications.

Except for the Cossack Regiment-of-the-Guard, there were no troops in Sebastopol. I decided to speak to the hands myself. I sent for their delegates and had a long interview with them. I told them that since April 9th the Directors' Council of the Administration had been considering how they could assist the workmen, and that at this very moment the Commission which was studying the question had decided to raise the laborers' wages to the same level as that of the lower officials. In future, workmen's wages were to be raised whenever the salaries of these officials were raised, and in the same proportion. The wages fixed in this way were to serve as a basis for the calculation of the salaries of skilled employees. Furthermore, the laborers were to be given clothing and food from the Military Commissariat's reserve supplies, which would not be needed at the front. Prices were to be at the

Military Commissariat's usual rates. The balance on the clothes was to be payable in a year's time, and only half the price of the food was to be paid on purchase. A scheme had been drawn up arranging for the opening of governmental shops in the towns and workmen's centres, which were to sell the necessities of life, the maximum available amount of provisions, manufactures, and other necessary merchandise was to be concentrated in these shops. They were to sell goods to workmen at reduced prices up to the value of ten per cent of their monthly wages. To begin with, two such shops were to be opened in Sebastopol. And finally, I informed the workmen of the hopeless state of our treasury and the inadequacy of our resources, and expressed my belief that they would appreciate all that the Army was doing for them, for it was sharing its last farthing[1] with them, and that they would support their efforts by continuing their work.

When the workmen left me they were obviously satisfied. The strike did not take place, and future attempts at agitation met with no success.

[1] A "farthing" is an old British coin equivalent to one quarter of a penny or 1/960th of a pound sterling—PUBLISHER

CHAPTER X

THE AGRARIAN PROBLEM AND THE DISTRICT ZEMSTVO[1]

The Agrarian Reform Commission under the presidency of Senator Glinka, ex-adjutant to the Ministry of Agriculture and ex-director of the Emigration Department, had begun its work in Yalta, in co-operation with an Agrarian Reform Commission and a special committee in Simferopol, and was working very actively. But from the beginning a storm of discussion had arisen over the Commission's scope. The Press, representatives of the "democratic" societies, and the "conservative" supporters of big landed estates, had all stated their own particular point of view with considerable violence. Some claimed recognition of "the conquests of the Revolution" and the free re-allotment amongst the poor peasants of all land belonging to the State or private owners. Others did not favor forcible appropriation, but wanted compensation for the dispossessed, declaring that "property is sacred," and that restrictions of any kind imposed on big properties could only hinder the economic regeneration of the country. It was not easy for the Commission to proceed with its work in such an atmosphere of discord, especially as its members were themselves in disagreement. The Commission did not consider itself competent to settle the agrarian question for the whole of Russia, and furthermore, it was not capable of estimating the influence that certain agricultural measures would have on the fight against Bolshevism under prevailing revolutionary conditions. In its efforts to steer a middle course and find some sort of solution, the Commission confined its work to elaborating measures which applied only to the Crimea (especially to the Northern districts which were rich in land) and which were adapted to local needs.

Newspapers mentioning the work of the Agrarian Commission found their way across the Red frontier. Peasants from the southern districts of Northern Taurida sneaked across the frontier and came to Sebastopol. They told us something about the situation and the opinion of the peasants beyond the frontier; they wanted to know how the new Commander-in-Chief proposed to deal with the land question and the problem of local government.

I invited some who called themselves representatives of the peasant Soviets to come and see me, and I had a long and detailed interview with

---

[1] Zemstvo = Effective District Council.

them. Later, I ordered Senator Glinka to coordinate and tabulate their demands, so that the Commission could take them into account, provided that they were not opposed to any of our general principles. The peasants told me that the whole population of their district was tired of the Soviet system and Communism—all, that is, except the beggars and the disorderly elements. The peasants wanted peace, order, and a normal state of affairs to be restored to the countryside. They wanted laws concerning the land and self-government to be promulgated, putting local government and the administration of the land into their own hands, they promised to act wisely, economically, and justly, without cheating anyone or destroying the large landed estates which were still intact. On these conditions only, they declared, would the peasants agree to recognize the cause of the Russian Army as their own and as the national popular cause.

These interviews caused me to make up my mind. I immediately told Senator Glinka to draft an Agrarian Law as soon as he could, and indicated its main outlines to him.

A glance at the general situation will show the urgent need there was for these measures. Throughout the territory which had been occupied for nearly a year by the Volunteer Army, as well as throughout that which had not come under General Denikin's legislative measures, total uncertainty reigned as to the legal situation, whilst lack of security in the countryside had led to complete economic disorder.

The revolutionary wave which had engulfed the landed property of the nobility had also demolished the bases of the agrarian organization of pre-revolutionary Russia. It had swept away the estate-owning aristocrats, but at the same time it had torn the small peasant proprietors from their small plots of land, ruined the farmers, disorganized lease-arrangements, and carried to the height of their power those obscure forces which called themselves the "poor peasantry;" these creatures preyed on the countryside, terrorizing all the hard-working populace, and relied for support on the Soviet Power.

Abstract considerations on one side, actual conditions did not at the moment permit of a restoration of the old system, pure and simple. The old arrangements were all disorganized, the evaluations destroyed, and the conditions of recruitment of manual labor changed; there was no longer any standard for the assessment of rural leases, whilst the personal safety of country landowners was by no means assured.

The prime necessity was to reinstate the hard-working peasants and set them up on their land again, to weld them together and rally them to the defence of order and national principles. It was an especially good opportunity to make a favorable impression on the peasants, and snatch away the enemy's principal weapon of propaganda against the White Army and its cause. We had to allay the peasants' suspicion that our object in fighting the

Reds was no other than to restore the rights of the great landed proprietors, and take reprisals against those who had infringed these rights.

I decided on the plan of publishing a Prikaze concerning the Land, based on the pressing needs of life as I had already defined them in my dispatch of April 8th. This Prikaze had to be elaborated, promulgated, and executed without further delay if the peasants were to know what the Russian Army which was freeing them from the Bolshevist yoke could and would do for them. The White Movement had to define its attitude to the agrarian question in an unmistakable manner, and emphasize the sincerity of the National Power's intentions.

The fundamental principles of the reform were set out later in some of my dispatches—

> The land for the people, and liberty in the structure of the State (Prikaze of May 20th, No. 3226)

And again—

> The owners of the land shall direct local administration, and be responsible for its management and good order (Prikaze of July 15th, No. 94)

As soon as he received my instructions and official order, Senator Glinka proceeded with the work I had entrusted to him, and soon finished it. Towards the middle of May, the first drafts of the Land and Local Government Laws were ready, and I had ratified them. Later, they were discussed by my Council, under my presidency. By May 18th G. V. Glinka had communicated his drafts to the members of the Council, and I suggested that they should express their opinion on the main points. Opinions differed very much. The majority were alarmed by the size of the task, and feared the obstacles that stood in the way of its realization. Only the military members of the Council, who reflected the opinion of the Army and were supported by the commanders of the troops at the front, fully realized the important psychological effects that the immediate promulgation of this measure would have on the Army and the civil population.

A. V. Krivochein arrived two days later, and he too understood the psychological importance of the decision I had taken, here again he displayed his keen sense of political realities and the elasticity of his mind.

"This draft is far from perfect," said M. Krivochein, "but it will make the success of the Army easier and will win the sympathies of the peasants. Since the Army is expecting a decisive pronouncement on the agrarian question, there is no time to be lost, life itself will add all the necessary amendments in the future." He did insist, however, that the "Prikaze concerning the Land" should be published in the form of a dispatch, and advised me to call the Agrarian Commissions provided for in the Law "Agrarian Soviets." A dispatch drawn up in the martial atmosphere of a military camp was not expected to be so perfect in form as a law promulgated under normal conditions.

The Prikaze concerning the Land was published on May 25, 1920, together with an official *communique* giving a detailed explanation of the causes and conditions which had inspired its promulgation, and indicating its tenor and importance.

It was promulgated, together with the Regulations and the Temporary Statute which was attached to it, on June 27th in a slightly altered form. It was done by means of a ukase of the Senate which was functioning as three departments; it had been reconstituted in the Don area under General Denikin's Government, and had since been transferred to Yalta.

The Senate had deemed it useful to add the following declarations to its ukase—

> The Prikaze of the Regent, who possesses plenary powers, gives the land to its cultivators, who will till it in perpetual hereditary ownership, but they are not to obtain it free of all charge. The new owners will have to pay the State, who will reserve the proceeds as compensation for the old owners.
>
> Such a process of change, redivision, and final reallotment of the land fits in with our people's conception of justice, and with the historical development of Imperial agrarian legislation.
>
> From now on, a regular agrarian system and the material well-being of the workers on the land will be assured to the countryside. The new law will be executed with the cooperation of the cultivators themselves, under the supreme control of the Regent and Commander-in-Chief.
>
> The object of the agrarian law is the general welfare of the State, and it will serve as the basis of Russia's economic power.
>
> Henceforth the disputes, the discontent, the many dissensions over the agrarian question, will be silenced! Every loyal son of our martyred country is bound not only by law, but by conscience, to use all his strength and wisdom to forget his personal interests, and cooperate with the Regent and Commander-in-Chief in putting the Land Law into effect as quickly and as completely as possible.

The entire agrarian reform was based on one idea—the consolidation of the law of private property without distinction of social class. It is true that a change of owners was provided for. Landed property was to undergo a new division, because national interest always takes precedence over the interests of private property. Nevertheless, the new agrarian system was based on the solid bond which binds the owner to his land—his right of ownership, which not only leaves him in safe possession to enjoy it, but gives him the right to dispose of it freely. Furthermore, until an effective redivision took place, he had the right to ask for an allotment of his part of the land.

All the land which passed to the owner-cultivators was to become their own property on condition that they paid an indemnity to the State, this was assessed at a rate favorable to the purchasers, and gave wide facilities for easy payment.

The selecting of the landowners who had the right to share in the redivision of land and the fixing of the maximum size of the lots, was to be done by the local representatives of the land, the Agrarian Soviets of each district. The composition of these Soviets was such that the peasant proprietors, the most stable element of the rural population, acquired a decisive voice in the adaptation of the law to local economic conditions.

The Prikaze concerning the Land, therefore, rejected the idea of making a general reallotment of the land, or of making a free gift of it. It did not promise a portion of land to everybody who wanted some, nor did it undertake to transform the whole rural proletariat into landowners, not to mention the urban proletariat who had lost all contact with agriculture. Furthermore, it negatived the idea of a redistribution of all the land on a national scale, aiming at the equality of all cultivators, and provided for in one law applicable to every province of Russia. On the contrary, each district was to decide for itself the question of redistribution of land within its own boundaries. This local character was the outstanding characteristic of the Prikaze, and combined all the practical advantages as well as the disadvantages of the system. It was the very opposite of those huge, unrealizable schemes for a general redistribution of all the land amongst all the people, which would necessitate the forcible transfer of great masses of the rural population from north to south and from west to east, across one-sixth of the surface of the globe.

Because no maximum size for property had been fixed, the possibility of retaining some of the old estates cropped up, especially if, in the opinion of the people of a district, local conditions demanded their maintenance in the interests of internal peace and the stability of the local economic system.

The actual holders of the land coming within the scope of the Prikaze were to pay their redemption fee into the treasury in corn or coin. Payments were due from the moment when the Prikaze was applied to the land of a given district, without waiting for the completion of all the formalities of consolidation. These payments were to be discharged afterwards by instalments to be fixed when the property was consolidated, and were to continue until the sum due to the State for the repurchase of the land had been paid off. In the case of nonpayment after a specified period, the plot of ground, consolidated or not, which was held by a defaulter, was to be handed over to another by permission of the Agrarian Soviet, and this new holder could claim consolidation of the property for himself (Arts. 8 and 10 of the Prikaze).

The head of the Financial Department was requested to draw up and present to the Commander-in-Chief for ratification with all possible speed, a draft of the bases for the assessments, the formulae and time-limits which were to govern the relations between the state financiers and the owners who took over land, expropriation, and ways of recovery by the Treasury of sums of money used in this relationship. This question of payments seemed to be the only one which would provoke some discontent. The peasants had nothing against the principle of repurchase, but they did not appreciate the advantages to themselves and the disadvantages to the State involved in the system of payment in corn, and insisted that the repurchase prices were too high and must be reduced.

The methods for applying the Prikaze were planned on the one hand to avoid any arbitrary proceedings against those who had taken possession of the land during the Revolution, and to prevent any future illegal seizure, and on the other, to enable the reform to be carried through with the minimum amount of damage to rural economy, which was still sound in some places, and without mining existing cultivation or decreasing the agricultural output. Paragraph i of the Prikaze enunciated the principle that in the regions occupied by the Russian Army "all de facto possession of agricultural land, independently of its legal title and the person of the possessor, is to be protected against violent seizure. All land is to remain in the possession of those who are working it, or using it in any other way." Thus the Land Law could be applied automatically to the whole area occupied by the Russian Army from the moment of its submission to the authority of the Commander-in-Chief, without a special order being enacted. Existing de facto possession was declared inviolable. It was the starting-point for all subsequent applications of the Prikaze.

In accordance with the Temporary Statute of Agrarian Institutions, each District Agrarian Soviet was to be composed of five or ten members whom the District Agrarian Assemblies were to elect, the members themselves were to elect one of their number as president. The officials, such as the surveyors and agronomists, were to be attached to the Agrarian Soviets as their technical advisers, but they were to have only consultative powers (Temp. Stat, Arts 2,5,6, and 8).

The District Agrarian Soviets, under the presidency of the local agrarian mediator, were to be composed of the President of the Zemstvo of the same district, the Justice of the Peace, a delegate from the Ministry of Finance, and at least four representatives elected by the District Agrarian Assemblies (Temp. Stat., Art. 10).

To these two institutions, one composed exclusively of representatives of the local population and the other of more than half, I gave the widest powers for the application of the Prikaze. They were to settle every question, oversee the organization of inquiries, fix standards, settle cultivators' rights to the confirmation of their claims of ownership, redistribute the land, set up boundaries between the allotments, return to its lawful owner land which had been acquired illegally, and do a dozen other things.

So that the Central Authorities should retain sufficient influence over the course of the reform, it was stipulated that the decisions of the District Agrarian Soviets could be annulled by their superiors, the provincial authorities, but only in case of a breach of the general laws and by order of the administration, or in the lawful interests of private persons, society, or the State (Temp Stat, Art 14).

The Prikaze, therefore, very effectively submitted the whole agrarian problem to the decision of the agricultural population itself. The functions of the Government officials who were to superintend agrarian questions and of the official mediators for the districts and provinces were limited to consolidating the work of the district agrarian institutions and supporting them in their activities so long as these were within the law.

On July 15th my Prikaze concerning the Local Zemstvo was published.

PRIKAZE ISSUED BY THE REGENT AND COMMANDER-IN-CHIEF OF THE ARMED FORCES OF SOUTH RUSSIA

SEBASTOPOL.. No 94. July 15-28, 1920.
(Civil Branch of the Administration.)

The remission of the land in full ownership to the cultivators who work on it, and the division of the great estates into small holdings, necessitates a modification of the structure of the Zemstvo.

The large new class of small landowners drawn from the erstwhile laboring class must be given a part in the difficult and responsible work of restoring the Zemstvos to regular working order again.

Those with land are to control local institutions and be responsible for their good order and management. I consider that only a Zemstvo organization based on this principle can be of any real help in the rebuilding of the State.

I am convinced that the great mass of the peasants who are now called upon to play a predominating part in the new organization of the Zemstvos will respond unanimously to this appeal, using their best efforts for the work, and will collaborate in the work I require of them for the welfare of their country. Until some National Power can promulgate a general and definitive Statute concerning the Zemstvo, this Temporary Statute is to be introduced into all territory occupied by the troops of the Commander-in-Chief of the Armed Forces of South Russia.

(Signed) GENERAL WRANGEL.
SENATOR GLINKA.

The elaboration of the regulations for the constitution was worked out in cooperation with representatives from the Zemstvos together with several experts.

The leading ideas of the Prikaze concerning the Land were expounded in a masterly fashion in an interview which my adjutant, M. Krivochein, ex-Minister of Agriculture, gave to the editor of a newspaper called the *Velikaia Rossia.* It appeared in the form of an editorial called "Launched on the Agricultural Campaign".

> The Commander-in-Chief (said M. Krivochein) is calling new forces into free and creative action, he is posing the question of decentralization of local administration on a huge scale, for a large new class of small landowners has been created and consolidated by the Prikaze concerning the Land.
>
> I have certain knowledge that these measures, together with other circumstances, have induced France to recognize our Government, and General Denikin could not obtain this recognition even when his troops had advanced as far as Orel, nor Admiral Koltchak when he was master of all Siberia
>
> The Prikaze concerning the Land obliges us to proceed to a second measure: the reorganization of the administration and the local Zemstvo.
>
> The Commander-in-Chief has boldly decided to give the small peasant proprietor a share in the control of the local Zemstvos. The modest title of this law somewhat obscures the enormous importance of the general reform of the Zemstvos which we have planned.
>
> The Revolution has uprooted all the foundations and modified all the conditions of life.
>
> We realize clearly that the forms of local administration must also be modified.
>
> After our law is passed, the district will become the centre of the Zemstvos' activity.
>
> Considering the enormous size of Russia, this measure alone is a very progressive step. We are giving the small peasant proprietors

> not only the management of the Zemstvo, but also administrative powers.
>
> Our legislation is thus more advanced than any other in Western Europe.
>
> As to the district Zemstvo, in future it is to exercise the functions of the provincial Zemstvo.
>
> We are prepared to go even farther on the same lines.
>
> What will be the attitude of the small landowners and peasant classes towards national and cultural problems now that they have a hand in the administration of the Zemstvo? The whole future depends on the answer. Can these classes surmount the difficulties of their task? Can they take care of the Church? What will happen to the schools, the hospitals, and Justice, under their rule? The course of all future reforms depends on this.
>
> I have worked with P. A. Stolypin (added M. Krivochein) at improving economic conditions for the Russian rural population, and I have great faith in its patriotism. I want to keep my faith.
>
> Very soon we will take the daring but necessary step of laying the foundations of the future Zemstvos and the Russian State.
>
> We believe that it will lead to the recovery of the creative forces of national culture.

After this information reached them, the Army and the peasants gave the Temporary Statute concerning the Zemstvo and the Prikaze concerning the Land a very good reception.

Right up to the last moment of our occupation of our native soil the peasants were very favorably disposed towards our troops. The population realized that the Authorities really did want to be guided by popular opinion, and were doing their utmost to put into execution the measures they had drafted.

When our troops left the Crimea, the new agrarian system and the Zemstvo Statute, conceived, elaborated, promulgated and executed within the remarkably short time of six months, had been gradually introduced into ninety of the one hundred and seven districts under occupation.

It is possible that if this unanimity of opinion between the Army and the peasants had been achieved at the time when the Russian Army had been advancing victoriously on Moscow and nearly half of Russia was still free from the Red yoke, the fate of the White Movement would have been quite different. Who knows? Perhaps the days of the Soviet Power would have been numbered.

By the middle of June the necessary preparatory work for the application of the Prikaze had been done.

The largest tracts of land liable to expropriation were in the most recently occupied territories, Melitopol, Dnieprovsk, and part of Perekop, the application of the Prikaze to the land in this area, which was the one nearest to the enemy, obviously assumed special importance. Therefore it was decided to appoint district agrarian mediators in these districts first, and only later on to districts farther south. The new agrarian organization was not set up in Yalta, because there were no great estates in that district, and the coast was given up to popular seaside resorts. Later, a District Agrarian Soviet was set up in the district of Baidary, and was attached to the one in Simferopol. As soon as Berdiansk was occupied, an agrarian mediator was appointed there.

At the beginning of July the agrarian mediators, with adequate staffs of adjutants, surveyors, and agronomists, set out for their districts and began work. Towards the end of July the elections for the District Agrarian Soviets had been held in a large number of districts, in spite of great difficulties which were the results of the times. Although it was the season when field-work is at high pressure, the peasants voluntarily took part in the elections. It really seemed as if the worthiest representatives of the countryside were returned to the Soviets. Of those elected a fairly high number were intellectuals—schoolmasters, justices of the peace, or agriculturists, as well as landowners, sometimes there were even some of the great landed proprietors.

The Agrarian Soviets set to work immediately after the elections, they worked on the returns of the reserve lands liable to redistribution amongst the cultivators, the fixing of the maximum amount of land assignable to new owners, a census of the average figures of the crops for the last ten years, and so on.

The normal maximum for the plots differed widely, according to economic conditions, and these were very varied, there was not the same amount of reserve land in any two districts, but in every case land was allotted with an eye to the necessities of life. The allotments varied in size from thirty to seventy deciatins,[1] and were even as large as one hundred or one hundred and fifty deciatins. In the Berdiansk district alone they were as small as twenty deciatins, and a few plots in the Simferopol district were only ten deciatins; here fruit-growing and market-gardening predominated.

When calculating the amount of land that the old owners were to be allowed, the Agrarian Soviets generally fixed it at one hundred to one hundred and fifty deciatins, but in a few cases they found it necessary to take the size of the owner's family into consideration, or the part he had played in the Civil War, or, above everything else, his personal administration of his estate, and whether or not he had improved agriculture on it. In a large

[1] A Russian unit of measurement equivalent to two and a half acres—TRANSLATOR

number of cases these considerations resulted in the amount of land left to the old owners being raised to two, three, four, or even five hundred deciatins, and in Simferopol even to six hundred! In revenge, there were also isolated cases in which the old owners did not get even as much land as the peasants.

All this is abundant proof that the new agrarian institutions were applied with the utmost freedom, giving scope for local needs, ideas, and agrarian theories, and that the representatives of the Central Agricultural Authority, who were the colleagues of the local workers, had absolutely no idea of putting pressure on the work.

It would be less than just not to mention here the zealous, energetic, and tactful work of that small staff who were recruited from amongst those who had helped in the execution of Stolypin's agrarian reforms and emigration schemes before the Revolution, they were all experienced men devoted to their work. Unfortunately, many of them decided to remain in the Crimea after the evacuation, and paid for their adherence to the White Cause and their services to the people with their lives.

When I submitted the agrarian question to the decision of the local institutions, I explained to the population the significance of my action and appealed to them to work with the Army. At the same time I expressed my belief that the new institutions, in performing their functions, would take the interests of national economy and national needs into consideration (*Government's Communique on the Agrarian Reform*). My hopes were fully realized. The Agrarian Soviets responded enthusiastically to my appeal and did their work with scrupulous care, they were very anxious to settle the difficult problem before them equitably and in a way that would foster the development of the national economy.

Little by little the new power was revealing itself, and the populace realized that its face was terrible only to miscreants and traitors. Therefore it inspired greater and even greater confidence. The flow of money from the depots into the savings-banks, which were continuing to function in spite of the high cost of living, was a striking proof of this confidence.

On May 29th an appeal to the Russian people was published.

APPEAL

People of Russia, hear why we are fighting! We are fighting for broken faith; for violated sanctuaries, for the liberation of the Russian people from the yoke of communist rogues and convicts who have shattered Holy Russia to her depths, for the ending of the Civil War, for the giving of the land in full ownership to the peasant who tills it, that he may devote himself to peaceful work, for the sovereignty of real liberty in Russia, so that the people may choose their master for themselves.

People of Russia, help me to save our country!

GENERAL WRANGEL

CHAPTER XI

ON THE EVE OF THE OFFENSIVE

Since my arrival in the Crimea I had been working ten or twelve hours a day, and I expected my colleagues to do the same.

My day began at seven o'clock am, at eight o'clock I received the chief-of-staff, the commander of the Fleet, the chief of the Military Administration, and any other visitors. This went on until one o'clock, when I dined. From two o'clock till six I received reports from other branches of the administration, and between six and eight, when I had supper, I nearly always fitted in interviews with people who had come to Sebastopol and with whom I wanted to have long talks—people such as representatives of the Allied Missions and so on. On the very few days when I had a free hour before supper I used to go round the town with my aide-de-camp and visit the hospitals and houses of refuge. In the evening I attended the meeting of the Council of the directors of the administration, or read dispatches, or attended to my vast correspondence. I never went to bed until eleven o'clock or midnight.

During the first week or so visitors were especially numerous. They came to see me about the most trifling questions. On two occasions I even had to deal with lunatics.

On one occasion I was told that there was an engineer, a naval mechanic, amongst the list of visitors, he wanted to see me about his invention, which, he said, had considerable importance at the present stage of the war. The inventor would not share his secret with anyone but the Commander-in-Chief. I received him. He was quite a young man, and looked puny and ill. He seemed very excited, I invited him to sit down, and told him I had heard of his invention and wanted to know what it was.

"Your Excellency, I would not have troubled you at all did I not believe that my invention could be useful to you, especially now that you are having such difficulties; treason is prowling all round you, and you can trust no one. This simple instrument that I have invented can be of enormous service to you. It is a kind of compass. You can fix it to a corner of your desk so that it is invisible. Now suppose you are talking to someone about whom you know very little. You just press the button of my instrument, quite imperceptibly, and the needle will show you on this screen who the person is—whether he is a Germanophile, a supporter of the Entente, a Bolshevist, a Democrat, or a Monarchist. I have all the rough sketches of the instrument here..." And he began to open his portfolio!

Another time the manager of an officers' cooperative society, an old retired colonel, was among the visitors. He explained the object, of his visit very clearly and in great detail I promised to help him, and as I was saying goodbye I asked him where he had served previously.

"In the old days I was an instructor at a military school in Petrograd." He mentioned its name. “I had the good fortune to show the Czarevitch over our Museum." After a moment's silence, he leant over to me and continued in a mysterious manner. "How he has grown, Your Excellency! I would not have known him the last time I saw him, he is taller than I am. He is quite well and cheerful, the Czar and the Grand Duchesses are also well, thank God!"

"Where and when did you last see the Imperial Family?"

"Well, it was last year, at Rostov. I was walking along the Sadovaia, when suddenly I saw the Czar in ordinary clothes. I scarcely recognized him. He greeted me, and later I called on him several times and saw him, the Czarina, and their children."

I had difficulty in changing the subject, but as soon as we began talking of something else, the colonel became perfectly normal again.

The 12th, 15th, and 16th Soviet Armies had been beaten by the Poles, and were retreating all along the front without putting up any resistance. For several weeks, the Poles, backed up by Petlioura's Ukrainian formations, had been sweeping over an immense territory, extending from Polotzk on the Drina to the upper reaches of the Dnieper, the Kiev region, and a large part of the right bank of the Ukraine. The Red Command were throwing all their reserves on to the western front as a remedy for their disastrous situation. The cavalry were the first to be transferred. The 1st Army, under "Comrade" Boudenny, was moved from Caucasia, it was the strongest of all the Red Cavalry formations. They even transferred the only cavalry division on the Crimean front to the south-west Polish front. The railways in South Russia had not yet been repaired after our retreat, so the transporting of the Red troops was a slow business, for they used the highroads. At the same time, the fact that we had seized the Crimean Passes had shown that the remains of the Russian Army had not lost all their military prowess. Also, the intensive military reorganization and the re-establishment of order in the Crimea had not escaped the attention of the Red Command, and although they were devoting all their attention to the Polish campaign, they no longer disregarded the menace in the Crimea. As early as April they had begun to send reinforcements for the 13th Army. By May its effectives had risen to twelve thousand bayonets and three thousand sabres.

A staff-colonel, the Lett Pauka, had been put at the head of the 13th Army. The Bolshevists were proceeding with intensive fortification works all along the front. The fortified positions were furnished with large quantities of artillery. Information came through concerning the Bolshevists' behind-the-line organizations and the repairing of the railways at the front. By May the Russian Army was already a considerable force. The total number of combatants at the front, in reserve and behind-the-lines, was forty thousand men. All those who were fit to fight were in regiments. The material equipment had been put in order. We had ten tanks and twenty-one aeroplanes—although they were old models and all of different types. Fortification works were in progress all along the front. The troops had been able to rest and recuperate. All the units were being drilled. The general strategic situation had become more favorable for us: not only could we set our minds at rest over the fate of the Crimea for some time to come, but we could again come to blows with the enemy. The difficult economic situation would not allow us to remain in the Crimea much longer. It became of vital importance that we should find an outlet into the rich southern districts of Northern Taurida. This move, should it succeed, would have a favorable repercussion on our political situation.

On April 30th the forcible requisition of four thousand horses at a price fixed beforehand was ordered, for this purpose the Crimea was divided into five sections corresponding to the five districts. The actual purchase of the horses was made by Remounts Commissions, one for each district. With the horses thus bought, we were able to supply the artillery and part of the transport, and mount a cavalry regiment four hundred strong.

On May 15th the mobilization of recruits born in 1900 or 1901 was ordered. In anticipation of the resumption of military operations, and because I attached special importance to questions affecting the railway-transport of troops and the regular running of the food-trains, I put the management of all the railways into the hands of the Chief of Military Communications. I had cause to congratulate myself on this measure later.

Simultaneously with these military orders I was issuing a series of measures for the civil administration.

A Temporary Statute concerning chiefs of the Civil Branch and Army Corps commanders was promulgated on May 11th. It gave an advance guarantee that regular administrative machinery would be set up immediately after occupation of new territory by our troops, and that a check would be put upon the arbitrary whims of military chiefs who were often completely ignorant of their work. Henceforth the general administration of the freed territories was to be controlled by the Army Corps Commanders through the chiefs of the civil branch, who were to have the powers of provincial governors. Such a chief of the Civil Branch was to be directly responsible to the Army Corps commander for the government of his district, and was to receive his general instructions from the chief of the Civil Administration. Within the Army Corps' area he was to see that the district chiefs and the personnel of the town-and-country police forces (which were responsible to him), the circuit-chiefs, and the inspectors of the volosts worked together.

He had to organize the town-and-country police in the newly occupied territories, working through the district chiefs.

At the service of the chief of the Civil Branch were the plenipotentiaries of the Finance, Justice, Commissariat, and Agricultural Departments, they had to carry out his instructions within their own spheres, receiving them as general instructions from the chiefs of their respective departments. This measure was later said to be very efficacious and useful.

The police force was reorganized on a new basis. The department for the repression of offences against the common law was separated from that for the repression of political offences and was able to devote itself to its main task—the pursuit of common-law criminals. The rumor in the Press that all the refugees evacuated from Novorossiisk and Odessa were being recalled to the Crimea annoyed me very much. Some of these refugees were in a truly lamentable situation, especially those living on the desert island of Lemnos, where the rate of infant mortality was shockingly high. They wrote desperate letters from there which aroused well-founded fears in the hearts of their relations.

Russians are inclined to pass in one moment from complete depression to the most radiant optimism. Those who had said not long ago that the Crimea was a tomb, now regarded it as an impregnable fortress. Every day we received hundreds of demands and petitions, begging that such and such a person should be allowed to return to the Crimea. The columns of the newspapers were full of articles entitled "Let us rejoin our families," "Will they never let us come back!" and so on.

Although I quite understood that officers and officials could not keep their minds on their work if they were anxious about the fate of their nearest and dearest all the time, I also knew that our situation was not yet absolutely safe, and that the return of the refugees would only aggravate the crisis in the Crimea. Therefore I put off the solution of this problem.

Life behind-the-lines was gradually becoming more normal, goods were coming in from abroad, shops, theatres, and cinemas were opening again. Sebastopol was becoming more like its old self, and order reigned there. The soldiers in the streets were properly dressed and never failed to give the military salute.

At the end of April I gave several dinners for the representatives of the Foreign Missions—English, French, American, Japanese, Serbian, and Polish, and accepted invitations to dine at the English, French, and Japanese Missions. I was on the best of terms with the representatives of every Mission. During my interviews with them I always emphasized the importance of our fight, not only for Russia, but for all Europe, insisting that the menace of world-Bolshevism was not yet over, and that Europe could not be easy in her mind so long as representatives of the International dwelt in Moscow, for they had set themselves the task of spreading their doctrine to all parts of the world. The economic equilibrium could not be re-established so long as one-sixth of the globe had no access to the world-market.

Although I was taking every possible measure to enable us to continue the struggle, I did not for one moment forget how necessary it was to provide for the evacuation of the Army and the populace in case of failure.

I was determined to launch an offensive in the near future, and wanted to do all I could in advance to frustrate the machinations of England, who most certainly wanted to prevent us doing so. At the same time I wanted to be able to use our victory, should we achieve one, to gain the support of France. I requested P. B Struve to return to Paris.

On May 2nd, General Milne, Commander of the English Army of Occupation, arrived in Sebastopol. He came to see me. The special object of his visit, he said, was to see for himself the results of the great reorganization in the Army and behind-the-lines in the Crimea, of which his agents had told him. His personal impressions in Sebastopol, he added, had entirely confirmed everything that he had been told.

During our interview I touched on the difficult economic situation in the Crimea.

The British Government, which had taken the initiative in the negotiations with the Bolshevists, had not arrived at any definite result. Meanwhile, continued occupation of the Crimea would mean starvation for the Army and the populace. Under these conditions I could see no other course but to try and enlarge our territory. General Milne was obviously interested in what I said, and attempted to investigate my intentions further, but I led the conversation into other channels.

May 16-29th, General Percy, Chief of the English Military Mission, sent me on the following Note—

BRITISH FORCE TO PERCY DENMISS

May 25th

> You will send the following communication to General Wrangel in writing on behalf of the High Commissioner, and no conversations on this subject are to take place between you and General Wrangel. The British Government instructs me to make it clear to General Wrangel that no change whatsoever is to be expected in British policy as a result of the Polish offensive. His Majesty's Government is determined to endeavor to bring hostilities in South Russia to a close as soon as possible. The Soviet have accepted Britain's proposals for negotiations on the basis of a general amnesty, and Lord Curzon is replying that he is anxious for these negotiations to begin with as little delay as possible. The British Government thinks that all negotiations should take place in South

Russia. His Majesty's Government has asked me what I consider is a suitable place, and I shall be glad of General Wrangel's opinion on this matter. I am instructed to explain to General Wrangel that he is not being left to negotiate alone with the Soviet Government. Lord Curzon is sending out a political officer as soon as possible to assist General Wrangel. Meanwhile, the Soviet Government has agreed to the participation of the British military representative. *Ends Acknowledge*

BRITISH MILITARY MISSION, SEBASTOPOL.
May 29, 1920

To the Commander-in-Chief of the Armed Forces of South Russia

YOUR EXCELLENCY,

The above telegram received from the Commander-in-Chief of the British Army of the Black Sea is forwarded for your information.

PERCY (*Brigadier-General*),
Commanding English Military Mission

Whilst the English continued to seek a compromise with the Soviet Government and insisted on the cessation of fighting, the French Government, supporting Poland now as ever, had quite a different point of view. In General Mangin's interviews with M. Struve, his successor Prince Troubetzkoy, and myself, he had more than once raised the question of eventual collaboration between our troops, the Poles, and Ukrainians. On 4-17th May, Prince Troubetzkoy wrote to General Mangin—

> You wished General Baron Wrangel to be informed that you would like to know his opinion on the question of eventual co-operation between the Armed Forces of South Russia and the Polish and Ukrainian armies.
>
> The Commander-in-Chief requests me to reply, and acquaint you with the policy he has decided to adopt hereafter, should events lead him to consider such cooperation.
>
> General Wrangel wishes to state first of all that he does not want to broach the political side of the question, nor to take his stand on the recent news of the political agreement between Poland and the Ukraine. The aim of the Armed Forces of South Russia is the essentially practical and military one of fighting the Bolshevists. If this is clearly understood, the Commander-in-Chief is ready to accept all the collaboration which offers itself, and will be more than willing to cooperate with the Polish and Ukrainian forces. He thinks

it advisable that each of the armies fighting the Bolshevists should be given definite zones of action, and suggests that the area bounded on the west by the Dnieper and on the north by the town of Ekaterinoslav would be the district in which the Russian Armies could be of most use.

It must be understood that to preserve good order in military spheres, the civil administration must be controlled by the military occupation authorities in each area.

On May 21st-June 3rd Admiral Hope arrived in the Crimea on board the English cruiser *Cardiff.* He sent me another Note from the British Government.

H. M. S. "CARDIFF". No 335. June 3,1920.

SIR,

I beg to inform you that I have received a message from the British High Commissioner at Constantinople directing me to inform you that H. M. Government is a good deal disquieted by rumors of your intention to take the offensive against the Bolshevist forces. I am also directed to inform you that, if you attack, the scheme for negotiations with the Soviet Government conceived by H. M. Government will inevitably fall through, and H.M. Government will be unable to concern itself any further with the fate of your Army.

I have the honour to be, Sir,

Your obedient servant,

G. HOPE (*Rear-Admiral*).

To GENERAL WRANGEL,

Commander-in-chief of the Armed Forces of South Russia

I answered these two English Notes on May 23rd-June 5th in a letter to the British High Commissioner.

I have had the honor of receiving two messages from Your Excellency, the first was sent to me by General Percy on May 16th-20th, and the second by Admiral Hope on May 21st-June 3rd. I hasten to reply as follows—

I still negative the idea of my participating directly in the negotiations with the Bolshevists which the British Government has undertaken, therefore it is for the British Government to choose the place at which the interviews with the Soviets shall take place.

Also, I have not yet received an answer to my telegram of April 11th-24th sent more than a month ago, in which I pointed out the necessity of using the resources of the southern parts of Northern Taurida to feed my troops and the Crimean population.

Force of circumstances now compels me to promulgate measures for the enlargement of the zone occupied by my Army, so that I may ward off a severe crisis. Before I received your last message I ordered the Army to launch an offensive to achieve this. Part of this offensive consists of a disembarkation which is already under way. It is obviously impossible to stop it.

I like to believe that when H. M. Government understands the situation and considers the new factors, it will realize that neither from the point of view of the commissariat question nor from the military standpoint had I the choice of any other course but an offensive. Should my Army be victorious, it will help the British Government enormously in its negotiations with the Soviets.

There is also another essential consideration of a different nature, and I feel I ought to draw the attention of HM Government to it. The very admission of the possibility of an entente with the Bolshevists renders the question of bona-fide guarantees to ensure the honoring of the agreement very vague. I think it absolutely essential that they should be defined, and I would be extremely grateful to the British Government if it would give me its opinion on this question. The recent examples of Bolshevist behavior in the Kuban and Georgia, with whose Governments the Reds have just signed treaties, are sufficient exemplification of the well-known Bolshevist rule of regarding all judicial and moral obligations as so many bourgeois prejudices.

In any case, I will allow myself to express the hope that so long as the primordial question of guarantees is not explicitly settled, the British Government will not refuse me the support it promised, which is so precious to me.

A. V. Krivochein had a series of interviews with representatives of the French Government just before he left Paris, some of them were very old friends of his. As a result, the following letters passed between A. V. Krivochein and M. Paléologue, Under-Secretary for Foreign Affairs.

On May 7th A. V. Krivochein wrote to M. Paléologue—

MY DEAR AMBASSADOR,

I propose to leave for the Crimea in a few days' time, General Wrangel has summoned me for an interview. It would give me great pleasure were I in a position to assure him that he has the sympathies

> of the French Government in the continuation of his fight against the Bolshevists, in which he would welcome the cooperation of the Poles and of any other force capable of taking part in the conflict. It would be very valuable to him if he knew for certain that authoritative circles in France recognize the importance of the existence of a piece of Russian territory, however small, on which normal government can be preserved for the future, a territory which remains faithful to the Allies and organizes a Government on European principles of law and liberty, where non-Bolshevist Russian elements can find a natural refuge. It is no less essential that General Wrangel should be able to count on help from France in the form of war materials, and eventually, if it should prove impossible to continue the struggle, on French help in the evacuation of the Crimea.

The next day he received the following answer—

> PARIS,
> *May* 8, 1920.
>
> *Ministry of Foreign Affairs, General Secretariat*
> MY DEAR MINISTER,
>
> I have not failed to submit your letter of yesterday to the President of the Council, the Minister for Foreign Affairs.
>
> I am pleased to be able to assure you that the French Government recognizes the importance of a territory which has become the last refuge of Russian patriots and the only sanctuary for law and the Russian conscience. So long as General Wrangel lacks the necessary guarantees for the safety of his troops, we will endeavor to assist him with food and equipment with which to defend himself against Bolshevist attacks, whilst our Black Sea fleet will continue to prevent any disembarkation on the shores of the Crimea. Finally, should further resistance become impossible, we will help with the evacuation in every possible way.
>
> With my very kindest regards,
>
> PALÉOLOGUE.

Krivochein also had a series of interviews with Russian Statesmen and politicians—M. N. Giers, the oldest member of the Russian Diplomatic Corps, V A Maklakov, who had been the Provisional Government's Ambassador in Paris, Prince Lvov, A I Goutchkov, Baron Nolde, P. N. Miliukov, Adjemov, and many others. All of them except Goutchkov tried to dissuade him from associating himself with the hopeless Crimean enterprise.

Miliukov and others of his party put forward the following idea—

In view of the smallness of the fragment of Russian territory to which the struggle was now confined, the Commander-in-Chief of the "White" forces should not speak in the name of the Russian nation. He ought to be the Commander-in-Chief of the White troops only, the Russian nation should be represented by a committee of Russian politicians resident in Paris, the centre of European politics. Under these conditions, the fact that M. Krivochein agreed to become my adjutant naturally weakened their position, for he had considerable influence in foreign circles. His personal participation in our work would raise our prestige abroad, and this was not at all to the liking of those who considered themselves "the salt of the (Russian) earth."

"You are the only statesman whose authority is recognized by all parties without exception, your work is necessary for the future of Russia. If you associate yourself with General Wrangel's hopeless undertaking, which is practically a gamble, you will be lost to Russia forever"—was Miliukov's argument.

M. Krivochein saw a party of our compatriots once again before he left. Nearly all of them considered that our campaign was irreparably lost, and did not believe that it was possible for us to go on, they thought that all our efforts had been in vain.

M. Krivochein was an experienced man and a judge of human nature, and he knew quite well that these doubters would support the Army immediately if it won a success. Also, he fully realized what an effect a success, however shortlived, would have on the attitude of foreign powers, especially France.

I kept him informed of all the details of our military situation and our preparations for the offensive; we expected great things from this, should it succeed. Yet M. Krivochein hesitated to believe in success, he warned me of the dangers of a risky operation.

The offensive was to be launched on May 25th-June 7th. On the 21st I left for Feodossia, where General Slachtchov's Army Corps was to embark and undertake coastal operations.

I had been in the Crimea two months. When I arrived there the foul Red wave was about to submerge the last strip of Russian ground, and hundreds of thousands of Russians who had been driven to the sea saw the end approaching.

The remains of the Army which had been fighting for its country for two years were rent by internal dissensions and had lost faith in their leaders, the military environment even was gone. Crowds of old men, women, and children were begging for help, terror-stricken, ragged, and starving. . . .

Death was stretching out its bony hand towards them.

Two months had gone by, and the Russian soldiers were united once more under their national flag. Our tricolour was raised from the dust again, the regiments were armed with bayonets and were defending their native soil with their bodies, ready to renew the struggle for its liberation.

Under their protection the populace breathed freely once more, despair had given place to hope, and love of country had been kindled in their hearts. In place of the grisly spectre of death flamed the radiant image of victory.

CHAPTER XII

FORWARD!

By May 25th the enemy had brought up fifteen to sixteen thousand bayonets and three to four thousand sabres against the Russian Army. We had received recent information that the Red Command were preparing to launch a serious offensive in a few days' time. Numerically, our Army was slightly superior to the enemy's, and their morale was excellent. The troops had been reduced to four Army Corps—

General Koutepov's 1st Army Corps
General Slachtchov's 2nd Army Corps
General Pissarev's mixed Army Corps
General Abramov's Don Army Corps

We had twenty-five thousand combatants, counting bayonets and sabres, the fleet contributed one-fifth to one-sixth of our total effective force. Only General Morozov's 2nd cavalry division of two thousand swordsmen, which formed part of the 1st Army Corps, and the mixed brigade of Terek and Astrakhan Cossacks, had horses. The mixed and the Don Army Corps had only a mounted detachment of one hundred and fifty to two hundred swordsmen. The rest of the cavalry regiments were on foot.

My order of May 21st put the following objectives before the troops—

General Slachtchov's troops had been relieved by General Pissarev's on the Salkovo front, so were to embark at Feodossia, make a coastal attack in the Kirillovka-Gorieloie area, cut off the Salkovo-Melitopol railway, and later cooperate with General Pissarev's troops and operate against the rear of those Red forces massed along the Perekop front.

Generals Pissarev and Koutepov were to attack the enemy at dawn on May 25th, beat them, and drive them back towards the Dnieper. General Abramov was to keep the Don Army Corps in reserve at my disposal near Djankoie Station.

One section of the fleet had entered the liman[1] of the Dnieper to support our left flank during the operation. The exact moment for the opening of hostilities and the place fixed for the disembarkation had been kept secret. The General Staff had purposely spread the rumor that a disembarkation was

[1] Liman = long shallow bay at the mouth of the Dnieper—TRANSLATOR

to take place near Novorossiisk or Odessa. General Slachtchov was not to unseal his orders until he was in mid-sea with his troops.

On May 20th I signed the following appeal to the people—

ORDER OF THE REGENT AND COMMANDER-IN-CHIEF OF THE ARMED FORCES OF SOUTH RUSSIA

SEBASTOPOL No. 3226 May 20, 1920

The Russian Army is about to free its native soil from the Red yoke.

I call upon all the Russian people to help me.

I have signed the Law concerning the local Zemstvos, and I have reconstituted the Zemstvos in the occupied territories.

The agricultural land belonging to the State or to private owners will be given by the local Zemstvos themselves to those who till it.

I call every Russian citizen to the defence of his country and to the works of peace, and I promise to pardon all wrongdoers who now return to our side.

For the people—the land, and liberty in the framework of the State!

For the land—a master chosen by the will of the people!

May the blessing of God be upon us!

GENERAL WRANGEL

This appeal was made public on May 25th.

The Prikaze concerning the Land had already gone to press.

I arrived at Feodossia on the morning of the 22nd, and found General Slachtchov's troops embarking. The troops made an excellent show. General Slachtchov himself was optimistic and self-confident. I spent only two or three hours in Feodossia. I visited all the ships which had troops on board and spoke to the officers and soldiers. I then gave my final instructions and went back to Sebastopol.

On the evening of May 23rd my General Staff and I left for Djankoie, near the front.

A radiogram arrived on the evening of the 24th, announcing that General Slachtchov's troops had disembarked successfully near Kirillovka, although the disembarkation had been accomplished under extremely difficult conditions and during a raging tempest.

In the dawn of May 25th, the Army opened the offensive all along the front. General Pissarev's units attacked the Reds after a short prelude by the artillery, supported by tanks and armored cars, whilst General Slachtchov's coastal force was approaching the railway by forced marches. Attacked from the front and threatened in the rear, the Reds fled almost without resisting. We took several hundred prisoners and two guns. Simultaneously General Koutepov's Army Corps attacked the bulk of the Soviet forces on the Perekop front. Tanks and armored cars went ahead of our troops to destroy the barbed wire. The Reds put up a fierce resistance. The Lett units were the most obstinate fighters. The Red artillerymen posted their guns between the houses in the villages they were occupying, and fired almost point-blank on our tanks. Many were wrecked, but, nevertheless, the infantry used them to seize all the fortified positions. In this one day we took fifteen big guns and three armored cars, not to mention the prisoners and machine-guns.

Heavy fighting continued on May 26th. General Slachtchov's units fought their way to the railway towards evening, and took one thousand prisoners. General Pissarev's mixed Corps and General Koutepov's command continued to advance, though the Reds put up a desperate resistance.

During these two days of fighting, the 1st Army Corps took three thousand five hundred prisoners, twenty-five guns, and three armored cars. Our own losses were very heavy, especially amongst the officers. In one of the regiments of the 1st Army Corps all the battalion and company commanders had been killed or wounded.

On May 28th General Slachtchov took Melitopol Station and succeeded in holding the town in spite of furious attacks from the Reds, who brought up fresh reserves from Alexandrovsk. The Red forces at Perekop which were retreating on Kahovka had also been reinforced. The Red Command sent a division of sharpshooters, marching along the Don to the Polish front to attack the units which had encountered the 13th Army. The Reds strove to resume the offensive, but we repulsed their every attack.

On May 29th and 30th there was still heavy fighting under Melitopol. The 1st Army Corps and the mixed Corps held their positions.

The transport and part of the Red infantry had been forced to retreat across the Dnieper and blow up the bridges.

Between May 25th and the 30th the 13th Soviet Army had lost eight thousand prisoners, thirty big guns, and two armored cars, besides a large number of machine-guns and huge stocks of ammunition. On May 30th I ordered all the troops to complete the overthrow of the enemy by a vigorous pursuit.

At four o'clock in the afternoon I left for Sebastopol.

In the last few days the Red position at the front had changed. Whilst our Army had been attacking them, the Bolshevists had been launching an offensive against the Poles.

On May 27th the Red troops took Bielaia Tserkov, thus penetrating the Polish front.

On May 30th they occupied Fastov and forced the passage of the Dnieper sixty versts to the north of Kiev, thus cutting off the Kiev-Korosten railway. On May 31st the Polish troops abandoned Kiev.

The Bolshevists made great play with their recent successes against the Poles, but kept as quiet as they could about their defeat in the south.

Urgent measures were indispensable if law and order were to be established in the newly occupied territories. Much had already been done. In some places there was already a certain amount of civil machinery centred in the Army Corps commanders, for the Army carried high the flag of law and order. Isolated cases of breaches of the law by the troops were immediately and mercilessly punished. Military judicial commissions and representatives of the people kept a jealous eye on legality at the front. And yet still stronger measures were necessary.

One of the most urgent needs was the regularization of the counter-espionage system (especially the supervision sections). On May 28th an order was promulgated.

The unique character of the counter-espionage organs and the grave charges which their actions had, not without reason, provoked in the days of my predecessors, made it absolutely necessary to submit them to strict supervision. We decided to go back to the pre-Revolutionary system, which submitted inquiries brought against political criminals by a constable to the control of the Attorney. The Military Attorney General was to cooperate with the Chief of the Department of Justice, and regulations defining their powers were drawn up in great detail. My Prikaze of July 8th (No 91) entrusted the task of supervising criminal inquiries and political crimes to members of the Military Attorney's department at the front, and to the Civil Attorney behind-the-lines. The above-mentioned magistrates had to supervise all inquiries into political matters, give as much help as they could, watch the legality of all arrests, and be responsible for the criminals under arrest.

This was the first time in three years of Civil War that political actions had been submitted to the control of the Attorney.

On May 31st a Prikaze was published appointing chiefs of Military Jurisdiction, one was to be attached to the General Staff of each Army Corps.

The work of Bolshevist agents had been much less effective lately. In April some of the members of the Central Communist Organization at Simferopol had been arrested. At this time "Comrade" Nicolas Babakhan was their leader, he had come from Soviet Russia. This organization had set its hand to the willful destruction of railway communications, the members did their utmost to damage the tracks and the points, and blew up bridges and armored trains. A large quantity of explosives fell into the hands of the police as a result of the raid on the C.C.O.'s premises. This organization was in close touch with the Bolshevist section of the 7th Reserve Battalion garrisoned in Simferopol, the armored-car detachment near the Commander-in-Chief's

Headquarters, and the "Greens" skulking in the mountains under Captain Orlov's leadership, whom I have already mentioned.

At about the same time, a Bolshevist organization at Kertch was successfully rooted out, and a machine-gun, some rifles, and a large number of pyroxylin cartridges[1] were confiscated.

Since the beginning of the spring the Bolshevists had been conducting their activities from the woods, merely keeping on rooms in the towns and other settlements to serve as meeting-places for the conspirators—an essential thing if they were to keep the Communist sections in touch with themselves and with Soviet Russia. The bands of "Greens" consisted largely of the riff-raff of the population, deserters, common-law criminals, and Bolshevists who had been transported from Kharkov to the Crimea, but who had escaped from Simferopol prison[2] during the winter.

There were not more than a couple of dozen men in these bands altogether, but we knew that the Bolshevists were taking advantage of the fact that no effective watch was being kept on the Crimean shores from the sea, and were preparing to reinforce the "Greens" with new recruits and to supply them with weapons and money. Motor-boats came from Anapa and Novorossiisk carrying men and guns, which they disembarked at some deserted spot at dead of night, leaving them to take the mountain road and join the "Greens."

The battle against enemy propaganda behind-the-lines needed an energetic and experienced man as its leader. I decided to entrust it to General Klimovitch, ex-director of the Police Department.

At the front the enemy were retreating in hasty disorder. The 13th Soviet Army had suffered heavy losses during the fighting which had lasted from May 25th to June 4th. Almost seventy-five percent of the effectives of some of their regiments had gone. During the retreat the enemy units had been thrown into great confusion, they had lost touch with one another and with their General Staffs. Enormous quantities of reserve stores had fallen into our hands. The most fertile districts of Northern Taurida were freed, and immediately the cost of food-stuffs in the Crimea fell.

Our cavalry obtained horses. A large amount of paper money was issued just at a useful moment, and the units paid cash for the horses at current market prices.

The Commissions of Military Jurisdiction punished all cases of arbitrary requisitioning without mercy. In the majority of cases the offender was a Don

---

[1] Pyroxylin is a highly flammable compound used as a gunpowder replacement in primitive explosives—PUBLISHER.

[2] When the sick and wounded, the officials' families, and the most valuable of the stores had been abandoned, the criminals in the prisons had been evacuated behind the lines.

Cossack, for the Cossacks were unaccustomed to fighting on foot, and did their best to obtain horses without troubling very much about the means they employed. In the early days complaints against the Cossack troops had simply flowed in, but after two regimental commanders had been forcibly discharged and the Commissions of Military Jurisdiction had given several very severe verdicts, complaints ceased altogether.

In spite of our heavy losses, the troops, stimulated by our victory, were full of enthusiasm. The population had been suspicious of us at first, fearing molestation and pillaging, but they were soon convinced that the Russian Army had changed its character, and that our units had nothing in common with those of a few months ago, who had been indistinguishable from Bolshevists. Many a time on my journeys I would stop to chat with the peasants in the villages, and I never heard anything but good of our troops.

I went from Tchernaia Dolina to Kahovka, where I inspected the cavalry regiments of General Barbovitch's division. General Barbovitch was an excellent cavalry commander, he understood his work thoroughly, and was a very brave and high-spirited man with an exceptionally fine character; he was as hard on other people as on himself, and had earned the respect and affection of his subordinates.

Every section of the Crimean Press was unanimous in its rejoicing.

When M. Krivochein arrived, General Chatilov had been appointed chief of my staff. I had foreseen this appointment long ago, but I had put it off until a propitious moment should arise, as I did not want to upset the whole organization of the staff immediately after I took over the command.

General Makhrov was appointed military representative in Poland. It was urgently necessary that we should coordinate our operations with those being conducted on the Polish front, but the political situation excluded any possibility of a direct understanding with the Polish Government, and demanded extraordinary tact on our side. We had to cooperate with the Poles in military operations, without tying ourselves down to any political agreement. General Makhrov was capable of coping with this complicated political and military situation.

On June 4th I went to Melitopol, and arrived there at twilight. I went straight from the station to the Cathedral, where I heard the *Te Deum*. After the service, I spoke to the people outside, and explained to them that the Russian Army was bringing them not vengeance and reprisals, but liberation from the Red yoke, peace and quiet and order; and that soon every working-man would be able to live in safety and enjoy the fruits of his labors under the protection of the Russian Army. I explained briefly the essence of the measures we proposed to take for the organization of the district Zemstvos and the redivision of land amongst the peasants. At the same time I emphasized the fact that the authorities, friendly as they were towards all classes of the population, would not tolerate any breach of the law, and should any occur, would punish them mercilessly.

A huge crowd of several thousand listened to me in complete silence. When I finished speaking, the square echoed with loud cheers which burst from thousands of throats.

CHAPTER XIII

IN NORTHERN TAURIDA

Our success had alarmed the Bolshevists. The Soviet Press was sounding the alarm, and insisting that "the Lord of the Crimea" must be suppressed altogether, or at least made to confine himself strictly to the Crimea once again. The Red agents redoubled their activities behind-the-lines. Lately, there had been a fresh epidemic of unrest amongst the workmen of the port. The workmen had advanced a number of claims, and since these had not been satisfied, they had gone on strike. But by now the authorities were strong enough to take energetic action. I ordered all the strikers to be disbanded, and had those who belonged to the mobilized classes sent to the front immediately. At the same time I let it be known that, should there be any more trouble, it would be suppressed with the utmost severity. The firmness which the authorities displayed sobered the malcontents. A few dozen turbulent young workmen were sent to the front, and as a result, the rest devoted themselves to their work, in spite of the difficulty of getting raw material, until the end of our occupation of the Crimea.

We received good news from the newly occupied territories. The Agrarian Law was being received very sympathetically, the Prikaze concerning the Land was read in the local Assemblies, and the peasants voiced their approval unmistakably. But at the same time some regrettable incidents occurred. Many of the local representatives of the central authority, and by no means the least important ones, had no sympathy with the new law, and did what they could to circumvent it by giving it arbitrary interpretations. This tendency had to be checked immediately.

Other equally regrettable demonstrations compelled me to issue an order prohibiting the appointment of landowners to administrative posts in their own districts, this prevented the landowner administrators from attempting to turn the situation to their own advantage, or to improve their personal relations with the peasants.

A State Police Force was being organized in the newly occupied areas, and the salaries of its members were based on the Army Standards.

There were large reserves of corn in Northern Taurida, and harvest-time was at hand. Therefore we would be able to supply the whole of the occupied area and still have a surplus of corn to exchange for other things which we needed: clothing, ammunition, petrol, oil, and coal were only to be obtained from abroad.

Our finances were still in a hopeless condition. Our tiny territory could not feed the Army. We had nothing to export except a small quantity of corn and perhaps salt. Local industries were almost non-existent, for the barest essentials were lacking, and nearly everything had to be imported from abroad. Our rouble continued to fall in spite of the increase in taxation. The negotiations which M. Struve had been conducting abroad with a view to raising a loan had come to nothing, for no one really believed that our cause would be successful.

The Red troops were following up their success on the Polish front. The Polish Army was in rapid retreat. French public opinion, which had been supporting Poland, was obviously very deeply shaken. France showed an increasing interest in our affairs, realizing perfectly well what a priceless boon our victorious offensive had been to their allies the Poles, for whom things had been going so badly. M. Struve, who was in Paris, took very skilful advantage of the situation. He gave a number of lectures on our struggle, telling of our success, emphasizing the new direction of the Supreme Command's policy, and dwelling on the latest agrarian and administrative reforms. The French Press reported some of these lectures and commented sympathetically on the "broad liberal policy of the South Russian Government."

M. Struve had a series of interviews with various public men, and finally M. Millerand, President of the French Council, received him. He showed great interest in the struggle in South Russia, and asked M. Struve to draw up for him a written account of the Regent's point of view on the Russian Question.

Therefore on June 7th-20th M. Struve sent M. Millerand the following letter—

HEAD OF THE DIPLOMATIC DEPARTMENT OF THE COMMANDER-IN-CHIEF OF THE ARMED FORCES OF SOUTHERN RUSSIA

PARIS,
June 20, 1920

The Commander-in-Chief of the Armed Forces of South Russia has directed me to communicate his ideas and intentions to you, in addition to his views on the present situation in Russia. I have already had occasion to give Your Excellency a verbal account of the principles underlying General Wrangel's internal policy. These principles epitomize the whole of the experience gained from the Russian Revolution, and are as follows—

I. Seizure by the peasants of land belonging to landed proprietors must be recognized wherever it has taken place.

This is to be the basis of wide agricultural reforms which will assure full and complete ownership of the land to the peasants who cultivate it. The peasants' Agrarian Revolution would thus be legalized and turned to the profit of the new owners of the soil, and an agrarian organization would be set up on the principle of private ownership, which is undoubtedly what the peasants want.

II. The future organization of Russia must be based on an agreement between the existing new separate entities. These various new entities in Russia are at present hostile to one another, but they must unite into one great federation based on an arrangement to which they have all freely consented, this shall be the outcome of their common interests and economic needs. Our policy would in no wise seek to impose union by force.

III. Whatever the future relations of the different parts of Russia which are now separate entities may be, the political organization of these countries and the constitution of their federal union must be based on the free expression of public opinion in representative and democratically elected assemblies.

Turning to the present situation in war-wracked Russia, the British Government's present Russian policy is based on the desire to put an end to the Civil War before anything else. Britain means by this that the Russian elements under General Wrangel's command, as well as all those who have preserved their independence against the Soviet Powers, should surrender to her and to the Red Army. If the British Government wants to hasten the end of the Civil War, this is neither an effective nor an honorable means of doing so, for it would force the best elements in the Russian Army into an unwilling surrender, and put the whole of Russia under the terrorist dictatorship of Militant Communism incarnate in the Soviet Government and its Red Army. On the other hand, if the Civil War be brought to an end by the two parties to the struggle, it would not under present conditions take the form of the surrender of the Armed Forces of South Russia to the Red Army, but of a delimitation between Soviet and anti-Bolshevist Russia calculated to assure the necessary conditions of life to the territories under both Governments. Whatever one's opinion may be as to the possibility of enduring peace between the two Governments, the cessation of the Civil War will be an aid to peace only if this plan is adopted, a surrender of one party to the other will be of no avail. The

Commander-in-Chief of the Armed Forces of South Russia would agree to the termination of the Civil War by some such arrangement as the above, but he cannot possibly consider surrendering to Soviet Russia.

Any agreement must guarantee the inviolability of the territory occupied by General Wrangel's Army within limits which will ensure the satisfaction of the elementary economic needs of the population, especially in the way of food production. Moreover, the encroachments which the Soviet Power have made on Cossack territories must be entirely retracted. General Wrangel has once more acknowledged their historic autonomy and peculiar form of government by an agreement with the Atamans who are elected by the Cossacks.

General Wrangel thinks that the political entities of Caucasia ought also to be guaranteed against all Soviet aggression.

Turning to the question of the resumption of economic relations with Soviet Russia the belief that such a course of action would exercise a pacific influence on the situation is certainly well founded, but if it is to succeed, it must be earned out methodically and consistently. This policy of establishing relations between Russia and the rest of the world must be based on two fundamental principles of civilized economic life—

(a) The law of private property
(b) Economic freedom.

The application of these principles, even though it be to foreigners only, implies the need for judicial and police organizations to guarantee them. Unless these principles are given effective recognition and put into practice, the resumption of economic relations with Soviet Russia will be but a dead letter. Recognition of private property in the future necessarily implies its recognition in the past, that is to say, it implies recognition by the Soviet Powers of all the rights and interests of foreigners in Bolshevist Russia, and of all the public debts, state and municipal, previously contracted by the Russian State. Here I must stress the point that if foreign Governments now agree to recognize a Russian Government which does not consider itself bound by the financial obligations of the Russian State, all future Russian Governments, however moderate and wise they may be, and however clear it may be to them that Russia's best interests demand the respecting of her engagements, will have enormous psychological difficulty in recognizing these debts whose negation has been explicitly or implicitly sanctioned by the Governments of the creditor states.

I hope that Your Excellency will find this an adequate explanation of the ideas of the Commander-in-Chief of the Armed Forces of South Russia. He considers the above course of action to be his duty, for he is the representative of the elements in the Army which have remained loyal to their military honor and alliances, and of a population which recognizes that there are principles of public life which are common to all civilized peoples. General Wrangel realizes the difficulties of his own and of the international situation. He is far from believing that the restoration of order and liberty to Russia can be accomplished by a purely military effort. He understands that hard work after the peace will be essential, and that before anything else, the needs of the peasants must be satisfied, for they form the vast majority of the Russian population. They do not want the restoration of the old order, but neither do they want the Communist tyranny. To uphold the interests of the peasant population, to purify the moral life of the country, to reconstruct the economic system, to give order and therefore unity—these are the Commander-in-Chief's aims, and he believes that their realization will lift Russia from the present state of anarchy into which the Communist regime has plunged her, making her the victim of monstrous social experiments hitherto unknown to history.

Yours faithfully,

P. STRUVE.

Whilst France was obviously drawing closer to us, England's policy was still hostile. Lloyd George continued to flirt with the Soviets. The meeting of the Supreme Council of the Allies which was discussing the proposals to be made to Germany on the subject of Reparations was also dealing with other urgent political questions of the moment. England and France held radically different views on the Russian Question.

The British Government had declared that it was taking no further responsibility for the continuation of the struggle in South Russia, and the English Military Mission had been recalled, nothing had been left in the Crimea but a little information bureau. General Percy, the head of the English Military Mission, had behaved like a perfect gentleman all through the negotiations. When he had heard that England intended to negotiate with the Bolshevists, he had telegraphed to his Government that he refused to take part. I knew that in his dispatches he had also urged the impossibility of my countermanding the offensive.

I gave a farewell dinner to the Mission just before it left. In a few words I expressed the regret the Russian Army felt at parting from its sincere friends, General Percy and the officers of the Mission. I said that, politics on one side, Russian and English officers and soldiers were bound together by the blood which they had both shed in the same cause during the Great War, and by the ideals of chivalry and honor dear to every soldier, which were incarnate in the Head of the English Mission and his officers. This community of feeling had been especially precious to my companions-in-arms and myself since the Army had been alone in its struggle.

General Percy said in reply that he regretted having to leave the Army which was struggling so heroically not only for the Russian cause but for the whole world. It deserved the highest respect of every impartial spectator. As a soldier, he had nothing to do with politics, but as an English citizen he hoped that the English people would not abandon their erstwhile ally, the Russian Army, in its heroic struggle. He and his officers considered it their duty to bear witness to the gallant exploits of the Russian patriots, who were so misunderstood in Europe. After dinner he told me that he was going to do his utmost to draw the attention of his Government to the fatal consequences which would ensue for all Europe if the abandoned Russian Army was definitely lost.

"I am hoping that my Government's policy will change, and I have not yet abandoned all hope of returning to you here at the head of another Military Mission. If this does not come about, there will be nothing for it but to devote myself to my farm," he added, half jestingly.

I attached no importance to his last remark, but a few months later I received a letter from him. He wrote that, since he was convinced of the disastrous character of his Government's present policy, he had left its service and refused the divisional post that had been offered him, he had gone to Canada, where he intended to devote himself to his farm. Later on, my English friends confirmed these facts.

In the meantime we had received news that "Comrade" Jloba's cavalry troop was drawing near to our front on the eastern side. The Army Corps units came up from Caucasia by rail and detrained at Volnovakha, Rozovka, and Tsarevokonstantinovka Stations.

I decided not to allow the enemy to complete their concentration, but to wrest the initiative from them. I gave the troops orders accordingly.

On June 15th the enemy launched a vigorous offensive against the Don Army Corps—they were a cavalry division and a half strong, and were supported by cars and armored trains. After heavy fighting with the rearguard, the Don troops retreated. The 2nd Army Corps undertook an offensive to ease the situation, but found difficulty in advancing.

On June 16th the Reds attempted to cross the Dnieper, but were driven back to the right bank after a short struggle. On the afternoon of the 17th they again tried to force a passage at Kartachinka, but were again repulsed, losing prisoners and machine-guns.

From the 17th until the 19th the Don troops continued to retreat, and Jloba's cavalry to advance towards the south-west. Jloba avoided day-time marches and went forward only by night, for he had suffered heavy losses from our aeroplanes. Meanwhile the struggle was still going on along the front where the 2nd Corps was stationed, thus General Slachtchov was not in a position to be of any assistance to the Don troops, who were exhausted by fighting. However, on June 17th the 2nd Corps won a definite success, General Slachtchov's troops attacked the enemy and inflicted a severe defeat on them. On the 19th our troops at last succeeded in occupying the positions which had been assigned to them for this operation.

Our fighting force numbered ten to eleven thousand bayonets and sabres altogether, whilst the approximate number of our troops at the front totaled fifteen thousand bayonets and six thousand five hundred sabres. Jloba's principal cavalry troops with which the enemy were attacking us numbered seven thousand five hundred cavalry and six thousand infantry. The 13th Soviet Army's total figure was twenty-five thousand bayonets and ten thousand cavalry.

At six o'clock in the evening of June 19th I gave the following directions—

> *To General Abramov* Leave a covering detachment, and before dawn on June 20th, attack the enemy in the south with your principal forces and try to surround their left wing.
>
> *To General Koutepov* First carry out the necessary regrouping, then, before the dawn of June 20th, strike a decisive blow on the north and north-east against the right flank and rear of the enemy.
>
> *To General Slachtchov* Hold the enemy in check on your front.

The directions ended with the following warning—

> The success of this operation depends upon its secrecy, for it must be completely unexpected when it does come, as well as upon the well-concerted action of the troops.

I telephoned instructions to the Commander of each Army Corps.

At dawn there was a skirmish on the front where the Don troops were stationed. The Cossacks' offensive had clinched with the Red offensive. I wired to the Don troops to hold out, cost what it might, in order to give the 1st Army Corps a chance to turn the enemy's flank and rear. I thanked the Don Cossacks for their recent gallantry and expressed my belief that they would do their duty.

The booming of the guns could be heard distinctly at Melitopol Station. Groups of citizens laden with their belongings had gathered nearby, and were asking if it was not time to leave the town. The General Staff was proceeding with its work as usual, but even their nerves were at very high tension. I still had a reserve force—the regiment composed of pupils from the military schools; they were posted at Voznessenskoie, covering Melitopol.

At midday the tension reached its height. The several Army Corps were in action, and we were not in direct communication with them. The barrage became louder and more distinct. . .

At last the whirring of a screw . . . an aeroplane flew over the train at a low altitude and sent a rocket up and a dispatch down, the enemy was absolutely beaten and hemmed in by our troops. General Tkatchov announced "the complete downfall of the enemy."

The 1st Army Corps had attacked after a rapid march. Our artillery had been stationed in the open country and had opened fire on the Red troops who were attacking the Don Army Corps. Our armored cars had broken through the ranks of Jloba's cavalry and fired point-blank on the Reds, and simultaneously a squadron of aeroplanes had deluged the Red cavalry with a rain of machine-gun fire. "Comrade" Jloba had stopped the offensive against the Don troops and launched all his forces—nearly five cavalry brigades—against the 1st Army Corps. But our troops had received the Red cavalry attack with rifle fire, reinforced by shells and machine-gun fire. Our artillery had taken up an exposed position and opened fire on the enemy's flank, and at the same time the Don troops, who had recovered very quickly, had made a dash northward.

Attacked in front and on their flank, and overwhelmed by the machine-gun fire from our squadron of aeroplanes, the mass of Red cavalry had been thrown into confusion and had taken to flight in all directions. The biggest detachment, with Jloba himself at its head, had made for the north, where the reserves of the 2nd Army Corps and the armored cars had met them and fired point-blank on the disordered mobs. Jloba had fallen back towards the south, but there again had come beneath the scourge of the 1st Army Corps, whose troops were pursuing the enemy in wagons, barring their path, and sprinkling it with machine-gun fire. . . . Our cavalry had come up with the remnants of the Red divisions and had finally dispersed them. A second group of Red cavalry had been hurried northwards, but, colliding with the troops of the 1st Army Corps, they had been greeted with a murderous fire, so had fallen back towards the east, only to meet with the Don troops. Our advance-guard cavalry had pursued the fragments of the defeated enemy troops for a long time, the Reds putting up no resistance, many of them had abandoned their weary horses and lay hidden in the hamlets or ravines.

"Comrade" Jloba's cavalry troop was wiped out. The enemy's whole artillery force, nearly forty big guns and two hundred machine-guns, as well as two thousand prisoners, fell into our hands. We also took three thousand horses, and the regiments of the 2nd Cavalry division and the Don were remounted with them. We took prisoner the General Staffs of two Red cavalry divisions.

On June 19th and 20th the Reds had again attempted the passage of the Dnieper, and had actually seized one or two positions, but they were repulsed with heavy losses almost immediately. At the same time General Slachtchov's Army Corps was repulsing fierce attacks from the Reds.

Then our troops took up the offensive all along the front. On June 23rd the enemy began a general retreat. The operations near Orekhov and Alexandrovsk on June 10th and 23rd had given us three thousand more prisoners and many trophies. Altogether, between June 15th and the 23rd (during which period the tenth really big operation of the Russian Army had taken place), we had taken more than eleven thousand prisoners, sixty big guns, three hundred machine-guns, two armored cars, and a huge collection of firearms and bayonets. The Red Command's scheme for "purging" Northern Taurida of the Russian Army had proved a complete fiasco.

I took advantage of the lull at the front and went to inspect the Don Army Corps. The regiments had all been remounted, and had been able to re-equip themselves adequately from the enormous stock of horses, saddles, and arms taken from Jloba's cavalry troop. Only a few days previously the Cossacks, who were unused to fighting on foot, had given a very poor performance in battle, but now the Cossack cavalry had become a force to be reckoned with once more. As I watched the orderly movements of the Cossack ranks marching past me, I felt that this magnificent resurrection of Russia's cavalry must be a dream.

The mobilization which I had ordered was being carried out successfully. Five weeks of incessant and heavy fighting had put large numbers of men out of action. The ranks of the Army were melting away, and the reinforcements could not make up for all the losses. New sources of recruitment had to be found. A certain number of soldiers and officers could still be brought up from behind-the-lines, by dint of hard work, General Staff's and numerous military administrations had been gradually suppressed. In the last two months no fewer than three hundled and sixty institutions had been wound up. Notwithstanding this, I hoped to reduce them still further by another hundred and fifty at least. A series of orders emanating from the civil and military administration commanded the immediate transference to the front of all able-bodied soldiers employed behind-the-lines, their positions were to be given to men unfit for active service. An exception was made for specialists of all kinds and for chiefs of sections and their superiors.

The Comptroller-General was to check off the numbers of effectives in the different military formations, and cut down the soldiers' rations to the minimum. Nevertheless, in spite of all these precautions, the proportion between the number of combatants and the number of mouths which the Commissariat had to feed was still one to five. The enormous number of wounded and prisoners, as well as considerable numbers of evacuated inhabitants who had returned—mostly old men and invalids of one kind or another—all added to the number of mouths to be fed behind-the-lines. Only a very small number of the unfit were still useful as reinforcements for the reserve regiments which acted as military instructors to the new recruits and some of the prisoners (from whose ranks we always drew a large number of recruits). In most cases the commanders of the units and the divisional chiefs would make the first selection from amongst their prisoners, and use them partly for service behind-the-lines and partly for active service. The rest of the prisoners would be consigned to concentration camps under the supervision of counter-espionage agents, the Communists would be eliminated and the rest drafted into the reserve regiments.

But even so, all these sources of recruitment could not make up for our losses, especially amongst the officers. We had to find still further sources. Find them we did in the remnants of the Armies of the north-west and the north, and also amongst General Schilling's troops which had withdrawn into Poland under General Bredov's command, and had been interned there. I ordered all our military representatives to do their utmost to send able-bodied soldiers and officers to the Crimea. Negotiations with Poland and Rumania on the subject of the return of General Bredov's detachment were proceeding satisfactorily.

The area which we had just occupied was rich in horses, therefore we were able to mount the regular cavalry regiments and the Kubanian Cossacks, and horse part of the artillery. Nevertheless, we still lacked horses for our transport, and I was compelled to order a supplementary mobilization of three thousand horses. It was especially difficult for the population to furnish such a large number as field-work was in full swing. I was anxious to lighten the burden for the population as much as I possibly could, to this end I ordered the troops to assist with the harvest-work and the winter sowing of corn; men who were free at the time were to help, and the transport-horses were to be used. Those chiefs of the civil administration who were in closest touch with the Army Corps were to collect information concerning the number of horses and vehicles necessary for gathering in the harvest. Thereupon the Army Corps commanders were to give the necessary instructions; the commanders of the units were to be responsible for their execution, whilst the divisional and Army Corps Chiefs were to supervise. Every Army Corps was to send me a weekly report of what had been done. I warned the troops that I should hold the chief of a unit responsible if I found that the harvest had not been gathered in from the fields near which his unit was stationed.

In view of the enemy's enormous numerical superiority, technical aids to warfare, such as aeroplanes, tanks, and armored cars, acquired particular importance for us. In the recent engagements, our aeroplanes had rendered us inestimable service, but all the machines, twenty or thirty of them altogether, were in such a state of disrepair that they would be unfit for use for a month or six weeks to come. The tanks and armored cars were in a similar ramshackle condition, and it was a tribute to the courageous doggedness of our officers that they were still in use at all.

Petrol, oil, and rubber were only to be obtained from abroad, and that only with the greatest difficulty; we felt the shortage very severely indeed.

We bought all our necessaries in Rumania, Bulgaria, and Georgia. Our attempts to utilize the Russian stocks in Trebizond were fruitless—the difficulties were insurmountable. England put all kinds of obstacles in our way, and held up our cargoes on a thousand and one pretexts. By using all kinds of expedients and working on the goodwill of the British representatives in Constantinople, we managed to avoid these obstacles. But we squandered a great deal of time and effort.

There was also a much more serious difficulty—we had not the necessary foreign currency for our purchases. Our financial situation was growing steadily worse. Our small reserves of foreign money were melting away, and we were not receiving any more; our rouble was still falling. Corn was our sole exportable commodity, and our only way of ensuring the re-equipment of the Army with war material was to exchange corn for ammunition. The idea of a monopoly in the export of corn had to be very seriously considered. Such a measure would inevitably provoke discontent in certain commercial circles whose first care was personal profit, but from the national point of view no other course was possible.

Northern Taurida gradually became more settled, and the Zemstvo resumed its work. The whole of its complex machinery had been disorganized, and had to be built up again from the very beginning.

The lack of men had become serious. Already it was rare to find experienced officers in the regiments. Penury was still very widespread in the civil administration. In my predecessor's time the administration had been overrun with a personnel which had been chosen at random. Later, when the Armed Forces of South Russia had collapsed, a large number of these officials had left the country, and the only ones still left in most branches of the administration were those who had been unable to go abroad for some reason or another, and those who had a family, and therefore were obliged to go on drudging, whatever the penalty. Almost without exception, they were all "twentieth men."[1] Under such conditions it was difficult to demand creative work from them.

Since the beginning of his activities as my adjutant and President of my Council, M. Krivochein had addressed a large number of people, urging them to work. But nobody could bring himself to devote his energy to a cause which was, in the opinion of everyone, hopeless. Most of them refused, on

[1] In old Russia, officials received their salaries on the twentieth of every month—TRANSLATOR

some pretext or another; some pleaded reasons of health, others urged personal reasons, others again declared that they had lost faith in the cause, and in themselves too. In his interviews with me, M. Krivochein complained bitterly of the conditions under which he was made to work. "Nobody gives me any help," he said "I have to bother about all kinds of peccadilloes." He worked twelve hours a day, but never lost heart. Our recent victories had reassured him considerably.

"Everything depends on our continued success," he said. "If we increase our territory and seize the oil and petrol areas of Caucasia, foreigners will support us, we shall have money, and then we shall be able to obtain all we want."

We discussed the present situation at great length, seeking a way out. The little Crimea could not continue to feed an army for very much longer. Our base was too small, and we could not possibly undertake widespread operations against the Soviet Armies from it. It was necessary to enlarge our base and seize new areas rich in natural wealth, which could give us new sources of re-equipment and ensure foreign credit. But before we could enlarge our territory we had to increase the size of our Army, and this seemed an impossible task in view of our lack of technical equipment, arms, and ammunition. Thus it seemed to be a vicious circle. The Poles were retreating all along the front. During the last few days their retreat had degenerated into a disorderly flight. It was already possible for the Red Command to detach troops from the Polish front and send them south. Just lately we had noticed many new divisions on our front; they had come up from the west. In a very short time the Reds would be finished with the Poles and would be able to launch all their forces against us.

The only possible source of recruitment still open to us was the Cossack territories. When General Denikin's armies had dispersed, tens of thousands of Cossacks had returned to their native villages, taking with them horses, arms, and ammunition. Enormous stocks of ammunition had been abandoned in Northern Caucasia and the Don. In spite of the bloody warfare which had been raging in the Don and Caucasia for so many years, these districts were still rich in natural resources. Everything seemed to point to our carrying the struggle into Cossack territory. The information which we received from our Intelligence Service in the Kuban and the Don seemed favorable. In many villages the Cossacks had revolted against the Soviet Power. The population hid our scouts and supported them whenever they had the opportunity. It is true that we also learnt of the measures which the Red Command had taken to disarm the population; many of the Cossacks had been deported to Central Russia.

The campaign which was to enlarge our base by extending it to Cossack territories could only succeed if it were supported by local bodies, as our troops arrived; there would have to be a general rising of the population. We could not spare very considerable forces for this campaign, for the defence of our granary, Northern Taurida, was a matter of life and death for us. We would only be able to recall the troops to the Crimean isthmus later on, when and if we won great initial successes and conquered the fertile districts of Northern Caucasia; then we could fortify our position and throw the greater part of our troops towards the east to consolidate and develop the successes already won there.

After deep reflection, I adopted the following plan: when the Army had been reorganized and order had been restored behind-the-lines, we must strike out at the enemy on the northern front and so free our hands. Then, whilst maintaining ourselves in Northern Taurida, we must detach a section of our forces (the Caucasian Cossack regiments) and send them to the Kuban, relying on the support of the Cossacks of that area, and sweep the whole of the Kuban free of the Bolshevists. Later still we must abandon Northern Taurida, leaving the defence of the isthmus to the 1st Army Corps, and send the Don troops to help those in the Kuban.

Since we were contemplating a campaign to free the Cossack districts from the Red yoke, the "Cossack Question" had to be settled once and for all. The relations between the South Russian Government and the Cossack Government had to be defined. I thought it desirable to preserve a wide autonomy which could work through the existing machinery of local Cossack administration; yet at the same time I felt that I ought, in the interests of the cause, to keep the essential weapons of national power in my own hands—weapons such as the departments for the Army, Finance, Communications, the Postal Service, and the Telegraph.

The situation was favorable for an agreement with the Cossacks. Separatist tendencies had lost credit amongst them, whilst the Cossacks at the front were frankly hostile to Separatism. The Atamans and their Governments felt that the troops at the front distrusted them, and found themselves in complete dependence on the South Russian Government; therefore they did their utmost to effect a reconciliation with the Supreme Command.

The Press, except for the official paper—the *Velikaia Rossia*—gave a very imperfect impression of the impotence of our national struggle, and the South Russian Government's point of view on internal and foreign questions. Quite often, whether consciously or unconsciously, through the fault of the editor or merely simple carelessness, or perhaps because of the incompetence of the censor, the Press published news-paragraphs or articles which produced the most unfortunate impression abroad.

A paper with monarchist leanings, the *Rousskaia Pravda*, which appeared in Sebastopol, published a series of articles wrongly advocating pogroms. Admiral MacCully, the American representative, and Major Etiévant, who was representing France now instead of General Mangin (he was equally well-disposed towards us), came to me one after the other, each with copies of this paper in his hand, and warned me that the articles they had marked would produce a very bad impression on public opinion in their country. I immediately gave an order censuring the censor and suspending the paper.

In view of the complicated political situation and the preponderance of democratic tendencies in the western countries on whom we were absolutely dependent, we had to be particularly circumspect. Emigrant Russian circles who were hostile to us were carrying on a treacherous campaign and deceiving democratic Europe. They wished it to be thought that we were not fighting for the National Cause but for nationalist tendencies, and that not liberation but restoration was our object. They made capital out of every possible event, the word "master" printed in large type in my Appeal to the Russian people on the eve of the offensive had raised a tempest in the Press of the Left. Unfortunately, such papers as the *Rousskaia Pravda* gave them many a pretext. On July 5th, an interview which I had given to one of their reporters appeared in the *Velikaia Rossia*; it read rather like a declaration—

"WHY ARE WE FIGHTING?"

> There can be only one answer to this question (said General Wrangel). We are fighting for freedom. On the other side of the northern front despotism, oppression, and slavery reign supreme. One can have the most varied opinion as to the opportuneness of such and such a regime, one may be republican, radical, socialist, or even Marxist, and still realize that the so-called Soviet Republic is nothing but the expression of an unprecedented, sinister despotism, which is sending Russia into a decline. Even the so-called governing class, the proletariat, are oppressed as much as the rest of the population. Europe no longer regards it as a mystery—the veil has been torn from the face of Soviet Russia. Moscow is the heart and centre of the reaction, for there live the tyrants who treat the people like beasts. As for ourselves, anyone who treats us as reactionaries must be either blind or dishonest. We are fighting to free our people from a bondage such as they have never experienced before, even in the darkest epochs of their history. For a long time Europe did not understand this, but it seems that she is just beginning to understand what we realize so clearly—the world-wide significance of our Civil War. If our sacrifices are to prove in vain, European society, European democracy, will be forced to take up arms to defend its cultural and political possessions against an enemy who is drunk with success.

"THE MASTER"

The word "Master" has made its fortune. It is in ready circulation. But Russia at this moment has no "master." I do not regard myself in this light at all, and want to say so in an unmistakable manner. But neither can I see Russia's "master" in the "Sovnarkom" usurper, that creature who has submerged Russia in anarchy. The "master" is none other than the Russian people themselves, and the State will take any form they wish; if they want a king, Russia will be a monarchy; if they think a republic will be most useful to them, we shall have a republic.

But give the people an opportunity to voice their opinion free from the Tcheka[1] and out of range of machine-guns! The Bolshevists have dissolved the Constituent Assembly and imprisoned or even assassinated many of its members, they dread any form of lawful representation capable of voicing the will of the people. But we, on the contrary, want to establish a modicum of order, so that the people may, if they so desire it, meet together and freely voice their opinion. My personal inclinations count for nothing. From the moment when I accepted my present position I repudiated all my own ideas on the question of government and subjected myself absolutely to the will of the Russian people.

"THE JEWISH QUESTION"

(I asked General Wrangel's opinion on the Jewish Question)

A recrudescence of animosity against the Jews is indeed apparent amongst the people, he said. Feeling is running very high indeed, especially amongst the masses, and is turning rapidly against the source of Bolshevist infection. The people do not single out the culprits, they see Jewish Commissars and Jewish Communists, and do not stop to realize that they form only a part of the Jewish population, and have perhaps broken with the other part who do not share their Communist views nor accept the Soviet Power. I believe that anything tending to lead to a pogrom, and all propaganda in this direction, is a misfortune for the State, and I will oppose such things by every means in my power. All pogroms demoralize the Army, the troops who take part in them become absolutely undisciplined. In the morning they attack the Jews, in the evening they pillage others. The Jewish Question is an age-old, miserable, difficult problem; it can only be solved by time and social legislation, and then only if this

[1] Soviet Government's secret police force—TRANSLATOR

> is promulgated by a strong power relying on law and supported by real force. In a land where anarchy and despotism reign supreme, where the inviolability of person and property is trampled underfoot, the way is open for one part of the population to perpetuate every kind of violence against another. The revival of anti-Semitism amongst the people is perhaps a sign of their loathing for Communism, with which they quite mistakenly identify all the Jews. The recrudescence of Bolshevist activity in any country in the world will bring similar anti-Semitic tendencies in its train.
>
> "RUSSIA AND EUROPE"
>
> I am longing for the end of the Civil War with all my soul. Every drop of Russian blood which is shed wrings my heart. But the struggle must go on until men's consciences awake and they realize that they are fighting against themselves and their liberty, and that they are committing a senseless act of political suicide. Until there is a normal power established in Russia—no matter what its complexion so long as it is based on those principles which centuries of human thought have hallowed—legality, respect for personal rights and for private property, and the inviolability of international engagements—Europe will see neither peace nor any amelioration of economic conditions. No international treaty, however unstable, can be concluded nor any question definitely settled. One day history will appreciate the self-abnegation and the labors of a handful of Russians in the Crimea who gave up everything, and strove for the good of humanity and the distant centres of European culture on this last strip of Russian territory. The Russian Army in the Crimea stands for a great liberating movement. It is a Holy War for freedom and justice.

The Bolshevist success on the Polish front had considerably strengthened the position of the Soviet Government in London. England was bringing strong pressure to bear on the Poles to induce them to sign the peace. Italy was also inclined for an *entente* with the Soviets. France and America alone remained faithful to their former policy.

The preliminary condition on which the French Government insisted before it would enter into any negotiations with the Bolshevists with a view to an alliance, was that the Bolshevists should recognize all the obligations of former Russian Governments. Lloyd George was ready to come to terms even on this point. France therefore abstained from taking part in the negotiations, and the English Government sent a Note to the Soviets, advising them to conclude an armistice with the Poles and refer the question of the Russo-Polish frontier to the Allies.

Should this plan be adopted, the Polish troops were to withdraw at once to the line which the Peace Conference had fixed a year previously, that is, the Brest-Litovsk line which had been fixed as the boundary of incontestably Polish territory. The Bolshevists were not to pass beyond a line fifty kilometres to the east of this. Should an armistice be arranged, England proposed to call a Peace Conference in London at the beginning of August. Besides Poland, Finland, Esthonia, Lethonia, Lithuania, and Eastern Galicia were to take part, and all were to be given this opportunity to affirm their independence. If the Bolshevists accepted this proposition, the English Prime Minister promised to allow them an absolutely free choice of their representatives for the Conference.

M. Giers, who informed us of all this, telegraphed—

> They want to extend this armistice to Wrangel's front, and make him withdraw to the Isthmus of Perekop.

On July 7th I instructed M. Neratov to telegraph to M. Struve—

> To demand the withdrawal of our troops to the Isthmus is to condemn the Army and the population to death by famine, for the peninsula cannot feed them.

Tchitcherin answered Lloyd George's armistice proposal by saying that he would reject English mediation between Poland and the Soviets or on the question of the Soviets' relations with the rebel Wrangel, to whom he could promise nothing but his life should he capitulate.

Force of circumstances compelled the new Polish Coalition Cabinet under the presidency of the peasant Vitos to negotiate an armistice directly with the Soviets.

I strove to hasten General Makhrov's departure for Poland by every means in my power. At last, after a whole month of negotiation, we obtained the consent of the Polish Government to his appointment as our military representative at Warsaw, and he set off for Constantinople on board an American destroyer.

On the evening of the 8th I went back to Djankoy. The next day M. Krivochein telephoned me—

> A telegram has just come from M. Struve (he said). The French Government has consented to a *de facto* recognition of the South Russian Government. It is a great political victory.

Yes, it was indeed a great triumph for our foreign policy; it was the crowning point of three months' work. M. Giers had telegraphed on July 7th—

> Struve begs to inform General Wrangel that M. Millerand summoned him today and told him that he would agree to recognize the Government of the Armed Forces of South Russia as a *de facto* Government on the following conditions—
>
> 1. That we recognize explicitly all the financial obligations of the old Russian Government which touch that part of Russia now occupied by our Armies.
> 2. That we recognize the division of the land amongst the peasants which took place during the Revolution, and confirm the peasants in this land in individual ownership.
> 3. That we promise to call a popular assembly elected on a democratic basis at the first suitable moment.
>
> This declaration must be put in the form of a request for *de facto* recognition addressed to M. Millerand, President of the Council of the French Republic.
>
> Struve strongly advocates the immediate acceptance of M. Millerand's offer, because *de facto* recognition by France will be an immense step forward in the consolidation of our international position, and will greatly facilitate re-equipment. We ought to recognize the entire Russian Debt, and not merely that part of it which applies to the territory which we are occupying, because, as Struve pointed out to M. Millerand, we look upon ourselves as the representatives of the national idea and of the whole Russian State, he has agreed to this interpretation. M. Millerand's communication is strictly confidential.

Two days later, on July 9th-22nd, Giers telegraphed—

> Struve begs to inform General Wrangel of the text, as reported in the official newspaper, of President Millerand's speech to the Chamber of Deputies on July 20th—
>
> Let me describe the position of General Wrangel, who is struggling so bravely and successfully against Bolshevism in the Crimea and Taurida, at the moment, circumstances are favoring him. A real *de facto* Government has been set up, and has won the support and sympathies of the population by enforcing the agrarian reform of dividing the land between the peasants, furthermore, at this very

> moment it is drafting a scheme for calling a popular representative assembly. When this *de facto* Government asks for recognition, it is quite understood that a preliminary condition will be its unanimous and responsible declaration that it accepts all the obligations contracted by previous Russian Governments with foreign states.

I instructed Prince Troubetzkoy to telegraph to Struve—

> Authorize Giers to make the required declaration to M. Millerand in the form that you consider best. It is desirable to emphasize that whilst we, as upholders of the national idea and the traditions of the Russian State, accept all the obligations of former Russian Governments, we expect that out corresponding rights will also be recognized.
>
> Concerning the agrarian question: The Prikaze concerning the Land, issued by the Commander-in-Chief on May 25th, gives the land back to the peasants in full ownership—that is to say, we have already complied with one of the conditions in advance. Furthermore, the Commander-in-Chief authorizes you to say that, in full accordance with his earlier declarations, he considers his principal task to be the creation of a situation which will make it possible for the people to voice their opinion freely on the essential problems of the form of government which is to be established as soon as circumstances permit. With this aim in view, the Prikaze of July 15th has already put local administration into the hands of the district Zemstvos which are elected on a democratic basis.
>
> Please convey to M. Millerand the Commander-in-Chief's sincere gratitude for his friendly references to us. The support which the French Government is giving the National Cause in Russia in these difficult times is of a piece with the traditional friendship of the two Allied Powers, and undoubtedly re-establishes their close union for the future, based as it is on their mutual interests and political aims.

Meanwhile the enemy were still reinforcing their effectives and sending new units to our front from Eastern Russia, Western Siberia, Caucasia, and the Polish front. On the northern section of our front the enemy's forces numbered eleven infantry and six cavalry divisions—thirty-five thousand bayonets and ten thousand sabres in all. The total number of men in the enemy's Army had grown to two hundred and fifty to three hundred thousand (counting both those at the front and behind-the-lines). I ordered my troops to attack the Reds and thus prevent them from completing their concentration and resuming the initiative. From July 12th to July 20th fighting had been in progress all along the front, with varying success. It was not until the 18th that we definitely gained the upper hand, by the 20th the enemy were already in full retreat, and we had taken more than five thousand prisoners, thirty big guns, one hundred and fifty machine-guns, four armored trains, and quantities of war material.

On July 22nd the following convention was solemnly signed between ourselves and the Atamans of the Don, Terek, Kuban, and Astrakhan—

> In view of their joint undertaking to free Russia from the yoke of Bolshevism, the Regent and Commander-in-Chief of the Armed Forces of South Russia and the Atamans and Governments of the Don, Kuban, Terek, and Astrakhan have unanimously concluded the following convention, as an elaboration of their agreement of April 15th of this year—
>
> 1. Complete independence in home affairs and administration is guaranteed to the States of the Don, Kuban, Terek, and Astrakhan.
> 2. The Presidents of the Governments of the Don, Kuban, Terek, and Astrakhan, or their deputies, shall sit in the Regent's Ministerial Council and have the right to vote.
> 3. The Commander-in-Chief shall assume plenary powers over all the armed forces of the Don, Kuban, Terek, and Astrakhan for military operations and all questions of army organization. The States of the Don, Kuban, Terek, and Astrakhan shall order a mobilization of those classes which have already been mobilized on the territory occupied by the Armed Forces of South Russia, as the Commander-in-Chief shall direct.
> 4. Everything necessary for the re-equipment of the Armed Forces of South Russia in their struggle against the Bolshevists shall, upon an order from the Commander-in-Chief, be supplied by the territories occupied by the Armed Forces and the States of the Don, Kuban, Terek, and Astrakhan—the share expected from each will be settled in advance.
> 5. The administration of the railways and the principal telegraph lines shall be in the hands of the Commander-in-Chief.
> 6. Arrangements and negotiations with foreign Governments on political and economic questions shall come within the province of the Regent and Commander-in-Chief. In cases where such negotiations affect the interests of one of the

four Cossack States, the Regent and Commander-in-Chief shall first consult with the Ataman of that State.

7. A tariff and a common indirect tax shall be established. All barriers and visits by customs officials are abolished between the parties to this convention.
8. One currency only shall be in circulation throughout the territories of the contracting parties. The Regent and Commander-in-Chief shall exercise the right of issuing it. The elaboration of the monetary system and the division of the money as it is minted are reserved for a later convention. The standard for the new currency is to be settled by the Regent's Ministerial Council with which it is compulsory that representatives of the States of the Don, Kuban, Terek, and Astrakhan shall cooperate. The Regent and Commander-in-Chief shall ratify the scheme.
9. When the territories of the States of the Don, Kuban, Terek, and Astrakhan are freed, this convention shall be put before the Cossack Representative Assembly and the local Radas for ratification, but it shall come into force immediately as it is signed. It is to remain in force until the Civil War is definitely over.

It became more and more obvious that the negotiations between the Poles and the Bolshevists would come to nothing. The Soviet Powers kept putting off the conclusion of the negotiations on all manner of pretexts, apparently wishing to gain time for the Red troops who were advancing victoriously, so that they could defeat their enemy at leisure. It is true that Lloyd George was still making desperate efforts to arrange a compromise with the Soviets, but even he seemed to realize the hopelessness of his attempts. In one of his speeches in the House of Commons he declared that England had done her utmost to prevent "the need for resorting to extreme measures arising."

French policy was unchanged. France was preparing to support Poland by every means in her power and was sending out military instructors, arms, and ammunition.

As for America, she had squarely refused to enter into any negotiations whatsoever with the Bolshevists.

The day when Europe would open her eyes and realize the world-danger of the Red International seemed to be approaching.

We had another telegram from M. Giers on July 22nd-August 4th. He wrote—

> In view of the urgency of the situation and the turn which the armistice question has taken, General Miller[1] has begun negotiations with the French military authorities, and will report the results directly to you
>
> GIERS

It was clear that the rupture was complete, and that henceforth all questions would have to be settled by force of arms and not by diplomatic Notes.

General Chatilov and I were sitting on the terrace of the palace one clear, peaceful evening, the sunset was already fading, and all the colours of the rainbow were mirrored in the sea. As twilight crept upon the town, the street-lamps began to twinkle.

We had often sat upon this terrace for hours, exchanging ideas and discussing the future, or talking of the part. But we seldom, if ever, revealed our most intimate thoughts to one another.

In these difficult days, when it seemed that there was no way out, we had tacitly agreed to spare one another's feelings. We spoke only of the immediate facts of the situation or of practical questions. It was only when we spoke of the past that we mutually confessed the doubts and mental anguish which until now we had kept zealously hidden in the very depths of our beings.

On this particular evening we talked more intimately and sincerely than usual. All the circumstances combined to put us in the mood for intimate outpourings—the serene loveliness of the dying day, the temporary lull after months of bloody warfare, and the rift which seemed to be opening in the black clouds which had enveloped our external situation on all sides.

"Yes," mused Chatilov pensively, "you and I cannot sufficiently appreciate the miracle in which we have been both onlookers and actors. It is now three months since we came here. You believed that your duty called you here to the Army, I came because I could not leave you. I do not know if you thought that success was possible, I know I considered that everything was absolutely lost. It is only three months ago." He paused.

"Yes, an immense amount of work has been done in that time," he continued, "and it has not been done in vain, whatever the future may hold for us, the honor of the national flag which was trailed in the dust at Novorossiisk, has now been redeemed, and this heroic struggle will fail, if indeed it does fail, in a blaze of beauty."

"And yet the failure of our struggle is no longer a foregone conclusion. Just as, three months ago, I was convinced that our cause was lost, today I am equally convinced that we shall succeed. The Army has achieved a new birth, and although it is small in numbers, its spirit has never been stronger.

[1] Our military representative in Paris

I do not doubt the success of the Kuban campaign—the Army will increase its numerical strength in this area as well as in the Don. The population is on our side now, they have faith in the new regime, and realize that it is fighting to free Russia and not to punish her. Europe herself understands that we are fighting for a cause which is not merely Russian but European. No, the failure of our cause is not to be thought of now."

I listened in silence while my friend and brother-in-arms was talking. An enormous amount of work had indeed been accomplished. Three months ago the Army had been driven down to the sea, and had been on the point of extinction on the last strip of native soil, the people of Russia had disowned it, seeing it only as an oppressor, not as a liberator. Europe had turned her back on us, and had been ready to regard the usurpers who had seized Russia as a Power representing the Russian people. The end had seemed imminent and inevitable—but behold! Our troops had gone forward and triumphed, their souls purged by suffering, they had marched on, spreading order and a spirit of lawfulness wherever they went. The new regime had the confidence of the people, its face had been unveiled for all to see. The world which had been on the point of forgetting us was already beginning to understand us, and the struggle of a handful of Russian patriots was becoming an important factor in international politics. Yes, this was all true enough, but how small was this scrap of free Russia compared with the vast Russian territories in the power of the Reds! How poverty-stricken we seemed compared with those who had pilfered our country of all its great wealth! How unequal were the two parties in territory, strength, and resources! Our ranks grew thinner daily; behind-the-lines were crowds of wounded, our best and most experienced officers were out of action, and there were none to take their place. Our weapons were wearing out, and our stock of ammunition was dwindling, our technical engines of war were becoming useless, and without them we were powerless. Buy more? We had not the necessary means at our disposal. Our economic position was growing more and more difficult. Had we the strength to hold out until help should come? And, another thing, was help coming? Would not those who were willing to send it demand too high a price in return? For we could not expect any entirely disinterested help.

It would be useless to look for high moral considerations behind Europe's policy, for it was inspired solely by a desire for gain. I have my proofs to hand. Only a few days before this, I had let it be known that, to stop contraband of war from being smuggled into the Black Sea ports, I had ordered mines to be laid at the entrance to the Soviet harbors. The commanders of the Allied Fleets, both English and French, had protested against this measure, and had telegraphed to me that it was superfluous, because they themselves had forbidden all traffic with the Soviet ports. Four days later, the wireless station at our Marine Department intercepted a wireless message from the French torpedo-boat *Commandant Borix*, which had been sent, it seemed, at the request of the Co-operative Union of Odessa. It ran as follows—

> The Ship (its name was indecipherable) leaves for Genoa on August 5th with four thousand tons of corn. Send the ship back with drugs, apparatus for shipment, and surgical instruments.
>
> (Signed) RANDONI

What guarantee had we that those who needed us at this particular time would not abandon us at the critical moment? Had we the time to become strong enough to be able to continue the Struggle with only our own forces, if need be, when this moment came?

The future was still uncertain, and it was better not to investigate it too closely, we had no choice—we had to go on fighting as long as we had the strength.

CHAPTER XIV

IN THE KUBAN

My preparations for the projected campaign in the Kuban were all made. On July 29th the embarkation of the troops was to begin simultaneously in Feodossia and Kertch. At dawn on August 1st the invading detachment were to disembark near the village of Primorsko-Akhtarskaia, and leaving some troops to cover them on the north, were to advance rapidly on Ekaterinodar. They were to rally the rebels on their way and stir up the Cossacks of the surrounding countryside.

This detachment numbered about four thousand five hundred bayonets and sabres, one hundred and thirty machine-guns, twenty-six big guns, some armored cars, and eight aeroplanes. A separate detachment of five hundred bayonets and a hill battery of two guns had been ordered to make a demonstration landing near Anapa, and to cooperate with the rebels of this area.

Our agents informed us that the Cossacks were everywhere hostile to the Soviet Power. We had received the following information concerning the enemy, their principal forces were in the area lying between Novorossiisk and the Tamana peninsula. From the north of this peninsula to Yeisk the coast was guarded only by very small detachments. If the enormous body of rebels be taken into account, our numerical strength was still a little inferior to the enemy's. All the circumstances led us to hope that, given secrecy and speed, we would be able to carry out our disembarkation without much opposition. Then afterwards our troops would advance on to their native soil on which dwelt a sympathetic population, rallying numerous detachments of rebels as they went, thus they would seize Ekaterinodar, the heart and centre of the Kuban, and sweep the Reds of the north right off Kubanian territory before the Red Command had had time to concentrate their very considerable forces.

The Kuban once occupied, I intended, as I have already stated, to transfer the whole Don Army Corps to Taman and withdraw our troops to Perekop. Once I had made sure of a base in the Kuban, I intended to begin dealing the Don region.

The command of the invading detachment had been given to General Ulagay, nobody else could have taken it. He had great influence with the Cossacks, and he alone could "raise the alarm," stir up the Cossacks, and win them over to his side. Everything, it seemed, would follow from that. Ulagay was an excellent cavalry commander, well able to cope with difficult situations, for he was daring and energetic, and was capable of performing prodigies of valor at the head of his cavalry. I was not ignorant of his weaknesses, however, his lack of organizing ability, and his abrupt moods of enthusiasm which would as abruptly veer round to the deepest despondency.

I gave General Ulagay and his chief-of-staff a general outline of the campaign, explained the problem to them, and told them what forces and resources I could spare them. I left it to them to elaborate the details of the operation, such as the distribution of the troops, the division of the different tasks between the units, the organization of the Commissariat, etc., whilst I entrusted the general supervisory work to General Chatilov. Later on, I was completely absorbed by political questions and the directing of the troops on the northern front, and so gave very little attention to the execution of the plan. I had delegated to Generals Chatilov, Ulagay, and Dratzenko. This was a great mistake, as the future was not slow in proving. I myself realized it by July 29th when I arrived at Feodossia to witness the embarkation of the troops. General Ulagay's enormous General Staff was hampered by its unnecessary size, and gave the impression of being an unorganized mob of men selected at random, with no bond of union whatsoever between them. This was inevitably a heavy burden for the troops.

The plan for the disembarkation in the Kuban had not been kept secret. The Ataman of the Kuban had heard of it, and had informed the members of his Government and the Rada. The rumor that we were "going to the Kuban" was current everywhere behind-the-lines and even at the front. Nobody seemed to believe the rumors that the General Staff spread about to the effect that the disembarkation would take place near Taganrog, to support Colonel Nasarov's detachment.

An enormous number of Kubanian refugees were trailing along in the wake of the troops. When the embarkation took place, the rabble was indescribable. According to General Kazanovitch, some young pupils from the military schools fainted for lack of air. Sixteen thousand men and four thousand five hundred horses were embarked, although the troops numbered only five thousand bayonets and sabres. All the rest were members of behind-the-line organizations or refugees.

It was too late by then to make any changes. I went the round of the ships and spoke to the troops, then I sent for their leader and gave him full instructions once more.

"The detachment base is the Kuban," I told him. "Do not keep looking back for your ships, and, above everything, avoid scattering your troops. Only a brisk advance can bring us success, the slightest delay, and you will be lost."

A few days before I had gone to Feodossia, some of our troops had landed there under the leadership of General Bredov, they had retreated to Odessa in Poland during the winter of 1920 and had been interned there. After long months of negotiation, they had been sent to the Crimea by way of Rumania. They had been living under the most terrible conditions in Poland. They had been confined to small camps, had lacked suitable clothing, and had been almost without food. After I had inspected the troops which were about to embark, I went to see the newly arrived "Bredovians." They were a sorry sight—tattered, barefooted, and some of them dressed only in filthy rags. After they had rested and been re-equipped in Feodossia, these units were to be sent to reinforce the 2nd Army Corps.

During the last days of July we received many intimations that the Red forces were concentrating on the right bank of the Dnieper. From day to day we had to be ready for a considerable detachment of Reds, should they attempt to force the lower reaches of the Dnieper. The information we had received from our agents and the wireless messages we had intercepted led us to suppose that the principal blow would be struck at the Berislavl area (opposite Kahovka) by three or four divisions. Acting on this information, I gave instructions to Generals Koutepov and Slachtchov.

On July 25th the Reds landed near Malaia Kahovka under cover of artillery fire from the right bank of the Dnieper, which dominates the sandy plain on the left bank. Immediately they began to construct a pontoon-bridge. Simultaneously, another Red detachment crossed the river under cover of the artillery near the Korsunsky monastery and Alechky. By midday they had finished the pontoon-budge, and towards evening they occupied Bolchaia Kahovka with a detachment of two thousand men and several light batteries.

Our units kept the enemy in check stubbornly, but they were decimated by the artillery from the right bank, and faced by forces considerably larger than their own, so that they were forced to abandon the counter-offensive.

According to the report of the commander of the division which had fought in this area, he had lost not less than half his contingent, he wrote that "the fighting-power of the troops had been very greatly reduced."

On July 26th the Reds continued their offensive, but this time they met with a repulse.

On July 27th the fighting was still in progress. The enemy completed the passage of the river near Kahovka, and transported their heavy artillery and cavalry units across to the left bank, deploying their forces along a wide front. They then launched an offensive in the south, striving to turn our cavalry's flanks.

On July 28th General Slachtchov's Army Corps took up a fortified position from which it could defend the principal route, the Perekop road, simultaneously, we managed to concentrate our cavalry, so that they might strike a blow at the enemy's left wing.

Whilst the cavalry and the units of the 2nd Army Corps were preparing to strike a blow at the Reds on the left bank of the Dnieper, the situation became threatening on the front where the 1st Army Corps was stationed. The Reds had concentrated the 2nd Cavalry Army, and the 1st, 3rd, and 46th divisions of light infantry, reinforced with the Communist units and a brigade of pupils from the Red military schools, and were making desperate efforts to break through our front.

Time and again our gallant 1st Army Corps repulsed the Red attacks, but our losses were enormous, especially amongst the officers. In these circumstances, it became absolutely necessary to finish with the Red group which had crossed the Dnieper as soon as possible, and thus leave the cavalry free to go to the assistance of the 1st Army Corps, which was wasting its strength in an unequal fight.

At dawn on July 30th, General Barbovitch's cavalry units advanced against the enemy's rearguard, which had discovered our cavalry movements and begun to retreat all along the front, pursued by our infantry. General Barbovitch overtook a retreating Lettish brigade. Our cavalry rushed upon the enemy, absolutely defeated them, and took two thousand prisoners and three guns complete with ammunition wagons, but in spite of gallant General Barbovitch's profitable venture, which had inflicted this severe defeat on the enemy, General Slachtchov could not win a decisive success. He had scattered the units of his Army Corps, and so could not make use of any of our cavalry's success, indeed, he gave the enemy time to recover themselves.

In the meantime the 1st Army Corps continued to repulse the fierce attacks of the Reds, shedding nearly every drop of their blood in the effort.

The fighting which continued throughout the day of July 31st ended in a fresh failure. Our units suffered heavy losses, the enemy put up a stubborn opposition, the Letts fought especially tenaciously. The enemy worked relentlessly to reinforce their position.

At last, on the 1st Army Corps' front, they seemed to be losing their breath. Their attacks grew visibly weaker. From the morning of August 1st a calm began to settle over the greater part of the front. General Koutepov was optimistic about the future. In the evening a telegram came to say that our troops had succeeded in landing near the hamlet of Akhtarsky.

Although a rumor of the raid on the Kuban had most certainly leaked through to the enemy owing to the indiscretion of the Kubanians in charge, the Red Command were ignorant of the exact landing-place, and the raid had been accomplished without any losses.

On the evening of August 2nd General Slachtchov telegraphed that he would be forced to give up his attacks on the enemy's fortified position. The head of the Kahovka bridge was in the hands of the enemy, and this put a considerable number of our troops out of action, besides constituting a menace to our left flank on our most important route—the Perekop road. Nevertheless, the enemy had not been able to win a decisive victory. Northern Taurida remained in our hands, and the units which had been detached from our main army had earned out the first part of their task, they had landed, and marched rapidly on to Kubanian territory.

In view of the development in the operations at the Kuban, I decided to transfer my Headquarters to Sebastopol, and to amalgamate the commands of the 1st and 2nd Army Corps, putting them both into the hands of General Koutepov. Koutepov could cope with any situation, he was a man of great military prowess and exceptional tenacity in the pursuit of his ends. He had won the friendship of officers and men alike, and was an incomparable instructor for the troops.

On August 10th M. Millerand, in a letter to M. Easily, counsellor at our Embassy in Paris, declared his *de facto* recognition of the South Russian Government.

PARIS,
August 10, 1920.

To the *Chargé d' Affaires.*

SIR,

In a letter of August 8th. you asked me if I did not consider it opportune to give effect to the statements I made to you on the subject of the *de facto* recognition of the South Russian Government. You ask me to take into consideration, on the one hand the consolidation of the internal Government and General Wrangel's military successes, and on the other the assurances contained in your letter of August 3rd.

You also point out the advantage of our having a diplomatic agent at Sebastopol, who will be able to exercise effective moral influence at least by reason of his personal authority.

I have the honor to inform you that the Government of the Republic has decided to accord *de facto* recognition to the Government of South Russia, and will send a diplomatic agent to Sebastopol as you suggest, at the same time notifying the Allied and Associated Governments of its decision.

I must add that I think it advantageous that this decision should receive as much publicity as possible.

Yours faithfully,

MILLERAND.

To M. BAISLEY,
Russian Chargé d' Affaires.

On August 3rd I had telegraphed to the President of the French Council—

> HIS EXCELLENCY M. MILLERAND, PRESIDENT OF THE COUNCIL, MINISTER OF FOREIGN AFFAIRS, PARIS
>
> In view of the Republican Government's decision to recognize the South Russian Government, I beg to offer you my warmest thanks for the invaluable help you have given the national cause of Russia at a supremely trying moment. We are straining every effort to accomplish our pre-ordained task of re-establishing a Russia based on the great principles of liberty and progress.
>
> GENERAL WRANGEL.

A few days later, the American Government's Note setting forth the views of the United States on the Russian and Polish Questions, came to our notice. Greis communicated it to us in several telegrams—

> The American Government has published a Note elucidating its point of view on the Russian and Polish Questions. Polish territory is not to be touched. America is sympathetic towards the Powers' negotiations for an armistice between Poland and the Soviets, but opposes the convocation of a general conference which would probably finish by recognizing the Bolshevists and the partition of Russia. America has pronounced in favor of the unity of Russia, and wants the settlement of all questions relating to the sovereignty of the territories of the old Russian Empire to be postponed. Therefore she has already refused to recognize the independence of the States which have been set up on the frontier, with the one exception of Armenia. She states that the frontiers of Armenia were definitely fixed with the cooperation and consent of Russia. The same cooperation is necessary to deal with the Near Eastern Question. The United States will recognize neither the Soviet Government, which is the very negation of all International Law, nor the principles of any of those nations which are striving for world-revolution by means of the Third International.
>
> The American Note has been very well received here. It releases France from her painful position of political isolation, and gives her solid moral support in her anti-Bolshevist policy, which is crippling Lloyd George's stubborn desire to come to an understanding with the Soviets. The Cabinet here in Paris has taken advantage of America's Note to declare openly, in a Note published today, its complete agreement with the democratic and national principles which America has voiced in the Russian Note.

> It was the adoption of these principles by the South Russian Government that led France to accord it recognition. The essential point for us to notice in America's action is the fact that the United States are upholding the principle of the territorial integrity of Russia.

I instructed M. Struve to see that our Ambassador at Washington conveyed to the American Government our sincere gratitude for the support it had given us by its declaration..

The situation on the Polish front seemed hopeless. The Red Army had continued its advance, and was now approaching Warsaw. The front was within fifty kilometres of the capital, which was being evacuated with all speed. Simultaneously, under the stimulus of patriotism, a huge number of volunteers from all classes of the population were joining the Army. General Weygand, who had just reached Poland, was doing his utmost to reorganize the Polish Army with the help of the French Staff officers he had brought with him. The Army was being regrouped with the object of launching an offensive at the first possible moment and of wresting the initiative from the enemy.

The Kuban operation was progressing favorably. General Ulagay's units had absolutely defeated the Red Caucasian cavalry division and had taken many prisoners, including the divisional staff and its commander, "Comrade" Meyer, and all the artillery. Then they had effected their junction with Colonel Skatun's rebels. Two thousand Cossacks from the freed villages had joined our troops.

The favorable military situation, our latest success in the field of foreign relations, and the gradual establishment of normal order in the country, all strengthened the people's confidence in us as the new rulers. Things began to settle down, the economic situation alone showed no signs of improvement. The maintenance of the Army, which was very large in proportion to the size of the territory it occupied, under conditions of economic disorder which were inevitable during a Civil War, was a heavy burden on the country. Our ordinary expenses were more than covered by direct and indirect taxation; but our military expenses, since it was impossible to obtain a loan at home or abroad, swallowed up the last remnants of our fund of foreign securities.

In case the operations which were in progress in the Kuban should make the northern section of our front an independent theatre of war, I decided to amalgamate the troops of the 1st and 2nd Army Corps and the Cavalry Corps and call them the 1st Army, putting General Koutepov at their head I gave the command of the 1st Army Corps to General Pissarev, and put General Vitkovsky at the head of the 2nd Army Corps instead of General Slachtchov.

General Slachtchov, who had long been a slave to drink and drugs, had now become completely unhinged as a result. On August 5th he arrived in

Sebastopol. He was a terrible spectacle. His face was deadly pale and his mouth never ceased to tremble, while tears streamed from his eyes. He sent me a dispatch which was abundant proof that I was dealing with a man in the throes of mental sickness.

I had difficulty in calming him. I was as friendly as I could be, and tried to persuade him how necessary it was that he should take care of himself. I assured him that once he had taken a rest and was better, he would again be able to serve our cause; I promised to do all I could to prevent his departure from being interpreted as a dismissal.

General Slachtchov seemed touched beyond words. He thanked me in a trembling voice, broken by tears. I could not look at him without feeling the deepest pity.

That same day he and his wife paid a visit to my wife. The next day we returned their visit. Slachtchov was living at the station in a railway-carriage. Incredible disorder reigned in his compartment. The table was covered with bottles, and dishes of *hors d'oeuvres*, on the bunks were clothes, playing-cards, and weapons, all lying about anyhow. Amidst all this confusion was Slachtchov, clad in a fantastic white dolman, gold-laced and befurred. He was surrounded by all kinds of birds; he had a crane there, and also a raven, a swallow, and a jay . . they were hopping about on the table and the bunks, fluttering round, and perching on their master's head and shoulders.

I insisted on General Slachtchov undergoing a medical examination. The doctors diagnosed an acute form of neurasthenia which necessitated strict treatment obtainable only in a sanatorium. They advised Slachtchov to go abroad and take care of himself, but all attempts to persuade him to go away were in vain. He decided to settle down in Yalta.

The regrouping of the Polish forces had been completed, and waves of obstinate fighting rolled up to the very walls of Warsaw. On some sections of the front the Poles were victorious, the Bolshevists beaten.

On General Koutepov's front, fierce fighting had begun again on August 5th.

In the meantime, on August 5th, our units in the Kuban had occupied several villages on the Ekaterinodar road, but had gone no farther. The latest news of the enemy we had received mentioned a concentration of Red forces. New units were making their appearance on General Ulagay's front. It was obvious that the enemy had begun to collect their forces to attack our invading detachment. There was no time to be lost, every day we wasted gave the enemy another day in which to bring up fresh troops. Yet General Ulagay did not stir on August 6th, 7th, or 8th.

General Siegel, Chief of the fortified area at Kertch, reported that our scouts in the Taman peninsula had sent word that the enemy were retreating. He had ordered a detachment, hastily formed from the reserve units and those behind-the-lines at Kertch, to land in Taman.

On the morning of the 10th I left for Kertch. The unforgiveable delay in the movements of General Ulagay's units was alarming me, and my brain was racked with anxious thoughts. At Vladislavovka Station General Chatilov got into my compartment. His gloomy expression warned me immediately that he was bringing bad news. Silently he handed me a telegram from General Ulagay. It said that the situation had become serious, for fresh enemy units had come up, and the enemy now enjoyed an overwhelming numerical superiority. Therefore he begged that ships might be sent as soon as possible to the hamlet of Akhtarsky to pick up the expeditionary force. My presentiment had not been a false one. The short sentences of the radiogram did not give a complete picture of what had happened, but it was obvious that every operation we had undertaken had failed. The indispensable condition of success—unexpectedness—was already lost. The initiative had been allowed to fall from our hands, and the chief of the detachment had lost all faith in the possibility of success.

Yet, at the same time, the enemy's retreat from the Taman peninsula still gave us a little hope that all was not lost. If General Ulagay could manage to defeat the forces which were coming up against him from Taman, and if he could transfer his base to the Tamanan peninsula, our position would still be fairly good. Unfortunately we lacked the necessary troops for keeping our hold on the peninsula until General Ulagay's troops should arrive. General Siegel had succeeded in getting together a mixed company and about one hundred plastounes[1] with just one gun at Kertch. But these troops were deficient alike in quantity and quality, and did not constitute a real force. The intensive fighting which was still in progress on the northern front did not permit of the transfer of a single man from there.

On the morning of August 11th I went to the village of Tamanskaia, where I was present at the singing of the *Te Deum*, I also addressed a public meeting. The village was almost empty. The few Cossacks who remained were in a state of absolute terror, they had no faith in our success, and expected the Reds to come back at any moment. Our units were already ten versts to the east of the village, and the enemy were retreating without putting up any resistance.

On my return to Kertch I found a wireless message from General Babiev, the gallant commander of the 1st Kuban Cossack division. He reported that he had just won a fairly big success near the villages of Brynkovskaia and Olghinskaia. He knew about the telegram which General Ulagay had sent me the previous evening, but all the same, he thought that our position was now a favorable one, and he saw no reason why we should give up the operation which we had begun. His lines of communication with General Ulagay had been cut, that was why he had sent this report straight to me.

[1] Cossack infantry—TRANSLATOR

I sent General Babiev's telegram on to General Ulagay by aeroplane, adding a word of my own to the effect that I considered it necessary to go on with the operation, at the same time bearing in mind the possibility of transferring our base to Taman. I asked him for a detailed communique on the situation.

On the morning of the 12th I received another telegram from General Ulagay. The situation had changed slightly, and it was no longer necessary to send the ships. The telegram reassured me only very slightly. The commander's abrupt change of arrangements was clear proof that he had lost his head altogether. That evening the airman returned with the detailed report on the situation for which I had asked.

In spite of the words he himself had addressed to the commanders of the units—"Only an energetic offensive can bring us success. The Kuban is our base, we have burnt our boats"—General Ulagay unfortunately encumbered himself with enormous rearguard impedimenta. Great reserves of arms, ammunition, and provisions had been left at the landing-stage, near the village of Primorsko-Akhtarsky. The refugees and the soldiers' families who had followed the Army to the Kuban had also remained there. Thus, even whilst they advanced, our units were compelled to look back all the time. We received information that the Reds were concentrating their forces, General Ulagay feared for his base and began to vacillate. General Babiev and others urged an immediate march on Ekaterinodar, for, according to some fugitives, it was almost empty of Red troops, who had left in a panic. But Ulagay would not come to any decision on August 6th or 7th. On the night of the 10th General Ulagay gave the order to retreat, and simultaneously sent a telegram asking that the ships should be sent after all.

Meanwhile, on August 9th, General Babiev had struck a heavy blow at the enemy and taken one thousand prisoners and many machine-guns.

On the l0th and 11th the Reds attacked our expeditionary force, but met with no success.

Our units had followed up their advance in Taman. I had sent them the detachment which had landed at Anapa in the south at the same time as General Ulagay's troops, it had been attempting to win over the Greens who were operating in this area. The hopes that we had entertained of the Greens had not been fulfilled. The new detachment had been attacked by the Reds and driven down to the sea, where they were holding out only with the greatest difficulty. In spite of their heavy losses, the pupils of the military schools who composed it had cut a brave figure.

On August 13th we were still occupying several villages in Taman. But our advance began to meet with an ever more vigorous resistance. The enemy had driven back General Ulagay's units and so released some troops from the Taman area; these were now hastening to re-establish their position on this front.

On the Polish front the situation had changed radically. The Polish troops had passed to the offensive and inflicted a crushing defeat on the Reds. In the area between Narev and the German frontier many tens of thousands of Soviet soldiers had laid down their arms, whilst tens of thousands more had crossed the German frontier and been disarmed. The Bolshevist Armies were in retreat all along the front, and the Poles were pursuing them. Every day the Polish victory took on greater and even greater dimensions. The strategic situation changed with kaleidoscopic rapidity.

On August 9th-22nd M. Maklakov telegraphed—

> I have spoken to M. Paléologue. The Bolshevist attack having been crushed, Poland is about to conclude the peace, the Great Powers are to fix the frontiers on ethnographical lines. Paléologue realizes how necessary it is that you should have speedy help. Everything possible will be done.

The signature of peace by Poland would make our position infinitely more serious. The failure of the Kuban operation had robbed us of our last hope of finding a way of continuing the struggle on neighboring Russian territory. Abandoned to our fate as we now were, we would inevitably perish sooner or later. But I did not give up all hope that France who had just recognized us and had therefore taken up a very pronounced attitude towards the Soviet Power, would not leave us helpless. Maklakov's telegram strengthened my hope.

Since it was apparent that France might waver, we had to maintain her belief in the strength of our position. The news of the forced abandonment of the Kuban would have produced a particularly unfavorable impression abroad at such a moment, therefore it had to be hushed up.

I instructed M. Struve to send the chief of the French Mission a memorandum with the necessary explanations. At the same time Neratov telegraphed to Maklakov—

> By order of the Commander-in-Chief, Struve has sent the chief of the French Military Mission the following memorandum—
>
> General Wrangel wishes to submit to the French Government and High Command the following observations on the general military situation: Poland's great success in her fight against the Red Army makes it possible, for the first time in the course of this war, to strike a decisive blow at the Soviet Power by means of concerted action by the Polish and Russian Armies under the supreme direction of the French High Command. This would ensure the general tranquility and social peace of the whole world The conclusion of a separate peace between the Poles and the Bolshevists

will leave the question still open, and will not wipe out the Bolshevist danger.

These considerations have led the Commander-in-Chief to put before the French Government and High Command the problem of the establishment of one anti-Bolshevist front in cooperation with the Poles and under the general direction of the French High Command. In such an eventuality our strategical plans will have to undergo some modification, and the centre of operations will have to be shifted to the Ukraine. The Commander-in-Chief does not consider it advisable to modify his strategical plans until he is sure of the approval and cooperation of the French Government. But the situation at the front demands a rapid decision and its immediate execution. In General Ulagay's Army, in addition to the effectives who are more or less adequately armed and equipped, there are nearly five thousand soldiers who lack the great essential—rifles. Under such conditions as these, the Commander-in-Chief has to carry out a complex and difficult strategical operation.

The Commander-in-Chief's suggestions for a modification of his strategical plan are as follows—

If the Poles follow up the operations on their right wing, we must not push on towards the right, this would be to repeat the mistake which General Denikin made when, he did not effect a junction with Admiral Koltchak's troops. The Bolshevists have concentrated considerable forces in the Kuban, therefore we must send reinforcements there, but this is only possible if we evacuate the mainland of Taurida, although the general situation demands that we remain in occupation there. Should the Poles begin active operations on their right wing in the Ukraine, whilst we concentrate our efforts on our left wing, a continuous common front will result, and we will aim at destroying the Soviet Power once and for all, and restoring tranquility to Europe on the basis of a general peace. The Commander-in-Chief urgently requests a speedy answer. Will you arrange all the necessary measures with the French Government and High Command and telegraph the result to us?

On August 15th General Babiev's units once again attempted an offensive, but were unsuccessful. Already the enemy possessed an enormous numerical superiority. After heavy fighting which lasted throughout the day, General Ulagay ordered the troops to withdraw to Atchuiev. When I heard the news I ordered ships to proceed to Atchuiev to take the invading detachment on board. General Chatilov went over there on a torpedo-boat.

On August 17th our units began to embark near Atchuiev. The lay of the land made it possible for us to hold the enemy in check with a very small rearguard and to embark in absolute security. The troops came on board in perfect order. In spite of heavy losses, our effectives had increased considerably in numbers. For example, one of our divisions which had lost three hundred men and two hundred horses, had left Feodossia with one thousand two hundred men and two hundred and fifty horses, it came back with one thousand five hundred Cossacks and six hundred horses. All those who could were fleeing from the Red yoke. Towards evening General Chatilov came back and reported that the embarkation was going on quite normally, that General Babiev's cavalry was already on board, and that the rest of the troops were not far behind.

Meanwhile the situation on the northern front had become threatening. From the 9th to the 11th fierce and bloody fighting had been going on. The enemy attacked us without truce or intermission, and drove back the 1st Army Corps in several places. The Red cavalry came right down into our territory and threatened our railway communications. The 2nd Army Corps had been driven back to Perekop.

On the morning of the 17th the struggle was resumed with great fierceness all along the front. Until midday the issue was uncertain, General Koutepov thought that the situation was very serious. I decided to go to Melitopol. At Djankoy Station we were warned that the Red Cavalry patrols were approaching the railway. The signal-lights were put out, and our train went northwards in the twilight. I reached Melitopol late in the evening. In spite of the lateness of the hour, the streets near Staff Headquarters were crowded with people. Agony was limned on those gloomy, anxious faces. General Koutepov had not lost his coolness. Towards night, reports came in from most of the areas under fire. Although the day had ended in some success for us, the situation was still grave. The presence of the Red cavalry in our rear boded all kinds of unexpected results.

On August 18th the enemy again attacked, and were everywhere repulsed. On the 19th our troops in their turn launched an offensive. The crisis was over, and I could return to Kertch. The news of our success spread rapidly through the town of Melitopol. The streets were full of life, and joyful faces were to be seen everywhere. An enormous crowd greeted me with loud cheers.

On the 19th I reached Kertch. The embarkation at Atchuiev was progressing favorably. At Taman our troops had suffered a slight repulse. The chief of the detachment there reported that he had suffered heavy losses and must retreat.

Towards night this detachment reached the shore. I ordered it to be taken on board and back to Kertch.

The expedition to the Kuban ended in failure. We were driven down on to a little strip of Russian territory on the coast, and from there we had to continue the struggle against an enemy who commanded all the vast stretches of Russia. Our forces dwindled day by day, our resources were used up. The dead weight of failure was crushing my heart. Again and again I asked myself if it had not been my fault. Had I foreseen everything? Had all my calculations been accurate?

The heavy fighting on the northern front, where the Red menace had been checked only at the cost of enormous efforts, made it impossible to transfer any troops from this area to the seat of the Kuban operation. The direction mapped out for the raiding company had been well chosen. In spite of the indiscretions of the Kubanians in authority, whose idle gossip had threatened the secrecy of the operation, the exact landing-place had remained unknown to the enemy. The Reds had expected us at Taman and in the Novorissusk section. The troops had landed without loss, and three days later had taken the most important railway in Kuban, Timachevskaia Station, thus coming within forty versts of Ekaterinodar, the heart of the Kuban. If General Ulagay had not hesitated, but had marched straight on without a backward glance at his base, Ekaterinodar would have been taken in two days, and the northern Kuban would have been free. There is no gain saying this.

Yet at the same time, a great deal of what had happened had been my fault. I knew General Ulagay's strong points and his weaknesses. When I appointed General Dratzenko, whom I did not know, to the post of Chief-of-Staff, I should have arranged all the details of the plan and the preparations for the operation myself. I had, however, entrusted the task to General Chatilov, who was also very busy, and therefore had been able to devote but little time to it. I blamed myself bitterly and could find no excuses for myself.

The only positive result of the expedition was the large number of reinforcements, both men and horses, which we had added to our expeditionary force—it now numbered about ten thousand Cossacks. This not only compensated for the heavy losses we had suffered on the northern front, but even left us a large surplus.

The collapse of the Red troops on the Polish front became more and more definite. More than one hundred thousand prisoners fell into the hands of the Poles, whilst about the same number of men had been interned in Germany. At the same time, the probability of peace between Poland and Soviet Russia became greater and greater. Poland was said to have declared explicitly that "Poland sincerely wants peace." Riga had already been mentioned as the seat of future negotiations.

I left General Chatilov at Kertch and set out for Sebastopol on the night of August 20th. As soon as I arrived I took what steps I could to prevent our recent failure in the Kuban creating an unfavorable impression.

The day after my arrival, Admiral MacCully, the chief of the American Military Mission, paid me a visit. By order of his Government he submitted a series of written questions to me on the subject of the general policy of the South Russian Government.

OFFICE OF THE SPECIAL AGENT OF THE UNITED STATES
STATE DEPARTMENT FOR RUSSIA

SEBASTOPOL, RUSSIA
September 6, 1920.

YOUR EXCELLENCY,

For the information of the U S Government I would appreciate very much a fairly explicit and comprehensive statement by General Wrangel of his policy and aims. The following questions suggest the character of the information desired—

1. Is the policy of General Wrangel the restoration of Russia on the basis of a general expression of the will of the people, and is he pledged to the creation of a constituent assembly to be elected by the will of the people on the basis of general and direct national suffrage?
2. Does General Wrangel specifically disavow any intention to impose upon Russia any unrepresentative Government, ignoring the sanctions of popular assent and acceptance?
3. Is the interpretation of recent declarations of General Wrangel correct, that, recognizing the mistakes of the Denikin and Koltchak Governments and profiting by their experience, he does not regard the establishment of law and freedom in Russia as primarily a military task, that he places first and foremost the organization of production and satisfaction of needs of the peasants, who constitute the great majority of the Russian people, that General Wrangel is organizing and training an organization not for pursuing extensive war against Bolshevism along the type attempted by Koltchak and Denikin, but would agree to protect against attack the nucleus of national regeneration; that, in short, his attempt is to create a centre of political and economic order and consolidated effort, around which Russian groups and territories may gather freely and develop their own desired effect?
4. Information exists that General Wrangel is introducing behind the lines local self-government by means of popularly elected Zemstvos and other democratic agencies, and that, in particular, he is seeking to solve the land problem in an orderly manner by constitutional methods and by validating the ownership of the lands by the peasants. Is this information correct?
5. Are there not a considerable number of refugees now dependent on General Wrangel's protection against the

Bolshevists? Approximately how many such refugees are there, and to what classes and groups do they in general belong?

6. Would it be justifiable to conclude that General Wrangel, although believing his movement to be the present centre of Russia's efforts at self-restoration and recovery of unity and national life, does not at the moment profess or claim to be the head of an all-Russian Government, that he does not regard himself as authorized to make treaties intending to be binding upon any future Russian Government that may be set up, or to grant concessions or otherwise dispose of the national domains and resources?
7. Is the recent declaration of the policy of the U S Government satisfactory to General Wrangel, both as regards Poland and as regards the unity and integrity of Russia?
8. What are the safeguards which General Wrangel feels can be relied upon, and which may assure other nations that General Wrangel will be able to pursue the policy of building up the portion of Russia which comes under his jurisdiction without permitting its development into either a military adventure or a political reaction?

As definite and explicit a statement of his aims as General Wrangel may be good enough to make would be much appreciated.

N. A. MACCULLY,
Rear-Admiral, U.S.N.

TO HIS EXCELLENCY, M. PETER STRUVE,
Minister of Foreign Affairs,
South Russian Government

The Admiral, a sincere friend of our cause, was simply beaming when he delivered this questionnaire to me. He believed that the American Government's request for answers to its questions was a preliminary to America's recognition of the South Russian Government. On August 24th the following answer to the questions was sent to Admiral MacCully—

CONFIDENTIAL

1. General Wrangel has declared many times that his sole aim is to enable the Russian people to express their wishes freely on the subject of the future government of the country. Today, therefore, he can but affirm once again his intention

of establishing conditions which will permit of the calling of a National Assembly based on universal suffrage, through which the Russian people can decide on the form of government for new Russia.

2. General Wrangel has not the slightest intention of imposing a Government on Russia which would function without the cooperation of a national representative body, or the sympathy and support of the people.
3. The interpretation of General Wrangel's recent declarations in the sense that he does not regard the establishment of law and liberty in Russia as preeminently a military task is perfectly justified. On the contrary, the series of reforms which have already been carried out prove that General Wrangel attaches primary importance to reconstructive work in the State and to the satisfying of the needs of the peasants who constitute the great majority of the Russian people. It is precisely because he wants to foster the peaceful development of creative governmental action that General Wrangel has refrained from bringing to the fore the question of the enlargement of the front on which his armies are fighting the Bolshevists. He has rather tried to assure the integrity of the economic and political centre which has been created by the Russian Army on occupied territory and in the Cossack regions with which he is in close alliance. The preservation of this healthy nucleus is indispensable, for it has to serve as a centre of gravity for the free development of the final efforts of the Russian people for national regeneration.
4. The information concerning the reforms which General Wrangel's Government has carried out by creating district Zemstvos, and in agrarian spheres, is absolutely accurate. The first of these reforms anticipates decentralization and safeguards the local economic interests of the population who will deal with economic questions through their freely elected agencies. The law concerning the district Zemstvos will be followed at a very early date by one concerning the provincial Zemstvos, both laws are to serve as a basis for a representative organ of a more general character. The Land Reform will deal with the agrarian problem in a radical way by allowing the legal remission by redemption of arable land to its cultivators who will become its owners, thus a strong class of small peasant proprietors will be created in accordance with the ideal of the Russian peasant.

5. The number of refugees who have sought General Wrangel's protection against the Bolshevists is very high. It greatly exceeds five hundred thousand in the Crimea alone, and there are almost as many again scattered through the Near East, Egypt, and Europe. Most of them are old men, women, and children. All these refugees are benefitting in one way or another from the support and help of the South Russian Government. Should the integrity of the territories of the South Russian Government be guaranteed, General Wrangel thinks it is his duty to facilitate the return of these refugees to their country and to allow them to devote themselves to productive work. This body of refugees is made up of the most diverse elements. They belong to all classes of the population, for men of all classes found it equally impossible to endure the Bolshevist tyranny.
6. General Wrangel considers that the Government of which he is the head is the sole remaining depository of the idea of national regeneration and the restoration of Russian unity. He thinks, however, that only a Government set up after the National Assembly has settled its nature should have the power to conclude treaties affecting the sovereign rights of the Russian people, or of disposing of the national patrimony.
7. The declaration of policy which was made recently by the Government of the United States coincides in every respect with General Wrangel's political programme. He is in complete agreement with the clauses dealing with the preservation of Russian unity and territorial integrity as well as with those dealing with Poland. General Wrangel would like to take this occasion to express his very deepest gratitude to the Federal Government.
8. General Wrangel realizes that if foreign powers accord recognition to the work already performed by his Government, they would like to be assured in some way other than by a verbal declaration that their fear that the South Russian Government's activities may degenerate into a military adventure or a political reaction is quite unjustified. As regards their fear of a military adventure, General Wrangel begs to remind you that he is ready to end the Civil War as soon as the integrity of the territory under his authority and the Cossack regions is guaranteed effectively, and as soon as the Russian people, now ground down beneath the Bolshevist yoke, are given the means of

> expressing their will freely. General Wrangel declares, on his side, that he is ready to promise the population of the territory which accepts his authority that they will be able to express their opinions. He is firmly convinced that this population will never pronounce in favor of the Soviets.

As for his personal affairs, General Wrangel has already declared openly that his object is to enable the people to express their wishes freely. He then will submit to the sovereign voice of the Russian nation without the slightest hesitation.

SEBASTOPOL,
August 24th-*September* 6, 1920

Heavy fighting was still in progress on our northern front. Our troops were pushing back the enemy towards Kahovka and drawing near to one of the fortified positions.

During the night of August 21st the units of the 2nd Army Corps attacked the enemy, but were received by furious counter-attacks and barrage-fire from the artillery. Our infantry attacked the fortified position with tanks and armored cars, and made a sudden incursion into the first line of the enemy's fortifications. In spite of heavy losses, our units hurled themselves against the second line of trenches which was defended by a large number of machine-guns. The Reds replied with a counter-attack in front, at the same time enveloping both our wings. Two of our four tanks were destroyed by artillery fire.

Before dawn our units were forced to return to their starting-place, for the enemy's fire had grown more and more deadly. At seven o'clock in the morning all the units of our attacking force were ordered to occupy the most advantageous positions possible, and limit themselves to an active defence

Our second failure before Kahovka demonstrated the strength of this position, the tenacity of the Reds in defending it, and the break-up of our infantry's dashing offensive.

To fill in the gaps made during the recent engagements I ordered a fresh mobilization and a requisition of one thousand five hundred horses. These repeated mobilizations and requisitioning of horses weighed heavily on the people, yet all through our struggle they manifested sincere sympathy towards us. But the recent military burdens had become insupportable, and cases of failure to mobilize became more and more frequent.

Although I fully realized the insupportable weight of the sacrifices I asked of the population, I was nevertheless compelled to enforce the impositions by every means in my power. The implacable struggle demanded sacrifices from everybody.

The enemy took advantage of the difficulty of the situation in our rear, and did their utmost to increase their propaganda behind-the-lines.

Towards the middle of July the Bolshevists succeeded in getting into touch with the Crimean Committee of the Communist Party by way of the sea. This organization had been dispersed for a time, but had renewed its activities towards the end of June. Motor-boats from Anapa and Novorissusk kept up communications with the Bolshevists outside the Crimea.

On August 5th a Communist detachment of about a dozen men, under the leadership of the sailor Mokrohussov, landed on the coast, having run their motor-boat close in to the shore. The detachment was armed with machine-guns, cartridges, hand-grenades, and a large sum of money—five hundred million roubles in notes called "Romanovs" (at this time a Romanov rouble was worth seventy roubles in our currency), as well as two hundred thousand pounds in Turkish money. Mokrohussov, with the aid of his confederates, succeeded in reaching the forests, he assumed the resounding title of "Commander of the Army of the Insurgents in the Crimea", and began to recruit every kind of rolling-stone into his ranks. Towards the end of August Mokrohussov had collected about three hundred men, whom he divided into three "regiments".

These bands behaved very daringly. During the night of July 30th a detachment of Greens had attacked a convoy of artillery, taken away the horses, and blown up the ammunition. On August 4th they had robbed the forest home of Massandra of a million roubles. During the night of August 20th they attacked the Bechui mines, robbed the strong-box, burnt down the explosives depot, and destroyed the shafts. On August 22nd Mokrohussov's bands invaded Kutchuk Ouzen and carried off the sergeant of the police and eleven policemen. On the 29th a band of one hundred and fifty men had attacked the market-town of Sudak with four machine-guns, but the convalescent officers and soldiers there had been warned in time and repulsed them, incurring heavy losses.

The regional "Revcom"[1] which had large sums of money at its disposal, was also working in the towns. In four months the "Revcom" had received from Moscow, through the Jewish courier Raphael Kurgan, surnamed "Folia," a million Romanovs in notes, ten thousand pounds sterling, and gold and diamonds worth forty million roubles. Communist Committees had been formed at Simferopol, Sebastopol, Yalta, Feodossia, Kertch, and Eupatona, and all were well provided with money. They all kept in communication with one another by means of a brisk service of couriers.

On August 2nd a Communist centre was discovered in Yalta; it was found to possess printing machinery, and had been maintaining communications with the Regional Committee. During August, two of the Regional

[1] Revolutionary Committee—TRANSLATOR.

Committee's couriers were arrested in the war zone, they were engaged in espionage. Almost simultaneously the Soviet spy-courier Simka Kessel was arrested at Perekop, he had wormed his way from the Crimea to Odessa.

A little later we managed to collect enough information to enable us to watch the people who were at the very centre of the new Regional Communist Committee. The watch we kept resulted in the arrest, on August 21st, of a certain Mordukh Akodice, who was trying to get through the forest to Sebastopol. He had received orders from the Regional Committee to re-establish the Revolutionary Committee in Sebastopol, for which work he had received sixteen thousand Romanov roubles which were found on him. At the same time the Jews Raphael Kurgan "Folia" and Naoum Glatmann were arrested in Simferopol, where they had been living under assumed names. They were the local representatives of the Regional Committee, in their rooms were found two hundred and fifty thousand Romanov roubles in bundles enclosed in wrappers bearing the stamp of the People's Bank of Moscow, a million of the Supreme Command's roubles, and gold and diamond objects officially valued at twenty-eight million roubles, there was also some party correspondence—financiers' accounts and notes on the political work of the Crimean Regional Committee. On the same day the Jews Hersch Gotzmann and Osman Gilert were arrested. In Gotzmann's house were found letters and the stamp of the Sebastopol Revolutionary Committee, which had hardly been used; in Gilert's rooms letters were also found, as well as three million roubles in every currency of the world, which was the property of the Party.

The material collected by raids on the houses of the aforementioned men, and the absolutely sincere and detailed confessions they made, enabled us to root out the whole network of the Bolshevist organization which had spread over the Crimea. The number of people formally subjected to the preliminary inquiry in the course of the month exceeded one hundred and fifty. The organization of our enemy's agents in the Crimea had been dealt a shattering blow.

I was indebted to General Klimovitch for the rapidity of the searches and the destruction of the Communist network in the district. The whole police force of the State, which was doing its duty very well and successfully, was under his authority.

The elections to the District Zemstvos were completed in an astonishing short space of time. There were already sixty-eight agrarian district Soviets. Almost everywhere inquiries into the land reserves had been completed and lists of people with a right to a plot of land in full ownership made up. Many of the agrarian Soviets had already arranged their scale for the distribution of landed property. Proprietors by right of the new law were already in existence. In the Melitopol and Dnieprovsk districts, the district agrarian Soviets had already begun to portion out several large estates.

The externals of life behind-the-lines no longer bore witness to the recent days of anguish. In spite of its proximity to the front, the negligence and debauchery so usual in towns behind-the-lines were conspicuous by their absence. The great number of officers behind the front had fallen back into disciplined ways. Life went on quietly as usual.

CHAPTER XV

"CONCENTRATE ON WRANGEL!"

Towards the end of August, the balance-sheet of the Bolshevist disaster on the Polish front was drawn up, nearly two hundred and fifty thousand men and tens of thousands of horses had been captured by the Poles or interned in Germany. The remnants of the Bolshevist Army were in precipitate flight towards the east, pursued by the Polish troops.

The Ukrainian units, who were advancing rapidly, were operating on the Polish troops' right wing. On the right bank of the Ukraine, revolts were flaring up everywhere. Companies of *franc-tireurs* were harassing the Red troops ceaselessly, and attacking convoys, trains, and echelons on the road.

We had succeeded in coming to an agreement with the Ukrainian *franc-tireurs*, we were to re-equip them with arms, ammunition, and money, I circulated proclamations amongst the population of the Ukraine urging them to rise and throw off the Bolshevist yoke.

During the last days of August a delegation from the largest company of *franc-tireurs* arrived. The commander of the company was an ex-officer of the old Imperial Guard, he was fighting for the moment under the yellow and blue Ukrainian flag. According to him, the population on the right bank of the Ukraine were exasperated with the Bolshevists, but the events of 1919 had left unfortunate memories of the Volunteer Army, these, combined with the able propaganda of the Ukrainians, did much to enlist sympathy for the Separatists.

The growing excitement in the Ukraine set Ukrainian circles outside the country in motion. I learnt that a delegation of Ukrainian-Federalists, composed of Messrs. Markotun, Tsitovitch, and Moghiliansky, had left Paris for the Crimea.

The strategical situation was as I had explained it to the French Government. Events on the Polish front made operations in the west of primary importance. If Poland should accept the peace which the Bolshevists were offering so insistently, and Lloyd George's Government was extolling, everything would be over for us. The three and a half Bolshevist Armies on the western front could then rush in on us, and the issue of such an attack could not be doubted. Our last batch of reinforcements—nearly ten thousand "Bredovians"—had been incorporated into the Army. We could not count on any others, except for a few officers who had been evacuated into different countries in 1919. Our local resources in men and horses had dwindled away to nothing. The sole source of recruitment still open to us was our prisoners, but their fighting value was only relative.

I did my utmost to convince the French and Polish Governments that the Poles must go on with the war, or must at least drag out the peace negotiations so that I could reinforce and re-equip my troops with the enormous booty which had fallen into the hands of the Poles, whilst the Red troops were being detained on the Polish front. I considered using the Red units which had gone over to the Poles or those which had been interned in Germany, in addition to the ammunition which the victors had seized. I proposed to form a 3rd Russian Army on Polish territory out of the remains of Bredov's command and the detachments of Bulak-Balakhovitch and Colonel Permykin. I intended to amalgamate the commands of the Polish and Russian troops and put the joint command into the hands of a French general who should work with representatives of the Polish and Russian Armies

I pursued these negotiations during my interviews with the French and Polish representatives, as well as through my representatives in Paris and Warsaw.

In the middle of September the chief of the Polish Military Mission informed me that the Polish Government had agreed to authorize the formation of a Russian Army eighty thousand strong on Polish territory.

The chief of our Foreign Communications telegraphed to Maklakov—

> We have just heard that the Polish Government has agreed to the formation of a Russian Army eighty thousand strong, to be recruited from amongst the Bolshevist prisoners. It has been pointed out to us that this measure will simplify the recruiting question, cut down transport expenses from Poland to the Crimea, and give the necessary tame for the development of our forces The Commander-in-Chief is in favor of this measure on the following conditions—
>
> 1. This new Army must be placed on the right wing of the group of Polish-Ukrainian Armies, so that in the course of the subsequent offensive it will be able to rejoin the left wing of our Armies.
> 2. This Army must be called the 3rd Russian Army. At the present moment the Russian forces in the Crimea are composed of two Armies.
> 3. The Commander of the 3rd Army must be appointed by General Wrangel.
> 4. The 3rd Army shall be subject to the Commander-in-Chief of the eastern anti-Bolshevist front until it comes into direct contact with the southern front,

> when it shall pass under the command of General Wrangel.
>
> Please inform the French Government and High Command of this.

The Polish Government appeared to be willing to meet us. General Miller, our military representative in Paris, telegraphed—

> The Poles agree to send their military representative to Paris to discuss the coordination of our military operations with us. The General you send ought to be fully acquainted with all your intentions and plans, and should have a thorough understanding of the situation and your forces

To hurry on the negotiations I decided to send M. Struve and General Yusefovitch to Paris, the latter was to control the formation of the Russian units in Poland, but until he arrived there the task fell upon General Makhrov.

MM. Struve and Yusefovitch were to deliver to the French Government a brief memorandum signed by my adjutant, M. Krivochein, detailing my propositions—

> ADJUTANT TO THE COMMANDER-IN CHIEF OF THE ARMED FORCES OF SOUTH RUSSIA
>
> SEBASTOPOL,
> *September* 15, 1920.
>
> *Confidential*
>
> When Poland's luck suddenly changed, the Russian Army was engaged in an attempt to liberate Northern Caucasia. The enemy had concentrated huge forces against our expeditionary force in the Kuban, therefore, if we were to follow up our successes there we had to send fresh units to the front from Taurida. This made the retreat to Perekop necessary. The Army was already preparing to retreat when the defeat of the Bolshevists on the Polish front made it possible to consider the formation of a united anti-Bolshevist front on the west. Should this plan be adopted, the protection of the Tauridan front will become of primary importance. It will compel us to send fewer reinforcements to the Kubanian front, and later will force us to abandon the operation in the Kuban altogether. Our expeditionary force, whilst still on Kubanian territory, was ordered to send troops into the Crimea. It came back not only unreduced, but with its effective force considerably increased. Later on, the Russian Army will prepare an offensive, but there can be no hope of

a decisive success unless the operation is undertaken in cooperation with the other anti-Bolshevist forces. Such cooperative actions are only possible by agreement. The amalgamation of the Ukrainian troops and the Polish Army is already an accomplished fact. For our part, a military convention with the Ukrainian Army is in course of preparation.

The time is now ripe for the Russian and Polish Armies to cooperate. Every subsequent success, every step forward, can result only from the formation of a common front. And here France assumes a dominating position. The safety of Warsaw, the very independence of Poland on the one hand, and the recognition of the South Russian Government and the help which has been given in the re-equipment of the Russian Army on the other, are the facts which make it obvious that the two Armies will freely consent to cooperate against the Bolshevists under the command of a French general, provided that he works with representatives of the two anti-Bolshevist Armies.

Poland's cessation of hostilities and entry into negotiations with the Soviet Government puts the Russian Army into a very difficult position. The Bolshevist forces now set free will be thrown on to the southern front, and in a few months we shall have three and a half new Bolshevist Armies arrayed against us.

But even under these conditions the Russian Army will not lay down its arms, it will continue the fight, hoping for success and trusting in its ally, France, to whom it has always been loyal, and who can now give it invaluable help. If the negotiations between Poland and Russia are prolonged, and if the troops of Bolshevist prisoners in Poland and Germany are sorted and transported to our front with all speed, together with the remains of General Miller's and General Youdenitch's Armies, we will be able to continue our struggle.

Negotiations must be prolonged until we have had time to transport the contingents from Germany and Poland and recruit the new units.

The contingents which are to be transported must be completely equipped and armed, and the new formations must be furnished with the necessary equipment, this can be supplied from the Bolshevist materials of war which the Poles have captured.

If all this were done, the Russian Army could continue the struggle against the Bolshevists, and, even if it were fighting alone, could be sure of ultimate success. Thus Poland could rest assured that the Bolshevists would be unable to violate the peace treaty.

> Over and above the delivery of materials of war to the Russian Army, this project will need still more important financial help in the form of a loan. The refunding of this loan, together with the payments for the materials of war, will be covered by a special treaty concerning the export of coin, coal, and other raw materials to France from the territories occupied by the Russian Army and those they intend to occupy.

We published articles expounding our point of view in many organs of the Russian Press abroad as well as in the newspapers of other countries.

At the same time, I decided to pay a visit to the front with the representatives of the Allied Missions, for on the one hand I wanted to show them how strong our position was, and on the other to prove to them by the evidence of then own eyes that we lacked technical equipment, and urgently needed help if we were to continue the struggle.

On the evening of August 30th I left for Sebastopol, accompanied by M. Krivochein, representatives of the French, Polish, American, English, Japanese, and Serbian Military Missions, and several Russian and foreign newspaper correspondents.

On the morning of August 31st the train stopped at Taganach Station, and we set off in cars to inspect a section of the fortifications. The fortifications were more nearly complete in this part of the front than anywhere else. There were heavy barbed-wire entanglements, armoured emplacements, a complex labyrinth of trenches, and skilfully-concealed batteries. The newly installed heavy siege-artillery was engaged in gunnery practice, and our aeroplanes were observing for it.

The visitors could see with their own eyes what an immense amount of work had been accomplished in the last few months in spite of the almost complete lack of technical equipment. When we returned to the train we went on as far as Akimovka Station, and there inspected the aviation park and General Babiev's splendid Kuban division, which was here in reserve. Our squadron of aeroplanes, under the direction of General Tkatchov, a bold pilot, executed a series of brilliant aerial manoeuvres, which were all the more remarkable because most of the machines were in a very bad state of repair, and only the incomparable boldness of the Russian officer made up for the deficiencies of his material. When the flying was over, the military agents gathered round the intrepid airmen and expressed their admiration. General Tkatchov reported that most of the machines were absolutely worn out, and that if we did not receive new ones very soon, our air force would become powerless. I took the opportunity to mention the efforts I had made to obtain some new aeroplanes and the insurmountable obstacles I had met with, not only from our enemies. For example, the aeroplanes I had bought, after the greatest difficulty, in a certain state[1] had been destroyed "by mistake" by one of the foreign Commissions of Control.[2]

The representative of the English Military Mission, the sympathetic Colonel Walsh, blushed furiously at these words.

General Babiev's division marched past in excellent order. After the review, the Cossacks showed off their horsemanship ("Djighitovka"), and their skill completely captivated the foreign visitors.

In the evening we reached Melitopol and joined the General Staff of the 1st Army. Its chief, General Dostovalov, gave us a short explanation of the general position, and informed us of the catastrophes which had dogged General Koutepov's troops in Northern Taurida. After supper we returned to out train and left for Fedorovka Station. From there we went by car to Kronsfeld colony, on the morning of September 1st. Here we inspected Kornilov's division, which was being held in reserve at the disposal of the Commander of the Army.

The ranks stretched from one end of the huge square to the other. An altar had been erected in the middle of the square, and the priests in glittering robes were performing their offices. The religious canticles soared up into the peaceful autumn air, and far up, a hovering lark mingled his song with them.

The faces of the soldiers were tanned and weather-beaten, their boots scorched and worn out, their shirts discolored and threadbare. Many of the men even lacked shirts altogether, and were wearing woollen vests instead There was one soldier dressed in a patterned cretonne shirt with canvas shoulder-pieces, old khaki trousers, and yellow English half-boots, another had no trousers at all, and was wearing nothing but a pair of woollen drawers. The terrible destitution of the troops simply leapt to the eyes. But with what care they had repaired their old garments, polished up their arms, and dressed their ranks! After the *Te Deum* I presented the 1st Kornilov Regiment with the Kornilovian flag, which had belonged to the first battalion to be named after General Kornilov. This flag, which had been preserved by an officer who had recently escaped from Bolshevist territory, was regarded as a precious relic by the regiment.

The units marched past. The ranks passed by, one after the other, all beautifully straight, the men's steps firm and vigorous, their faces contented and cheerful. It seemed as if they were the regiments of old Russia resurrected from the tomb.

After the parade, the divisional commander offered us dinner in the village, during the meal I complimented the representatives of the Allied Powers in the name of the Russian Army. In their reply, the foreign

---

[1] Bulgaria.

[2] The English.

representatives expressed their sincere sympathy with us, and their desire to come to our help. These military men, delighted with everything they had just seen, had ceased to be politicians for a moment.

After dinner we went out to inspect, the positions which Markov's and Drosdovsky's reserve divisions were occupying. We found the same appalling want, the same gallant resemblance to the old Russian regiments, the same confident, steady manner.

We returned to our train late in the evening. During the night M. Krivochein, the Allied representatives, and the foreign correspondents left for Sebastopol, whilst I went on to Yushun Station, from there I went by car, on September 2nd, to inspect the positions held by the 2nd Army Corps.

The regiments of the 2nd Army Corps had been severely tried during the fighting under Kahovka, and had recently been reinforced by units from Bredov's command and by reservists; as a result, they were still only imperfectly amalgamated, and then external appearance could not be compared with that of the regiments of the 1st Army Corps. But they were in a quiet and confident frame of mind. General Vitkovsky was working ceaselessly, doing his utmost to restore order to the Army Corps which his predecessor had so disorganized. On September 5th I returned to Sebastopol.

As our troops had evacuated the Kuban, the enemy could use some of their troops which were thereby set free for work on the Crimean front. New units were arriving from Caucasia and the interior of Russia, and making for different sections of our front.

The Red group on the right bank of the Dnieper, under the command of "Comrade" Eidemann, had received the title of the 6th Army. Its General Staff had arrived quite complete from the northern front. The 6th Army was made up of the 1st, 3rd, 13th (from Pskov), 46th, and 52nd divisions of sharpshooters, and "Comrade" Goff's cavalry brigade.

The 2nd cavalry Army, under the command of the ex-Voiskovoi-Starchma[1] Mironov, was also operating on the right bank of the Dnieper: it was made up of the 2nd, 16th, and 21st cavalry divisions and a special mounted brigade. The 7th and the 2nd cavalry Armies numbered fifteen thousand bayonets and six thousand sabres altogether.

The 13th Soviet Army was still operating on General Koutepov's front. It numbered thirty thousand bayonets and seven thousand sabres. The 7th, 13th, and 2nd cavalry Armies, together numbered forty-five thousand bayonets and thirteen thousand sabres. On September 1st our effective forces did not exceed twenty-five thousand bayonets and eight thousand sabres.

Having undertaken an operation in the west, we had first to fight the Reds on the northern and eastern sections of the front, and thus free ourselves for

[1] Cossack Lieutenant-Colonel.

an operation on the other side of the Dnieper. I decided to let the mounted troops of the Don Army Corps strike a blow and attempt to envelop the left flank of the 13th Soviet Army.

Fighting went on without pause throughout September. The troops had been unable to rest for months past, yet they performed prodigies of valor. In a series of brilliant engagements the Russian Army scattered the enemy's forces all along the front from the Sea of Azov to the Kitchkasse Pass. The task I had set it—that of freeing our hands for an operation on the other side of the Dnieper—was accomplished.

Whilst incessant fighting was in progress at the front, intensive work was going on behind-the-lines. I changed my quarters, left the house I had been occupying, and went to a much larger building called the Grand Palace, where the commander of the Fleet had previously had his quarters. My closest colleagues, M. Krivochein and General Chatilov, my chief-of-staff, were also at the Grand Palace.

Our working-day began at seven o'clock, and went on, almost without interruption, until eleven o'clock or midnight. Our attention had to be divided between the most varied problems the war, internal and foreign policy, economics, and finance. These last questions worried M. Krivochein and me more than anything else.

In spite of all our difficulties, we managed to cover our ordinary expenses with our ordinary revenue. But the extraordinary budget for this year showed a deficit of two hundred and fifty milliards[1]. It is true that, because of the depreciation of the rouble, this figure was less considerable than it seemed, but, nevertheless, it was still very large. The Crimea was poor in local resources, and certainly could not support the entire machinery and personnel of a huge Army. Although our effective fighting forces did not number more than thirty or thirty-five thousand men (not counting the fleet), the vast interior, the tens of thousands of wounded who filled the hospitals, the huge number of prisoners in the reserve formations, and the concentration camps, the military schools, the numerous organizations behind-the-lines, the administrative departments for War and the Navy, the fleet and the maritime departments, all added to the number of mouths that the Supreme Command had to feed—so that the grand total was something like two hundred and fifty or three hundred thousand. Feeding all these people cost more than all our wealth put together. We were doing all we could to get ammunition from abroad on the strength of our reserve securities.

Corn was now our sole export. The Government, through its agents, continued to buy it up in Northern Taurida. The Ministry of Commerce and

[1] A "milliard" is an anachronistic term for a thousand millions, most often referred to today as simply a "billion"—PUBLISHER

Industry had made contracts with different people between July 24th and September 16th to deliver ten million pouds[1] of grain. Nearly a million and a half pounds had already reached the ports, and almost a million had been exported. Not only was corn our sole export and therefore of great economic value, but the arrival of Russian corn from the Crimea on the markets of Western Europe had also great political importance. The Western Powers, especially France, who had suffered greatly during the war, were suffering from a lack of bread, and the arrival at Marseilles of a ship carrying two hundred and seventy-five thousand pouds of Russian corn was mentioned in nearly all the French papers.

The monopoly of the corn trade by the South Russian Government provoked violent criticism from one party in commercial circles which was direly interested in the question. The South Russian Government was accused of "impeding commerce" and "strangling private enterprise". We could not put a stop to these criticisms.

We still had only very faint hopes of obtaining a foreign loan, for the existence of the South Russian Government seemed very precarious, no one believed in its stability.

M. Krivochein thought out the scheme of convoking a special economic conference of industrialists, merchants and financiers at Sebastopol to discuss the possibilities of an economic and industrial revival in South Russia and discover some way of raising a loan. The date of the conference was fixed for the end of September, and the invitations were sent our accordingly. Many of those who were invited, including Count Kokovteov, Davydov, and Rittich, refused to come on some pretext or another, but others accepted the invitation.

The Poles began to negotiate with the representatives of Soviet Russia. The Polish delegation arrived at Riga on September 5th-18th. From the very beginning, a complete divergence in their views was obvious. Each side seemed to postulate conditions which the other could not possibly accept; nevertheless, negotiations were not broken off. Behind the backs of the negotiating parties the clash of interests of the other Powers could be distinctly felt.

It appeared that the Bolshevists had a very clear view of the situation. They foresaw that they would reach an agreement with the Poles in some way or another, and so the Soviet leaders decided to settle accounts with their other enemy. They sent round the watchword "Concentrate on Wrangel!"

The remnants of the Red Armies had flowed back towards the east without a pause before the Polish troops, but the Red Command now launched all its available reserves against the south.

---

[1] The poud is a Russian measure of weight roughly equivalent to forty English pounds—TRANSLATOR.

In mid-September we began to receive information that Boudenny's cavalry (the 1st Cavalry Army) was coming south from the south-west section of the Polish front.

Unexpected changes had taken place in the French Government. M. Deschanel, the President of the Republic, had fallen seriously ill and had been compelled to resign. M. Millerand had been elected in his place. M. Leygues was appointed President of the French Council. MM. Petit and Paléologue, the colleagues of the ex-President of the Council, who had supported the policy of a rapprochement with national Russia, had gone out of office. I sent the new President a telegram of congratulation.

On September 20th I went to Melitopol for a few hours and conferred with Generals Koutepov and Dratzenko. The preparations for the expedition across the Dnieper had been completed, and the operation was due to begin on September 25th.

On my return journey to Sebastopol, I escaped falling a victim to a plot by the purest accident. A quarter of an hour before my train was due, a mine had been discovered. A peasant had been mowing the grass near the railroad and had noticed an electric cable. He had had time to communicate with the signal-box on the line, and my train had been held up at the nearest station The detachment of sappers who were rushed to the spot uncovered a mine of considerable size. If the criminals had been able to carry out their plan, there would not have been much left of our train. Unfortunately, the criminals escaped. A most thorough inquiry was held, and it was established that a certain Stefanovitch-Stivenson knew something of the crime; he was arrested, but escaped from prison a few days later.

A delegation from the National Ukrainian Party arrived in the Crimea, it consisted of its president, Markotun, its secretary, General Tsitovitch, and a member of the Party, one Moghiliansky. The National Ukrainian Party was hostile to Petlioura's Separatist policy, it was spreading the idea of Russian unity with local autonomy for the Ukraine. The Party was working in close cooperation with the Ukrainian Government of Galicia, of which Petruchevitch, who had proclaimed the union with Russia, was president. The National Ukrainian Party had no real strength, but it was sympathetic to us, and had a few connections in the Ukraine and some in France. These could be used to counterbalance the Ukrainian Separatists. Therefore I made a point of showing the greatest attention to the delegation. I received it in the presence of M. Krivochein, M. Struve, the chief of the Ministry of Foreign Affairs, and General Chatilov, my chief-of-staff. I expressed my complete agreement with its principles as explained by the delegation, and declared that I based my whole policy on the union of all the Russian forces which were in arms against Bolshevism, and that I was ready to support the formation of autonomous national units on the same lines as those adopted in my agreement with the Cossacks, The Party also received some material help.

On September 18th the Atamans of the Don, Kuban, Terek, and Astrakhan organized a banquet in honor of the Ukrainian Party on the premises of the Seamen's Club. The Ataman of the Don, in the name of the Cossacks, welcomed the Ukrainian delegation, which was a personification of the idea of union under Russia, the mother of them all. He led a cheer for Russia. M. Markotun, replying, emphasized the fatal character of the Separatist tendencies which those foreigners who desired the partitioning of Russia were supporting. He dwelt on the results which the South Russian Government had obtained since it had abandoned its uncompromising attitude towards the different nationalities of Greater Russia, and had achieved the union of all the Russian forces in their struggle against the common enemy. In conclusion, he gave the toast of the Commander-in-Chief.

I replied to both speakers. In my speech I pointed out that Bolshevism was a menace not only to Russia, but to the whole world. To the Bolshevists, Russia was nothing but a funeral pile, with the help of which they hoped to set alight the whole of Europe. In our struggle for the cause of Russia we were saving Europe, and Poland owed her recent overwhelming victory largely to us. "The Polish Press had many times expressed the view that Poland is fighting not against the Russian people, but against the representatives of the International. I hope," I said, "that the near future will not give the lie to these declarations, and that Poland will not abandon those who are fighting for the common cause of culture and civilization."

M. Mikhalsky, the representative of the Polish Mission, emphasized, in the course of his speech, the fact, that although the Polish Government had not mentioned the aim of the war in its declaration, it was, in effect, a fight against the International. "The promise of a new frontier will not stop the war—our Government will not call a halt, for it is sure of victory!"

On September 20th the "Temporary Statute concerning the district Zemstvos" was published. The elections for the district Zemstvos were already over in some of the districts.

The population had shown great moderation and common sense at the elections. The disorganization of local life had given rise to a healthy tendency towards union. In most of the districts the wealthier peasants had been elected, some big landowners had also been returned. The district Soviets which were still in existence in those regions where they had not been replaced by Zemstvos were very hard at work. In most of the districts the inquiry into the redistribution of the land had already been held and finished, and the new terms of ownership sketched out. In some places the peasants' rights of ownership over the land on which they worked had already been consolidated.

In many of the richest districts the wealthier peasants were buying the land directly from the owners. The owners received full payment immediately, and the peasants were free from redemption-payments. The people manifestly wished to possess the land in full ownership, and to acquire it legally. The population was echoing the spirit of the new law.

The number of friendly transactions between peasants and landowners would doubtless have been still larger had it not been for the difficult conditions created by the Civil War and the continual mobilizations which deprived the peasants of manual labor and horses.

Whilst the reorganization of the Zemstvos was going on, the municipal governments were not forgotten. On September 23rd a conference met under the presidency of the Deputy-Director of the Administration of the Interior, it discussed a project concerning the elections for the municipal councils. The basis of the electoral system was to remain intact, the reform was to be limited to the methods used at elections.

On September 2nd, Admiral Sablin, the Commander of our Fleet, fell ill. He had been unwell for a long time, but had been fighting against his illness. Now he was compelled to take to his bed. His disease—cancer of the liver—grew rapidly worse, and his case became hopeless. It was a great loss for the fleet, for Admiral Sablin was energetic and able, and had set the fleet in order in spite of the extreme difficulty of the situation, the lack of material, and the varied composition of the crews which had been recruited haphazard, and were quite untrained. The ships had been cleaned up and repainted and the crews disciplined. Nearly all the damaged equipment had been repaired, and reserve supplies of fuel, amounting to five hundred thousand pouds of coal and one thousand five hundred pouds of oil, had been concentrated in the ports in case of an evacuation. The men-of-war of our squadron were keeping a strict watch on the coast and were covering our movements. Every air-raid that our aeroplanes had undertaken had been successful. There was no hope of Admiral Sablin's recovering, so I offered the post of Commandant of the Fleet and Director of the Ministry of Marine to Admiral Kedrov.

On September 20th we received a French wireless message from Batoum. The French representative informed us that several thousand Cossack rebels, commanded by General Fostikov, had retreated to the coast in the Sotchy-Adler Section, after an engagement with the Bolshevists; they wanted to take refuge in Georgia, but the Georgian Government had refused to let them enter the country. The Cossacks were asking for help. I immediately ordered cartridges, shells, and provisions to be sent off to them by transport-ship. I also sent a torpedo-boat to establish communications with the rebels. General Chatilov sailed on this torpedo-boat. He returned on September 22nd.

General Fostikov, who had been organizing his revolt since the summer, had collected several thousand Cossacks. After a series of victorious engagements, he had freed a large part of the Maikop and Laba districts from Red domination. But his position had become difficult after our failure at the

Kuban. He lacked ammunition, and little by little the Red troops had surrounded the rebels. General Fostikov foresaw that he would have to evacuate the Kuban, and so was trying to get into touch with me through Batoum, where a large number of the Kubanian leaders had congregated after the shameful capitulation of General Bukretov's Army. But all his dispatches had been intercepted by the Kubanian leaders and had not reached me. Finally, General Fostikov learnt from a Bolshevist newspaper which he had picked up at the front that France had recognized the South Russian Government, and so he had attempted to get into touch with me through the French representative at Batoum. This time I had received his dispatch.

Recently General Fostikov had been entirely surrounded by the Bolshevists, and had been suffering from a terrible shortage of ammunition, so he had decided to retreat to Georgia. He had persuaded all the Cossacks who had wanted to go back to their own homes to give up the idea and retreat with the others—a detachment of two thousand men—into the Sotchy area. He was having difficulty in holding out there. He had used up nearly all his provisions and ammunition. The Georgians had refused to let the Cossacks march through their territory. Immediate help was necessary. Unfortunately a storm was raging, which made it impossible for the transport-ship to leave. A few days later the man-of-war set out alone. In the meantime a wireless message arrived announcing that the Cossacks had retreated to Georgia under pressure from the Reds, the Georgian troops had surrounded and disarmed them. The Reds were demanding their extradition.

I ordered the torpedo-boat which was escorting the transport-ship to embark the Cossacks, cost what it might; should the Georgians put up any opposition it was not to hesitate to open fire on them.

At first the Georgians answered with a summary refusal to allow the troops to embark. After long-drawn-out negotiations, we arrived at a compromise. The Georgians feared the Bolshevists, and would only agree to the embarkation of the Cossacks on condition that we pretended to use armed force! The torpedo-boat hurled a few torpedoes into space, the Georgian detachment retreated, and the Cossacks came on board. I ordered General Fostikov's detachment of nearly two thousand men to be landed at Feodossia, where the Cossacks were given rest, clothes, and ammunition, which would enable them to be sent to the front again later on.

CHAPTER XVI

ACROSS THE DNIEPER

Preparations for the operation across the Dnieper had been in progress for nearly a month. The collection of the necessary material for pontoon-bridges was a very difficult task, for there was none in the Crimea. The operation had to be prepared with the utmost secrecy, because its success depended largely on its being a surprise attack It was necessary to make a detailed survey of the banks of the Dnieper, for the configuration of the lower reaches (the "plavnias") changed every year after the great spring floods. During the last ten days of September we were at last able to launch a pontoon-bridge on the Dnieper near Uchkelka, which is in the bend of the river just where the current ceases to flow westwards, and curves back towards the south-west.

The enemy, who had been defeated in the middle of September, were showing no signs of activity on the 1st Army's front. The demoralized units of the 13th Soviet Army were avoiding all contact with our troops, and were apparently combining with the reserves with a view to a future action. The cavalry of the 13th Army was continuing to reconnoitre on the eastern section of the front.

The Reds had concentrated considerable forces opposite General Dratzenko's 2nd Army. In spite of a well-organized espionage service, they did not succeed in discovering in advance the spot at which we intended to cross the Dnieper. But in anticipation of our march towards the west, the Red Command had massed their best units from the southern front on the right bank of the Dnieper. Boudenny's 1st cavalry Army was coming from the south-west front (on the borders of Galicia) by forced marches, and was making for this section of the line. It was expected on the southern front about October 16th. Before it arrived we had to defeat the enemy forces already massed across the Dnieper—(the 2nd cavalry Army reinforced by infantry units from the 6th and 13th Soviet Armies)—in order to make both its banks safe for us, this was an indispensable preliminary condition of our deeper penetration into the Ukraine.

During the night of September 25th our infantry crossed the ford at the Isle of Khortitza (near Alexandrovsk), they were up to their armpits in water and under artillery and machine-gun fire from the Reds, yet they seized the slopes and began to advance. The enemy retreated before our attack all along the front. On the night of the 26th, the pontoon-bridge on the Dnieper near Uchkelka was ready, and the main body of the 2nd Army began to cross.

From the 26th until the 28th, those units of the 2nd Army which had crossed the Dnieper followed up their advance and repulsed the Reds. Our cavalry broke through the enemy's lines and carried off many trophies. On September 28th they took more than three thousand prisoners, eight guns, six armored cars, and an armored train.

On September 29th General Babiev's cavalry troop advanced south-westwards in an attempt to circumvent the enemy's position at Kahovka. The operation developed favorably.

The Reds strove to check our offensive, for it threatened their principal lines of communication between the 6th and the 2nd cavalry Armies, they attacked us simultaneously on the east (where General Koutepov and the 1st Army were) and at Kahovka. The Red Command hoped to deflect our troops from their set purpose by this manoeuvre, the aim of which was to catch us in a vice, a similar manoeuvre had been tried several times during the summer campaign in Northern Taurida. The enemy drove back the units on General Koutepov's right wing and advanced on Melitopol. But a few days later the Reds were repulsed by the 1st Army all along the front. Local forces had retaken the position we had formerly held before Kahovka and in the Kherson section.

Meanwhile General Dratzenko's 2nd Army was proceeding with its operation. I was very dissatisfied with Dratzenko's conduct, he was behaving in an indecisive, timid manner, and was simply groping his way along. . . . His lack of clear, precise decision, and the absence of a strong lead from the commander of the Army, was having its effect. . . .

On the evening of the 30th I telegraphed to General Dratzenko demanding decisive action. I pointed out that through his indecision we were running the risk of losing everything we had won by our initial successes. Our air-scouts reported that the Reds were beginning to evacuate the armed fortress of Kahovka. I ordered General Vitkovsky's units to attack this position at dawn on October 1st.

I was awakened during the night. General Dratzenko reported that he had encountered a large force of the enemy's troops on the right bank of the Dnieper and had suffered heavy losses, not being willing to risk the complete annihilation of his army, he had been compelled to give the order to retreat to the left bank. . . . The whole operation had collapsed.

At dawn General Vitkovsky's units launched their attack on the armed fortress of Kahovka, but they were repulsed. Our units had reached the barbed wire, but had been unable to get through it, they had been forced to throw themselves on the ground, and had suffered heavy losses from the enemy's intensive artillery-fire. The tanks detachment had succeeded in getting into Kahovka, but had been killed almost to a man. The information we had received from our observation aeroplanes concerning the evacuation of Kahovka had been absolutely incorrect.

In spite of the repeated demands which I sent to the staff of the 2nd Army throughout that night, I could obtain no details of the events which had taken place on the left bank of the Dnieper. We merely learnt that the retreat had been effected on the north under cover of the Kubanian sharpshooters commanded by the gallant General Tayganok, and on the west, under cover of the Terek *plastounes* from Firsovka. The cavalry was in complete disorder, the artillery and transport formed a long ribbon which was winding over the bridges towards the left bank of the Dnieper.

At nine o'clock in the morning I received a laconic telegram from General Dratzenko. "General Babiev was killed by a shell today—September 30th." This explained everything. With the death of their adored leader the cavalry had lost heart, their nerve had gone, and with it their faith in then own strength. General Naoumenko, who had taken over the command, had also been wounded and was unable to save the situation. The regiments had fallen a prey to confusion. The units were making for the bridges with all speed. The enemy, much heartened, had resumed the offensive. The confusion in the ranks of the disabled cavalry grew still greater. There was no longer any possibility of restoring order.

Everyone was hurrying towards the bridges. The cavalry and infantry units mingled in the narrow forest paths and hollows. . . General Dratzenko, much moved by this spectacle, had given the order for a general retreat to the left bank of the Dnieper.

Towards the evening of October 1st, our units had retreated across the Dnieper. The pontoon-bridge had been taken apart and towed to the left bank. On the morning of October 2nd the Samur and Terek regiments, who had been covering the retreat, also retired, crossing the river in boats.

The Trans-Dnieper operation was over. It had been thought out carefully, prepared cleverly, and developed strictly according to plan, and yet it had ended in failure. Our failure was due partly to that disastrous accident, the death of General Babiev, and partly and more importantly to the inept manoeuvres of General Dratzenko, Commander of the 2nd Army. He acknowledged this himself with rare moral courage and quite winning honesty, and begged to be released from his command.

On September 26th we had received news that the Poles had signed an armistice. Hostilities had ceased on the Polish front, and the Red Command was free to hurl its entire forces against us. At the same time the negotiations which my representatives were pursuing with the French Government led us to hope that France would not abandon us and leave us helpless. M. Struve reported that he was negotiating a French loan for which the auspices were favorable, and that later on we might expect help in the form of ammunition. In a few days' time a French High Commission, accompanied by a Military Mission, was to leave for the Crimea. The Crimean representatives of the Polish Government continued to assure us that the Poles sincerely desired to reach an agreement with us, and gave us to understand that the signature of the armistice was only a forced concession to England, and was far from being a peace.

A daily paper reached Sebastopol containing an interview with Prince Lubomirsky, the diplomatic representative of the Polish Military Mission in the Crimea—

> Prince Lubomirsky, a member of the Polish Military Mission, has just arrived in Sebastopol from Warsaw. In an interview with our correspondent, Prince Lubomirsky discussed several interesting questions of the moment.
>
> The conclusion of the armistice with the Bolshevists was due to a whole series of reasons. The Polish Government wants neither the armistice nor a peace. In spite of the terrible Russo-German war which was fought out on Polish territory, the Polish people have nothing but hatred for the Bolshevists, they are ready to continue the war against them. The principal reason for the armistice is that, except for France, the Western countries not only refuse to support Poland, but even insist on the cessation of the war with the Soviets.
>
> Europe's policy is dictated by the following causes: the post-war industrial revival demands raw materials, there is a shortage of the materials which formerly came from Russia, and the gap cannot be filled from elsewhere. In the West they imagine that the moment they conclude a peace with the Soviets, Russia will begin to flow with rivers of milk and honey. It is the Bolshevists themselves who have fostered this attitude, hiding the truth from the West. In addition to this principal cause, circumstances of a technical kind have also exerted an influence on the signing of the armistice. The Czechs would not let material of war and ammunition come through into Poland. The free town of Dantzig was holding up all goods addressed to Poland. The Polish troops were very short of shells in spite of the help which their gallant friend, France, had given them. All these reasons taken together have forced the Polish Government to conclude not a peace but an armistice.

On the subject of an alliance between Poland and General Wrangel, Prince Lubomirsky said:

> Polish administrative circles are very sympathetic to the idea of an alliance with General Wrangel, I am certain that such an alliance will be concluded in the very near future.

Although the Polish Armies had suspended hostilities, the Polish Government was still able to help us very effectively by prolonging the negotiations and so detaining the Red forces on the western front. We kept open our lines of communication with the Poles only with the greatest of difficulty. We only managed it at all through the intermediary of France. Our attempts to establish communications with Warsaw by wireless came to nothing. In spite of all my demands, the Inter-allied High Commissioners categorically refused to give us permission to set up a wireless station on the site of the old Russian Embassy at Bouyouk-Dere.[1]

Although I cherished no great illusions about our "foreign friends," I did not give up hope that the Polish Government, under pressure from France, would delay the conclusion of the peace as long as possible, in order that we might complete the formation of our Army on Polish territory, or at least have time to transfer Russian troops to the Crimea.

Once we had received reinforcements and materials of war and had arranged the projected loan, we would be able to continue the struggle. With this goal in view, it was essential that we should keep our hold on Northern Taurida. A retreat beyond the isthmus into the Crimean peninsula would not only condemn us to hunger and every kind of privation, but would be the confession of our powerlessness to continue an active struggle, this would deprive us of all future help from France. Once we were shut up in the Crimea, we would cease to be a menace to the Soviet Government, and therefore to be of any interest to the Western Powers.

The failure of the Trans-Dnieper operation was having its inevitable reaction on the spirits of the troops. Our recent heavy losses had still further weakened our effective forces, and we could not fill in the gaps immediately. The fortified camp at Kahovka was a continual menace to us. The enemy all along our front were receiving reinforcements daily. Boudenny's cavalry was expected to reach one of the sections on the right bank of the Dnieper the second week in October. When the 1st cavalry Army arrived, the enemy's forces would be three or three and a half times greater than ours, their effective cavalry force was five times that of ours. Furthermore, their artillery and technical equipment was vastly superior to ours.

On October 1st I summoned Generals Koutepov and Chatilov to a conference. I proposed that my most intimate colleagues and I should discuss every aspect of the following question: ought we to risk a battle in front of the Crimean Passes, or should we evacuate Northern Taurida and retreat behind the isthmus? We took into consideration all the prevailing conditions, and were unanimous in our decision to risk a battle in Northern Taurida. It was a last desperate venture, but any other decision would inevitably have led straight to the final crash. At Sebastopol I found news awaiting me that

[1] Near Constantinople.

Poland had signed the peace. It had been signed by Russia and the Soviet Ukraine on one side, and Poland on the other. The independence of the Ukraine and of White Russia was guaranteed, and both parties waived their indemnity rights. Poland received compensation for all property evacuated from her territory since August 1, 1914. The treaty containing the preliminary peace terms had been signed on September 29th, and the interview with the Polish diplomatic representative which had appeared in the papers on October 1st had been given after the signature of the peace treaty. The Poles were consistent in their duplicity.

The news that Poland had signed the peace did not create much of a stir amongst the largest classes of our population. The majority of the people did not realize its direct bearing on the future of our struggle, nor did they understand the importance of the failure of our Trans-Dnieper operation. The General Staff's communique on the trophies taken during the five days' operation—thirteen thousand five hundred prisoners, twenty-seven guns, six armored cars, and one armored train—saved the population from realizing that we had suffered a serious defeat. I did my utmost to prevent the news of our failure from becoming current. It was now more necessary than ever that foreigners should be convinced of the stability of our position.

The last sitting of the Financial and Economic Conference took place on October 4th in my presence. I thanked the members of the Conference for the support which they had given the South Russian Government, and expressed my conviction that when they went abroad they would not slacken in their support of the Russian National Cause. I mentioned the difficult struggle which we were undertaking and the privations which the Army was suffering, and remarked casually that the enemy's numerical superiority—for they could now use their entire force against us—and our own lack of ammunition would oblige us to retreat into the Crimea, "but soon, when we have rested and reorganized, we intend to renew the struggle."

I could foresee that the decisive battle in Northern Taurida would turn out badly for us, and I was preparing public opinion in advance.

On October 5th the Financial and Economic Conference finished its work; it proposed a series of practical financial and industrial measures, and adopted a resolution declaring amongst other things that—

> The Financial and Economic Conference cannot but bow respectfully to the huge task and the civil and military exploits which the South Russian Government are accomplishing at this very moment, and to the results which they have achieved in so short a time. In a country ravaged by war and the crimes of the Bolshevist Government, the bases of a free economic life and a new civil order are rapidly being established.

The same day I gave a supper in honor of the members of the Conference. MM P. Bark, V. Riabuchinsky, V. Gourko, and others spoke. M. Riabuchinsky's speech was particularly brilliant and vigorous. I read my order to the Army referring to Poland's peace treaty with Soviet Russia.

ORDER FROM THE COMMANDER-IN-CHIEF OF THE RUSSIAN ARMY

SEBASTOPOL. NO. 3697. *October* 6-19, 1920.

TO EVERY RUSSIAN SOLDIER

> The Polish Army which has been fighting side by side with us against the common enemy of liberty and order has just laid down its arms and signed a preliminary peace with the oppressors and traitors who designate themselves the Soviet Government of Russia. We are now alone in the struggle which will decide the fate not only of our country but of the whole of humanity. Let us strive to free our native land from the yoke of these Red scum who recognize neither God nor country, who bring confusion and shame in their wake. By delivering Russia over to pillage and ruin, these infidels hope to start a world-wide conflagration.
>
> It is now nearly three years since the Russian Army set its feet on the path to Calvary. Weak in numbers but strong in spirit we bore our cross, unshakably convinced that our just cause would triumph in the end. Scarcely six months ago we were on the very brink of the abyss, and the infidels were already preparing to celebrate their triumph with our blood. By the united effort of all the loyal sons of the Motherland, we tore victory once again from the hands of the enemy, and for the last six months we have fought them without cease.
>
> Soldiers! The freed lands of Russia look upon you with love, our brothers in the Red butchers' dungeons put their faith in you; and I, your old comrade-in-arms, trust my invincible eagles. This is not the first time that we have waged unequal warfare. God is not on the side of might, but of right.
>
> GENERAL WRANGEL

On October 6th I received a telegram from Ataman Semenov who was in command of the fighting in the far east of Russia. It ran as follows—

> I understand the character of the Cossacks, the native tribes and the peasants who live on the borders of eastern Russia, and I have

> come to the irrevocable decision, that not only must I recognize in your person the Government of South Russia, but also that I must submit to you as to the successor of the legitimate Russian Power, whilst I remain the chief authority in far eastern Russia and retain the powers of Commander-in-Chief and Pokhodny Ataman[1] of the Cossack troops of Transbaikalia, Amur, Oussouria, Yenissey, Siberia, Orenburg, and Bachkiria, the last four States having become our property, together with their Governments.
>
> The rural population which was intoxicated with the delights of Bolshevism has already begun to grow sober again, the volunteer Cossacks, the native tribes, and the peasants, are returning to our side. The units of my Army find this state of affairs in Transbaikalia, the Oussourian region and Northern Mongolia. In my own name and in that of my troops and the population which is subject to me, I compliment you on the great services which you have rendered to your country.
>
> COMMANDER-IN-CHIEF AND POKHODNY ATAMAN,
> LIEUT-GEN. SEMENOV

Gallant General Babiev's funeral took place on October 5th, I was oppressed with sadness as I followed my old comrade's coffin. Still another of our glorious heroes was dead. Yet another name had been added to the long list of Russian warriors who had expiated their country's shame with their blood.

On October 6th the French Mission, with the Count de Martel at its head, arrived on board the cruiser *Provence*. A guard-of-honor formed of Cossacks of the Guard was awaiting it on the quayside. General Viazmitinov, Chief of the Military Administration, and M. Tatichechev, Deputy-Director of the Ministry of Foreign Affairs, welcomed the Mission in my name. A large two-storied house was reserved for it.

The following day I received the Count de Mattel in the presence of my adjutant, M. Krivochein, my chief-of-Staff, General Chatilov, and M. Tatichechev. The Count de Mattel brought with him Admiral de Bon, Commandant of the Mediterranean Squadron (the cruiser *Provence* was his flagship), his chief-of-staff, General Brousseau, the chief of the French Military Mission, and Colonel Buchenschutz, its chief-of-staff.

When he gave up his letters of credit, the Count de Mattel said to me—

> My Government has appointed me its representative to Your Excellency under the title of High Commissioner of the French Republic, and thereby seeks to emphasize the importance it attaches

---

[1] A Cossack title corresponding to Commander-in-Chief of Cossack troops.

> to the alliance and sincere friendship which has always existed between the French and the Russian people in spite of all trials and tests. We can never forget the invaluable help which Russia gave us at the beginning of the war, when the waves of the German invasion were breaking over our frontiers. We know that the Peace of Brest-Litovsk was the work of a distinct minority, which alone was responsible for that piece of treachery. France has never attempted any compromise with the Soviet Power, which of its own free will has put itself outside all known laws.
>
> France is the sincere friend of all true defenders of liberty, law, and order, that is why she has recognized, with the sincerest sympathy, that Your Excellency has established a democratic Government which respects the rights of national minorities and relies for support on an Army which is in close touch with the people.
>
> France, who is still working to repair the ravages of the war, and has not yet rebuilt all her own ruins, has decided to give you her full moral support, and as much material help as possible.
>
> You know the President of the Republic's feelings for Russia. M. Leygues, the head of the French Government, has defined his policy clearly in the following words, which he addressed to the Parlement: "We want the Russian people, who are so simple and good, so interesting, so worthy to live an honorable and powerful life, to find peace, order, and prosperity once again."
>
> It is as the representative of such feelings that I have come to the Crimea. Most cordially and sincerely I put my support and help at your disposal, both as a conscientious executor of the wishes of the French Government and as a sincere friend of the Russian people.

I replied to the Count de Mattel's speech in the following words—

> It gives me the deepest pleasure to welcome France's representative to Russian territory. National Russia is bound to France by traditional feelings of friendship and affection. I would like to express my profound gratitude to the Republican Government for taking the initiative in declaring itself unequivocably in favor of the cause of Russian regeneration.
>
> At the very moment when the shameful conspiracy overthrew every vestige of law and order in Russia and forced the country into making a dishonourable capitulation to the enemy, Russian patriots were already engaged in the struggle against the enemies of their country. That struggle has been going on now for nearly three years, and we are firmly resolved to fight it out to the finish, not because

> we are animated by any warlike spirit, but because we are inflexibly determined to free the people of Russia from the tyranny which is oppressing them, and to make it possible for them to decide their own destiny.
>
> You can rely upon us giving you our most whole-hearted support, and you may rest assured that we most sincerely wish to second you in the execution of the high task which has been entrusted to you.

At four o'clock on the same day I visited the Count de Martel on board the cruiser *Provence*.

On October 8th I invited the members of the Mission to dinner. After dinner I mingled with my guests. The hall was brilliantly lighted and decorated with flowers and the resplendent uniforms of the guests, it hummed with animated conversation. I went up to General Dragomirov. "Well," he said, "we are about to set out on the highroad."

I forced myself to give him a pleasant answer, but my thoughts were far away, out in Northern Taurida, where our fate was being decided. Amongst all this brilliant merry-making, gloomy forebodings clutched at my heart.

On October 9th Admiral de Bon held a lunch in my honor on board the cruiser *Provence*, which was leaving the same day for Constantinople. Admiral de Bon was a charming old man and quite captivated me. He was Russia's sincere friend, and remained so later when we were in exile. After lunch, M. Krivochein and I had a long conversation with Admiral de Bon, the Count de Martel, and General Brousseau, we explained our opinions and our needs to them. The Admiral was going straight to Paris from Constantinople, and once there, he hoped to be able to get our most urgent needs satisfied.

The negotiation of the loan was going on quite satisfactorily in Paris. Maklakov telegraphed—

> Struve wishes to inform you that on October 20th he was received by M. Leygues, President of the Council, and on the 22nd by the President of the Republic, to whom he explained the financial situation and our plans for the loan. His attitude was very friendly, and there are great hopes of success.

The transport-ship *Rion* was on its way to the Crimea with a cargo of warm clothes, ammunition, etc., for the troops. It seemed that the long-awaited help was about to arrive at last. But was it not now too late?

We received news from the front of the continual arrival of the enemy's reinforcements. All the reserves at the disposal of the Red Command which could be transferred from the interior of Russia, Western Siberia, or the Polish front, were now being sent southwards. The bands of the famous "Father" Makhno, who up till now had been "working" behind the Red lines, suddenly realized the possibility of profits to be made from plundering the Crimea, and joined the Soviet troops. The enemy's forces grew larger every day. The General Staff of the 4th Red Army, which had been beaten by the Poles at the battle of Warsaw, when some of its divisions had been interned in Germany, had arrived in Alexandrovsk from the western front.

Nature herself seemed to be against us. An intensely cold spell set in, a most unusual thing for this time of the year. Our troops, who were thinly clad, suffered appallingly from the cold, many soldiers had frost-bitten limbs. The temperature fell yet lower. The troops dwindled away.

At the same time as the Red Command was throwing all its available forces southwards, it was also taking measures to increase its propaganda work behind our lines.

Lately, the Greens had redoubled their activity. There had been a recrudescence of military espionage inspired by the Registration Bureau ("Registrod") on the Caucasian front, which had its headquarters at Rostov on the Don. The "Registrod" sent scouts into our midst under registration marks, numbers five and thirteen were stationed at Temriuk in the Kuban, and there were special numbers on the shores of the Taman peninsula. From Temriuk and by way of Taman the Red spies crossed the narrow Kertch Pass, landed on the Kertch peninsula, and set out for the Crimea, later they returned by the same route.

In one month alone six Soviet spies were caught in the town of Kertch and its suburbs, and the liaison service which the Bolshevists had organized between our territory and the Tamanan Coast was discovered. In Kertch and the hamlet of Yurgaky (on the Sea of Azov) this service was preparing secret stations equipped with signal-lights, spherical mirrors for signaling by heliography, and materials for chemical writing. On one of the spies we found, amongst other documents, an order to "rouse Mokrohoussov" with instructions how to find him.

Under the expert direction of General Klimovitch, our counter-espionage service foiled each of the enemy's attempts. The enemy agents who fell into our hands were court-martialed and mercilessly punished. I fought with all my might against these attempts at subversion, yet at the same time I strove to uphold the authority of the machinery of justice and its independence from all representatives of the administrative authorities, however highly placed these might be.

An order published on October 9th definitely established the independence of the Military Jurisdiction, which until now had been, in the person of the Attorney-General of the Army and Navy, subject to the chief of the Military Administration, and obliged to take its orders from the Ministry of Marine on questions concerning the fleet.

Groups of the so-called "Democratic Opposition," filled with fumes which had been generated at the beginning of the Revolution, were still committing and defending the mistakes which had been committed in every phase of our struggle. Blind and obstinate in their defence of "the conquests of the Revolution," which gave them an alluring semblance of prestige and influence, these groups were inclined to regard every measure which they did not initiate as a menace to these "conquests." These groups included some elective organizations (several Zemstvos and Municipalities), and also some of the professional syndicates and the most considerable of the Co-operative Unions—the Tsentrosoyouz and its branches—the Tsentrocektzia, the Dnieprosoyouz, and the Zdravsoyouz.

From the very fast days of the March Revolution these organizations had made a rule of recruiting their staffs from amongst those who had served a term in revolutionary politics. Therefore the great majority of their organizations were packed with elements which understood Bolshevist and semi-Bolshevist ideas, however much they camouflaged them, much better than the ideals of the Russian Army, which had adopted the principle of military dictatorship as an aid to success in its fight to the death.

These groups did not hesitate to give surreptitious protection, or even active help to our enemies, whenever this did not conflict with the "morals of the party" or its commercial interests.

In this connection the activity of the Tsentrosoyouz and its branches merits special mention. In 1919 it had been proved by documentary evidence that when the Volunteer Army was occupying Odessa, Kiev, and Kharkov, the Tsentrosoyouz, the Tsentrocektzia, and the Dnieprosoyouz had been in communication with the Soviet Government, received subsidies from it, and carried out its orders, supplying the Red Army and the provinces of Northern Russia with materials and provender. An examination of the account-books of the Tsentrosoyouz and its Kharkov branch and those of the Popular Bank of Moscow established the fact that the Tsentrosoyouz had received fifty million roubles from the Soviet Government, whilst merchandise destined for Soviet Russia had been found in the Tsentrosoyouz's local depots. Amongst the other co-operative organizations, the Tsentrocektzia (Workmen's Co-operative), the Dnieprosoyouz, and the Zdravsoyouz enjoyed the special favor of the Soviet Government, and had received important subsidies from the Soviets for putting themselves at their service, for this service they had used their branches on the territory occupied by the Russian Army!

A "General Plan of Work for the Year 1920", found in September 1920 during a police-raid on the Tsentrosoyouz Offices at Kertch, will serve as a specimen of the Tsentrosoyouz's activities in the Crimea in the Bolshevist interests. This plan had been sent to the office at Kertch by M. Dobrovolsky, manager of the Tauridan counting-house of the Tsentrosoyouz, and was followed by a letter from M. Vonov, a director of the southern section of this organization, it mentioned the following achievements—

1. Buying up of raw materials and sending them untouched to the northern provinces and abroad
2. Preparation of semi-manufactured goods and sending them to the north to be finished in the Tsentrosoyouz's factories
3. Production of manufactured articles and sending them into Northern Russia

Some goods had been sent to Northern Russia by way of Batoum and Georgia, and some by a ruse, merchandise would be accumulated in localities which it was believed that the Volunteer Army was about to evacuate, then the abandoned goods would be sent immediately to Soviet Russia, credited to the branches of the Tsentrosoyouz.

A Soviet law of March 20, 1920, had changed all the co-operative organizations of Soviet Russia into "communal distributive organizations." The central organization of the Tsentrosoyouz at Moscow had come under this law. It had been transformed into a central organ for the provisioning of Soviet Russia. Naturally the owners of the Tsentrosoyouz had not given up their capital and independence with a good grace, but they had been compelled to do so by sheer force and other measures of repression. For some time the co-operative organization abroad (the Inocentre), which was in London, under the management of MM. Berckenheim and Salheim and Mme. Lensky, was the only branch to keep its independence besides the branch in the Crimea.

It would have been natural under these conditions if the Inocentre in London had collaborated with the Russian Army to prevent the total absorption of the co-operative organizations by the Bolshevists. Nothing of the kind had happened. On the contrary, when the Soviet delegation led by Krassin, Noghin, and Razumovsky had arrived in London, Berckenheim had communicated with them and offered his good offices to obtain a commercial treaty for Soviet Russia.

This last action unmasked the Tsentrosoyouz's real policy at a moment when its Crimean representatives were assuring the South Russian Government of its devotion to our cause.

These tendencies explain the hostility which the Tsentrosoyouz showed towards us in all its "non-commercial" activities, to which this organization devoted five per cent, of its capital. These "non-commercial" activities, which consisted of organizing libraries and conferences and editing books and pamphlets, had been developed on quite a large scale.

In later days, when we had been compelled to leave the country, some of the men who had been in charge of the South Russian branch of the Tsentrosoyouz, and had played an important part in politics, were to be found amongst the members of the Soviet Mission to Constantinople, whilst others of their colleagues in the Tsentrosoyouz took posts as Soviet representatives in Trebizond, Zunguldak, and even London.

On September 25th the activities of these people were investigated. The houses of several of them were raided, which caused a veritable panic. The leaders of the Opposition in the municipality of Sebastopol, with the Mayor of the town, a Revolutionary Socialist, at their head, drew up a memorandum and sent it to the French High Commissioner, it was one long calumny, and was intended to discredit the South Russian Government in every way in the eyes of the French representative. The facts cited in the memorandum were either distorted or entirely fictitious.

In spite of all the precautions which these traitors took, we managed to obtain a copy of this memorandum. I made up my mind to put an end to this game whilst it was still in its early stages.

A Press Congress was to be held in Sebastopol on October 30th. A group of journalists asked me for an interview in connection with it. I took the opportunity to tell them how important the recognition of France was to us in our present circumstances, especially now that Poland had signed the peace. I pointed out that we could rely on help from France only if her Government was convinced of the justice of our cause, and I expressed my indignation at this document, which was the work of Russian men who put their personal or party interests before the common cause, and were base enough to serve the enemy by endeavoring to destroy foreign confidence in us. In proof of my charges, I showed the journalists the memorandum which the Mayor of Sebastopol and others had sent to the French. I saw that they were sincerely indignant.

By the next day the shameful story had gone all round the town, rousing general indignation against the Mayor and several of the municipal councilors. The Mayor attempted to offer me his "explanations", but I refused to receive him. He bowed to public opinion, resigned his mayoral office, and left Sebastopol.

The Don Cossacks were holding their "Krug"[1] at Eupatona. I went over there with Count de Maud, at his invitation, to attend the sitting on October 14th.

In my reply to the president's address of welcome, I again made a short reference to the possibility of a "temporary" retreat of the Army towards the isthmuses. After the sitting, the members of the Krug invited us to dinner at the Hotel Beyler. In reply to the Ataman's address, the Count de Martel made a long speech—

> Gentlemen, I am indeed happy to be in your midst at this grave and decisive moment in the life and destiny of your country. France

[1] "Krug" = Cossack Regional Parliament.

has ever been Russia's friend, and now it grieves her deeply to see your rich and beautiful country ruined by the violence of a handful of individuals.

France has never compromised with the Bolshevists. She has always been at the head of the world-wide anti-Bolshevist movement, and she greets General Wrangel's accession to power with delight, for he has undertaken to weld together all those men who wish to continue the struggle and defend the rights of the Russian people in spite of innumerable difficulties. France realizes that although the war against Germany has been brought to a victorious conclusion, there will be no general peace until there is peace in Russia, and Bolshevism, which was imported from Germany, is swept from Russian soil. France realizes too that the Cossacks have always been in the vanguard of the Civil War, and that they will continue this fight against the enemy, however difficult and murderous it may be. You are fighting to save millions of Russian men who have been condemned to death, a handful of men whose egotism is unparalleled in all the annals of history will dispose of them mercilessly, as they would ruin the Crimea tomorrow were it not defended by such a vigorous Commander-in-Chief, a knight "without fear and without reproach," who is entrusted with the task of keeping order and peace, and of safeguarding the rights of every citizen. I wish very sincerely that your land which is still occupied by the enemy may soon see the realization of its hopes. You have chosen the only sane course—that of union another effort, and you will reach your goal, you will achieve peace for the Don and your villages.

I cherish the hope that my expectations may soon become accomplished facts, and I have pleasure in conveying to you the best wishes of France, and fraternal greetings from your friends and allies, who will spare no effort to come to your help wherever it is possible for them to do so.

In the evening we left for Sebastopol.

On October 13th the enemy had begun to cross the Dnieper near Nikopol. Fighting was also in progress on other sections of the front.

On October 15th the Reds launched a general offensive all along the front.

CHAPTER XVII

THE LAST VENTURE

The total number of Red troops on the southern front was something like fifty-five to sixty thousand bayonets and twenty-two to twenty-five thousand sabres, counting only combatants, the complete figure, including formations behind-the-lines, reached six hundred thousand men.

The proportion of the Red troops to the Russian Army was at least three or three and a half to one. The Red Command's plan of campaign provided for the application of "pincers" to the living force of the Russian Army, and a sudden irruption into the Crimea by way of the isthmuses.

I forestalled the Red Command's plans, and, collecting an attacking force, I launched an operation consisting of consecutive attacks at the enemy's main body, my attacking force maneuvered on the operative lines in the interior.

When I reached the front, General Koutepov's and General Abramov's units were fighting for the third day in succession. The weather was colder than ever, there had not been such a frost in the Crimea for dozens of years. The number of its victims increased daily. The men muffled themselves up in any clothes that came to hand; some of them swathed themselves in straw underneath their shirts.

In spite of the real gallantry of our troops, the infantry of the 1st Army Corps was driven back from the banks of the Dnieper, and the enemy set foot on the left bank and began to push southwards. On October 15th the units of the 2nd Army Corps had also been driven back by the enemy's troops which emerged from the armed camp at Kahovka. We had been expecting the principal attack to come from this direction.

In the course of the morning of October 16th, the temperature fell to fourteen degrees below zero, A thick fog enveloped us; nothing could be distinguished a few steps ahead. In the evening a dispatch arrived from the 2nd Army Corps: hard pressed by the enemy, the units were retreating to Perekop, Large masses of Red cavalry had turned the right wing of the 2nd Army Corps and were advancing rapidly towards the east.

The 1st Red Cavalry Army had thrown all its forces behind our troops and was striving to cut off their retreat into the Crimea. In the meanwhile, General Koutepov was marking time. I sent him a wireless order to march on Salkovo with all speed, and do his utmost to check the enemy troops which had penetrated our lines at Sivache. All the same, it was clear that the enemy would reach the isthmuses before General Koutepov's troops could arrive. The enemy were on the march and were not meeting a single obstacle, they could be expected at Salkovo on the evening of the 17th. The fortified positions which guarded the approaches to the Crimea were garrisoned only with very small look-out patrols. The Red troops could easily seize the Salkovo Pass at one bound and cut off all communications between our Army and the Crimea. It was absolutely urgent that we should occupy the Salkovo Pass.

During the night of the 16th I ordered General Abramov to send the infantry division which was concentrated at Melitopol to Salkovo, under cover of armored cars. But the railroad was blocked, and the movement was earned out very slowly. The temperature fell to twenty degrees below zero. The water froze in the pumps at the stations, for they were not constructed to stand such intense cold. The echelons were held up on the march. One hour of anguish succeeded another. I had no troops at my command—the entrance to the Crimea was open to the enemy. During the day of the 17th I sent everyone who could bear arms to Salkovo—the Simferopol Military School, the Artillery School, and my own escort. I sent to Feodossia for General Fostikov's Kubanian units, even though he had not yet had time to reorganize them.

At twilight, the Red cavalry units came up to Salkovo and discharged a fusillade at our meagre units. At nightfall the Red cavalry dismounted and attempted an attack on foot, but were repulsed by our rifle and artillery fire.

During the night I managed to establish wireless communications with General Koutepov. I ordered him to quicken his movements as much as possible, get into touch with the units of the 2nd Army, which was retreating along the line of the railway, take the command into his own hands, strike at the enemy in the north, and try to check them at Sivache.

On the morning of the 18th, General Abramov's units came up from Rykovo Station and came to grips with the enemy. Towards midday General Koutepov's units came up from the west. The position of "Comrade" Boudenny's cavalry could have become very serious, for it had been driven back from the north-east and the north on to the semi-frozen salt marshes of Sivache. General Abramov's infantry units threw themselves with all their strength upon the enemy, who were not expecting an attack from this side. Boudenny's cavalry were taken unawares whilst the regiments were resting in the villages and the horses were unsaddled. The Red cavalry dashed about in utter disorder. The squadrons formed up hastily and rushed about in all directions, passing between our infantry units. One of the enemy's batteries with all its equipment and a great deal of transport fell into the hands of General Gusselchtchikov's Cossacks. The way into the Crimea was still open to our troops.

If General Koutepov had acted more energetically, the fine flower of the Red cavalry, "Comrade" Boudenny's Army, would have suffered the fate of Jloba's cavalry. But the successful beginning of this offensive bore almost no fruit. Our troops had no base, they were surrounded on all sides by the enemy, and were still shaken by the hardships they had endured; as a result, they fought but spiritlessly. The officers themselves no longer manifested their former bold assurance. The main body of the Red cavalry was able to file off eastwards without hindrance, and outstrip General Koutepov's cavalry.

On October 20th, General Abramov's troops were fighting in the pass. Later on, General Koutepov's units came up, closely followed by the Red cavalry.

The decisive battle in Northern Taurida was over. The enemy had become master of all the territory we had taken from them during the summer. An enormous amount of booty had fallen into their hands: five armored trains, eighteen guns, nearly a hundred wagon-loads of shells, ten million cartridges, twenty-five locomotive engines, several trains loaded with provisions and ammunition, and nearly two million pouds of corn from Melitopol and Guenitchesk. Our troops had suffered heavy losses, many had been killed, wounded, or frozen. A large number of prisoners and stragglers were in the hands of the enemy. The stragglers were mostly the soldiers of the Red Army whom we had incorporated into our units at different times. There were several cases of wholesale surrender: a whole battalion in Drozdovsky's division gave itself up. But the Army as a whole was still intact, and our troops in their turn had taken fifteen big guns, nearly two thousand prisoners, and many rifles and machine-guns.

The Army was intact, but its fighting-power was no longer what it had been. Could this Army rely on our fortifications for support, and withstand the enemy's attacks? Six months' intensive work had resulted in the erection of fortifications which made it very difficult for the enemy to enter the Crimea: trenches had been dug, barrages of barbed wire erected, heavy artillery emplaced, and machine-gun posts constructed.

All the technical equipment in the fortress of Sebastopol had been put in use. The branch-railway which had been extended to Yuchun made it possible for our armored trains to keep the approaches to the fortifications under fire. The armor-plating, the dug-outs, and the huts for the troops were the only things still unfinished. Lack of manual labor and wood had delayed the work. The intense cold, which had set in exceptionally early, had given rise to a particularly unfortunate situation, because our line of defence lay along a practically uninhabited area, so that the question of billets for the troops became extremely acute.

In the very first days after Poland had signed the peace, when I had first decided to risk a battle in Northern Taurida, I had foreseen the possibility of an unfavorable issue, and had visualized the probability of the victorious enemy invading the Crimea on the heels of our troops. However strong a position may be, it is bound to fall if the spirit of the troops who are defending it is broken.

Therefore, I had at the time ordered General Chatilov to verify the plan of evacuation which the General Staff had drawn up in cooperation with the Admiral of the Fleet. This plan had provided for the evacuation of sixty thousand men. I had ordered the figure to be altered to seventy-five thousand men, and had directed that the coal and oil needed to complete our reserve supplies of fuel should be delivered immediately from Constantinople.

As soon as our retreat into the Crimea seemed inevitable, I had ordered ships to be prepared immediately in the ports of Kertch, Feodossia, and Yalta to embark thirteen thousand men and four thousand horses. I had explained away this measure as a preparation for a raid on Odessa, the object of which was to join the Russian troops operating in the Ukraine.

To mask my real intentions even more completely, I did everything to substantiate the rumors that a raid was to be made. The General Staff was ordered to spread the rumor that a landing in Kuban was being planned.

The number of troops to be mentioned was chosen in proportion to our effective forces in such a way that even those who knew the exact number of our troops could not be suspicious. I ordered the ships to be loaded with provisions and ammunition.

Having in this way secured a certain quantity of free tonnage in the port of Sebastopol, I could, in case of misfortune, very quickly embark forty to fifty thousand men in the principal ports (Sebastopol, Yalta, Feodossia, and Kertch), and under cover of the retreating troops save the women, children, wounded, and sick entrusted to my care.

On the evening of the 20th General Koutepov came to see me. Although he was outwardly calm, his words betrayed his anxiety. Amongst other things, he asked me if I had prepared for a possible misfortune. My answer obviously reassured him. On the 21st, General Abramov arrived. I consulted the two Army Commanders, and on the 22nd I issued an order to the troops entrusting the defence of the Crimea to General Koutepov and amalgamating the Command, putting it entirely into his hands.

During the night of the 22nd I left for Sebastopol. The slightest panic behind-the-lines would spread to the troops, this had to be avoided at all costs. Immediately I arrived, I summoned the Press agents and gave them a general explanation of the situation.

On the evening of the 22nd there was a sitting of the South Russian Government I presided. I gave a detailed report of the recent fighting, and pointed out the difficulty of our troops' situation owing to the enormous numerical superiority of the enemy. I dwelt upon the particular difficulties of the troops and the population in the besieged Crimea, and the intensive work which would be necessary on our part; at the same time I assured them that we would defend the last scrap of native soil, and that, once we were rested, re-equipped, and reinforced, we would attempt to wrest victory from the hands of the enemy.

My timely measures had lulled the anxiety which had been aroused. All was quiet behind-the-lines, for everyone believed the Perekop lines to be impregnable. On October 26th, a conference of representatives from the towns met at Simferopol and adopted a resolution approving the policy of the South Russian Government and promising it whole-hearted support. A Press Congress was to meet in Sebastopol on October 30th. Life was going on as usual. The shops were crowded with customers, the theatres and cinemas were packed.

On October 25th, one of our military societies organized a musical evening in aid of some charity. I accepted an invitation to attend it, burying my desperate anguish deep in my breast, for I thought that my absence from such a party, organized as it was by a regimental society on whose books I figured, would give rise to panicky comments. I remained at the concert until eleven o'clock, listening to the music without hearing it, and making a great effort to say a friendly word to a wounded officer or pay a compliment to one of the ladies who had organized the affair.

Our troops had completed their regrouping. The intense cold had frozen over the salt marshes of Sivache, and our line of defence was therefore considerably lengthened. The lack of housing accommodation and of fuel increased the number of victims of the cold. I ordered all the reserve supplies of clothing that could be found in our depots to be distributed amongst the troops.

At this moment, the large transport-ship *Rion* arrived with winter clothing for the troops, but it was too late.

CHAPTER XVIII

INTO THE UNKNOWN

On the evening of October 26th I was presiding at a meeting of the Government, when an orderly came into the room and handed General Chatilov a Hughes telegram from General Koutepov. After he had read the message, General Chatilov handed it to me. General Koutepov reported that the enemy had penetrated our lines below Perekop and were now threatening to surround us, therefore he had been compelled to order a general retreat to our second line of fortifications. Neither the matter nor the manner of this message left room for doubt that we were on the brink of disaster. I pretended that I had to speak to General Koutepov on the telephone, delegated the chair to M. Krivochein, and went into an adjoining room. General Chatilov followed me. It was as clear to him as it was to me that the troops were incapable of offering any further resistance, the Army's stock of endurance was already overdrawn, and no fortifications could check the enemy any longer.

Urgent measures were necessary if the Army and the population were to be rescued. I sent for Admiral Kedrov, who was at the meeting in the other room, and in a few words I described the situation to him.

An involuntary exclamation escaped the Admiral.

"My God! Why did I accept this burden?" he cried.

But he quickly regained his composure. He had tonnage at his command for sixty thousand men. The additional coal and oil reserves had just arrived from Constantinople. This made it possible for us to increase out tonnage and bring the number of men we could embark up to seventy to seventy-five thousand. We had not the tonnage for a greater number than this. I ordered every vessel capable of putting out to sea to be utilized. I demanded the immediate return from Constantinople of every ship that could be mobilized. Finally, I had all the foreign trading-vessels in the Crimean ports detained, so that we could use their tonnage also.

M. Krivochein, who had a presentiment that disaster was in the air, now came out of the council chamber. He was visibly moved. We strove to calm him, and assured him that every possible measure had been taken in anticipation of disaster I begged him to reassure the other members of the Government as much as he could.

For myself, I decided to set out for the front and take stock of the situation I left at three o'clock on October 21st, and reached the front just as day was drawing in General Abramov and his chief-of-staff entered my compartment at Simferopol. Since the command of the Crimean troops had been unified and put into General Koutepov's hands, the 2nd Army's General Staff had been stationed in Simferopol.

When I reached Djankoy, I at once received General Koutepov, who explained the general situation to me.

Our troops had been forced to retreat to our last line of fortifications.

General Koutepov still intended to attempt a counterattack the next morning, and win back our lost lines, but he had very little faith in our chances of success. According to him, the spirit of the troops was broken. The best of the superior commanders were out of action, and it was impossible to count on success. I agreed with him absolutely, nevertheless, I insisted that we must hold the lines at all costs, so that we might at least gain the five or six days which were necessary for loading up the fuel, distributing the ships between the different ports, and embarking the interior organizations and the sick and wounded from the hospitals, etc. General Koutepov promised to do his utmost, but his answers made me realize that he despaired of the troops being able to hold the lines.

The storm was approaching, our fate was hanging by a thread, we had to strain every moral and intellectual force. The slightest irresolution, the most insignificant mistake, and all would be lost. The first essential was to keep order in Sebastopol. There were almost no troops stationed there. My escort, which had been on guard in the town, had been sent a few days previously to the Yalta section, to settle with "Comrade" Mokrohoussov's Greens who had been driven back into the mountains. I telegraphed for a company of pupils from the military school to be sent to Simferopol Station to meet my train, and for the necessary number of extra carriages, so that the company could entrain for Sebastopol.

At Simferopol I received the deputy-governor and explained the situation to him. I ordered General Abramov to take all the preliminary measures for the evacuation of the military and civil administrations in Simferopol, the officers and pupils of the military schools, the sick, and wounded, the families of the officials, and anyone else to whom the arrival of the Bolshevists would be a special menace. All the preliminary measures were to be earned out secretly as far as was possible, in order to avoid premature disturbances. I promised that the evacuation order should be sent the moment it was needed, and that a sufficient amount of rolling-stock should be put at the disposal of the Simferopol authorities.

At nine o'clock on the morning of October 28th, I reached Sebastopol with an escort of pupils from the military schools. I went straight from the station to the Palace. I summoned M. Krivochein, General Chatilov, and Admiral Kedrov, and gave them their final instructions. I ordered that the public buildings which housed the postal and telegraphic services should be occupied by the troops, and that patrols should be stationed at the railway station and on the quays. I made final arrangements for the disposal of the tonnage, ships capable of carrying twenty thousand men were to go to Kertch, thirteen thousand to Feodossia, ten thousand to Yalta, twenty thousand to Sebastopol, and four thousand to Eupatoria. I gave instructions for the order of embarkation—first the interior organizations were to go, then the sick and wounded, then supplies of provisions and the most valuable of the equipment. Thus, when the order was given, the embarkation could begin immediately.

At ten o'clock I received the French High Commissioner, the Count de Mattel, and the representatives of the other foreign Missions—Admiral MacCully, Colonel Walsh, and Major Takahashi; I begged them all to interrogate the representatives of their Governments at Constantinople on the question of assistance for us from foreign ships, for we would need it if it came to an evacuation and we were obliged to leave the Crimea.

During the day I invited representatives of the Russian and foreign Press to call, and explained the situation to them; the Army, which was fighting not only for the honor and liberty of its own country, but for the common cause of culture and civilization throughout the world, the Army which had just stayed the bloody hand which the butchers of Moscow had raised against Europe, was now abandoned by everyone and at the end of its tether. A handful of heroes, half-naked, starving, and exhausted, was continuing to defend the last strip of native soil. Our resources were dwindling away, and every day it was possible that we would be driven into the sea. We would hold out until the bitter end, protecting those who had sought refuge behind our bayonets. I had taken the necessary measures for the evacuation of all those who would be threatened with murderous reprisals. I had the right to hope that the nations by whose side our Army has fought for a common cause, would not refuse hospitality to unfortunate refugees.

The alarming news spread through the town with the speed of lightning. The telephone never ceased from ringing, nor people from calling at the Palace, to ask for information on the situation.

Late at night some news came through from the front that morning our units had begun a counter-offensive and had seized the positions they had abandoned the night before, but they had not been able to maintain them for long. They had fallen back on to their original position, hard-pressed by the enemy's larger forces. Our reserves had dwindled away. During the day the Reds had brought up reinforcements and followed up their advantage; by the evening they had wrestled the last line of fortifications from our troops.

The situation had become critical. The hours still left to us for the completion of our preparations for the evacuation were numbered. The work was going forward rapidly. Coal was being loaded day and night, gangs of non-combatants were formed, recruited from amongst the members of the administrative bodies, etc., to help the coal-heavers. Provisions and water were being loaded on board with all speed. The transport-ships were making for the ports which had been assigned to them. The General Staff and the administrative bodies were working very hard, sorting out the archives and packing up the records.

At two o'clock in the afternoon, the French cruiser *Waldeck-Rousseau* arrived from Constantinople, escorted by a torpedo-boat. Admiral Dumesnil, temporary Commandant of the French Mediterranean Squadron, was on board. He and the Count de Martel called on me, and the Admiral impressed me very favorably, he was a man of strong will and unshakable nobility of mind. Our interview lasted two hours, the conclusions we reached are summarized in the following letter which the Admiral sent me it is dated October 29th-November 11th—

Light Division,
Rear-Admiral,
No. 9 AM.

On board the *Waldeck-Rousseau*,
November 11, 1920

REAR-ADMIRAL DUMESNIL,
COMMANDANT OF THE LIGHT DIVISION

TO HIS EXCELLENCY GENERAL WRANGEL,
Commander-in-Chief of the Armed Forces of South Russia.

Dear General,

I have the honor to communicate to Your Excellency a summary of our interview of today's date, and to request you to endorse it, so that I can be sure that it is correct before I submit it to the French Government—

Your Excellency regards the situation at the front as hopeless, and sees no other solution than to evacuate the whole of the civil population desirous of fleeing from Bolshevist reprisals, together with the remnants of the White Army, wounded or able-bodied. You ask my help in accomplishing the evacuation, for it cannot be effected completely without the protection of the ships which are under my orders and the help of several French transports or tugs.

Your Excellency considers that if France will not promise you transport, and junction with the Army on the Russo-Polish front (should she promise this, you are ready to continue the struggle on this theatre of war with the evacuated troops), your troops must cease to play a military role. You ask for help and assistance from the French Government for them as well as for all the civil refugees; the provisions they are taking with them from the Crimea are sufficient for only twelve days, and nearly all the refugees are absolutely devoid of resources.

The means which the Crimean Government have at their disposal for meeting the expenses of the evacuation of the refugees, their maintenance, and then eventual settlement, include a fleet of warships and a fleet of mercantile marine.

These are free from all financial burdens, and your Excellency proposes that they should be handed over immediately to the French Government as security.

Yours very sincerely,

DUMESNIL

Our troops were continuing to retreat, hard pressed by the enemy. I issued the following orders—

The troops were to break away from the enemy and march to the ports of embarkation, the 1st and 2nd Army Corps were to make for Eupatona and Sebastopol, General Barbovitch's cavalry troop for Yalta, General Fostikov's Kubanians for Feodossia, the Don troops and the Terek-Astrakhan brigade for Kertch. The heavy transport was to be abandoned, the infantry was to pack into the wagons, the cavalry was to cover its retreat.

At the same time I signed the order announcing to the population that we were about to leave our native land.

ORDER FROM THE REGENT OF SOUTH RUSSIA AND THE COMMANDER-IN-CHIEF OF THE RUSSIAN ARMY

SEBASTOPOL,
October 29, 1920

People of Russia! Alone in its struggle against the oppressor, the Russian Army has been maintaining an unequal contest in its defence of the last strip of Russian territory on which law and truth hold sway.

Conscious of my responsibility, I have tried to anticipate every possible contingency from the very beginning.

I now order the evacuation and embarkation at the Crimean ports of all those who are following the Russian Army on its road to Calvary, that is to say, the families of the soldiers, the officials of the civil administration and their families, and anyone else who would be in danger if they fell into the hands of the enemy.

The Army will cover the embarkation, knowing that the necessary ships for its own evacuation are ready and waiting in the ports

> according to a pre-arranged plan. I have done everything that human strength can do to fulfil my duty to the Army and the population.
>
> We cannot foretell our future fate.
>
> We have no other territory than the Crimea, We have no money. Frankly as always, I warn you all of what awaits you.
>
> May God grant us strength and wisdom to endure this period of Russian misery, and to survive it.
>
> GENERAL WRANGEL.

Simultaneously, a Government *communiqué* appeared—

> Whilst proceeding with the evacuation of those of the officers, officials, and their families who wish to leave the Crimea, the South Russian Government considers it its duty to warn everybody of the severe ordeals which await those who are about to leave Russia. Owing to the lack of fuel, there will be severe overcrowding on the ships, the time spent on the sea and in the roadstead will necessarily be a long one. Furthermore, the future fate of the evacuated is quite uncertain, for up to the present, none of the foreign Powers have promised to receive them. The South Russian Government has no means of helping them, either during the journey or later on. All these considerations compel the Government to advise all those who will not suffer directly from the violence of the enemy to remain in the Crimea.

The order and the *communiqué* were telegraphed to all the towns, so that the entire population might know their contents.

Late on the evening of the 29th, the last sitting of the Government took place under the presidency of M. Krivochein. On the morning of the 30th the embarkation of the many departments of the civil and military administration was to begin. M. Krivochein gave his final instructions and sailed for Constantinople on board the English cruiser *Centaur*. I urged him to speak to M. de France, the French High Commissioner at Constantinople, and to secure his help in case we should arrive in the Bosphorus. At the same time I charged him to do all he could to organize help for the refugees who would arrive there, also to interest the Russian organizations in this work, and foreign institutions too, if possible I was counting very largely on assistance from the American Red Cross.

I finished my work late that night and went to bed, but I was soon awakened. The Admiral of the Fleet had sent Captain Machukov, his chief-of-staff, to me. Our wireless station had received a message from the Soviets, the Red Command proposed that I should surrender, they guaranteed the life and personal inviolability of every member of the High Command, as well as of all those who would lay down their arms. I ordered all the wireless stations to be closed down, except one where the officers were running the service.

My order and the Government's *communiqué*, which had been printed overnight, were posted up in the streets of Sebastopol on the morning of the 30th

The population was in the throes of violent agitation for the first few hours, but this soon subsided. The people felt that authority was still in the hands of strong men who had not lost their heads, whose actions were deliberate and based on a settled scheme, they felt that they could all count on the support of the representatives of authority, and that all confusion would be nipped in the bud. Several persons who were attempting to create disorder by anarchistic acts were immediately arrested, and one of them, a soldier from a mechanical detachment, was court-martialed and shot two hours later.

The embarkation of the staffs from the hospitals and the numerous administrations was proceeding in perfect order. Long strings of wagons were winding along the streets which were crowded with men carrying their possessions. The employees of the military authorities, followed by patrols which had been organized with the help of the pupils from the military schools and the soldiers of my escort, were scouring the streets, seeing that order was maintained amongst the transport, and supervising the embarkation. All those who wished to leave had to notify the General Staff. The numbers were huge. Our calculations were exceeded by large numbers, and we realized that we had not nearly enough tonnage.

It was not so cold now. The sea was dead calm, and Admiral Kedrov decided to use every ship and boat that would hold water, taking some in tow. In these difficult hours, when he was overwhelmed with intensive, feverish work, the Admiral displayed rare organizing ability, and worked ceaselessly day and night, attending to everything himself, and demanding the same amount of work from his subordinates. An enormous amount of work fell also to the General Staff, they too were unable to snatch even a moment's rest.

In the evening, a representative from the municipality came to see me. He begged me to take measures in good time to ensure the safety of the town, the factories by the harbor, and the artillery magazines after our departure. He offered to take charge of the supervisory work and to organize a service recruited from amongst the workmen. I willingly gave my consent, and promised to distribute arms amongst the workmen in good time, this was done later.

The Count de Martel and Admiral Dumesnil came to see me. The Count consented to take everyone who left the Crimea under the protection of France. The French Government accepted the Russian tonnage as security for the money for the maintenance of the refugees.

On October 31st:, an exchange of official letters on the subject took place—

SEBASTOPOL,
October 31st-*November* 13, 1920

At this moment, when circumstances compel me to leave the Crimea, I must consider if and how I can use my Army on the territories which are still occupied by the Russian forces which have recognized my authority. Whilst reserving to my troops their ultimate freedom of action for use when facilities have been granted for returning to our native land, I must take into account the fact that France was the only Power to recognize the South Russian Government and give it moral and material support, therefore I place my Army, my Navy, and all those who have followed me, under the protection of France.

I have issued an order to this effect to the different units of the military and mercantile fleet of Russia, I am sending you a copy of it with this letter.

I regard these ships as securities for the payment of the expenses which France has already incurred or will in future incur in giving the help which our present circumstances make necessary.

GENERAL P. WRANGEL

SEBASTOPOL,
November 13, 1920.

I have the honor to acknowledge the receipt of your letter of today, in which you inform me that circumstances compel you to leave the Crimea, and that you must consider if and how you can use your Army on the territories which are still occupied by the Russian forces which have recognized your authority.

Whilst you reserve to your troops their ultimate freedom of action for use after you are granted facilities for returning to your native land, you take into account the fact that France was the only Power to recognize the South Russian Government and give it moral and material support, therefore you now place your Army, your Navy, and all those who followed you, under the protection of France

You have sent me a copy of the order to this effect, which you have issued to the different units of the military and mercantile Russian fleet, you add that you regard these ships as securities for

> the payment of the expenses which France has already incurred or will in future incur in giving the help which your present circumstances make necessary.
>
> Together with Admiral Dumesnil, Commandant of the French Fleet at Sebastopol, I have the honor to inform you that, subject to subsequent confirmation,[1] I accept your decision and the arrangements you suggest in the name of my Government.
>
> COUNT DE MARTEL
> DUMESNIL

I decided to spend the night of the 31st at the Hotel Kist, near the Tsarskaia quay. The operative section of my General Staff was there.

I was preparing to leave the Palace when I was told that the "Revolutionary Committee of the town of Eupatoria" wanted to speak to me on the telephone. I took up the receiver.

> "The town is absolutely quiet. A newly formed Revolutionary Committee has taken over power. The troops and all the citizens who wished to go have been embarked. The ships have put out to sea," I was told.
>
> "Do you know anything about the Red troops?" I asked.
>
> "Nothing at all. There are no troops whatsoever in our town," was the reply.
>
> "Thank you for your information. Good luck," I said.
>
> "Good luck," was the answer.

Towards midnight, a fire broke out in the warehouses of the American Red Cross. The population attempted to pillage them, but a detachment of my escort arrived on the spot and quickly restored order. The night passed without any other untoward incident.

Since the morning of October 31st, the echelons from Simferopol had been embarking in their turn. The wounded were loaded on to the transport-ship *Yalta*, which had been transformed into a hospital-ship. M. Ilyin, the head of the Health Department, was supervising everything personally, although he was so ill that he could hardly stand; he was receiving the wounded as they arrived and organizing their disposal on the ship.

The ships which had taken on board the administrative bodies from Sebastopol the evening before, had put out to sea loaded to the utmost of their capacity. Fortunately the sea was perfectly calm. The transport-ships intended for the units of the 1st Army were in the bay. On my orders they

[1] The confirmation was given later—TRANSLATOR.

were equipped with sentries from the different units. Our Armies were continuing to retreat according to the orders they had received at ten o'clock in the morning, the front was drawing near to Sarabuz. During the retreat we scarcely came into contact with the enemy.

Towards midday I walked through the town with my aide-de-camp. The streets were almost deserted, and most of the shops were shut; now and then we met a straggling transport-wagon, or an isolated pedestrian hurrying towards the harbor. Everyone we met saluted me respectfully, as usual. I became more and more convinced that the embarkation would be accomplished smoothly and that everybody would get away in time.

General Koutepov and his General Staff arrived at twilight. The troops were retreating in perfect order. Those who wished to remain behind had been given full leave to do so, but only very few took advantage of this permission. General Koutepov calculated that the embarkation would be finished by about ten o'clock in the morning.

I ordered the troops to occupy the line of fortifications which had been used in 1855,[1] in order to cover the embarkation. The Admiral of the Fleet was ordered to finish embarkation operations by midday on November 1st. At one o'clock in the afternoon the ships were to make for the roadstead.

At ten o'clock on the morning of November 1st, I went the round of the ships in a motor-boat, accompanied by the Admiral of the Fleet. The embarkation was nearly finished. There were only a few hundred men still on the quayside, waiting their turn. As our motor-boat passed along, cheers rang out from the crowded ships and the quayside. Hats and handkerchiefs were waved. My heart contracted painfully, and a wave of compassion, pity, and love for all these men who were so dear to me, filled my soul.

The last outposts had retreated, and the pupils from the military schools were drawn up in the market-square. A crowd of townspeople were waiting in front of the Town Hall. I saluted the pupils from the military school and thanked them for their magnificent services. I said: "The Army, which has shed its blood in great torrents in fighting not only for the Russian cause but for the whole world, is now leaving its native shores, abandoned by everybody. We are going into exile, we are not going as beggars with outstretched hands, but with our heads held high, conscious of having done our duty to the end. We have the right to claim help from those who owe their continued freedom and even their continued existence to us, we have sacrificed much for their cause."

I gave the pupils from the military school the order to embark, and made for my motor-boat. There was a flutter of handkerchiefs in the crowd, and I saw that many people were weeping. A young girl came up to me. She was sobbing and pressing a handkerchief to her lips.

---

[1] During the Crimean War—TRANSLATOR.

"God bless you and keep you, Your Excellency," she said.

"Thank you. Are you remaining here?" I asked.

"Yes I have a sick mother, and I cannot abandon her," she replied.

"God bless you too," I said.

A group of municipal councilors approached. I was very much astonished to recognize some of them, especially as they were members of the Opposition.

"You have spoken the truth, Your Excellency," said one. "You can indeed leave here with your head held high, knowing that you have done your duty. Let me wish you a good journey."

I shook hands and expressed my thanks.

Admiral MacCully, the Chief of the American Mission, came up to me with a spontaneous movement. He wrung my hand very heartily and said—

"I have always been one of your admirers, today I am more so than ever."

The last of the sentries were embarked. At twenty minutes to three, my motor-boat left the quay and made for the cruiser *General Kornilov*, which was flying my flag. A tumult of cheers went up from the crowded ships.

The *General Kornilov* weighed anchor. One by one the ships put out to sea. Every vessel that was watertight left the shores of the Crimea. None were left in Sebastopol except a few useless tugs and old warships whose machinery was so damaged that they could not be used for transport. All the rest had been utilized. We cast anchor in Strieletzky Bay, and remained there until half-past two at night, waiting until the last men in Strieletzky Bay had been embarked and the last ships had put out to sea. At last we weighed anchor and made for Yalta, which we reached at nine o'clock on the morning of November 2nd.

The embarkation was already finished here. The tonnage had been found adequate, and everyone who wanted to leave had been embarked. Everything was quiet in the town, the streets were almost deserted. I went on shore with the chief-of-staff of the Fleet, and made the round of the ships, chatting to the officers and soldiers. Our cavalry had kept the enemy in check, covering the infantry's retreat, then they had broken right away from the enemy and reached Yalta by forced marches. They had left the Red troops a long way behind them, the enemy were not expected to arrive before the next day at the earliest. I returned to the cruiser *General Kornilov*.

Towards midday the transports began moving. The crowded ships passed before me, cheers filled the air. The Russian spirit is great, and the Russian soul unfathomable.

At two o'clock in the afternoon, we weighed anchor and made for Feodossia. Admiral Dumesnil was following us on board the cruiser *Waldeck-Rousseau*, escorted by a torpedo-boat. Shortly afterwards, we met the enormous transport-ship the *Don*, we were greeted with shouts and cheers; whilst we were still a long way off we could make out the *papakhas.*[1]

General Fostikov and his Kubanians were on board the *Don.* I ordered one of our ship's boats to be launched and went over to the transport-ship. The embarkation had been less successful at Feodossia. According to General Fostikov, the tonnage had been insufficient, and one of the Kubanian divisions had not been able to embark; it had set out for Kertch. General Fostikov's report raised well-founded doubts as to the measures which he had taken. I returned to the cruiser *General Kornilov* and sent a wireless message to Kertch, directing General Abramov to wait for and embark the Kubanians at all costs.

On November 3rd, at nine o'clock in the morning, we anchored in the roadstead outside Feodossia. We received a wireless message from General Abramov—

> Kubanian and Terek troops have arrived; the embarkation is proceeding smoothly.

The chief-of-staff of the Fleet left for Kertch on board the ice-breaker *Gaidamak*, followed by the transport-ship *Rossia*, which had just arrived from Constantinople, and could take a party of troops on board in addition to its ordinary passengers.

The recent cold spell had broken. The weather was fine once again; it was even quite hot in the sun. The sea was as clear as a mirror and reflected the transparent blue sky. Groups of white sea-gulls were wheeling through the air, and the coast was enshrouded in a pink haze.

At two o'clock in the afternoon, the *Waldeck-Rousseau* weighed anchor and fired a salute of twenty-one guns—the last salute to the Russian flag in Russian territorial waters. The *General Kornilov* replied to it.

Shortly afterwards, we received a wireless message from the chief-of-staff of the Fleet, who had gone to Kertch—

> Embarkation finished. Everyone on board to the last soldier.

At twenty minutes to four, the *Gaidamak* reappeared. The embarkation had been carried out brilliantly. The troops which had been on barges had been transhipped to the *Rossia* and the ships had put out to sea.[2]

---

[1] Fur caps which Cossacks wear —TRANSLATOR.

[2] One hundred and forty-five thousand six hundred and ninety-three men, not counting the crews of the ships, had been evacuated on one hundred and twenty-six ships. With the exception of the destroyer *Jivos*, which went down in the storm, all the ships arrived safely at Constantinople.

I felt an immense weight fall from my mind. For a few moments my thoughts escaped quite involuntarily from the sad present and the uncertain future. God had helped me to do my duty. He would bless our journey into the unknown. I gave the order to make for Constantinople. The *General Kornilov* received a wireless message from the *Waldeck-Rousseau*—

TO GENERAL WRANGEL FROM ADMIRAL DUMESNIL

> For the last seven months the officers and soldiers of the South Russian Army under your command have given a splendid display of gallantry. They have fought an enemy ten times more numerous than themselves, and have striven to free Russia from shameful tyranny. The struggle was too unequal, and you have been compelled to leave your country. I realize the anguish this step has cost you. But you must find some satisfaction in the knowledge that the evacuation has been conducted in an exemplary manner. The French Fleet which has given you its whole-hearted support, rejoices to see the evacuation so brilliantly terminated. Your struggle has not been in vain, the population of South Russia will soon begin to compare your just and beneficent rule with the vile government of the Soviets. Thus you will be instrumental in awakening and regenerating your country. I most sincerely hope that this awakening may come about as soon as possible. The Admiral, the officers, and the sailors of the French Fleet do reverence to General Wrangel and pay homage to his valor.

Soon afterwards, we intercepted another Soviet wireless message from Sebastopol to Moscow, urgently demanding that "experienced propagandists" be sent at once, because there were none left in the Crimea. A singing testimonial to General Klimovitch!

Night is falling. The stars are gleaming in the darkening sky, the sea is all a-twinkle. The lonely lights on my native shore glow fainter, and then vanish altogether, one after the other. And now the last one fades from my sight.

Farewell, my country!

SEREMSKY-KARLOVIZY, *December* 30, 1923

Part III

The White Armies: In Russia and Later

CHAPTER XIX

THE WHITE ARMIES: IN RUSSIA AND LATER

A speech delivered by General Wrangel at a political conference in Brussels and published in the "English Review" of October 1927, this article is, by the courtesy of the Editor of that journal, here reprinted as the final part of the Memoirs.

At the end of the year 1917 the Government of Kerensky could no longer retain the executive power in their feeble hands. It was seized by a set of people who built on the lowest sentiments of the populace, operating as demagogues do, and promising peace and plenty with idleness. None of these promises were kept. That did not matter to the Bolshevist ringleaders. Russia in its quality of a national state was no concern of theirs. What they sought was a base whence to diffuse their unholy influence over the whole world.

The moment that the Bolshevists laid hands on the executive power, Russia, as a national entity, ceased to exist. Even the name which served to describe it disappeared. All the interests of the State, as such, were sacrificed to those of the Red International. Everywhere this International waged determined war against every element of the national spirit, aggravated class conflicts, and destroyed all the foundations of morality—religion, the fatherland, the family.

Yet, in spite of all, Russia still exists as a nation. Immediately after the Bolshevists seized the reins of power, a few men, stirred by love for their country and jealous for its greatness and glory, raised the national flag that had fallen in the mud. They started in the south of Russia an implacable struggle against the oppressors of their country.

Their appeal was heard; a crowd of officers, soldiers, students, intellectuals, politicians, workers, and peasants flocked to the Don. All those whose hearts were right and courageous, and who could not admit that Russia was dead, gathered under the national flag. There were men of every class and condition of life, of the most varied ages and political views. Enrolling themselves in the ranks of the National Army, they forgot every item of political or social divergence.

They were all united by the same warm love of their country, and the same desire to sacrifice themselves for her.

Such, in November 1917, was the birth of the White Army. It was the incarnation of the national sentiment, of the revolt of Russian patriotism. United under the folds of the tricolour, they fought from that time for the national cause. This Army, loyal to all the obligations taken over by previous national governments, still continues the struggle for the honor of its country's name, for the resurrection of Russia as a Nation. Its way of fighting has altered; the outward forms which properly belong to armies have gone, but the idea which directed its making has remained untouched.

What is this idea? It is life devoted to the fatherland, eagerness to save her at the expense of life itself, a passionate desire to tear the red flag down from the Kremlin and hoist in its place the National flag.

The struggle which began in the south of Russia soon raised echoes elsewhere, in the north, the north-west, and Siberia. I will not pause here to tell you past history, I will only recall the brilliant successes with which the White Armies began. The troops of General Denikin occupied a third of Russia and advanced within a short distance of Moscow. In the north-west General Youdenitch was already in sight of the fires of St. Petersburg. In the west, Admiral Koltchak had almost reached the Volga.

Yet victory was not in reserve for the White Armies. The troops of the north were driven to the sea and forced to give up the territory they occupied. Some of them perished, while others were obliged to take refuge in Norway. In the northwest the Army of General Youdenitch had to retire to Esthonian territory on which it was interned. The army of Admiral Koltchak in Siberia had to fight in retreat and was dispersed. Finally, in the south of Russia the troops of General Denikin retired to Novorossiisk. What was left of them passed into the Crimea. After a year of heroic struggle this last strip of Russian soil was abandoned.

The failure of the White Armies was due to a number of reasons, and I will not weary the reader by examining them in detail. I will confine myself to mentioning the chief of them. A prominent place is due to the political and strategic errors of the leaders who did not sufficiently regard the state of feeling among the masses of the people. They exaggerated the importance of their early successes. They did not think sufficiently about securing the possession of the territories they occupied, organizing them, raising new levies to fill the gaps in their ranks, and looking after the provision of victuals and munitions.

The political ignorance of the people accounted for a good deal. They had not yet lost their illusions concerning the Bolshevist power, they still went on believing in the lying promises of the Maximalist agitators. Lastly, the Bolshevist Armies had at then disposition all the resources of an immense country, its reserves of food, its stocks of arms and munitions.

On the other side, the White Armies were short of everything. During the first months of the struggle the only arms and munitions we could draw on were those taken from the enemy. Support from outside was indispensable. It could only come from those by whose side the Russian Army had fought during the Great War. The White Armies who had refused to recognize the shameful peace of Brest-Litovsk and were loyal to their alliances thought they had the right to count on this support.

But the Western Powers were far from realizing the essence of the Bolshevist idea, the danger it threatened to the world. They did not consider fairly the importance of the struggle the White Army was carrying on. They did not understand that this Army, in fighting for its own country, was also fighting for civilization and the culture of Europe. Not only did the White Armies fail to receive sufficient help in time to be of use, they had even on several occasions to run foul of obstacles raised by the former Allies of Russia.

It must be noted that the English alone afforded material assistance to the White Armies. But this help was slow in arriving and inadequate. Support in the shape of armed forces, to a very small amount, to tell the truth, was given by the English, and in part by France. Unfortunately there was never any certainty that this help would not be abruptly withdrawn, and often this happened without any previous warning.

The result was the loss of thousands of lives and immense stores left to plunderers. In the north-west the English, while they supported General Youdenitch and promised him their help, were combining at the same time in his rear with his political enemies, thus giving them the chance at the decisive moment to stab General Youdenitch in the back.

In the south, the French forces under General d'Anselme, which had occupied in 1919 the port of Odessa, gave up the town when the enemy approached. This action without any warning made the position of the Russian troops and the civil population desperate. Lastly, there can be no excuse for the handing over of Admiral Koltchak to the Bolshevists by General Janin. The Admiral had put himself under General Janin's protection. Handed over to the Bolshevists, he was immediately shot.

In the spring of 1920 the White Armies of the north, north-west, and Siberia had to admit defeat. In the south the troops of General Denikin were thrust on to the Black Sea. The British Government had up to this point lent assistance to General Denikin in the shape of arms and munitions. Foreseeing the success of the Bolshevists, and judging from it that the time had come to pass from the struggle in arms to a rapprochement with the enemy of yesterday, it now requested the head of the White Army to cease all hostilities.

The Government of Mr. Lloyd George took upon itself to enter into negotiations with the Bolshevist Government concerning the amnesty to be granted to the White Army and the peoples of the Crimea. It threatened, if we on our side refused, to deprive us of all assistance.

At this moment our situation seemed desperate The remains of the Armies which had fought in the south of Russia, after evacuating Novorossiisk, numbering about thirty-five thousand, had fled into the

Crimea. It was no longer an Army, but a disorderly crowd which had grown slack in its discipline and was morally and physically exhausted after a retreat for hundreds of miles in the height of winter, and a series of defeats. Munitions, artillery stores, and cavalry had been abandoned at Novorossiisk for want of sufficient ships to carry them. In the north, the Crimean Peninsula was covered on the Isthmus of Perekop by weak detachments of no more than five thousand five hundred men. The Army found itself pinned on to the sea, on a scrap of ground, lacking the chance to revictual and fill up its losses in men. The Commander-in-Chief, General Denikin, was so broken by all this that he retired from his duties. The post of Commander devolved on me. Fate had reserved for me a heavy charge. While I fully understood the weight of responsibility that I was taking on, while I knew the difficulties in the grim conditions of continuing the struggle, I judged that I could not decline the post. I could not promise the Army victory; all I could do was to promise it should come out of an almost hopeless position without loss of honor.

In the answer I sent to the British Government I could not consider the possibility of direct negotiations with the enemy. I left the initiative to Mr Lloyd George, and made Great Britain responsible for its decisions.

Meanwhile I worked feverishly to restore the morale of the army and increase its fighting power. I wrote to King Alexander of Serbia, then heir to the throne and Regent, and begged him to give my Army shelter in case of need. I arranged at the same time that measures should be taken to make evacuation easy, if that course became inevitable. As might have been easily foreseen, the negotiations started by the English with the Bolshevist led to no result. The Government of the Soviets evaded all answer on the business and demanded a series of political concessions. The British Government, informing me of this, insisted that I should enter into direct negotiations. They warned me that a continuation of the struggle might have fatal results, and that in any case I could not count on any assistance from them. It was clear that the British Government, which sought closer relations with the Bolshevist Government, wished above all to see hostilities come to an end. It did not apparently consider that the result would be the sacrifice of thousands of lives.

The Army was already pretty near reorganization, and I answered these threats in May 1920 by ordering the offensive. The troops, by this time rested and reconstituted, showed their old bravery, and the first encounters with the Bolshevists brought victory back to our ranks. The British Government followed this up by recalling their representatives and Military Mission from the Crimea. Between the two parties in the struggle, Mr. Lloyd George did not hesitate to fix his choice on our enemies. The course of events since has shown how unsound his calculations were. Very different was the attitude of the French Government. It declared its disapproval of any approach to the

Bolshevists and expressed its sympathy with my action. Unfortunately this attitude did not lead to a true understanding of the international danger presented by Bolshevism. France wished to create a strong Polish State as a means of support against Germany. At the time when hostilities began between Poland and the Government of the Soviets, France thought it necessary to support the White Armies, which might attract to their front a portion of the Red forces. Later, M. Millerand, the French President, made a public acknowledgment that the help which had been lent to the White Armies had no other aim beyond the saving of Poland. It was said, particularly in an article that appeared in the official newspaper, *Le Temps*, that France had used every means to save Poland, and that one of these means "was the establishment of a threat to the rear of the Bolshevist Armies which was backed by the forces of General Wrangel. The pressure brought to bear by General Wrangel's forces helped to save Warsaw."

The French Government was led by these considerations to recognize in June 1920 my *de facto* Government. This recognition had an especial moral effect, but France had not the time to bring material help of an effective sort into the fray. However, it was this official recognition that enabled the Army to receive a part of the Russian stores available since the Great War in various countries.

Fighting continued successfully in the south of Russia during all the summer and autumn of 1920. All the exertions of the Bolshevists proved futile. But after the defeat before Warsaw of the Armies of the Soviets, the egoistic and shortsighted policy of Mr. Lloyd George, then acting as mentor to the political world of Europe, had a new success. Hostilities were prematurely suspended on the Polish front, and once more the Bolshevists were saved.

Our Army was abandoned to its fate.

It was evident that after the Armistice and the conclusion of the peace with the Poles the Bolshevists would direct their forces against the Crimea, and the White Army could not struggle against such odds. What happened was that the Soviet Government concentrated on the front occupied by my troops more than five hundred thousand men with all their cavalry. Exhausted by long months of incessant fighting, and weakened by all sorts of privations, the White Army was overwhelmed. To save the remnant of the troops and the people who had put themselves under their protection, I gave the order in October 1920 for retreat. The troops fell back by forced marches on the seaports and embarked according to a plan previously arranged. The civil population, those who served in the rear, the sick and the wounded, women and children, were the first to be put on board. The evacuation took place in perfect order. I inspected personally on the cruiser *Kornilov* the harbors used, and I was able to assure myself that all who wished to quit Russian soil found it possible to do so.

Three years of determined struggle, of fighting and suffering, of heroism, victory, and defeat, followed by fresh victory, then came to an end. We left the last strip of the land of our fathers.

In my order of the day concerning the evacuation I did not conceal the fact that our future fate was unknown to me, that we had no longer any Russian territory to move on, and that we had no resources left. I gave everyone full freedom to settle his own destiny. This order of the day, which warned everyone of the future to be expected, stopped nobody. From October 31st to November 3rd one hundred and twenty-six ships left the ports of the Crimea, carrying one hundred and fifty thousand men who refused to live under the Bolshevist yoke. We left our country for thc unknown, for privations, sorrows, and sufferings.

The number of those evacuated was one hundred thousand officers and soldiers and fifty thousand civilians, including among these thirty thousand women and seven thousand children. Of the one hundred thousand officers and soldiers, fifty thousand belonged to the fighting troops, forty thousand to those who served in the rear. There were three thousand pupils from the military schools, and more than six thousand were ill, invalided, or wounded. The fifty thousand civilians included all ranks of society, amongst them peasants and workers. It was no emigration of privileged classes and professions. It was the exodus of National Russia with all the elements that go to make it, its civil organization and its Army. These exiles cherished in their hearts profound faith in a victorious return to the land of their fathers. Of this crowd of *émigrés* it was the Army that from the national point of view formed the most valuable part. It was the only group organized and consolidated by the blood all had shed, the idea they shared. Its new existence showed that the fight for the honor of the country and the remaking of Russia as a nation was not yet ended. It was evident that the Army ought to become the centre to gather round it the Russian *émigrés* scattered in all countries. It was indispensable to keep this nucleus intact.

The moment evacuation was over, the following problems confronted the High Command: provision for all those who had left the Crimea without a roof over their heads, food, or medical assistance, the reorganization of the Army to meet these new and exceptional circumstances, the taking of measures to start by degrees arrangements which would allow them to provide for their existence by their own work without burdening the finances of the countries which would afford them shelter, the regathenng round this nucleus of all the scattered portions of the old Russian Army and of those who had taken part in the struggle against the Bolshevists on the various fronts, and finally, the concentration round the Army of all the other elements of the nation.

After their arrival in the Bosphorus, the one hundred and fifty thousand refugees were divided into several groups. The principal one, composed of the military units, was portioned out into military camps twenty-five thousand men at Gallipoli; fifteen thousand at the island of Lemnos, fifteen thousand at Tchataldja, in the neighborhood of Constantinople. Finally, more than thirty thousand men were sent off to Serbia, Rumania, Bulgaria, and Greece. The sick and wounded were distributed among Russian and foreign hospital ships. The vessels of the Russian Fleet with their crews, amounting to five thousand men, were sent to Bizerte. The remainder of the civilian refugees were distributed in camps and barracks and maintained at the expense of Russian charitable organizations.

The Russian troops, distributed into camps, maintained at my urgent request their organization with its military ranks and discipline. Realizing the importance of the preservation of order, of the maintenance of discipline and submission to regulations, the representatives of the French Government at Constantinople consented to the complete preservation of the military organization and left the troops the use of their own arms and colours.

But this state of things did not last long. Short-sighted politics, politics of a day-to-day sort, went on. This kind of politics, when dealing with old allies, was thoroughly immoral. The Powers of Western Europe yielded to the demands of their crowds of workers, who were fascinated by the success of their Russian comrades. They stopped all assistance to forces which had fought the Bolshevists. They went further: they put themselves in the way of closer relations with the Soviet Government. England opened the way, Italy followed, and then France. In the last days of November 1920, M. Leygues, President of the French Senate, declared that "he was disposed to authorize commercial operations between French and Russians, and that he did not think it necessary to continue the embargo against the Russian Soviets." "So far as the Government of General Wrangel is concerned," he added, "the defeat of his Army being admitted, France regards herself as relieved of all obligations to him, and will only assist his soldiers on humanitarian grounds." Clearly, in these conditions, the Russian Army was bound to be considered not only useless, but even a nuisance. It offered, in fact, an exceptional case from the standpoint of international law, and formed an obstacle to the creation of relations and friendly ties with the group of Soviets. The results of this change of politics were soon felt. In January 1920, at Constantinople, General Charpy, commander of the French troops in occupation, issued an order of the day that the principal thing to be considered at the moment was the evacuation of the military and civil camps as quickly as possible. The General indicated a series of measures to be taken for that purpose. In accordance with these directions the commanders of the French camps published in February notices encouraging the men to return to the Russia of the Soviets. It was explained that the French Government had taken all the necessary measures to guarantee the safety of those who returned. At the same time the dwellers in the camps were warned that revictualling would shortly be cut off. In spite of the efforts I made to warn the men of the danger they would incur if they returned to Russia, this threat to cut off their provisions induced something like one thousand five hundred men to sign on the lifts for repatriation. These were sent in the middle of February to Novorossiisk. Some time later, proposals were made to the Russian officers and soldiers that they should emigrate to Brazil as colonists of the State of Sao Paulo. They were promised—on no particular authority—financial help and the grant of free concessions by the Brazilian Government. On this occasion, thanks to my warnings, those who signed were hardly any. Shortly afterwards it became clear that the promises did not coincide with the facts; all those who allowed themselves to be caught were punished for their excess of trust. Those who, in spite of my advice, left for Russia, underwent all sorts of trials. Some of them were shot.

Those who embarked for Brazil became slaves or something near it—not colonists.

I protested, but in vain. In the middle of March the French High Commissioners renewed, with threats about stopping provisions, their demands that the Russian refugees should choose one of three solutions out of the difficulty: return to Russia, emigration to Brazil, or discovery on the spot of work to support their needs. None of these solutions could be accepted. A return to Russia, as earlier experience proved, was risking one's life. Brazil did not take colonists. Looking for work in the desert of Gallipoli or Lemnos was a cruel jest. At this point it will be well to explain that these demands were not due to the question of money. The number of men who found themselves revictualled by the French had materially decreased, for nearly twenty thousand had already left for Serbia. Further, after the evacuation of the Crimea, I had remitted to the French Government, as a guarantee for the expenses in which it might be involved, securities which amounted in all to one hundred million francs. I protested again, and explained that, if the French Government insisted that my Army should be annihilated, the most honorable means would be to allow that Army to return to Russian ground weapon in hand, so that it might at least find death with honor. A series of measures was aimed against the refractory Russian General-in-Chief; my orders to the troops were intercepted, and I was deprived of the chance of visiting the camps.

Finally, I was invited to leave for Paris on the invitation of the French Government. I answered that I was ready to leave on condition that during my absence the dispatch of my men to Russia and Brazil was suspended, and that I was allowed a free return to Constantinople. The answer I received was that the dismemberment of my Army was inevitable and could not be further delayed. Carrying out the orders of the High Commissioners, the commander of the camp of Lemnos, General Brousseau, demanded an immediate answer with a choice of one of the three solutions I have mentioned above, and asked for a list of those who wished to leave for Russia. Subordinates, unfortunately, took measures deeply offensive to the Russian command. Violence was even used during the embarkation. Some men who were thrust on shipboard threw themselves into the water and got back to the shore. These incidents made a very painful impression everywhere and in the Russian Press. A series of protests was raised against the operations of General Brousseau.

This tragedy of the defenders of Russia as a nation found an echo in part of the French Press. It protested against the violent treatment of those who a few months earlier were fighting under a flag recognized by the French Government. The Government found itself obliged to explain. An official Note published by the Havas Agency declared that the measures taken to propel the Russians towards Russia were dictated by "humanitarian" considerations (!).

At the same time the Government made known its resolve to remove those who had evacuated the Crimea from their dependence on the authority of General Wrangel, who was opposed to the measures taken. "All the Russians who find themselves in the camps," said the Note, "should know that the Wrangel Army no longer exists, that their former commanders have no orders to give them, that their decision depends on nobody; and that revictualling cannot last any longer." It was easy to declare on paper that the Army of General Wrangel did not exist and the orders of its chiefs had no effect. It was less easy to translate these affirmations into fact: Bound by the same idea, by their faith in their chiefs, united by the blood they had shed and the privations they had endured in the camps of Gallipoli and Lemnos, the troops went on considering themselves under arms, subject to their officers, and in the first place to their Commander-in-Chief.

"The Army which for seven years shed its blood for the common cause with France," I wrote to the High Commissioners, "is not the Army of General Wrangel, but it is the Russian Army, unless the French Government recognizes as such the Army whose chiefs signed the peace of Brest-Litovsk. The desire of the French Government to see the disappearance of the Army of General Wrangel and the discipline of his troops cannot compel the soldiers and officers of Russia. They will never consent, out of deference to the French Government, to betray their flag and their chief."

At last, towards the month of April, General Pellé came to Constantinople as the French High Commissioner. He verified one after another the ineffectiveness of the orders dictated from Paris, took the Russian question in hand, and changed completely the attitude hitherto adopted. The threats to deprive the Russians of provisions stopped; rations, however small, continued to be served. General Brousseau was removed, and relations with the Russian Army palpably improved.

I cannot, however, pass in silence over a detail characteristic of the attitude of the States of Europe towards the White Army. During the negotiations I started to distribute my Army in various countries. There was a question about transferring it to Hungary. The Hungarian Minister of National Defence, in answer to my request, wrote that, in spite of the sympathy a country like Hungary, newly freed from the Bolshevist yoke, felt for the soldiers of General Wrangel, it was impossible for him to authorize such a step without ascertaining the sentiments of the Governments of the Entente, the signatories of the Peace of Versailles. The conference of the representatives of the Entente examined this question on July 21, 1921, and communicated its answer by Note a month later. In this document, signed by the High Commissioner of Italy, Prince Castagnetto, the High Commissioners of the Entente Governments called the attention of the Hungarian Government to the fact that—

> The entry of the Army of General Wrangel into Hungarian territory could not fail to excite commotion and facilitate anti-Bolshevist intrigues which are contrary to the true interests of Hungary and of all the civilized world.

So the Allied Governments testified that it was not Bolshevist, but anti-Bolshevist organizations which represented a danger to the interests of Hungary and of the civilized world...

And this was said to a country which had gone through the horrors of Bolshevism and suffered the massacres of Bela Kun!

The effect of the period of existence at Gallipoli and Lemnos with its many privations was to bring the men still closer together, to eliminate the weak and the waverers, and to give those who remained the strength to overcome all the privations which eventually awaited them. Thrown, in the middle of winter, without shelter or clothing, on the desert shore of Gallipoli or the arid island of Lemnos, unity of feeling tightened the ranks of the Russian Army.

Shortly on the site of the camps rose a little town built by the Army. Each stone, each bit of wood, each tent was carried by hand, for want of vehicles. The camps were adorned with odd churches, made out of the most unexpected materials. Choral songs, orchestras, and stages were organized. The ruins of Gallipoli were ornamented with drawings recalling the Fatherland. The approaches to the camps were brightened with regimental emblems marked out by the help of pebbles. Inscriptions bore witness to the deep love of the Fatherland, the sentiment of duty—

Remember that thou belonged to Russia
Russia knows that thou wilt do thy duty
Thy duty will only cease with death

Everything vouched for the fact that life at Gallipoli or Lemnos among the ruins, the destitution and the cold, with quite insufficient rations, could not injure the morale of the Army or reduce its bravery.

After my arrival at Constantinople I took measures to organize the Army, so as to allow it to manage to satisfy its own needs by its own work. The principles which guided me were these: "The Army, not wishing to be a burden to the countries which gave it a place of refuge, feeds itself by working, till the day when it will be called to arms to do its duty to its country."

The negotiations lasted long and met with great difficulties. At last, in the spring of 1921, the Government of the kingdom of the Serbs, Croats, and Slovenes agreed to employ a large part of the cavalry to guard the frontiers, and the Cossacks of Kuban, as well as the engineers, for various works of public utility. A little later Bulgaria agreed to welcome almost the whole of the rest of the forces. The transport of the troops began in May 1921, and by the beginning of 1922 they were already distributed in Serbia, Bulgaria, and Czecho-Slovakia. The last detachment left Gallipoli in the spring of 1923.

With the arrival of the Army in the Balkans a new period of its existence began. To set troops to work and make them change their weapons for the spade and the pickaxe is a delicate business psychologically and difficult in practice. This was done by slow degrees, in accordance with a plan of minute detail prepared in advance, and, even so, there were great obstacles to get over. The Balkans are, from the economic point of view, but little developed. They do not offer enough things to take up, and cannot supply work to large numbers of people. We have to arrange work on our own account. That was made possible by the organization of the Army all ready to hand. While waiting for its psychological adaptation to the new ways, it was impossible, without injury to the morale of the troops, to distribute the men into too small groups. Gradually the Army got to work, and the number of men who were paid for by the High Command decreased. At the beginning the High Command had to be responsible for the needs of all the officers and under-officers whose whole time was taken by general organizing. As the various units got to work, and the men got accustomed to the new order of things, the cost of keeping the chiefs lessened; officers and under-officers set to work in their turn, and the number of persons whose needs the High Command saw to was reduced. At present all the chiefs without exception are gaining their livelihood. The Russian officers and soldiers themselves gain their bread, with no difference between them, by heavy work in the mines, factories, and yards. The support of the families of the soldiery, the women, the wounded, and the sick who had been incapacitated for work during their services in the ranks, required a large expenditure. But this help was regarded by the Army as a debt of honor. At first the charges were borne by the High Command. By slow degrees the troops at work supported their families and the sick.

I took measures to form a fund for help in each unit. These funds were maintained at first by the savings made out of the advances by the High Command. Later they were made up with money kept back from the men's pay. The men readily recognized the necessity for this arrangement, and supported if with the utmost goodwill. A part of these sums is the property of the regiment. It provides the expenses of *liaison* and secretarial work, and is used to help men who are unemployed. The other part is the property of each man, and is advanced to him in case of illness or urgent need. It is returned to him if he leaves the regiment. The formation and increase of this capital, guarantee the man against anything that can happen, cover the expenses of removal to look for new work, and allow of the organization of infirmaries, the support of those out of work, etc.

In all this there is a formal principle, always maintained. No chief can receive any assistance, whether it be a salary or relief, at the expense of the deposits made by his men.

When the Army had got to work, it became clear that economic conditions and the smallness of the pay would not allow it to stay long in the Balkans. The necessity of a wider distribution in the countries of Western Europe, where industry is better developed, became beyond doubt. This prospect was no longer to be feared, for the Army had adapted itself to its new conditions and the danger of disorganization was removed. I started negotiations to send small detachments to France. These departures continued regularly from this time and still go on. The men who isolate themselves and leave their useful work, and the small groups who change their country in search of it, remain united to the Army. After their removal they rally round the nucleus existing on the spot, or form new groups. No man, no detachment, remains isolated. Small units and individuals are bound up together.

At the head of the new groups, chiefs are selected who secure connection with the central services of the Army. The military organization of these groups of workers offers many advantages. The men do not feel isolated. They retain a bond with their comrades, with all those who have shared their ideas for years. They do not feel lost in an environment which is strange to them. They can assist each other, improve their position, organize funds for mutual aid, evening lectures and libraries, and meet for religious services. This system of holding together has, further, a practical reason in its favor, for it influences the improvement of wages. The organization and discipline of military groups of workers make inevitably an impression on the managers of the businesses concerned. Very often these are ready to spend considerable sums to improve the position of the group. In numerous instances the management give a favorable hearing to the requests of the leader of the group, and grant large sums for the creation of churches and libraries, and to house the officiating minister and give him a salary. A joint request by the members of the group, conveyed through the medium of its chief, is commonly accepted, when individuals would ask in vain.

While the Army was geographically distributed to facilitate its search for work, I attempted to rally round it all the military figures who had taken part in the Great War, not only on the Russian front, but also in France and at Salonika, as well as those who had joined in the fight against the Bolshevists on the various fronts and found themselves scattered over all the countries of the world. All these men were linked together by a single idea—a boundless love of their country; they were attracted to each other, and to the Army, the only organized national centre. Anticipating these sentiments, I took measures to form out of all these men a single whole. My efforts resulted in 1924 in the foundation of the General Union of Old Soldiers of Russia, which brought together all the officers' organizations and all the units of the Russian Army in exile. This General Union of Soldiers is regulated by Statute. This Statute, which admits certain variations demanded by local conditions, is formally recorded in the countries where those affiliated to the Union happen to be. The Union is, then, a legal organization existing under the protection of the laws of the country where it operates. It counts among its members more than forty thousand men with strong ties of union. It is an entire Army, an Army of workers with a flexible organization and a very strong sense of discipline, though that is entirely voluntary discipline is a matter of personal choice, for there is no means of punishment apart from purely moral measures. It is an order of knights.

All the members of this Army of workers live by their own labor. They give up a part of their pay to support the system, and help those who are ill or unemployed. Here is a thing unique in our practical and commercial century: an organization whose members not only receive no pay, but pour out their pennies gladly to remain in its ranks! These sums are almost enough for the needs of the Army, yet the organization to be kept up is huge. It has cost unheard-of efforts and the strongest of wills; but the Russian Army in exile is today indestructible. It has no fear of poverty; it is used to the hardest work. Since it modified its outward form, it has no more fear of those who wish it ill, for it is under the protection of the laws of the countries which have given it shelter. It fears only one thing, the idea of ceasing to be the Russian Army. That is why it cannot give up its chief mission—the fight for the resurrection, the honor, and the glory of the fatherland.

The General Union of Old Soldiers of Russia is an organization of evident weight. It is the only national Russian organization which represents abroad with lively strength the idea of the nation; it forms the counterpoise to the International, which has seized the land of Russia and bent it beneath its yoke. As it owes no allegiance to any political party or any foreign Government, it represents by itself a great political force. The Union of the Old Soldiers of Russia preserves and maintains the orders of the old Imperial Russian Army at the moral level it desires by means of lectures, conferences, and clubs during the brief hours of leisure, and keeps up military attainments among its members. It brings together under the inspiration of one idea some tens of thousands of men, it unites them in a single military family with the motto, "All for one, one for all," it supplies them with a means of mutual help; and so it makes life easier for Russian patriots, and helps them to bear the calamities that have fallen upon them. There can be no doubt that, as soon as the Bolshevists fall, however that may happen, the Union is destined to play a decisive part in the resurrection of the national force in arms and in the reestablishment of law and order. The Red Army, which is a political organization intimately connected with the political regime whence it sprang, cannot survive it, and will disappear with it.

Today the Russian emigrants are divided into several political clans which go on talking with passionate zeal. These discussions surprise foreigners, they do not realize that the very existence of these differences shows that the difficult life of the exile has not killed his spirit, that we are seeking eagerly the larger hope, and that our sentiments turn with ardour to our country. In these wide divisions of emigrants the Union of Old Russian Soldiers has found general sympathy, and at this moment it counts friends and supporters in all the political camps of the Russian Dispersion.

What is, then, the programme of this organization? What are its political ideals? They are to fight to the death against the Communist power which has subdued Russia, to deny any possibility of treating with it; to believe in the Russian people, and the conviction that this people alone has the right to choose the forms of its future government and to arrange its country on its own lines.

Representing national Russia, we do a unique service to our country. Owing no allegiance to anybody, we are ready to advance with all those who are against Communism and Socialism. We seek nothing for ourselves, and do not desire the restitution by force or the old preferential rights of the governing classes. As servants of our country, we are ready to join all the Russians who have fought and are fighting now against the Bolshevists, and all those who to this day have been forced to remain in Russia under the yoke of the power they hate and are obliged to obey.

Six years have passed since the day when we left our native soil. By painful work the Russian Army gains its bread, enduring affronts and humiliations. But in spite of all its privations and misfortunes it has not lost its faith in the approaching triumph of the sacred cause. Slowly the eyes of Europe are being opened to the real meaning of Bolshevism. The nations of Europe are beginning to understand the danger of the Red madness, of the risk the world of civilization runs in the existence of an international hot-bed which uses the immense resources of our land to keep up its destructive work. The heart of our country has been quickened by the forces of sanity, they will grow and cannot be stopped. We are no longer alone in our struggle, owing our existence to none but ourselves, we wait calmly for the day when our forces will be recalled by our country, and we shall give them to her joyfully. The other day I visited the grave of the Unknown Soldier. What a magnificent symbol of heroism, love, and an Army's self-sacrifice for its country! Passers-by uncovered to pay homage to the hero. Every country has put up similar monuments. Everywhere the memory of the hero and patriot is commemorated. The Russian Army alone is forgotten. Its high deeds, its privations, and its sufferings are nowhere remembered. Deprived of its country, hunted and disowned, it is forced to earn its bread by hard work, in the mines, the factories, the yards. The unknown Russian soldier, who has shed his blood so lavishly for the common cause, still waits for the moment of his honoring. His tomb is deserted. He has no crown, no flame of remembrance. But we are confident that the hour of recognition is at hand.

History, which knows no favoritism, will tell the importance of our struggle, the capacity of our sacrifices. It will know that the fight we carried on for the love of our country, for the resurrection of Russia as a nation, was indeed at the same time to safeguard the culture of Europe, the struggle for an age-long civilization, for the defence of Europe against the Red terror. On that day the nations of Europe will salute the Russian Army, paying homage to its valor, its sufferings, and its death agonies.

ABOUT THE AUTHOR

General Baron Pyotr Nikolayevich Wrangel was a Russian engineer and military leader born on April 27, 1887. Volunteering for the cavalry at a young age, he distinguished himself with bravery and tactical ingenuity in the Russo-Japanese War. He was promoted rapidly, commanding a cavalry squadron in World War I. Wrangel was one of the first Russian officers in that war to be awarded the Order of St. George (4th degree), the highest military decoration of the Russian Empire. As political turmoil swept through his country, Wrangel was a trusted confidant and advisor of many high ranking officers, even briefly serving as the Czar's aide-de-camp.

After resigning his commission rather than serve under the failed Kerensky government, Wrangel briefly retired to private life until he was almost murdered by a Bolshevik terror squad. He then joined General Denikin's Volunteer Army, where he rose to international prominence for his many victories and integrity. Eventually forced out of the Volunteer Army after clashing with Denikin, Wrangel was abroad when the White Army collapsed after its failed assault on Moscow.

While others scrambled to save themselves, Wrangel returned to Russia from his safe exile to rebuild the anti-communist movement. Under the command of Wrangel, the White Army retook Crimea and the surrounding area from a communist force many times its size. Afterwards, they fought a series of brilliant holding actions while trying to build international support. When victory finally became impossible, Wrangel led the orderly evacuation of White forces and civilian refugees.

Once abroad, Wrangel continued his career of service, working to improve conditions for the White émigrés scattered across the globe. He died suddenly on April 25, 1928. His family believed that he was poisoned by Soviet agents. He was survived by his beloved wife Olga and his four children Peter, Alexis, Helene, and Nathalie.